nouilh
e Plays

Léocadia, Antigone, The Waltz of the Toreadors, The Lark, Poor Bitos

A selection of the most enduring work of one of this century's best-known French playwrights. Anouilh's fondness for re-working myth, history and legend is well demonstrated in *Antigone* (the mythical Greek heroine), *Poor Bitos* (who is transported back to the French Revolution) and *The Lark* (the Joan of Arc story retold); while *Léocadia* and *The Waltz of the Toreadors* represent another talent – for ironic modern comedy. *Léocadia* and *Antigone*, the two earliest plays in the volume dating from the early forties, are in new translations by Timberlake Wertenbaker and Barbara Bray respectively. The other three plays appear in the well-established versions which reached the London stage: *The Lark* by Christopher Fry, and *Poor Bitos* and *The Waltz of the Toreadors* by Lucienne Hill.

The volume is introduced by the BBC radio producer Ned Chaillet, who was formerly a theatre critic on *The Times* and the *Wall Street Journal* – Europe.

JEAN ANOUILH was born in Bordeaux in 1910, but went to Paris when he was still young, began to study law, then worked for an advertising agency. In 1931 he became secretary to the actor-manager, Louis Jouvet, and his first play, *The Ermine*, was staged the following year. *Antigone* firmly established his popularity in France in 1944, and Peter Brook's 1950 production of *Ring Round the Moon* (1947) in Christopher Fry's translation made his name in England. Of his other plays, which he himself has categorised as 'Plays Black', 'Plays Pink,' 'Plays Bright' etc., the best known in English are: *Restless Heart* (1934); *Dinner with the Family*, *Traveller without Luggage* (both 1937); *Thieves Carnival* (1938); *Léocadia* (1939); *Point of Departure* (1941); *Romeo and Jeannette* (1945); *Medea* (1946); *Ardèle* (1948); *The Rehearsal* (1950); *Colombe* (1951); *The Waltz of the Toreadors* (1952); *The Lark* (1953); *Ornifle* (1955); *Poor Bitos* (1956); *Becket* (1959); *The Fighting Cock* (1966); *Dear Antoine* (1971); *The Director of the Opera* (1973); *Number One* (1981).

in the same series

Aeschylus (two volumes)
Jean Anouilh
John Arden
Arden & D'Arcy
Aristophanes (two volumes)
Peter Barnes
Brendan Behan
Aphra Behn
Edward Bond (four volumes)
Bertolt Brecht (three volumes)
Howard Brenton (two volumes)
Büchner
Bulgakov
Calderón
Anton Chekhov
Caryl Churchill (two volumes)
Noël Coward (five volumes)
Sarah Daniels
Eduardo De Filippo
David Edgar (three volumes)
Euripides (three volumes)
Dario Fo
Michael Frayn (two volumes)
Max Frisch
Gorky
Harley Granville Barker
Henrik Ibsen (six volumes)
Lorca (three volumes)
Marivaux
Mustapha Matura
David Mercer
Arthur Miller (three volumes)
Anthony Minghella
Molière
Tom Murphy (two volumes)
Peter Nichols (two volumes)
Clifford Odets
Joe Orton
Louise Page
A. W. Pinero
Luigi Pirandello
Stephen Poliakoff
Terence Rattigan (two volumes)
Ntozake Shange
Sophocles (two volumes)
Wole Soyinka
David Storey
August Strindberg (three volumes)
J. M. Synge
Ramón del Valle-Inclán
Frank Wedekind
Oscar Wilde

JEAN ANOUILH

Five Plays

Introduced by Ned Chaillet

Léocadia
translated by Timberlake Wertenbaker

Antigone
translated by Barbara Bray

The Waltz of the Toreadors
translated by Lucienne Hill

The Lark
translated by Christopher Fry

Poor Bitos
translated by Lucienne Hill

Methuen Drama

Methuen's World Dramatists

This collection first published as a Methuen paperback original
in 1987 by Methuen London Ltd.
Reprinted in 1993 by Methuen Drama,
an imprint of Reed Consumer Books Ltd
Michelin House, 81 Fulham Road, London SW3 6RB
and Auckland, Melbourne, Singapore and Toronto
and distributed in the United States of America
by HEB Inc., 361 Hanover Street, Portsmouth, New Hampshire NH 03801 3959

British Library Cataloguing in Publication Data

Anouilh, Jean
Jean Anouilh : five plays. —— (World
dramatists).
I. Title II. Series
842′.912 PQ2601.N67

ISBN 0-413-14030-X

Printed and Bound in Great Britain by
Cox & Wyman Ltd, Reading, Berkshire

Introduction

Literary reputations are too often like hemlines, rising in the youth and declining with the increasing age of the author. Before the vogue of Ionesco, Genet and that sometime Frenchman Beckett, Jean Anouilh was proving that success in the French theatre could be translated into success in the English-speaking theatre; moreover, he was recognized as a major playwright, inventive and original and not at all a guileless perpetrator of middle-class whimsy – that reputation can only have arisen when critics looked at his popularity rather than his plays. However amusing, there was always the touch of the poison pen to his portrayals of bourgeois life.

The French discovered him with the production of his play *Traveller Without Luggage* (*Le voyageur sans baggage*) in 1937 and *Thieves' Carnival* (*Le bal des voleurs*), an earlier play, when it was produced in 1938. The Second World War prevented any early discovery of his work in Britain or the United States, but in 1945, with the end of the war in Europe, New York was to see his ambiguous political allegory *Antigone* only a year after the first performance in Paris.

In those days, far from representing the traditions of Boulevard writing, Anouilh was placed at the forefront of new French drama, even by Jean-Paul Sartre, who dragged him rather forcibly into the existentialist company of Albert Camus, Simone de Beauvoir and Sartre himself. In a lecture called 'Forgers of Myth', given during Sartre's second visit to the United States in 1946, the subject was ostensibly French theatre under the Occupation, but the real subject was the bruised reputation of the theatre of 'character' which new French writing had abandoned. In plays such as Anouilh's *Antigone*, Sartre found moral and metaphysical preoccupations which reflected the severity of French life and which represented a 'true realism because we know it is impossible, in everyday life, to distinguish between fact and [what is] right, the real from the ideal, psychology from ethics.'

An early advocate in Britain was the young Peter Brook, who directed the British première of *Ring Round the Moon* (*L'invitation au château*) in 1950 and *Colombe* in 1951. In the preface to the published edition of *Colombe* Brook indicated the different prejudices that had to be overcome in Britain:

> The reaction of a great number of Englishmen, including many serious critics, to all the post-war school of French plays has been one of suspicion and reserve. Their authors' philosophies have been mocked, their view of life dismissed as 'cynical' and 'pessimistic', labels have been rushed on to the plays as an insulation to preserve us from being gulled by their ideas. Each new French play is treated as a Wooden Horse: critics toil like Trojans to smell out and warn us of the enemy concealed under the benign exterior.

And this was the reaction he found at a time when new French plays were regularly produced on the London and New York stages, rather a far cry from the 1980s.

Anouilh cracked those prejudices for a while, with a fresh, idiosyncratic approach to stagecraft and a gallery of unfamiliar characters, though Brook found traditional virtues in the writing:

> He conceives his plays as ballets, as patterns of movement, as pretexts for actors' performances. Unlike so many present-day playwrights who are the descendants of a literary school, and whose plays are animated novels, Anouilh is in the tradition of the *commedia dell'arte*. His plays are recorded improvisations. Like Chopin, he preconceives the accidental and calls it an impromptu. He is a poet, but not a poet of words: he is a poet of words-acted, of scenes-set, of players-performing.

Many different plays would emerge after Brook wrote those words, in his preface to *Ring Round the Moon*, particularly in such very different confrontations with history as *The Lark*, *Poor Bitos* and *Becket*, but Anouilh's fundamental theatricality and conscious artificiality remained a guidepost. While the audience might be invited to laugh, and even to show sympathy from time to time, it was never invited to get very close. As Sartre described it:

> To us a play should not seem too *familiar*. Its greatness derives from its social and, in a certain sense, religious functions: it must remain a rite; even as it speaks to the spectators of themselves it must do it in a tone and with a constant reserve which, far from breeding familiarity, will increase the distance between play and audience.

The opportunity to meet Anouilh afresh, when the plays tumbled into the English repertoire in the early 1950s, was a great advantage held by his first English and American audiences. With a stock of significant work behind him, Anouilh was able to reveal himself first in part and then in whole, and against any failures there were plays where the magic was bound to work. For a time he found himself in the happy position of being a foreign writer known and admired by a British audience, with a welcome extended for his new work which included a production of *Becket* by the Royal Shakespeare Company in 1961.

American audiences were a little harder to cultivate, and Anouilh found some of the reasons in 'a certain incomprehension with regard to my plays produced in the States. They have been weighed in the balance of realism and found wanting whereas they are not realistic, but a poetic and imaginative interpretation of reality.' In addition, there can be found in his work those usual Gallic preoccupations which notoriously bewilder British and American audiences: while sexual infidelity seems to be universally comprehensible, cuckoldry, for instance, with its continental imagery of horns on the head of the betrayed lover, does not translate. Those of his plays that have best endured on English-speaking stages tend to touch on myth and history, yet from time to time translators have succeeded in opening up his particular view of the world of French bourgeois values as well, and Lucienne Hill's version of *The Waltz of the Toreadors* (*La valse des toréadors*), where sexual obsessions abound, is an admirable introduction to one of the richest strains of his work.

In recent years, Anouilh has suffered from the cultural incuriosity of commercial managements, but he has been far from alone in that neglect. London's West End theatre, while in many ways healthier than Broadway, has largely abandoned plays which are not British or American, and Broadway tends to accept foreign work only when it is translated into musical comedy. However, in 1984 *Le nombril* – in a translation by Michael Frayn called *Number One* – did make it to the West End for a short time, glamorously cast with Leo McKern as a playwright making a farcical summation of his life. It rounds off an important area of Anouilh's work, and could be taken as an invitation to audiences to reconsider his career.

For readers of this volume, with new translators tackling the challenges of bringing his plays into English, the opportunity is very like that moment in the 1950s when he sprang fully formed onto the stages of New York and London. There is a great body of work awaiting rediscovery now, including the plays of his maturity and several of the most crucial are brought together here. For theatre-goers, there will be fewer options until theatres commit their resources to restaging some of the major plays, and perhaps exploring the by-ways. Such rediscoveries are often posthumous.

'Je n'ai pas de biographie'

Time has caught up with Anouilh's most famous statement about his life. 'I have no biography and I am very glad of it', he wrote to the critic Hubert Gignoux in 1946. He did not begrudge adding the simple facts that he was born in Bordeaux on 23 June 1910, and that he came to Paris when he was young. He also shared a few details about his education, at the Colbert Primary School and Chaptal College. He even went so far as to acknowledge a year and a half at the law faculty in Paris and two years with an advertising agency before he determined to make his living from the theatre following the production of his play *L'hermine* (*The Ermine*) in 1932. 'The rest is my life', he concluded, 'and . . . I shall keep the details to myself.'

At the end of the Second World War, it was possible for the playwright to gently disengage from public scrutiny, for his work was diverse and the public perception contradictory. A country which had been divided by the German occupation saw in him the divisions of French society and Anouilh seemed content not to resolve the differing impressions. *Antigone*, which he wrote in 1942, had been seen by audiences in occupied Paris as both collaborationist and as part of the resistance. If Antigone's stubborn insistence on burying her brother against the state's decree was regarded as a covert statement of support for those fighting the Germans, the tyrant Creon was seen to be altogether too plausible and rational, a justification for adherence to the imposed laws of a dictator. But the apparent ambivalence of Anouilh's stance could not long survive the hardening divisions of post-war France and his instinct for conciliation isolated him from both the left and the Gaullist right.

Within two years of his response to Gignoux the man without a biography had installed a new character in his plays, a creation described by J.W. Lambert as "a rampageous mouthpiece, the dramatist off the leash, another Père Ubu . . . always cursed with a mad wife and a voraciously contemptuous group of family and friends." The character was often to go under the name of Saint-Pé, although not always, and was eventually to emerge rather blatantly as a playwright who was nearly as disconcerting in his uninhibited utterances as Alfred Jarry's alter-ego, Ubu. Through him an audience could begin to discern a very intimate picture of the writer at work. Perhaps the playwright was still denying his audience the final confirmation of biographical statement, withholding real names, real dates and real information in the form of newspaper-style facts, but from the time of the composition of *Ardèle* in 1948 a fictional public persona began to emerge and it survived with remarkable consistency into the 1980s.

Rather than no biography, Anouilh had come to have a most literary autobiography; one in which details of fact might be lacking, but in which much is revealed about the writer. In apparent recognition of inescapably belonging to the public domain, Anouilh finally published the first volume of his memoirs in 1987. The title, *The Viscountess d'Eristal Has Not Received her Mechanised Carpet Cleaner*, refers to his first job in the complaints department of a Paris store, and to the first complaint he had to handle.

In the course of his long and active career in the theatre, never the most reclusive of professions, many details had already become public; through the press, through scholars and through the occasional theatrical memoir. A friend and fellow student at Chaptal College was the actor and director Jean-Louis Barrault, who describes the young Anouilh as a 'spick and span' youth – compared to the 'scruffy' young Barrault – who was already dreaming of theatre and writing plays before he was 19. Anouilh himself was proud to let us know that his father was a tailor, an artistic trade which earned his respect. In his mother, too, we can discern an artist who was also an artisan: as a violinist she played in the orchestra of the Casino at the seaside resort of Arachon where one of his relatives was a director and where Anouilh spent at least three months in 1919 listening to operettas night after night. He consciously brought a similar mastery of basic skills to his own craft, describing himself as a man who makes 'plays as a chairmaker makes plays. Chairs are made to be sat on and plays are made to be played . . .' Through such practicality he became, in Barrault's words, 'the most expert playwright of our generation. He knows the theatre to the tip of his nose and his pen.'

While working at the advertising agency, he met the actress Monelle Valentin and married her when he went to work for the actor and director Louis Jouvet as a secretary in 1931. He was later divorced from Valentin, though she was to create the roles of many of his heroines including Antigone, and despite being intimately involved with the work of Jouvet's company he received little encouragement from his employer. Following the production of his first play *The Ermine* by another troupe in 1932, he committed himself to full-time writing and encountered fairly steady poverty. Writing titles for silent films provided some support, but with the modest success of his play *Once a Prisoner* (*Y avait un prisonnier*) in 1935, and its sale to Hollywood, the risk proved justified.

Even while still reluctant to reveal the events he deemed private, Anouilh was careful to credit his artistic influences. When explaining his sympathetic comprehension of poverty in his third play, *La sauvage* (*The Restless Heart*), he points to the truly wretched childhood of his first wife, Valentin. In a tribute to Jean Giraudoux at his death in 1944, Anouilh named the playwright as one of his two masters, though on only one occasion had he met Giraudoux for more than five minutes. It was Giraudoux's play *Siegfried*, seen by Anouilh in 1928, that provided him with the artistic revelation that made him write as he did – and though he does not say so in his tribute, the set of the production was to provide him with the first furniture of his marriage when it was loaned to him by Jouvet. His other master was Georges Pitoëff, whose production of *Traveller Without Luggage* provided Anouilh's breakthrough into popularity, running for 190 performances in 1937. Pitoëff offered inspiration in his other productions as well, by producing the plays of Luigi Pirandello and George Bernard Shaw, both of whom helped shape Anouilh's theatre.

Apart from contributing to the theatre through his own plays, and often sharing in the direction of them, he also turned his hand to directing plays by others. In 1962, for instance, he staged and brought belated acclaim to *Victor*, an influential play by Roger Vitrac which Anouilh first saw in 1947. He claimed that by producing the play he was trying to rectify an injustice. Elements of *Victor* had found their way into his play *Ardèle* and had stayed there with Vitrac's enthusiastic permission. Anouilh did not forget such kindness any more than he forgot slights from others.

Despite withdrawing to the shores of Lake Geneva in his later years, Anouilh continued to pursue his interest in new writing by reading the work of younger playwrights and indeed sometimes seeing them through into production and print.

Number One

When Michael Frayn translated *Le nombril* (1981, literally *The Navel*) as *Number One*, he chose a title which gave an exact English emphasis to the central character of the play, the playwright. Léon Saint-Pé as playwright is very much the character who emerged as General Saint-Pé in *Ardèle*, and while his first concern is indeed 'looking after number one', it is also the concern of every character who populates the play. In retrospect, it has been the concern of nearly every character in all the Saint-Pé plays. Saint-Pé's weakness in such a universe is his moral hesitancy; while others act promptly and ruthlessly in their own interests, he pauses to try to preserve a personal honour. In *The Waltz of the Toreadors* it costs him a virginal mistress he has chastely cherished for seventeen years. In *Le nombril* it chiefly costs him his peace of mind, as the latter-day Saint-Pé finds it hard to feel much concern for the loss of yet another mistress who is constantly on the lookout for greener pastures.

As a late testament from the perspective of his seventies, *Le nombril* does not exactly boost Anouilh's reputation as a serious dramatist. It does not return to his exploration of modern life from the perspective of myth as in, for instance, *Eurydice* or *Antigone*; it does not explicitly confront the implications of political action as in perhaps his angriest play, *Poor Bitos*. There is not even the cavalier revision of history that marked his plays on Joan of Arc or Thomas Becket and Henry II, making us more aware of the world we live in by reshaping the past. On the face of it, the play is simply a comic and venomous rumination about the playwright's family, his friends, the literary establishment and literary aspiration. In fact, it is splendidly frivolous about anything serious: Saint-Pé has decided, because he likes the title, that his next play will be called *Les misérables*. Yet through Léon Saint-Pé it is possible to measure something of the total achievement of Jean Anouilh.

For those who know his other Saint-Pé plays, or who have met Antoine de Saint-Flour (or Antonio di San Floura in *The Director of the Opera*), the tyranny of the ordinary will be a familiar theme. While the concerns are defiantly domestic and cantankerous, they are concerns which have been used throughout Anouilh's career to take the measure of great and momentous events in private lives. From the time of *La sauvage* in 1934 his characters were already talking about fleeing from happiness – something which continually emerges as a dubious aspiration – and throughout his work love is clearly something which cannot fail to be corrupted. The young people in his earliest plays are prepared to die to preserve love, which seems to be the only way it can be preserved, and by the time of *Ardèle*, where the chief diversions are sexual and even so unsatisfactory, it is blatantly explained by General Saint-Pé that life is the enemy of love. The lovers in that play, hunchbacks as it happens, take their own lives.

When *Ardèle* was first performed in 1948, it was accompanied by a curtain-raiser, or impromptu, entitled *Épisode de la vie d'un auteur*. A wry look at the domestic distractions which interfere with the creative process, it was eventually printed with *Le nombril*. From the first performance it was evident that the character of the Author, speaking with his own voice, could be interchangeable with Saint-Pé, and both characters begin to appear regularly among the more imaginary of Anouilh's creatures. Taken over time they emerge as a single intact comic creation, as individual and archetypal as any of the characters of the *commedia dell'arte* (and just as prone to express discomforting feelings). Anouilh was himself very early to acknowledge a 'family resemblance' among his plays.

The Waltz of the Toreadors (1952) marks Saint-Pé's second appearance, still as a general. We meet him as his mad wife is shouting her jealous suspicions at him from her sick bed and soon see him recounting his war memories to his secretary. In a short time his chaste mistress of seventeen years, who had fallen in love with him as they danced 'the waltz of the toreadors', arrives to prove that his wife is in love with his best friend, the doctor who attends her. She hopes finally to free him from his marriage and marry him herself. The situation is farcical because the general dithers in his affair as he dithers in all his relationships for the simple reason that: 'I can't make people suffer.' The doctor's response is: 'Then you will make them suffer a great deal my friend, and you will suffer a great deal yourself.' The giving and the getting of pain is inescapable, even in comedy.

Although the play is comic, the laughter springs from a view of the war between men and women which is very near to August Strindberg. Take, for instance, the general's speech:

> My bits of fun – do you think they amuse me? . . . It's my terror of living which sends me scampering after them. . . . When you see them swinging by with their buttocks and breasts under their dresses you feel I don't know what wild hope surge up inside you. But once the dress is off . . . it's such a sorry thing, a woman's body, so stupid

> suddenly, lying there gaping at you when you don't really feel any desire for it.

That is hardly the stuff of a run-of-the-mill farce, and the heart of the play, where even attempted suicide is used as a mocking taunt, consists of a vicious duet between Saint-Pé and his wife, rounded off with a conscious invocation of the dance of death when the wife cries for her husband to 'dance with your chronic invalid, your old bag of bones'. But in an abrupt change of gear, Saint-Pé, finding it impossible to shake off his wife, suddenly finds that he is to lose his loyal mistress to his secretary, who will be revealed as his illegitimate son. After the final bluster and confusion and with all the accumulated paraphernalia of a Feydeau farce, the play finishes with Saint-Pé strolling into the garden with the new maid.

Stung as he rarely was by attacks on the play at its Paris opening, Anouilh published a defence of it and later declared that its failure in Paris had been, for him, a fatal accident causing him unconsciously to switch tracks. *The Waltz of the Toreadors* was the sort of theatre he wished he had continued to write. Although he was to soften his new-found jarring style as a result of its reception, he was very far from willing to give up the disconcerting figure of Saint-Pé.

Along with further appearances by the general and his descendants, appearances by the Author, named as the Author, became dramatically challenging in themselves. In *La grotte* (*The Grotto*), of 1960, a character called the Author took the blame for revealing the ugly version of life which was on offer. It is the Author who presents the play as something incomplete, and though announced as a conventional detective story, something in the style of Agatha Christie perhaps, the investigation of a murder continually reveals unsavoury complications. Crime may have its simple solutions, and murderers might be charged, but human relationships and social divisiveness make a fair apportionment of guilt impossible. The crime is not resolved, the play is never finished.

Anouilh's merging of dramatic characterization and author's private voice was halted between the production of *The Grotto* in 1961 and the production of his next work in 1968, although older pieces and adaptations appeared in Paris. He attributed to personal and public reasons the causes of his relative silence: Charles de Gaulle was again in power – to Anouilh's disgust – and he decided to attend more closely to the needs of his family. When he returned with new plays, it was ironically the family which became the object of derision. His use of the theatre as dramatic metaphor, with plays within plays as in *Cher Antoine* (*Dear Antoine*), saw him succeed in reclaiming his public, but there is no mistaking his disillusion with the family as social unit. His early plays had attributed the dilemmas of some characters to unhappy childhoods. In the later plays it is the family which is devouring the father, making demands on his time (and money) which prevent him from fulfilling his life.

In *Le nombril*, though it is perhaps a gesture at signing off from further commentary, the Author has given up trying to resolve the problems of the family. His sole intention is writing, and the sole action consists of invasions on his privacy. He is not safe from his former wife, an unhappily married daughter or her stupidly happy husband, or from his own mistress. Typically, there are also workmen and deliverymen in the house and a complaining housekeeper. Chaos is all the Author can expect, and he accepts it fatalistically.

Frayn's version, markedly different from the original, ends when the Author idly decides to extend his own afflictions to his tormentors. The unexpected success of his friend, Gaston, an envious and amiable sponger who has just won the Prix Goncourt, provides Saint-Pé with the motivation to take his revenge by writing them all into his play as they watch. To Gaston, he gives his own gout; and then sends all the scavengers who were pursuing him in pursuit of Gaston's new wealth. But even as he types that Léon is inspired, the housekeeper arrives as she did at the beginning of the play, reporting on a terrible leak in the bathroom.

Anouilh's ending is both less polished and more typical. Utter farcical chaos descends with the arrival of journalists and a sudden violent row between Léon and Gaston while the mistress poses for a photographer. The ageing playwright Saint-Pé, in 1981, is no more capable than the ageing General Saint-Pé, in 1951, of making people suffer. It is life itself that causes pain.

Plays Black and Otherwise

The length of Anouilh's tenure in the front ranks of French dramatists has ironically made him seem part of the past, despite his continued productivity. Younger by four years than Samuel Beckett, it was none the less Anouilh who used his authority to boost Beckett's career as a playwright; it was not until *Waiting for Godot* in 1953 that Beckett became a dramatist and an article by Anouilh gave the play support. Again, it was the 'boulevardier' Anouilh who spoke up for the new voice of Eugène Ionesco. Although Ionesco was only two years younger, his was also a voice that was only raised in the French theatre after the Second World War.

Against such writers, taken to be more representative of the second half of the twentieth century, Anouilh has been perceived as simply a popular dramatist guilty of perpetrating light comedies and the occasional history. That can be misleading. It was Harold Hobson who reported Anouilh's sad denial of the accusation of popularity. 'No', he told Hobson, 'I am nothing like so popular as (André) Roussin (author of *La petite hutte – The Little Hut*). My plays don't run for a thousand nights.' Not exactly, perhaps, but in London *The Waltz of the Toreadors* ran for 700 and *Poor Bitos*, by no means an easy piece, ran for 336. *Ring Round the Moon* survived for 682 performances.

Emerging as he did before the Second World War, he might best be measured against the modern writers he took as his own masters: Shaw, Pirandello and Giraudoux. Unlike them, he did not stray from the theatre to write short stories or criticism in any quantity, or any novels at all. The theatre became his profession and he remained faithful. It is easy to see the source of some of the techniques which he fused into his own style. The poetic elements of his writing are chiefly inherited from Giraudoux: the freely acknowledged theatricality of the plays, with an author constantly in search of his characters, is an inverted debt to Pirandello; and the witty exchanges of his moral debates owe much to Shaw's example, including sometimes the tendency to talk too much.

From the early Shaw he also adopted the practice of gathering his plays in groups and giving them labels. Where Shaw had his 'Plays Pleasant' and 'Plays Unpleasant', Anouilh collected his plays under such headings as *Pièces noires* ('Plays Black'), *Pièces roses* ('Plays Pink'), *Pièces brilliantes* ('Plays Bright'), and *Pièces grinçantes* ('Plays Grating'). The group titles are indicative of the playwright's intention, though his critics would sometimes have preferred different groupings.

His plays did not appear in order according to colour. The earliest of the Black Plays was *The Ermine*, from 1931, which was followed by the earliest of the Pink Plays, *Thieves' Carnival*, in 1938, and not all the plays were performed near the time of their composition.

Of the plays included in this volume, *Léocadia* (1939) was published with his Pink Plays in 1942; *Antigone* (1942) appeared in the 'New Plays Black' of 1946; *Waltz of the Toreadors* (1952) and *Poor Bitos* (1956) were collected in the grating plays of 1956/57 and *The Lark* (1953) appeared in a new category, the *Pièces costumées* of 1962. There were also 'Plays Baroque' and 'Plays Hidden'.

Léocadia is the sort of play which Anouilh would not write again after his experiences of the Occupation and the Liberation. In great part, it is about his familiar themes of artificiality and the theatricality of life, areas which would continue to interest him, but in later plays the humour would be darker. His famous bitterness would be evident even in the laughter. To end *Léocadia* he asks for a tune that is not quite sad. It is just possible to see why he called it pink.

The character Léocadia was an opera singer, a woman who died after three blissful days of love with a prince who continues to mourn her. Every piece of their memory from the inn where they met to the taxi they used, the ice-cream van they visited and every bench they sat on, has been brought to the park of the Prince's aunt, the Duchess. Having no children of her own, she is desperate to sustain her nephew but sees that the artificially created world of his great passion is insufficient to last forever. Amanda is her solution, a milliner identical to the dead Léocadia, who might give the Prince a living relationship.

To give up his perfect love, the love that survived by dying, the Prince must take the false Léocadia knowing full well that the passion will die too. Neither does Amanda offer him any false hope. As she finally claims him she tells him 'You have such ordinary hands. . . . Hands love and then one morning they become strangers and can only be used for a greeting or to pat a cheek. And that's as it should be. Hold me, please.'

Anouilh's story of degenerate royalty in the twentieth century, a sweet-and-sour fairytale, is a tale of modern France despite its artificial timelessness. The old Duchess, in dismay at her nephew's melancholy which has led him to associate with the commoners who had witnessed his great passion, has preserved the royal prerogative by placing them on her staff. But she can only finally preserve the royal line and the Prince by matching him with the milliner, Amanda.

Antigone was always bound to join the black pieces, if only because classical fate had such a heavy hand in the story. The Prologue, by a very amiable Chorus, introduces us to the characters and tells us what will happen to them. Those in the audience who are not familiar with the original Greek myth, or the version of the story by Sophocles, are thus given all the information before the action starts. The thin girl who is going to die is Antigone, or more to the point, an actress who is about to become Antigone. Her crime will be offering her dead brother, the rebel Polynices, proper burial rites despite the decree by the king, Creon, that he is to remain unburied and unwept.

Even as early in the evening as the Prologue, there is speculation about the fate of Creon in the days after the particular story we are seeing, when the guards who serve him will serve their next master, and arrest Creon. But the play stops with Antigone's death, the death of her betrothed (Creon's son Haemon) and the death of Creon's wife: three suicides. The speech is colloquial, but the implications remain classical. As ever, Antigone will die for her pig-headed belief in her duty as an individual. She simply wakes up one day and embraces that as her fate.

Antigone is Anouilh's most popular play with amateurs, offering the reassuring touch of the ancient source, high emotion and very human characters. It also offers ideas, many of which are shrouded in the ambiguity which permitted both sides in occupied France to take comfort and offence from the drama. From a distance of decades after the event, it is easier to perceive the play's real perspective. In a typically ironical remark, Antigone is told by her sister that 'it's all right for men to die for their ideas. But you're only a girl.' The author's disdain for political action could be seen there, or more clearly when the Chorus says:

> But tragedy's so peaceful! For one thing, everybody's on a par. All innocent! It doesn't matter if one person kills and the other is killed – it's just a matter of casting. . . . In drama you struggle, because you hope you're going to survive. It's utilitarian – sordid. But tragedy is gratuitous. Pointless, irremediable. Fit for a king!

It is doubly ironic that it was the playwright's grand disdain which offered hope, for in the end everyone who 'had to die is dead: those who believed in one thing, those who believed in the opposite. . . . And those who are still alive are quietly beginning to forget them and get their names mixed up.' Anouilh's disregard for political action received formidable encouragement after the Liberation when he gave his support to a cause that failed. He emerged, as might be expected, deeply contemptuous of the Resistance.

During the war, the pink play *Léocadia* had appeared in print in a publication called *Je suis partout*. The editor of the magazine was the critic Robert Brasillach, a writer who was both pro-German and anti-semitic. Anouilh had little contact with his editor, but Brasillach's fate after the Liberation would colour all Anouilh's subsequent work and is the key to the bitter *Poor Bitos* which caused an uproar when it opened in France.

Brasillach was condemned to death on 1 February 1945. The evidence of his writing, where he had called for the death of men who were recognized as patriots after the defeat of the Germans, was proof enough of his treason, and there was no doubt that he was closely identified with the German cause. However, the execution of literary collaborators was far from a foregone conclusion, and Anouilh joined with others in raising a petition to spare Brasillach's life. He was executed five days later and Anouilh saw in his death a vendetta by the victorious left.

Poor Bitos has the subtitle *Le dîner de têtes*, or 'The Dinner of Heads', a phrase with a gruesome double meaning. At first it simply refers to the wig party which is the play's setting, where the guests appear with their heads dressed in the wigs of famous historical figures from the French Revolution: the second reference is to the baskets of guillotined heads in the Terror. A group of young aristocrats have invited Bitos, the austere and poor deputy public prosecutor, to the party, and he alone arrives in full costume as the revolutionary leader Robespierre. It is their intention to humiliate him.

In the vengeful wake of the Liberation, but ten years late, Bitos has ordered the execution of a boyhood friend for collaboration. Sentimentally, he sought to console the friend's daughter afterwards by spending half a month's wages on a doll for her. His hosts have decided to punish him for his behaviour by reminding him of just how close he has sailed to Robespierre's unforgiving example, and a guest, in the guise of the guard who shot Robespierre on his arrest in 1794, fires a blank in his face. Bitos then falls into a dream of himself as Robespierre, and Anouilh paints a fiercely accusatory picture of the mentality of left-wing idealism.

Interestingly, though the original French audiences saw the play as a right-wing attack on the left and were gratifyingly scandalized, the English audiences which did not see the play until 1963 found a balance in Anouilh's cruel portraiture of left and right. Without the coded references to the Brasillach affair it is indeed possible to perceive the play as another of Anouilh's attempts to cast a plague on both houses. Although it is said ironically, it is the character Brassac, representing capitalism, who tells Bitos: 'One thing's certain whether it's you or us –

and we may as well admit the fact – in France we dine off severed heads. It's the national dish.'

Poor Bitos cannot escape being analysed in a political light, although it can be experienced as a purely theatrical event thanks to the ingenious structure of the play and its striking use of dramatic imagery. *The Lark*, on the other hand, with its internationally versatile heroine, Joan of Arc, is often able to avoid a recognition of its political roots despite belonging unmistakeably to the same conflicts of Occupation, Resistance and Liberation. It even shares with *Poor Bitos* the primary act of judicial murder, which was how Anouilh viewed the execution of Brasillach.

But *The Lark* is an optimistic play, one which coincided with a new beginning in Anouilh's life symbolized by his marriage to the young actress Nicole Lançon. Although the entire play is dominated by history and seems to move inevitably to Joan's execution, Anouilh refuses to allow it to take place. Whereas Antigone's fate was predetermined tragedy, with everyone 'innocent' and doomed to the same end, Joan's story does not end with the burning:

> . . . The real end of Joan's story, the end which will never come to an end, which they will always tell, long after they have forgotten our names or confused them all together: it isn't the painful and miserable end of the cornered animal caught at Rouen: but the lark singing in the open sky. Joan at Rheims in all her glory. The true end of the story is a kind of joy. Joan of Arc: a story which ends happily.

By the time Anouilh turned his hand to dramatizing Joan, she had been bounced back and forth by political factions in France for the best part of a century. She had long represented national identity, and following the crushing of the Paris Commune (1871) various groups, religious and secular, had continually sought to claim her for particular causes, including both the Resistance and the Vichy government during the war. In addition, many great dramatists had already tackled the theme, including Schiller, Brecht and Shaw, and Anouilh had himself worked on the second of Ingrid Bergman's movies about Joan, *Joan at the Stake*, which came from the oratorio by Paul Claudel.

The structure of *The Lark* displays Anouilh's stage mastery perfectly. He offers us an empty stage which is gradually filled by actors in plain costumes who come to enact Joan's trial, but who also enact her life. There is no ultimate distinction between history and legend; all life is theatrical. By the end of the play the stage is full: a 'beautiful illustration from a school play'. But the author denies any new perceptions, or explanations. In the introduction to the first French production, Anouilh maintained that the play:

> . . . makes no attempt to explain the mystery of Joan. . . . Some nights, when I am feeling depressed, I try to be rational and I say: the situation – social, political and military – was ripe for the phenomenon of Joan. . . . If it hadn't been this one, another would have been found. . . . You cannot explain Joan, any more than you can explain the tiniest flower growing by the wayside. . . . There's just the phenomenon of a daisy or of the sky or of a bird. What pretentious creatures men are, if that's not enough for them.
>
> Children, even when they are growing older, are allowed to make a bunch of daisies or play at imitating bird-song, even if they know nothing about botany or ornithology. That is just about what I have done.

Except that, when writing about Joan, or Bitos, or Antigone, or about Saint-Pé or the melancholy Prince in *Léocadia*, Anouilh is always writing about France; and it just so happens that much of what he perceives about his country, regardless of the specific political impetus or social situation, translates into a theatricality which translates across cultures, evoking laughter, pity, bitterness and sentiment that is international. It is his private view of the world as stage that gives him public success, and ultimately it is that also which has preserved his work in the world repertoire.

The Translations

An odd thing happens to plays in translation. Usually, unless they have once been captured by a writer of equivalent gifts or fortuitously matched by a translator's sympathetic temperament to the same period in another culture, they age rapidly. The slightest mismatching of contemporary idioms will date a translation far faster than the original. Often, phrases which seem to capture the gist of the original text in the year of the translation are out of common parlance when the play is revived and because they have been grafted on to the translation the whole play can jar. The shelf-life of an ordinary translation is about ten years.

Anouilh is luckier than many playwrights, though many hands have been turned to his texts over the years. Very early on Peter Brook saw the need for a matching poetic sensibility which could bring the most lyrical of his plays into English. His choice as translator for *L'invitation au château* was Christopher Fry, then at the height of his powers, and his patience in waiting for Fry to finish his own work led to Fry's enduringly popular translation, *Ring Round the Moon*. That partnership was carried over to *The Lark*, a more literal but affectingly idiomatic version of Anouilh in English and that translation is included in this collection.

Lucienne Hill is responsible for both *The Waltz of the Toreadors* and *Poor Bitos*, two of the most popular of Anouilh's plays to emerge in translation near the time of their composition, and those versions are also included.

Barbara Bray, best known for her translations from the modern French theatre, has newly translated *Antigone*, in a version which was first heard on BBC Radio 3. Anouilh was deeply influenced by Marivaux (1688–1763), as well as by Molière, and Timberlake Wertenbaker, the most successful of Marivaux's translators into English and a playwright herself, is responsible for the new version of *Léocadia*, a translation which also made its first appearance on BBC Radio.

Ned Chaillet, 1987

LEOCADIA

translated by
Timberlake Wertenbaker

Characters

AMANDA, *a milliner*
THE PRINCE
THE DUCHESS, *his aunt*
THE BARON HECTOR
THE HEAD WAITER
THE TAXI DRIVER
THE ICE-CREAM VENDOR
THE INN PROPRIETOR
THE CLOAKROOM LADY
THE GYPSIES
THE BUTLER
THE GAME KEEPER
SERVANTS

Scene One

An oppressively luxurious drawing room. A young woman, AMANDA, *sits with a little cardboard suitcase at her feet. She seems to have been there for some time. She yawns and absent-mindedly caresses the statue of a Venetian Blackamoor, which stands on a pedestal next to her. Suddenly, she snatches her hand away: a little lady has come in, preceded by her lorgnette. She goes to the Blackamoor, adjusts its position and then marches on the young woman, who is now standing.*

THE DUCHESS. Is it you?

AMANDA. Yes, your Grace. I think so.

THE DUCHESS. Stand up straight.

AMANDA, *bewildered, straightens herself up.*

THE DUCHESS. Why aren't you taller?

AMANDA. I don't know. I do what I can.

THE DUCHESS (*peremptory*). You'll have to do better than that.

AMANDA *looks at her.*

I'm sixty years old, child, and I've never worn anything that wasn't Louis Quinze. (*She shows her heels.*) How tall do you think I am in my bare feet?

AMANDA. Five feet, your Grace?

THE DUCHESS (*annoyed*). Very well. I'm four foot nine. But it doesn't matter in the least because you'll never see me in bare feet. No one has ever seen me in bare feet. Except the Duke of course, but he was as blind as a bat. (*She goes to her, suddenly severe.*) And what's this?

AMANDA (*slightly disconcerted*). My gloves, your Grace.

THE DUCHESS. They're going to the dogs.

AMANDA. The dogs?

THE DUCHESS. It's a figure of speech. Actually, my dogs wouldn't want to have anything to do with them. Their taste has been coloured, if I may say so, by my hatred of green. They'd turn themselves into sausage meat rather than lie on a green cushion. There is only one green item in this house, child, and that's your gloves.

She throws the gloves into the fire.

AMANDA (*who can't help groaning*). I paid a lot of money for those gloves . . .

THE DUCHESS. That was a mistake. Let me see your hands. (*She takes* AMANDA*'s hand.*) Good. It's a fine hand. It may sew hats, but there's good blood there. In any case, who isn't sewing hats these days? I'm not, but then I belong to another age. By the way, did the telegram explain what you were being offered here?

AMANDA. I believe it was a job, your Grace.

THE DUCHESS. A job! A job! I adore that expression. Isn't she divine, Gaston?

Since they are alone in the room, AMANDA *looks around, a little surprised.*

That's the late Duke, my husband. He died in 1913, but I'm so absent-minded I can never remember not to talk to him. (*She looks at* AMANDA *and sits down next to her.*) Divine. (*She now speaks to her as she might to a little dog.*) And are you pleased, my little one, to have found a jobjob?

AMANDA. Oh yes, your Grace. I can tell you this because they've given me excellent references, but two days ago, I lost my job with the Reseda sisters.

THE DUCHESS (*who has risen and is now going towards the door*). I know. I arranged it.

AMANDA (*who has risen as well, is taken aback by this confession*). You arranged it? How dare you!

THE DUCHESS (*smiles at this word and leaves, shouting.*) Dare! Dare! Gaston, didn't I tell you she was divine!

The young woman collapses back on to the sofa. Her little suitcase is still at her feet and she looks around her, more and more lost, and about to burst into tears. A BUTLER *comes in and bows formally.*

THE BUTLER. Her Grace wishes to ask Miss if she would care to partake of a light luncheon before her Grace's return.

AMANDA. No thank you, I'm not hungry.

THE BUTLER. I hope Miss will forgive me, but I was only asking for the sake of appearances. Her Grace ordered me to serve Miss this luncheon whether Miss was hungry or not.

To the accompaniment of a merry little tune, SERVANTS *bring on an extraordinary luncheon, served on an insolent profusion of silver.* AMANDA *remains alone in front of too many cakes, sweets and jams to want anything. Finally, timidly, she helps herself to a tangerine and begins to peel it. The* DUCHESS *sweeps in, followed by* HECTOR, *a tall, gaunt, and rather decaying old gentleman. The* DUCHESS *snatches the tangerine from* AMANDA *and throws it into the fire.*

THE DUCHESS. You must never eat tangerines, child. No

oranges. No lemons. They make you thin and you can't afford to lose an ounce. Wouldn't she be ravishing, Hector, with a little more flesh on her?

HECTOR *puts on his monocle to have a look at* AMANDA *but does not have time to give his answer.*

You must have eggs and starches. Starches and eggs. (*She calls.*) Théophile!

THE BUTLER (*entering at once*). Your Grace?

THE DUCHESS. Take all this away and bring the young lady an egg.

AMANDA (*who now stands, resolute*). No!

THE DUCHESS (*turns to her, surprised*). No? And why ever not?

AMANDA. I don't like eggs. And I'm not hungry.

THE DUCHESS (*to* HECTOR *as she goes out*). She's divine.

HECTOR (*echoes as he follows the* DUCHESS *out.*) Divine.

They've gone, and this time, AMANDA *has had enough. She grabs her suitcase and seems about to break something or burst into tears. She shouts to the* SERVANTS *who are clearing the luncheon away under the* BUTLER*'s supervision.*

AMANDA. Is someone finally going to tell me why I've been brought here? Well?

THE BUTLER (*following the servants out*). I hope Miss will forgive me, but none of the staff knows anything. It would be best for Miss to apply directly to her Grace, or if that fails, to his Lordship, the Baron Hector.

AMANDA (*left alone, throws her suitcase on the floor and angrily stamps her foot*). Dash!

THE DUCHESS (*who has reappeared through another door*).

What an ugly little word, child. Say Damn. It's proper English. (*She sits down, the perfect hostess.*) I'm so sorry to have kept you waiting in the drawing room when you must be anxious to see your room and rest from the fatigue of your travels. But it could upset all my plans if you moved from here as there is someone who must not see you and who is expected back at the house at any moment.

AMANDA *sits, calmer now, and believes she is summing up the situation.*

AMANDA. I received a telegram from you this morning saying you could offer me a job. But I wonder if there isn't some misunderstanding.

THE DUCHESS. There certainly is a misunderstanding, child.

AMANDA. Yes. I'm a milliner. I only know how to make hats.

THE DUCHESS. And you've guessed, quite correctly, that I'm not the sort of woman who'd bring you all the way out here to mend my old fripperies.

AMANDA. If you're looking for a lady's maid or even a companion, I must tell you immediately that I have a skill, and it's a skill I intend to practise.

THE DUCHESS. You were right, Gaston, this child has great quality. (*She gets up and says to* AMANDA *as she leaves.*) Another point in her favour.

AMANDA (*getting up as well*). No. This time, I won't allow you to leave.

THE DUCHESS. Did you hear that, Gaston? We're not allowed to leave. It's just like the days of François the First.

AMANDA (*taken aback*). François the First?

THE DUCHESS. We were confined to our lands under François the First. It seems we died of boredom.

AMANDA. Your Grace: I arrived on the 2.16 train. It will soon be five o'clock and the only train that can take me back to Paris tonight leaves at 5.39. If there's nothing for me to do here, I'd like to catch it.

THE DUCHESS. No, child. You won't catch that train.

AMANDA. Why not?

THE DUCHESS. It's been cancelled.

AMANDA. But it's on the timetable.

THE DUCHESS. It may be on the timetable, it's been cancelled nonetheless.

AMANDA (*who now believes anything is possible*). You cancelled it. To keep me from leaving.

THE DUCHESS. I would certainly have done so under Louis the Fifteenth, my child, but my family has lost its influence since '89. Do you want to know who cancelled that train? The Freemasons. (*She makes her sit and begins.*) They noticed the locals were beginning to come and visit my basilica. We were beginning to make a little profit, what with admission charges and the sale of candles and souvenirs. I'm a modern woman and I've understood you can't do anything without publicity these days. And then, before I could even lift a little finger, they cancelled my train. But I've picked up the gauntlet: I'm going to make a deal with Citroen.

She's about to leave.

AMANDA (*who's had enough, follows her, sniffing*). Please, I don't understanding anything about freemasons and basilicas. I only know I've been waiting here for two hours. And I didn't even have breakfast before leaving this morning.

THE DUCHESS. What? No breakfast? But I ordered you an egg. Eggs and starches. Starches and eggs. That's not an old wives' tale, either. I had to pay a Viennese specialist one thousand francs for that information. What's happened to that egg? I'll go and get it.

She's about to leave yet again, but AMANDA *whimpers.*

AMANDA. No, your Grace, no. Don't go without telling me something. I'll go mad.

THE DUCHESS (*stops, solemn*). I see you're forgetting to be stupid, child. I have a confession to make: I'm not sixty, I'm sixty-nine. I've seen the beginning of air travel, the end of the corset, bobbed hair and the World War. When I tell you I'm a little old lady who has known the ups and downs of life, you'll have the kindness to believe me, won't you?

AMANDA (*exhausted*). Yes, your Grace.

THE DUCHESS. Well, the reason I've been coming in and out of this room like a jack-in-the-box is because I don't have the courage to tell you why I asked you here.

She goes and AMANDA, *stunned, finds herself watching her vanish once again.* AMANDA *then grabs her suitcase, half frightened and half angry.*

AMANDA. I've had enough of these lunatics. I'll go back to Paris on foot if I have to.

She opens a French window, looks around to see if she's being watched, and runs into the garden. The orchestra executes a tremelo. The stage remains empty for a few seconds and then the DUCHESS *and* HECTOR *come in.*

THE DUCHESS. Hector Hector! Where is she? I have a dreadful foreboding.

HECTOR (*who is stupidly looking under the furniture*). For once, your foreboding may be right. She's gone.

THE DUCHESS (*taking his arm*). Hector, if she meets him in the park, we're lost.

They go out quickly. Blackout. A short musical phrase ends with the chirping of birds. The lights come back on to reveal a rustic scene.

Scene Two

A crossroads in the grounds of the Château. There is a circular bench at the foot of an obelisk. In a corner, an old-fashioned taxi is stopped next to a big tree. Two legs are sticking out from under the bonnet. On closer inspection, it becomes clear that it is a rather odd taxi, ancient, washed out, and wrapped in ivy and honeysuckle. On its roof, a cock is crowing itself hoarse. Not far from the taxi stands a candyfloss-coloured ice-cream van. Legs are sticking out of that as well. AMANDA *runs on, suitcase in hand. She stops when she sees the taxi and lets out a little cry of joy.*

AMANDA. Thank God! What luck! A taxi! (*She looks around, doesn't see anyone, and then discovers the legs.*) Sir . . .

A VOICE (*coming from elsewhere*). Yes? What?

AMANDA. Are those your legs?

A kindly old man straightens himself up from behind the ice-cream van and asks calmly as he adjusts his lorgnette.

THE ICE-CREAM VENDOR. Which ones?

AMANDA, *speechless, shows him the legs sticking out from under the bonnet.*

THE ICE-CREAM VENDOR (*casually, as he goes back to his newspaper behind the ice-cream van*). No, not those ones.

AMANDA (*shouting to him as he disappears*). Please, Sir? (*The man turns around.*) Am I still in the grounds of the Château? I've been walking for such a long time.

THE ICE-CREAM VENDOR (*darkly*). Yes, Miss. You can walk as long as you like, you'll always end up in the grounds of the Château.

The birds, or the orchestra, make fun of AMANDA'*s fears. She has grabbed her suitcase and is running to the taxi.*

AMANDA. Taxi, taxi, are you free?

THE DRIVER (*hearing those words, gets out of his car, furious*). Am I free? What kind of a question is that? That's all I need. To be living in France in this day and age and not be free.

AMANDA. Dear God, thank you. I'm saved. (*She dives into the taxi and shouts.*) Take me to the station immediately.

The DRIVER *has watched her go into the taxi with a half surprised, half mocking expression. She comes out immediately by the other door, shouting.*

Driver!

THE DRIVER. Yes.

AMANDA (*going up to him, defeated*). There are rabbits in your taxi.

THE DRIVER. Of course there are rabbits in my taxi. (*He begins to get himself into a rage.*) What's wrong with rabbits? Can't I raise rabbits if I want to? You tell me who says I can't raise rabbits.

AMANDA (*moving backwards*). I didn't . . . you have the right to raise rabbits.

THE DRIVER. I'm a human being, like everyone else. Just because they pay me three thousand francs a month to do sweet damn all doesn't mean I'm not human, does it? I always swore I wouldn't be a private chauffeur, no, not for anybody. So they call me a mechanic. I'm a flunkey, that's what I am. A flunkey. A flunkey. Go on, tell me I'm a flunkey.

AMANDA (*still moving backwards*). I wouldn't dream of it . . .

As she walks backwards, she feels something cling to her and she cries out because everything frightens her now. She sees what it is, calms down, and gives the driver a little smile.

I'm so sorry. I'm a little jumpy today . . . (*She breathes out.*) It's some ivy.

THE DRIVER (*who has calmed down*). Of course it's ivy. What's wrong with ivy? I tried roses, climbers, but they wanted too much care, watering and pruning and all that. So I planted some ivy. It's cheerful and it takes care of itself.

AMANDA. What happens to it when you drive off?

THE DRIVER. What happens to what?

AMANDA. To the . . . ivy . . . (*She asks, blinking, because anything is possible here.*) Does it follow you?

THE DRIVER (*delighted by this notion*). Ha, ha, ha. You're a funny one, aren't you? Do you think my ivy's made of rubber or something? Do you think it's elastic? (*He calls.*) Hey, Joseph!

THE ICE-CREAM VENDOR (*reappearing*). What?

THE DRIVER. Did you hear what she just said? She asked me if my ivy followed me. Can you see me taking it for a piddle on the boulevards? (*He calls.*) Ivy, Ivy, come here you naughty little thing.

AMANDA (*who has been inspecting the taxi*). But your taxi doesn't work. It's full of roots.

THE DRIVER (*hurt*). What do you mean, my taxi doesn't work? I'll show you how well my taxi works. (*He cranks up the motor, which starts. He is triumphant.*) See that? Now tell me my taxi doesn't work!

AMANDA. Please, please don't drive off with the ivy. I'm going mad. I've seen too many strange things today. (*She goes up to the* ICE-CREAM VENDOR.) Are you really an ice-cream vendor?

THE ICE-CREAM VENDOR. Yes, Miss.

AMANDA. I don't suppose you could sell me some ice-cream? I'm dying of thirst.

THE ICE-CREAM VENDOR. It's been two years since I've made an ice cream, Miss. Even if I wanted to, I wouldn't know how anymore.

AMANDA. That's what I thought. I'm beginning to see some logic in this absurdity. I'd have been suspicious if you'd been a real ice-cream vendor who sold real ice cream. Ice cream that makes your mouth go all cold. Will you do me a favour?

She hands him something.

THE ICE-CREAM VENDOR. A pin? What am I supposed to do with a pin?

AMANDA. Would you prick me, please? Not too much, just to see.

THE ICE-CREAM VENDOR (*pricking her*). She's funny.

THE DRIVER. Funny? She's barmy, that's what she is.

AMANDA. Ouch! Thank you very much. You can give me back my pin now. A pin's always useful in life. Now I know I'm alive: when I'm pricked, I feel it. And since I have two legs, I can walk on them. I won't even ask the way to the station, I'll walk straight ahead of me until I find a signpost. Because in life, in real life, that is, there are always signposts. I'll read with my own eyes and walk with my own legs until I reach the station. There, I'll find the station master and he'll be a real station master. (*She takes her suitcase, on the verge of tears.*) At least, I hope so.

As she's about to run off, she bumps into the DUCHESS *who has swept in with* HECTOR.

THE DUCHESS. Thank God, we've found her. (*She collapses on the bench.*) My dear child, you almost made me die of fright. I'm worn out.

AMANDA (*who sits as well*). Don't try to make me feel sorry for you. I'm worn out too, and I've almost died of fright.

THE DUCHESS. You? What could you possibly be frightened of?

AMANDA. Of everything . . . and of you.

THE DUCHESS. Frightened of me? What a preposterous notion, Hector.

AMANDA (*animated*). And of this taxi driver whose taxi is rooted to the spot, and of this ice-cream vendor who doesn't sell ice cream and of these grounds no one can leave. Where am I? What do you want from me? I work for my living, I've never done anything wrong, I don't have any money, not even any savings, I don't have friends who could pay for my ransom – so why?

THE DUCHESS. Why what?

AMANDA. Why did you have me dismissed from the Reseda sisters? Why did you lure me here with the promise of a job? What sort of a job can I have with these bizarre creatures anyway? I suppose you want me to be a milliner who doesn't make hats. (*She gets up, resolute.*) Well, I'm not frightened of any of you. Where is the station? I insist you tell me where the station is.

THE DUCHESS. Hector, she's divine.

HECTOR. Divine.

AMANDA (*sits down again, at the end of her tether. She mumbles as she begins to cry*). Where is the station?

THE DUCHESS (*utters a cry and takes her hands*). No, no, whatever you do, please don't cry. I can't see anyone crying without beginning to do so myself. And if you're sensitive as well, I'll set you off again and we'll never stop. I understand your confusion, child, and I'll put an end to it immediately. The hour for explanations has struck, however difficult these might prove . . . I will now make everything clear. In a word, child, I have a nephew. I adore my nephew. His name is Albert. The poor child is the victim of the most acute melancholy . . . (*She begins to sniff.*) You'll have to continue, Hector. It's such a painful tale, I simply can't bear telling it.

HECTOR *gets up and stands formally in front of* AMANDA. *The* DUCHESS *introduces him in quite a different tone.*

My cousin, the Baron D'Andinet D'Andaine.

HECTOR *bows.* AMANDA *executes a little curtsey.* HECTOR *is about to speak, but the* DUCHESS *goes on.*

The Baron Hector, that is. Not to be confused with the Baron Jérôme, who's with the consulate in Honolulu, nor with the Baron Jasmin, the General's son. The Baron Hector.

HECTOR *bows once again and is about to speak. The* DUCHESS *interrupts.*

By the way, you needn't worry about confusing him with the Baron Jasmin, because the Baron Jasmin is dead. Speak, Hector, speak.

HECTOR. It's this. My cousin the Prince Troubescoi . . .

THE DUCHESS. Yes, my younger sister became a Troubescoi by her second marriage. It was when the Tsar came to Paris. The Slavonic charm, we all succumbed to it. My sister died of it in the end, poor thing. Do go on, Hector.

HECTOR. My cousin the Prince Troubescoi . . .

THE DUCHESS. Say Prince Albert. She could confuse him with the other one, you know, that idiot who married an Englishwoman: Patrick Troubescoi. (*She asks* AMANDA *quite naturally.*) Perhaps you've met him?

AMANDA. No.

THE DUCHESS. I'm surprised, he knows everybody. Go on, Hector.

HECTOR. A few years ago, my cousin the Prince Albert Troubescoi met, not far from here, in Dinard, a young woman . . .

THE DUCHESS (*cuts him off*). Stop, Hector. You're making this extraordinary love story sound utterly banal. I'll have to tell this young person myself, however much pain it may cause me. Two years ago, my dear little Albert fell madly in love with a woman of great beauty, of incomparable style, a woman you may have heard of: Léocadia Gardi.

AMANDA. The singer?

THE DUCHESS. Yes. The great, the unforgettable singer. The Diva. Ah, what a voice. When she sang the prelude to *Astarte*. (*She begins to sing.*) *'Salut, Seigneur, sur cette terre . . .'* (*She stops.*) Unfortunately I have no voice. I used to have a trickle of a voice. I was told it was an enchanting trickle, but one day I drank too much cold water and it dried up. Odd for water to have that effect, don't you think? I never tried to understand, doctors are such useless creatures. In any case, I now have no voice. Where was I?

HECTOR. Léocadia . . .

THE DUCHESS. Léocadia . . . So you were telling me you knew our dear little Léocadia well. That will help us enormously.

AMANDA. No, I didn't really know her. I read about her death in the newspapers.

THE DUCHESS. So you know how she died.

AMANDA. It was an accident, wasn't it?

THE DUCHESS. The dear soul always wore very long scarves. They were very her, very chic, and she had a remarkable way of tying them just as she was about to leave you. Now, she was in all things a passionate woman. One night, she was leaving some friends after a long discussion on the meaning of art and she tied her scarf as she was saying goodbye. But her gesture was too grand, even for her, and she strangled herself. She let out a cry – a strangled cry – and fell down, stone dead. (*She sniffs.*) Finish for me, Hector, I can't.

HECTOR (*who considers the story finished, repeats*). Dead.

THE DUCHESS. It was only three days before this that my little Albert had begun to love her. But those three days were to mark him for ever. Are you beginning to understand?

AMANDA. No.

THE DUCHESS. Then I shall have to go on. When he heard the dreadful news, Albert tried to throw himself out of the window. I held on to his lapels and kept him back, but that was only coping with the present. There was the future to contend with. I took him on the most expensive cruise I could find, one and a half times around the world. In vain. He spent those one hundred and twenty-one days in his cabin staring at a photograph of his beloved, and I spent them sitting in my cabin, watching him through a crack in the door to make sure he didn't jump out of the porthole. Ah, my dear child, would you like further details of my long martyrdom?

AMANDA (*who's had just about enough*). No.

THE DUCHESS. You're quite right, it would be too painful. Let me simply say that I, who am the soul of curiosity, went one and a half times around the world with my nose glued to a door. Sometimes, when we were in our ports of call, my thirst for knowledge overcame me. I'd glance through the porthole and perceive half a turban. Ah, I'd say to myself, India. Then a pigtail down someone's back: China. Smoke coming out of a mountain: Italy. It was only when we arrived in France and I'd put him in the care of some friends that I could think a little about myself. I'd lost thirty pounds from worry. But I'd gained thirty pounds from lack of exercise. So I was the same weight as when I left. We were in Marseilles. Are you following all this? I'm not talking too fast for you?

AMANDA. No . . .

THE DUCHESS. A point in your favour. We came back here as soon as we could to spend the rest of our holidays. I began to feel that Albert was no longer suffering as much, although his melancholy still worried me. I had him followed by my spies and his every movement reported back to me. I learned that Albert spent his days in Dinard, sometimes talking to a taxi driver, sometimes to an ice-cream vendor and sometimes to the proprietor of a dingy little inn. And every night, he went to the same gypsy nightclub and sat at the same table where he was served by the same head waiter. When September came and Dinard was empty, it was the only nightclub to remain open and Albert continued to spend his nights there, alone. I usually mind my own business, but I had to unravel the mystery . . . I soon found out that Albert was financing the nightclub himself just so he could sit, every night, at the same table. At first I was baffled. And then, I understood!

AMANDA (*who is beginning to be moved by this love story*). That's where they first told each other they were in love? . . .

THE DUCHESS. Ah, Hector, Hector, what sensitivity is to be found among the Common People. What we had so much trouble grasping with our intelligence has been sensed immediately by the heart of this young girl. Yes, child. Those people Albert kept going back to see had all witnessed his love for the Diva.

AMANDA (*dreamy*). How wonderful to love like that . . .

THE DUCHESS. Isn't it? But put yourself in my place. Albert is a Troubescoi and – of greater importance for me – a D'Andinet D'Andaine. It's not that I'm a reactionary old fossil: I even became a voluntary nurse in 1919 . . . but there really was no point in taking all that trouble to rule half of France during the middle ages, if seven hundred years later one's nephew were to end up gallivanting about with taxi drivers and ice-cream vendors . . . One might as well call oneself Dupont straight away and open a lace shop! . . . What was I saying?

HECTOR. You understood . . .

THE DUCHESS. Quite. I understood that all those people whose attraction for Albert had at first baffled me were simply his memories. I set to work and after two weeks of enquiries and hard bargaining, all those who had seen the couple together during their days of happiness came on to the staff here. And because I felt the décor was crucial to Albert's dreams, I also bought the taxi, the ice-cream van and every single bench they had sat on. I had to take the town to court over the benches, but I won. The inn and the nightclub were dismantled and rebuilt stone by stone in my grounds.

AMANDA. What a beautiful fairy tale!

THE DUCHESS. It was the least I could do. Thank God the poor dears hadn't visited any historical monuments. I may still have influence with the government, but that would have been very difficult.

AMANDA. You must love your nephew very much.

THE DUCHESS. I adore him, dear child, and when you know him, you'll do the same. And you see, I'm a stay-at-home and I like my creature comforts. And just as he has a barber who comes to shave him here every morning, I wanted Albert to be able to remember in the comfort of his own home.

AMANDA. I still don't understand what I'm doing here. I'm

ready to swear on my mother's grave – she's dead – that I never knew, never saw, and was never seen by your nephew – especially during those three fateful days – and I can't possibly be part of his memories. I've never set foot in Dinard and anyway, when Léocadia Gardi died, I was working at the Reseda sisters morning, noon and night. Miss Estelle from the workshop will confirm this. It was my first year there and I didn't even have any holidays that summer, so there's no way I could have gone to the coast to play at being a memory.

THE DUCHESS. Oh, Hector, she's so delightfully amusing.

HECTOR. She's sharp.

THE DUCHESS. She's not sharp, she's witty.

HECTOR. She has a sharp wit.

THE DUCHESS (*shrugging her shoulders*). A sharp wit, a sharp wit . . . don't pay attention, child. Ever since he's been having injections for his fibrositis, he thinks everything is sharp. You're witty and that's sufficient. Not everyone is witty these days.

AMANDA. Very well, I have wit. I even have a sharp wit if that pleases his lordship. But you can't have brought me here for the sake of my wit.

THE DUCHESS. No, child. (*She's suddenly embarrassed.*) What time is it? We've been chatting away . . .

AMANDA (*forces her to sit*). Please, your Grace. Answer me once and for all. Time can't matter that much to someone who's made me miss every train back to Paris.

THE DUCHESS. My dear girl, I've never been spoken to in that manner before.

AMANDA. And I've never been lured into the depths of Brittany before with the promise of a job no one can describe.

THE DUCHESS. We're being reviled, Hector, but we deserve it. (*She has a determined expression on her face.*) It is time to speak.

HECTOR (*without enthusiasm*). Let us speak.

THE DUCHESS. Let us speak.

There is an awkward silence, and they look away, embarrassed.

THE DUCHESS. Hector.

HECTOR. Yes.

THE DUCHESS. Are you a man?

HECTOR. No.

THE DUCHESS (*thrown*). What do you mean, no?

HECTOR (*pathetic, but firm*). You keep telling me I'm not.

THE DUCHESS (*craven*). I was only joking. You are a man. Speak to this child, who is suspecting the worst.

AMANDA. Yes, the worst.

THE DUCHESS (*sighs*). If only it were the worst, but it's worse than the worst. There must be an Italian word for it. Speak, Hector, we're listening.

HECTOR (*breathes in and is about to begin*). Well. (*He gulps. His voice catches.*) No, I can't. It was your idea anyway.

THE DUCHESS. Then let us speak together.

HECTOR. Together?

THE DUCHESS. We'll say the little prologue we prepared and learned by heart this morning.

HECTOR. Word for word?

THE DUCHESS. Word for word. I'll give the signal to start. Ready?

HECTOR. Ready.

THE DUCHESS. Fire!

They take a step forward and begin.

HECTOR/THE DUCHESS. Child – and we hope that in view of our great age and experience, you won't mind if we call you child. (*They look at each other, adjust their breathing and proceed.*) Child – what we have to tell you may appear indecent when pronounced by such respectable mouths as our . . .

HECTOR *has trailed off. The* DUCHESS *looks at him sternly.*

THE DUCHESS. Well, Hector?

HECTOR (*beginning to cry*). No, I can't . . . Even together, I can't!

THE DUCHESS (*scornful*). And when I think that one of our ancestors defended a bridge all alone against two hundred Albigensians.

HECTOR (*who no longer knows what he's saying*). Bring on this Albigensians and I'll defend a bridge if I must . . . But not this . . . my whole being revolts . . . not this!

THE DUCHESS. Very well, go. Since the head of the family is running away from the enemy, I'll take charge myself. Go.

HECTOR *goes out, his head down. The* DUCHESS *abandons her scornful expression and pulls* AMANDA *close to her. She starts again in a tone where there is much less clowning and where, under the humour, a real intelligence begins to show itself, which suddenly makes her almost human.*

Child, I know you think I'm an idiot. No, don't deny it. I will reassure you myself. I'm not an idiot, but you will find what I'm about to say offensive. You'll get up from this bench, pick up your suitcase and slip through my fingers. (*She looks at her and continues.*) If I had a daughter, I'd want her to do the same . . . And here we are, alone and quite alike now in this deserted park where the fading light subdues our appearance . . . (*She dreams a little.*) If I had a daughter . . . But I have no daughter. I couldn't have children. I don't know whether it was Gaston's fault or mine – when he died it was too late for me to check with anyone else. I have no daughter . . . but I have a nephew. And if I've been extravagant for his sake it's because I love him, and also, of course, because I'm frightfully extravagant by nature. (*She looks at* AMANDA *again and continues.*) If I had a daughter . . . Yes, of course. But we're given other duties, bit parts to play . . . mine is rather unexpected for a woman of my class . . . But you, you're all alone and naked under your ha'penny dress and it would be so easy for you to help a little old lady who has reached the end of her tether.

AMANDA (*murmurs*). I don't understand you very well . . .

THE DUCHESS. I'm doing it on purpose, child. I'm talking and talking until it gets completely dark and you won't see me blush. It's such a strange thing to blush. I haven't done it since I was a little girl in crinolines and frilly pantaloons and I was made to stand in the corner because I wouldn't salute General MacMahon.

She continues dreaming. The evening closes in.

AMANDA (*murmurs*). It's completely dark now.

THE DUCHESS (*abruptly, from the shadows*). Tell me, child, have you had lovers?

AMANDA (*takes a step backwards*). Lovers?

THE DUCHESS. Dancing around the maypole, you see a young man, you kiss him. What am I saying? I'm getting my eras mixed up. I meant a dance hall where all the young girls flock to these days.

Silence. AMANDA *does not answer.*

THE DUCHESS (*a little weary*). I suppose I've frightened you, or even worse, you're disgusted. I'm not asking you if you've been in love. I don't pry. I'm speaking of passing fancies . . .

AMANDA (*in a small voice, after a long silence*). Yes, of course I've had lovers. But I've never been in love.

THE DUCHESS. Life is full of surprises and perhaps you'll have that happiness one day. In the meantime, you must try to live as intelligently as you can, day by day. Then, when you finally do fall in love, you can seize it with both hands and be as stupid as you like. But let's leave love aside . . . (*A pause. She continues, softly.*) Albert is handsome, charming, and still young, despite his suffering. But if all he finds of Léocadia are old stones and idiots who don't know how to talk about her, he'll kill himself eventually. I'm a powerful old woman, despite the Republic, and fabulously wealthy, but I will have to watch him die without being able to lift a finger. And then I'll be all alone, like a useless old shoe.

AMANDA. Yes, but what can I do? You can't have thought . . . I'm not pretty. And even if I were, no one could come between him and his memory.

THE DUCHESS. No one but you.

AMANDA (*genuinely surprised*). Me?

THE DUCHESS. The world is stupid, child, and sees only surfaces, gestures, scarves. And no one may have told you this before. I cried out when I first saw you at the

Reseda sisters. To anyone who knew more of her than her ghost, you are the living image of Léocadia.

Silence. The evening birds have now taken over from the afternoon birds. The park is full of shadows and murmurs.

AMANDA (*very gently*). I can't . . . I may be nothing, but at least those lovers took my fancy.

THE DUCHESS (*also gently and now very tired*). Of course. I'm sorry.

She gets up with difficulty, like a very old woman. There is the sound of a bicycle. She starts.

Listen . . . there he is. Just lean against that pillar. This is where he first saw her. Let him see you, just this once, let him cry out, let him take an interest in something other than that dead woman, who'll take him away with her one of these days. (*She takes* AMANDA'*s arm.*) Please. I beg you. (*She looks at her, pleading, and suddenly adds.*) And you'll see him for yourself. I'm blushing again. Isn't life strange? I've only blushed three times in sixty years and the last two have been during the past ten minutes. You'll see him and perhaps he will have the happiness, just for a moment, of taking your fancy.

The sound of the bicycle is still heard in the darkness, but it's coming near.

AMANDA (*whispering*). What do I say to him?

THE DUCHESS (*squeezing her arm*). Say: Excuse me, can you tell me the way to the sea.

She hides in the shadows of the trees. It's about time. A spot of white appears: it's the PRINCE *on his bicycle. He passes very close to another spot of white:* AMANDA *leaning against the pillar. She murmurs.*

AMANDA. Excuse me.

He stops, gets down from his bicycle, takes off his cap and looks at her.

THE PRINCE. Yes?

AMANDA. Can you tell me the way to the sea?

THE PRINCE. It's the second on your left.

He bows, sad and courteous, gets back on his bicycle and leaves. The sound of the bicycle fades. The DUCHESS *comes out of the shadows, much aged.*

AMANDA (*softly, after a silence*). He didn't recognise me . . .

THE DUCHESS. It was dark. And who knows what she looks like in his dreams. (*She asks, shyly.*) You've missed your train, wouldn't you like to spend the night with us at the house?

AMANDA (*in an odd voice*). Yes, please.

It's completely dark now and they can no longer be seen. There is only the sound of the wind in the huge trees of the park.

Curtain.

Scene Three

The DUCHESS's *drawing room. It is morning. The* BUTLER *stands on the stage, motionless. He seems to be waiting. Another man, who looks like the butler's twin brother, comes on and the two exchange hostile glances.*

THE HEAD WAITER. Good morning, Sir.

THE BUTLER (*icily*). Sir: good morning.

They look at each other. The BUTLER *straightens his tie and the* HEAD WAITER, *despite himself, does the same.*

THE BUTLER. May I enquire why you are here, Sir?

THE HEAD WAITER. Her Grace summoned me for nine o'clock, Sir, to discuss business concerning the fictional establishment which I look after in the park.

THE BUTLER (*making sure he doesn't betray his bitterness*). Then I believe you may sit down, Sir.

THE HEAD WAITER (*sitting stiffly*). Thank you, Sir.

The BUTLER *leaves, after shifting slightly the statue of the Venetian Blackamoor, thus demonstrating this is his domain. At the door, however, he changes his mind and comes back.*

THE BUTLER. A word with you, Sir: I myself have always been in service in the houses of the Haute Bourgeoisie, indeed – if I may say so without appearing vain – in the very best houses of the Faubourg. But I have a brother-in-law – a man who in all other ways is of the utmost respectability – who has chosen – out of greed – hotel work. He has been at the Piccardy, at the Waldorf, at the Savoy . . . perhaps you know these?

THE HEAD WAITER. I know them, Sir.

THE BUTLER. Well, despite the fact that they have worked in the very best hotels, my brother-in-law and his colleagues have always betrayed a certain laxity, a – how can I put it – tendency towards familiarity, which cannot be avoided – no matter how well trained they may once have been – by those who are used to serving a client rather than a master.

THE HEAD WAITER (*impenetrable*). I do not follow your drift, Sir.

THE BUTLER. It is this. I have not been able to perceive the signs of this corruption in yourself, Sir. And yet, I have heard that the place where you served in Dinard was by no means of the very first order . . .

THE HEAD WAITER (*pale*). Many of the best people went there, but no, it was not of the very first order.

THE BUTLER. I know you could not possibly be imitating me, Sir. An eye as practised as mine would have detected this immediately. Please allow me to ask you a question: is it possible that you spent some years in the houses of the Bourgeoisie before . . . ?

THE HEAD WAITER (*lowering his head, with a sob in his throat*). Yes, Sir. Before. But one day . . .

THE BUTLER (*stops him with a gesture*). I wouldn't dream of asking what happened, Sir. I am only pleased to see that a true butler can always be recognised, no matter how low he may have sunk.

THE HEAD WAITER (*grateful*). Thank you, Sir.

THE BUTLER (*pleasant and superior*). We won't mention it again, my friend. And forgive me if I twisted the knife in the wound. I'll warn her Grace of your arrival.

He goes out. The DUCHESS *bursts in, as she usually does, followed by* HECTOR *and* AMANDA *who is wearing a Léocadia-type dress and accessories.*

THE DUCHESS. Dear friend.

THE HEAD WAITER (*who has risen quickly*). Good morning, your Grace.

THE DUCHESS (*in one breath*). Don't even say good morning. Look at this young woman, look at her carefully, look. What do you say?

The HEAD WAITER *is baffled and looks at* AMANDA *without understanding what all the fuss is about. Then he understands.*

THE HEAD WAITER. Oh!

THE DUCHESS (*forgets herself and takes his hands in her enthusiasm*). Thank you, dear friend, thank you for that 'oh'. (*To* AMANDA.) That 'oh' is a success, dear child, kiss me. (*She kisses* AMANDA *and turns back to the* HEAD WAITER.) Now you may wish me good morning.

THE HEAD WAITER. Good morning, your Grace.

THE DUCHESS (*distant and gracious*). Good morning. (*She shows* AMANDA.) Look. Isn't it disturbing?

THE HEAD WAITER. Haunting, your Grace.

THE DUCHESS. Haunting! Just the word I spent all of last night looking for. Haunting! Where did you find it?

THE HEAD WAITER (*looking at his hands, worried*). Find what, your Grace?

THE DUCHESS. That word.

THE HEAD WAITER. I don't know, your Grace . . . the papers?

THE DUCHESS. Quite. I never could read the papers. But it is the exact word. Haunting. (*She's delighted.*) Haunting. Child, you are haunting.

AMANDA (*pretending to shiver*). It might not be too pleasant in the mornings.

THE DUCHESS (*patting her cheeks*). She's such a little wit. You're only haunting for us, child, you're actually a Greuze. A little walking Greuze.

HECTOR. Or rather the girl in Boucher. The one the poet talks about . . .

THE DUCHESS. Tut, tut, you don't know what you're talking about, Hector, nor does the poet. This child is not a Boucher, but a Greuze. And when she smiles and looks a little surprised, she might be a La Nain. (*To* AMANDA.) Have you been told all this before?

AMANDA (*simply*). I've never even heard of those names.

THE DUCHESS (*who relishes this*). She is divine, Hector.

HECTOR. Divine.

THE DUCHESS. They're painters, child, great painters. (*She explains with her usual excess, as if she were talking to an idiot.*) Painters are people who paint pictures, with brushes and . . .

AMANDA (*who laughs a little*). I know what a painter is.

THE DUCHESS (*casually*). I have a dozen or so of their masterpieces in the Long Gallery, we'll go there later and compare. It'll be amusing. But now, we must get to work. (*She goes to the* HEAD WAITER.) I summoned you here because you can help us. Prince Albert has been told about this child, but he doesn't want to see her yet. When he does, I want him to be rooted to the spot. Rooted. And he will be. And yet, we can't expect a miracle. He'll be much more demanding than we are.

AMANDA. Please don't frighten me, your Grace. I'm already so nervous.

THE DUCHESS. We must face the difficulties of our task, child. We have a resemblance. Good. That's already a lot, but with a woman like Léocadia, that is not enough. We must have atmosphere. (*She goes to* HECTOR.) Where are the orchids?

HECTOR (*gets up, surprised, thinking he may have sat on them*). The orchids?

THE DUCHESS. How can we have forgotten that Léocadia never went anywhere without a bunch of orchids? I'll telephone Dinard and tell them to bring some immediately.

She goes out, followed by HECTOR. AMANDA *remains alone with the* HEAD WAITER. *They look at each other for a moment, embarrassed. Then* AMANDA *says to him with a smile.*

AMANDA. Haunting . . . (*He hesitates, not knowing what attitude to adopt and makes a vague and non-committal gesture.*) What odd jobs we have.

THE HEAD WAITER (*stiff and cautious*). There are no bad jobs, Miss.

AMANDA (*pleasantly*). No . . . one must live. How long have you been one?

THE HEAD WAITER. One what, Miss?

AMANDA. A memory.

THE HEAD WAITER. Almost two years, Miss.

AMANDA. Do they pay you well?

THE HEAD WAITER (*outraged by this brutal question makes the gesture of a waiter refusing a tip*). Oh, Miss. (*But* AMANDA'*s frank look unsettles him and he confesses.*) Yes, Miss, very well. (*Then he regrets confessing something one must never confess. He makes another gesture.*) That is, when I say well . . . if you think about it . . .

AMANDA (*laughs at his embarrassment*). And is it tiring?

THE HEAD WAITER. What?

AMANDA. Being a memory. (*The* HEAD WAITER *makes a gesture.*) What do you do all day?

THE HEAD WAITER. Nothing. I wait. I wait for him. I walk

around the empty tables and I think. (*Trusting now, he adds, after a silence.*) Thinking's a strange thing, Miss, it makes you sad.

AMANDA. I only saw him for a moment yesterday and it was dark. Is he pleasant?

THE HEAD WAITER. Neither pleasant nor unpleasant. All that can be said about him is that he doesn't seem to be there.

AMANDA. What does he do when he comes to your place?

THE HEAD WAITER. He always sits at the same table, the one they sat at that night. He orders a Pommery Brut 1923 and I bring him two glasses. Then he looks straight ahead of him in silence, sometimes for five minutes and sometimes for the whole night. Then he leaves.

AMANDA (*dreamily*). Poor thing.

THE HEAD WAITER (*darkly*). And then we finish the champagne.

AMANDA (*like a little girl who's never had much champagne*). How lucky you are!

THE HEAD WAITER (*blasé*). You get bored with it after a while, Miss. It gives me a stomach ache.

AMANDA (*who has been dreaming for a moment in silence*). What I don't understand is that they only saw each other for three days . . . I think you need more time than that to love. To love in the way I mean. (*She suddenly asks the dumbfounded* HEAD WAITER.) Did they make love, at least?

THE HEAD WAITER (*still taken aback*). Really, Miss, I can't answer that. Not at my place, they didn't. (*Then he adds.*) The people from the Inn say they did it there, but I think they're giving themselves airs.

AMANDA (*very gently*). And even if they had, once isn't much.

The HEAD WAITER *makes a vague gesture, indicating his incompetence in the matter.* AMANDA *is still pensive and continues.*

Suffering does exist, of course. I may be odd, but I think people either suffer more or they suffer less. Not the way he does.

THE HEAD WAITER (*very distinguished and sceptical*). Who knows what suffering is? I was in Monte Carlo when his Highness the Grand Duke Sosthène, in a sudden attack of neurosis, poured three hundred bottles of Veuve Cliquot, special vintage, into his drawing room and then forced all of his staff to dip their feet in it. And he was crying and asking for our forgiveness.

AMANDA (*gently*). I don't think that's real suffering either.

THE DUCHESS (*who has come in, followed by* HECTOR, *as always*). Good. We'll have two hundred orchids in ten minutes.

AMANDA (*smiling*). Isn't that rather a lot?

THE DUCHESS (*turns around, surprised*). A lot? Why?

AMANDA. I may not know much about paintings, but I once worked in a flower shop and . . .

THE DUCHESS. Two hundred may not be enough: Léocadia chewed orchids all day long. How long does it take a nervous person to eat an orchid?

AMANDA. I don't know. I used to sell daisies for chewing.

THE DUCHESS (*who is no longer listening to her*). Let's organise ourselves while we wait for the flowers. We must reconstruct for the benefit of this child Léocadia's entrance into the Blue Danube. (*She gets hold of an armchair*.) Let's start with the decor. Sit there, child. (*To* HECTOR.) Isn't she ravishing? And she already looks so right. (*She goes up to* AMANDA.) Ravishing!

AMANDA. I'm trying to look distinguished.

THE DUCHESS (*moving away*). No, no, don't do anything, we'll show you all that later. (*To the* HEAD WAITER.) I didn't want to rehearse in your place because Albert often walks in the park in the mornings, whereas he never comes here. And Théophile is on the look out anyway. (*She goes to* AMANDA.) Child, the more I think about it, the more I see that Léocadia's charm resided mainly in her eyes. She had a delightful way of looking at people. Between ourselves, it was simply that she was frightfully shortsighted. I suggest that while we're moving the furniture you practise blinking. That'll be your first lesson. (*She goes back to the* HEAD WAITER.) You can help me move this Blackamoor. Léocadia used to say he represented the gentle and teasing spirit of the morning. (*She can't help sighing as she moves it with the help of the* HEAD WAITER.) What a heavy beast. (*As she moves near* AMANDA.) Blink, child, blink. That's it. The last one was almost right.

The door opens without a sound. The BUTLER *watches in disgust as his rival, with the help of his mistress, disturbs the sacrosanct order of the drawing room and the young woman sits in the corner and blinks for no apparent reason. He shudders with horror and disappears.*

THE DUCHESS (*who is still moving the furniture*). This will be the musicians' platform. There's the table where they sat. Is that right?

THE HEAD WAITER. Yes, your Grace. More or less.

THE DUCHESS. Good, good. (*To* AMANDA.) Stop blinking

now, child, you'll get a cramp and later, when you have to do it properly, it won't look natural. (*To the* HEAD WAITER.) And now, dear friend, I expect you to tell us exactly what impression Léocadia made on you when she entered the Blue Danube for the first time.

THE HEAD WAITER (*delighted by this important role*). The impression she made on me?

THE DUCHESS. The exact impression. Take your time. We're among friends here and we want the truth, the whole truth and nothing but the truth.

THE HEAD WAITER (*carried away, raises his hand and shouts*). I swear, so help me God!

THE DUCHESS. What?

THE HEAD WAITER (*whose conscience may not be very clear, blushes*). Oh, nothing. I'm so sorry, your Grace.

THE DUCHESS. We're listening. (*To* AMANDA.) Don't blink any more, child, don't blink.

AMANDA (*who is blinking because she can no longer overcome her need to laugh*). I can't help it.

THE DUCHESS (*delighted*). Excellent. It means you're becoming her. Blink away, child, blink, blink. (*To the* HEAD WAITER.) We're listening.

THE HEAD WAITER (*who has had time to pull himself together*). Well, to be honest, when Miss Léocadia came for the first time into the Blue Danube, I think I can speak on behalf of all my mates who were there when I say that we received a shock.

THE DUCHESS. A shock. How very interesting. A shock. (*To* AMANDA) Make a note of that, child, do you have a pencil?

AMANDA (*who is no longer doing much to stop her*

giggles). I think I can remember that. (*She says in the same way as the* HEAD WAITER.) A shock.

THE DUCHESS (*repeats, delighted*). A shock.

THE HEAD WAITER. A shock. First of all, Miss Léocadia was very beautiful . . . And then she had a way of walking towards you, staring straight into your eyes, and just as you thought she was about to speak to you, nothing. She had distinction, arrogance, and if I may use words that best express my thoughts, your Grace?

THE DUCHESS. I insist that you do, my friend.

THE HEAD WAITER. She had a certain something.

THE DUCHESS (*enthusiastic*). A certain something. (*To* AMANDA.) Make a note of that, child. It's astonishingly accurate. This young man is of great value and very observant. Yes, all of Léocadia was in her walk, it was so distinctive, so *fin de siècle* . . . (*She imitates her.*) Her eyes staring straight into yours and then suddenly, that distracted look, she brushed past you without even seeing you. Unfortunately, I'm not like that at all. I'm short and I tend to hop. My friend, do you know what you must do to enlighten this child once and for all? You must demonstrate.

THE HEAD WAITER. What must I demonstrate, your Grace?

THE DUCHESS. Léocadia's entrance into the Blue Danube.

THE HEAD WAITER (*who is itching to do so*). I don't know if I dare, your Grace.

THE DUCHESS. I am asking you to, my friend.

THE HEAD WAITER. Very well, but your Grace must remember I do not wish to parody or to show the least disrespect. I am a man settled in my ways, no longer a youth, and it will therefore not be easy for me to . . .

THE DUCHESS. It's to give this young woman the right tone, that's all.

THE HEAD WAITER. Very well, your Grace. When Miss Léocadia came into the nightclub, the orchestra had just started a tune that was very popular that year: 'The Waltz of Love.'

THE DUCHESS. Hector will be the orchestra. Stand there on the platform, Hector, and hum the tune. You know it, you wrecked our ears with it two years ago.

HECTOR (*delighted with this role*). Shall I also imitate a violinist with my arms?

THE DUCHESS (*uninterested in this detail*). Do what you like.

HECTOR *will spend the rest of the scene humming and asking himself whether or not he should imitate a violinist with his arms.*

THE HEAD WAITER. If your Grace will allow it, I shall walk towards her.

THE DUCHESS. Excellent.

THE HEAD WAITER. Let's have the orchestra!

HECTOR *strikes up 'The Waltz of Love'. The* HEAD WAITER *solemly begins his imitation of Léocadia entering the Blue Danube. The* BUTLER *suddenly opens the door as if he had something urgent to communicate.*

THE BUTLER. Your Grace!

He stops, frozen. His rival has just passed in front of him without even seeing him and is reeling towards the DUCHESS, *staring into her eyes, as she exclaims.*

THE DUCHESS. That's it. That's it exactly. The man's a natural mime. Let's do it again while it's still fresh. Quick, child, walk behind him and do everything he does.

HECTOR *starts the waltz again and the* HEAD WAITER *repeats Léocadia's entrance into the Blue Danube.* AMANDA, *giggling, walks behind and imitates him. Having finished his own demonstration, the* HEAD WAITER *turns around and watches* AMANDA *walk towards him. He cries out, rapturously.*

THE HEAD WAITER. Bravo, Miss. Stay there. And now, walk towards me. Stare into my eyes, that's it, and now, insolence, insolence! I'm only a head waiter, I'm nothing, I'm dirt. You don't even see me.

But AMANDA *has stopped, blushing with embarrassment. Moving from behind the* BUTLER – *who has been stock still since his entrance, unable to utter a word – the* PRINCE *now stands in the doorway, pale with rage.* HECTOR *stops and the* DUCHESS *and the* HEAD WAITER *turn around, horrified.*

THE PRINCE. What is the meaning of this masquerade?

THE DUCHESS (*cries out*). Albert here! Théophile, what have you done?

THE BUTLER. (*bows his head, having aged ten years*). I came in to warn your Grace, but I was so upset by what I saw –

THE DUCHESS (*with a fearsome gesture*). You're dismissed, Théophile. Go!

The BUTLER *goes, having aged a hundred years.*

THE PRINCE (*to the others, harshly*). Leave us, please. I'm sorry, Aunt, but I would like to speak to this young woman alone.

HECTOR *and the* HEAD WAITER *beat a hasty retreat. The* DUCHESS *is about to leave as well. The* PRINCE *now looks at* AMANDA *for the first time. She doesn't know where to put herself. Suddenly he sees the Venetian Blackamoor and jumps.*

THE PRINCE. Who touched this statue?

THE DUCHESS (*from the door*). I did, Albert. I wanted to make room for . . .

THE PRINCE (*furious, puts it back in its place*). I said no one was ever, under any pretext, to touch anything she had touched.

The DUCHESS, *who isn't very frightened, leaves, making gestures of complicity behind* ALBERT*'s back to* AMANDA.

THE PRINCE (*looks silently at* AMANDA *and finally says to her*). I'm afraid my aunt has put you in rather an awkward situation.

AMANDA (*simply*). I'm afraid she has.

THE PRINCE (*without indulgence*). I suppose you were desperate for a job.

AMANDA. I wasn't. That is, I was after your aunt had me dismissed from the place where I worked.

THE PRINCE (*amused*). She did that? She's amazing.

AMANDA (*a little bitter*). Amazing, yes. (*She adds.*) But since yesterday, I've lost the habit of finding anything amazing.

THE PRINCE. You've been here since yesterday?

AMANDA. Yes. You even spoke to me yesterday near the pillar in the park.

THE PRINCE (*surprised*). Was that you? I'm sorry, it was so dark . . . Why did you ask me the way to the sea?

AMANDA (*gently*). It was something I was supposed to say to you.

THE PRINCE (*suddenly stupefied, murmurs*). Excuse me . . . can you tell me the way to the sea?

He sits in an armchair, no longer saying anything, dreaming. There is a long silence. AMANDA *coughs, makes some noise, but nothing works. She begins to tiptoe away, but the* PRINCE *suddenly shouts.*

THE PRINCE. Don't go. Come here. Stand in front of me. You're ugly. You have the gutteral accents of a Parisian. You don't look like her, you could never look like her, no one could. You're just a little shop girl, without class, without mystery, without aura.

AMANDA (*calmly*). What's an aura?

THE PRINCE (*explodes*). You don't expect me to work on your vocabulary as well, do you?

AMANDA (*who looks straight at him, with dignity*). I want to know if it's an insult.

THE PRINCE (*looks at her and can't help smiling. He says, more gently*). No, it's not an insult.

AMANDA. Good.

She looks at him with scorn and goes to the door with as much dignity as she can muster.

THE PRINCE (*can't help asking her*). What would you have done if it had been an insult?

AMANDA (*turning around*). I would have told you what I thought of you.

THE PRINCE (*softly, suddenly weary*). I don't care what anyone thinks of me.

He curls himself up in the armchair and remains silent. AMANDA *looks at him from the doorway, a shade of pity in her eyes. Suddenly, in the middle of his reverie, he murmurs, his eyes closed.*

THE PRINCE. Can you tell me . . . (*He stops and starts again, with another tone of voice, searching.*) Can you tell me the way . . . (*He tries again, but his voice is awkward.*) The way . . .

He stops, exhausted. Suddenly, his face relaxes. AMANDA, *who has tears in her eyes because she sees he is really suffering, murmurs behind him, as in the preceding scene.*

AMANDA. Can you tell me the way to the sea?

Silence. He asks gently, almost humbly.

THE PRINCE. Who taught you to imitate her voice?

AMANDA. No one. It's my own.

THE PRINCE (*after a pause*). Say that sentence again, please.

AMANDA. Excuse me, can you tell me the way to the sea?

THE PRINCE (*softly, his eyes closed*). It's the second on your left.

AMANDA. Thank you.

THE PRINCE (*his eyes still closed, calls out*). Excuse me . . .

AMANDA (*surprised*). Yes?

THE PRINCE. You dropped your glove.

AMANDA *looks down, surprised, then she understands that*

he is remembering the meeting of two years ago. She stammers, a little frightened.

AMANDA. Thank you, thank you very much.

THE PRINCE (*opens his eyes*). No. She didn't answer. She only smiled and disappeared into the night. (*He gets up, without looking at her and wipes something from his cheek.*) I'm sorry.

AMANDA. No. I'm sorry – for being here. (*Silence.* AMANDA *looks at him and says, very seriously.*) What I don't understand is why, when I said the same thing yesterday, in the same voice, you answered me so calmly. As if I were anybody and you were used to being asked, every evening, the way to the sea.

THE PRINCE (*in a strange voice*). It's odd, isn't it?

AMANDA. Yes, it's odd.

THE PRINCE (*a little constricted and still without looking at her*). You wouldn't be willing to stay here a little longer, despite all I've said to you and your opinion of me? Let's say three days . . .

AMANDA (*bows her head. She'd like to use her power, her anger. She tries to be dignified.*) Last night, I didn't want to. Then this morning, I said yes, but a moment ago, I was going to say no.

THE PRINCE (*turns towards her gently, for the first time*). Please say yes again. It will even things out.

AMANDA. I look like a fool who doesn't know her own mind.

THE PRINCE. What do you think I look like?

AMANDA. It doesn't matter for you. But I don't lead the kind of life that allows me to be round the bend.

THE PRINCE. What would happen if you were 'round the bend'?

AMANDA. Dreadful things. I'd ladder my stockings. My gloves would disappear. I'd miss my trains. I'd be dismissed from work. (*She stops and sighs.*) Mind you, all that has happened already.

THE PRINCE (*on the defensive*). You must have heard about my life. I suppose that to someone like you, for whom financial considerations are crucial, it must be irritating that I've spent so much money, energy and time just to worship a memory.

AMANDA (*softly*). When the man from the War Office brought that big letter which said my Dad wouldn't be coming home from the war, my mother – she was a cleaning lady – started sleeping in the kitchen on a cot. In the bedroom, she laid out all of my father's belongings and put his jacket next to her wedding dress on the bed. And each year, on the anniversary of his death, she spent more in chrysanthemums, comparatively speaking, than you have to build a whole town in your park.

THE PRINCE (*after a pause*). I must ask for your forgiveness.

AMANDA (*very correct*). No, no, but don't think that just . . .

THE PRINCE (*solemn*). I don't. I'm pleased you've told me all that because it makes what I'm about to say easier. My aunt is mad, however delightfully. But I'm sane. And if I allowed her to rebuild all the places I visited with Miss Léocadia Gardi, it was because I needed help in my struggle.

AMANDA (*who doesn't understand*). Your struggle?

THE PRINCE. It sounds stupid, but it's almost funny. Please try not to smile. The truth is that I'm forgetting.

AMANDA. Who are you forgetting?

THE PRINCE. I'm forgetting the woman I loved. I'm no longer certain of the colour of her eyes, I had completely forgotten her voice until a moment ago. I don't know what world I was living in last night . . . (*He hits his forehead angrily.*) My mind keeps drifting. To think you stood there, in the same place, at the same time, and with the same voice asked me the way to the sea and I didn't jump, I didn't cry out, I didn't . . . No wonder they all make fun of me. The Prince Albert Troubescoi built a whole town in the park in memory of the woman he loved but he can't even remember the first thing she said to him.

Pause. He collapses, exhausted.

AMANDA. What can I do for you?

THE PRINCE (*after a pause, very softly*). Stay a few days and let me see you in all the places I seek her in vain. Try – please don't mind if I ask you this – try not to be yourself any more, but her. Just for three days.

AMANDA (*who stands with her hand on the Venetian Blackamoor*). I promise.

THE PRINCE (*cries out*). Oh! Please don't move. She came to the house the next day to ask my aunt to lend her the park for a charity she was organising. My aunt was out and I spoke to her . . . I found her standing, just like that. She told me how much she liked that statue. We spent the whole afternoon chatting, and that same night she allowed me to accompany her to the Blue Danube. It was in that nightclub that we were to discover the next day that we loved each other. (*His eyes are closed.*)

The Blue Danube . . . it was the most pretentious and silly place, with a head waiter who took himself for a butler and that imitation Viennese music everyone liked that year. She hummed it all evening. (*He begins to sing the waltz, badly.*) Lalalala, what was that waltz? (*He searches.*) Lalala . . .

AMANDA (*helps him*). Lalalala.

THE PRINCE (*continues*). Lalalala.

AMANDA (*completes and they sing together*). Lalalalalala.

The orchestra takes over from AMANDA. *The lights dim and come back up on the fourth scene.*

Scene Four

The clearing in the grounds where the Inn of Sainte-Anne-du-Pouldu and the Blue Danube nightclub have been rebuilt, back to back, with their signs up. It is late at night and the inn is closed but the Blue Danube is open, displaying the charm of its antique decor under the brilliant light of rococo chandeliers. Three GYPSIES *who look like skating instructors from the Palais de la Glace, the* HEAD WAITER, *and a* CLOAKROOM LADY *who with her frills and flounces looks like an usherette from the Comédie Française, all flutter about like night moths preserved in some kind of phenol.* AMANDA *and the* PRINCE *have just arrived and the* CLOAKROOM LADY *is helping a surprised and delighted* AMANDA *with her furs. The* HEAD WAITER *takes their order.*

THE HEAD WAITER (*as if he didn't already know*). What shall I bring your Lordship?

THE PRINCE. The same as last night.

THE HEAD WAITER. Very good, my Lord. (*He writes.*) A Pommery Brut, 1923.

AMANDA (*thoughtlessly*). Oh, but before . . . I'd like . . . I'm so thirsty and I love the taste . . . could I have an anisette, please?

General panic. The music stops.

THE HEAD WAITER. That is . . . Miss Gardi never . . . you must excuse me.

AMANDA (*suddenly embarrassed*). No, no, you must excuse me. I don't know what I'm doing . . . Champagne of course, the same as last night, that is, the champagne we are supposed to have.

The music starts again, relieved.

THE PRINCE (*after a pause, a little stiffly*). If you're thirsty and you're so keen on it . . . bring us an anisette.

THE HEAD WAITER (*in a panic*). I'm not sure . . . Very good, my Lord. I'll manage.

AMANDA (*shouts after him*). With some water, please!

THE HEAD WAITER (*more and more panicked*). Water! No one warned us . . . we'll have to melt the ice.

AMANDA. Thank you, you're very kind. I'll drink it quickly.

THE HEAD WAITER (*leaves, reassured*). Yes. I'll take the glass away immediately and we won't mention it again.

AMANDA (*excusing herself with a smile*). It's not easy to suppress all of one's wishes for two days.

THE PRINCE (*a little harshly*). You'll be free the day after tomorrow. Try to be patient.

AMANDA. You know very well I don't need patience. It's

fascinating to become another woman so suddenly. (*She caresses her bracelets.*) A woman who's rich, who's loved.

Meanwhile, the anisette is being prepared with much milling about, confabulations, toing and froing. The CLOAKROOM LADY *and one of the* GYPSIES, *putting down his violin, join in what begins to look like a furtive and scurrying little ballet, danced to a musical theme that deforms the 'waltz' without changing it completely. At last, the* HEAD WAITER *brings the anisette.*

THE PRINCE. Yesterday wasn't too bad, was it?

THE HEAD WAITER. The anisette! (*He adds reproachfully because that's what has given him the most trouble.*) With water.

AMANDA (*who is really thirsty*). Ah, thank you! (*She takes a sip and looks at her glass.*) It's so pretty when the anisette hasn't completely mixed with the water.

She seems to want to be happy on her own account in the midst of the music, lights, perfumes and rare jewels, but she notices the PRINCE *and the* HEAD WAITER *looking at her coldly, waiting. She empties the glass in one go and screws up her face because it's too strong and she has almost choked. She hands the glass back to the* HEAD WAITER.

AMANDA. I'm sorry.

THE HEAD WAITER (*taking her glass, can't help saying, with a sigh of relief*). There.

THE PRINCE (*takes back his monocle, pleased that it's all over*). There.

AMANDA (*in an odd little voice*). There.

The orchestra, which had stopped for a moment, strikes up the 'waltz' again and the HEAD WAITER *immediately brings the champagne bucket. With great ceremony – it's a serious matter this time – he pours the champagne. The atmosphere has relaxed.*

THE PRINCE. Yesterday wasn't too bad for a first time, even if you did make some blunders. I hope this doesn't sound rude, but there's a touch of commonness in you, which is most attractive, but it did occasionally strike a wrong note.

AMANDA. I didn't use a single word of slang.

THE PRINCE (*casually, to a dismayed* AMANDA). Léocadia never used anything else. But we can't hope to copy her language. And then, we said so little to each other that first night. It was enough for me just to see you there, sitting opposite, eating those flowers.

AMANDA (*apologising gently*). I wasn't so good with the flowers, was I? I felt sick.

THE PRINCE. Sick?

AMANDA. I'm quite happy to chew the odd blade of grass, but to have the bittersweet taste of that flower all night long . . .

THE PRINCE (*dreamily*). Léocadia said it reminded her of the poppy, the mandrake root, drugged nights in the East . . .

AMANDA (*trying to get the* HEAD WAITER, *who is watching her coldly, to laugh*). I don't know anything about things like that, all I knew was that I had a stomach ache. Sorry. But this afternoon was better, wasn't it?

THE PRINCE. Much better. You may have noticed I don't often pay compliments.

AMANDA. I have.

THE PRINCE. I must tell you that on the boat – during that long and lazy trip upriver to Dinan – you evoked her ghost almost to perfection.

AMANDA (*pleased, with a triumphant look at the* HEAD WAITER). Thank you.

THE PRINCE (*adds, after a pause, for himself and with no malice*). It's true that she allowed her magnificent intelligence to lie dormant that afternoon.

AMANDA (*in a small voice*). Thank you anyway.

She doesn't dare look at the HEAD WAITER, *who leaves, mocking.*

THE PRINCE (*who hasn't noticed a thing, continues*). You were perfect. Possibly a little too lively, too flesh and blood.

AMANDA. It's a difficult habit to break when you're alive. I'll try to do better this evening. These meals are making me feel so light . . .

THE PRINCE. Léocadia always put her glove on her plate.

AMANDA. One of these days I'll end up eating my glove by mistake.

THE PRINCE (*dreamily*). Dear, ethereal Léocadia. Please respect this image which disturbs me so and don't describe all the meals you have brought to you after we leave each other.

AMANDA (*her head down*). I may be alive, but I'm not a cheat. I try to be this woman even when you're not looking at me. I swear to you I'm eating nothing but orchids and drinking nothing but champagne. I used to go to bed with the crow, but if you'd passed by my windows last night, you would have seen me lying on the *chaise longue*, reading Mallarmé by candlelight and trying to concentrate. In vain, I have to say.

THE PRINCE (*a little surprised*). Why? You knew I wouldn't try to see you after I had officially left you. Do you find this game amusing?

AMANDA. No. I find my own books amusing and I like to sleep. (*She stretches herself at the thought.*) Oh, how I'll sleep the day after tomorrow.

THE PRINCE. Why then?

AMANDA (*slightly flustered*). No reason . . . when I do a job, I like to do it well, that's all.

A short silence. They've turned away, unconsciously, and the GYPSIES *immediately feel they have to take up their instruments and start a Viennese tune. When the* PRINCE *speaks, the musicians trail off and sit down again.*

THE PRINCE (*returning to his own thoughts*). That second evening was to decide the rest of our lives . . . what remained of it, that is: a morning together and the end of an afternoon.

AMANDA. Is that when you realised you loved each other?

THE PRINCE (*curt*). Who told you?

AMANDA. I don't know . . . you probably.

THE PRINCE. No, not I.

AMANDA. Then it was your aunt . . . or I felt that's what would happen now.

THE PRINCE. That second evening, yes. As this strange night unfolded, like so many others with its music, lights, drink and talk . . .

AMANDA. What did you talk about before you talked about your feelings?

THE PRINCE. We talked about the houses we'd seen, the colour of the river, the dusk, her favourite poets and her favourite hats, the people around us who made her laugh . . . but we were always talking about our feelings.

AMANDA. Who spoke?

THE PRINCE. Both of us, I think. Or rather, she spoke. Why do you ask?

AMANDA (*curled up on the red velvet seat, softly, after a silence*). If I had fallen in love with you during that long, sunlit afternoon, I would have sat very still, letting my hot skin rest against the cold of my satin dress, and enjoying the freshness of these diamonds on my arms and this iced glass in my hand. I would have looked at you, without saying a word.

THE PRINCE (*has listened to her calmly and concludes*). That's because you're a primitive little being incapable of self-analysis.

AMANDA. Probably.

THE PRINCE. Just as well. There's no room for your self-analysis. You've played your part with perfect discretion, I must thank you for that. You aren't normally very talkative, are you?

AMANDA. I am. At the workshop I was called The Mouth.

THE PRINCE (*puts on his monocle*). The Mouth?

AMANDA. Because I always had some story to tell.

THE PRINCE. Then you have great tact, that's even better.

AMANDA (*laughs*). No, in the workshop where I was before, I was called The Foot.

THE PRINCE (*puts on his monocle and looks at her again*). The Foot?

AMANDA. Because I always put my foot in it.

THE PRINCE. You don't seem to deserve any of these names.

AMANDA (*smiles*). I'm being careful . . . I'd like these three days to succeed for you. I can't talk like Miss Léocadia Gardi, but at least I can be silent like her. There are so many ways of being silent while one listens to the man one loves. What was hers?

THE PRINCE (*lost in his memories*). She spoke more quietly.

AMANDA (*stupefied*). But she still went on?

THE PRINCE (*with complete naturalness*). Yes. She completed your sentence or embarked on her own answer. Sometimes she whispered words in Roumanian, her native tongue . . . These uninterrupted monologues were her greatest charm. She displayed in them the multiple facets of her mind like so many fireworks and she punctuated them with long throaty laughs, which started suddenly when they were least expected and ceased abruptly in a kind of cry.

AMANDA. I must seem very calm compared to her.

THE PRINCE. There's no need for you to imitate the verbal genius of such an exceptional being. It's enough that you have given me her silent image. (*He takes her hand at the end of this sentence, but drops it abruptly.*) Oh. I'm so sorry.

AMANDA (*taken aback, looks at her hand*). Why?

THE PRINCE. I was going to take your hand. She hated being touched.

AMANDA. Even by you?

THE PRINCE. Especially by me. She said I had the hands of

a peasant and that they were brutal.

AMANDA (*quickly takes his hand and looks at it*). The hands of a peasant?

THE PRINCE (*a little embarrassed, his hand still in hers*). I have callouses from yachting and tennis. And I can't hold a golf club with gloves on, can you?

AMANDA (*still looking at his hand*). How interesting. The hands of a man of leisure bear as many tool marks as those of a working man. Hold my arm.

He takes her arm, a little surprised. She closes her eyes and murmurs, with a little smile.

No. Your hands are hard but they aren't brutal.

The PRINCE *takes his hand away. There is a silence, and the* GYPSIES, *afraid of being caught out, seize their instruments. The first violinist comes to their table and plays his most amorous tune. The* PRINCE *says nothing and looks at his hand. After a moment,* AMANDA *ventures, shyly.*

AMANDA. What were you thinking?

THE PRINCE. I was thinking that if she'd said to me what you've just said, I would have been frightfully happy that night.

AMANDA (*gently*). She talked so much, she must at some point have told you she loved you.

THE PRINCE (*drops his head like a young man ill at ease*). Yes, of course, but she was so good at analysing herself, at seizing the slightest nuance of her roving mind that I couldn't tell you exactly how she said it.

AMANDA. If not exactly how, at least exactly when.

THE PRINCE. She was so mad that night. She spoke of everything, always interrupting herself. She pretended she was all the lovers of mythology and she saw me as a bull, a swan . . . she even forced me to smoke a cigar – I hate them – so that I would be surrounded by smoke and look like Jupiter disguised as a cloud. I was Siegfried as well, and a few other Wagnerian heroes.

The violinist has returned to his place and the music slowly stops. In the silence, AMANDA *asks in a small voice.*

AMANDA. Are you sure she never once said, very simply: 'I love you.'

THE PRINCE (*crossly*). Léocadia could never say, simply: 'I love you.' Not to her favourite greyhound, not even to the pet snake who followed her everywhere.

AMANDA. I don't expect her to say it to a snake, even a pet one. But to you! It makes me sad she never said, 'I love you, Albert.'

THE PRINCE (*who is getting more cross*). 'I love you, Albert. I love you, Albert.' You're ridiculous. Try to understand once and for all that this isn't some vulgar romance between a shop girl and a draper's assistant on a station platform.

AMANDA. Of course. (*Trying to console him, gently.*) Mind you, she may have said 'I love you' in the middle of all the rest and you didn't hear it.

THE PRINCE. I don't think so.

AMANDA. When you come here and try and make her live in your imagination, do you try to make her talk as well?

THE PRINCE (*softly*). Not immediately. Sometimes it takes me several hours just to get her in front of me, sitting still. She used to move about all the time. And then, details escape me. Her eyes . . . I can never find her eyes.

AMANDA (*gently*). They're here tonight.

THE PRINCE. When I finally do have her in front of me, then very carefully, I try to make her speak.

AMANDA (*sarcastically*). You mean go on and on.

THE PRINCE (*ingenuous*). That's impossible. Her image is so fragile the least thing destroys it. I make her say very simple things: yes . . . no . . . perhaps . . . I'll see you tonight. I also make her say my name. She used to shower me with nicknames, Paris, Eros, my Swan, but she never called me by my name. She thought it was a stupid name. She was right, of course, but it's still my name. So I have my revenge. I make her say Albert all night long, Albert, my darling Albert. But it never works. The only time she did say my name it was sarcastically and I always see the curve of her lips at that moment.

AMANDA. Why don't you make her say 'I love you' since you have her at your mercy?

THE PRINCE (*bows his head, ill at ease*). I don't dare. I can't imagine what she would look like saying it.

AMANDA (*almost tenderly*). Look at me.

He lifts his head, surprised. She murmurs, gently, looking at him.

AMANDA. I love you, Albert.

He goes pale and looks at her, his jaw clenched.

AMANDA (*repeats, gently*). I love you, Albert. Will you remember the shape of my lips? I love you, Albert.

THE PRINCE (*with a lump in his throat, a little harshly*).

Thank you.

He wants to pour the champagne, but his hand is shaking, he can't get the bottle at the right angle and he fails. The HEAD WAITER *has been watching him and comes quickly, misunderstanding the unfinished gesture.*

THE HEAD WAITER. Shall I bring you more champange, my Lord?

THE PRINCE. Yes, thank you.

The HEAD WAITER *takes the bucket away and the orchestra, which seems to have been waiting for just such a signal, strikes up a lively piece. The* PRINCE *gets up, furious, and shouts.*

No! Not that music!

The musicians stop, dumbfounded.

THE HEAD WAITER (*coming to the table*). If your Lordship will forgive me, your Lordship cannot have forgotten that we played that piece when we brought more champagne to your Lordship's table. It was a custom of the house to play that piece whenever more champagne was brought to a table and I can assure your Lordship that we did not fail to do so that night.

THE PRINCE (*exasperated*). I said I didn't want that music. I don't care what you did that night!

The nightclub staff look at each other, appalled by such sacrilege. The HEAD WAITER, *having returned with the champagne bucket, is trembling like a leaf. Only the sound of the bottle against metal can be heard in the silence. The* PRINCE *and* AMANDA *look at each other with hostility. The* HEAD WAITER, *trembling more and more, lets the cork escape. An explosion. The* CLOAKROOM LADY *lets out a shrill cry from her retreat. A flood. The* HEAD WAITER *mops up the champagne, perishing with shame.*

THE HEAD WAITER. Please forgive me, my Lord. It's the first time in thirty-seven years. It must be a bad bottle. I'll go and change it.

AMANDA (*to the* HEAD WAITER *as he leaves*). I'll have another anisette with water, please.

THE HEAD WAITER (*stumbles off, bumping into everything*). Another anisette!

THE PRINCE (*between his teeth, still staring at her*). Must you add insult to injury?

AMANDA. I'm not trying to insult you, but I find your sudden bad temper unbearable, so I'm becoming myself again for a moment. And *I'm* thirsty. And *I* don't like champagne.

THE PRINCE (*shouts*). I, I, I, how interesting it is to say I. Don't worry, you never ceased being yourself these past two days and laughing, like the rest of your kind, at what you can't understand.

AMANDA. You're lying. I've tried to be her as hard as I could. At the moment, I can't. Forgive me and let me drink my anisette.

THE PRINCE. Why did you make fun of me with those words she never said and which you knew would hurt me?

AMANDA. I hoped they would help you.

THE PRINCE. You're lying.

AMANDA. Yes, I'm lying. (*She gets up, and says, very simply.*) I'm sorry to hurt you, but it seems to me that to suffer for love is something so beautiful, so precious, it ought not to be wasted like this. You'll hate me for what

I'm about to say and send me back to Paris, but I'll go back less unhappy if I've told you what I think: she didn't love you. That's nothing. It's possible to give so much without return. And anyway, I think you already suspected that she didn't love you. But there is something more serious I must tell you before I go back to sewing hats: you're young, rich, handsome, and your peasant hands are not brutal. You ought to try to forget all this and be happy. Because the truth is that you didn't love her either.

Silence. They hold their breath. Then the PRINCE *speaks in a calm voice.*

THE PRINCE. You're an idiot, and insolent as well. Waiter, please bring this young lady's coat. The way to the house is dark, someone will take you back. Tomorrow, one of my aunt's stewards will settle your wages.

AMANDA (*placid*). Bringing money into this hurts no one but you.

THE PRINCE. Yes, I'd forgotten about the selflessness of the Common People. You'll have nothing if you insist.

AMANDA. I want my return fare to Paris and three days' wages at union rates. I can tell you exactly what –

THE PRINCE. Don't bother.

The HEAD WAITER *arrives, walking ahead of the* CLOAKROOM LADY, *with* AMANDA*'s cloak. He shivers with emotion.*

THE HEAD WAITER. Madam's coat.

AMANDA. Take it back to the house. *I* don't wear furs in the middle of the summer. In the middle of the summer, *I*'m hot.

She is about to make a dignified exit.

THE PRINCE (*catching hold of her*). Wait: I belong to a class which provides farce with its favourite characters . . . I was brought up by old ladies and priests. Once out of their hands, my world was restricted to a society that had little contact with what you call life. It's only natural you take me for a fool.

AMANDA. I never took you for a fool.

THE PRINCE. Yes, you did. I don't blame you, I just called you an idiot. One always calls people who see things differently idiots. But listen . . . there's a prejudice against the working-class drunk who brings the country to its knees, paralyses production, has loads of children and insists on playing darts twice a week – the man who doesn't understand the great or the sublime. There is, however, an equally strong prejudice against an unhappy young man who lives as I do in a sixteenth-century pile and holds twenty-two useless titles. This may surprise you, but it's as difficult for me to convince people I'm not a dolt as it is for the son of a working-class brute. At least if this son has brains and works hard, he'll get scholarships and he'll be encouraged to become Prime Minister. Not so for me.

AMANDA. I don't see what you're getting at.

THE PRINCE. Let's agree that neither one of us is an idiot. And yet, my love strikes you as bizarre. You can't believe I loved such a laughing stock as Miss Léocadia Gardi.

AMANDA. I didn't say she was a laughing stock.

THE PRINCE. Because you're a sweet little girl who has respect for the dead. But if she were here tonight, sitting where you are and looking just as you do, you'd burst out laughing. Wouldn't you?

AMANDA (*her head down*). Yes.

THE PRINCE. Sit down.

AMANDA (*sitting*). Why?

THE PRINCE. Because I'm about to embark on a long monologue. (*And indeed, he begins.*) Life is wonderful when it's in stories or history books, but it has one major drawback: it has to be lived. It's impossible to sleep for more than twelve hours, so there are time-honoured procedures, alcohol, drugs. But I found it disgusting to use medicines to create happiness. You might suggest the cheerful courage of the boy scouts, but it's a grace which God, like most other graces, has distributed parsimoniously. Another way is to get up on the right foot every morning and do Swedish exercises in front of the mirror while repeating how happy one is. It's a regime for the constipated. So, I was bored . . . 'Bored', shout the virtuous souls, 'with all that heaven gave you? When there are so many poor people in the world?' That's an absurd reasoning. Why not tell those poor people they should enjoy their sound stomachs because there are so many millionaires with ulcers? My case is no different. Comfort is a habit and only a boor would find happiness in it. I was bored . . . 'If you'd had to work an eight-hour day, you wouldn't say that, young man.' True. At a factory, or in front of a pile of accounts, I would have had the leisure to avoid thinking of myself during the week and would only have been bored on Sundays, like everyone else. But I was sent this trial of seven Sundays a week. I didn't want to cheat with charities or horsebreeding. And to work to make even more money would have been vile and immoral, you'll agree. What more is there to say? I'm not an artist. I don't have any special gifts. I have a good memory, but what's the point of memorising other people's exploits? What's left is a rational and unrelenting pursuit of pleasure, which is what most people in my world do. It's the life of a convict. If working people used half as much energy and imagination to make money as the leisured classes use to go yawning in the four corners of Europe, they'd soon be millionaires. I have no vices either . . . it must be a wonderful thing, a vice.

Silence. He stops at this thought and dreams.

AMANDA (*timidly*). Is that all?

THE PRINCE. Almost. Into that fog of boredom from which I never hoped to escape there came a being who shed light for three days. A mad being, surrounded by greyhounds and pet snakes, who lived on orchids, champagne and passion, and who strangled herself one night after she'd talked too much of Bach. But this madwoman, with her silly refinements, her frivolities, this woman was intelligence. (*He looks at her, insolent.*) Intelligence, another goddess you may not have heard of. It's for her sake I let the village boys run after me laughing, because that's what they must have done to her, wherever she went. During those three days, before she dropped me back into an empty world, she taught me the worthlessness of certain appearances. Such things as two beautiful lips which murmur I love you, a skin that's a delight to touch. She taught me the worthlessness of your quiet contentment in the sun with its litter of picnic papers and the sound of the band. And she taught me about our kind of bitter joy, which has nothing to do with your safe little happiness. (*A pause, then he suddenly shouts.*) I don't love you. You're beautiful, more beautiful than she was, you're desirable, you're gay and tender, you're youth, nature, life, and you may even be right. But I don't love you.

AMANDA (*after a pause*). Is that all this time?

THE PRINCE. Yes, that's all.

AMANDA. Well, I couldn't care less about anything you've said.

She gets up, crosses the nightclub with a haughty air and goes out, slamming the door behind her. She walks into the park with a firm step, and then, when she feels she is no longer being watched, she collapses on a stone bench in the darkness. The PRINCE, *his tirade over, remains very stiff, very proud of himself. He looks around him. He is alone. He goes mechanically to his table and asks pitifully of the* HEAD WAITER *who comes towards him.*

THE PRINCE. You never doubted I loved her more than anything in the world, did you?

THE HEAD WAITER (*pours the champagne, obsequious*). No, my Lord. How can your Lordship ask such a question? Your Lordship adored her. We often speak of it amongst ourselves, my mates and I. It was an unforgettable love, even for the likes of us.

And as the PRINCE, *his head in both hands, starts to dream again, the* HEAD WAITER *turns to the* MUSICIANS *and with a revolting wink, orders.*

THE HEAD WAITER. Music!

The MUSICIANS, *with a mocking air, vigorously strike up a waltz. The* PRINCE *slumps down, his head in his hands.* AMANDA, *in the darkness of the park, sobs quietly on the bench.*

Curtain.

Scene Five

The curtain rises on a pink and grey-hued dawn. A quivering in the air announces the sunrise. AMANDA, *having cried herself to sleep, has slipped off the stone bench on to the ground. The lights of the nightclub are out and the* HEAD WAITER *and the other night moths have vanished. In the disorder of the empty room, the* PRINCE, *in evening dress, still sleeps, sprawled among the empty glasses, his head in his arms.*

Gunshots are heard in the distance. After a few seconds, the sound of the gunfire draws near. The DUCHESS *and* HECTOR *come in, wearing old-fashioned hunting dress and carrying guns for duck shooting. They are followed by a game keeper, who carries a second set of guns and empty game bags.*

THE GAME KEEPER. Your turn, my Lord.

HECTOR (*shoots into the auditorium and cries, frustrated*). Missed!

THE GAME KEEPER. Your turn, your Grace!

THE DUCHESS (*shoots and cries delighted*). Missed! Excellent! I am always so happy when I miss. A bird flying with ease and contentment is such a beautiful sight, I've never understood why we're required to aim these little lead balls at them. (*She notices a spot of white at the foot of the bench and cries out.*) Oh, my God! What's that white thing on the ground? You haven't hit anything, Hector?

HECTOR (*flustered*). I doubt it, my dear.

THE GAME KEEPER (*who has gone to inspect*). It's the young guest, your Grace.

THE DUCHESS. Is she hurt?

THE GAME KEEPER. No, she's asleep, your Grace.

THE DUCHESS (*going to* AMANDA). Asleep . . . and hurt. Her face is bathed in tears.

AMANDA (*has woken with a scream and then recognises the* DUCHESS). Oh – it's you. No, I don't want to talk to anyone. I want to leave immediately.

THE DUCHESS (*gestures to the others to leave*). Why do you want to leave, child?

AMANDA. She has more power than I do . . . I don't care, you understand, because I know I have more power than she does. But she has more power than I do.

THE DUCHESS. She has power, child, but not as much power as you do. And between ourselves, she's under a great disadvantage for a young woman: she's dead.

AMANDA. She wouldn't even let him hold her arm. And yet, I know that his hands aren't brutal. They are hands made to take and to touch. If only he'd listen to his hands, but he won't. So I have to go because she has more power than I do.

THE DUCHESS. You're twenty years old, you're alive and you're in love: no one has more power than you do this morning. Stop crying over the dreams of one night and look around you: it's morning.

And indeed, the light has changed around them and more changes will take place as the DUCHESS, *talking more and more like a fairy godmother, describes them.*

The sun is rising. Everything is opening to the same rhythm and hope: flower buds, hesitant young leaves, people's shutters. Smell the day: earth and wet grass and coffee, man's homage to the dawn.

And indeed, the PROPRIETOR *of the Inn of Sainte-Anne-du-Pouldu has opened his shutters and now stands on the threshold, yawning and grinding his coffee. Later, he will bring out the shrubs and tables for the terrace.*

Here come the first colours of the day, true greens and pinks. And soon we'll have the first buzzing of the bees, the first warmth of the sun. Léocadia may have had the powers of the night on her side . . . you're twenty, you're alive, you're in love. Stretch yourself out in the sun and laugh. All the powers of the morning are with you.

The DUCHESS *vanishes. The sun is shining now and the music is triumphant.* AMANDA *stretches out and laughs in the sun. The music stops at the sound of her happy laugh. She goes to the inn where the* PROPRIETOR *has finished arranging the tables on the terrace.*

AMANDA. Excuse me!

The PROPRIETOR *acts as if he doesn't hear.*

AMANDA. Sir!

The PROPRIETOR *still ignores her.* AMANDA *taps on the table with a stone. He looks at her, checks the table to see she hasn't scratched it and wipes it with bad grace.*

AMANDA. Is this the Inn of the Sainte-Anne-du-Pouldu?

He points to the sign.

AMANDA. Thank you. Are you dumb?

THE PROPRIETOR. Yes.

AMANDA (*very natural, with a smile*). What is it like?

THE PROPRIETOR (*half vanquished by her smile, answers*

sulkily). Like everything else, you get used to it.

AMANDA. Were you very young when it started?

THE PROPRIETOR. Thirty-seven.

AMANDA. What do you do for it?

THE PROPRIETOR. I gargle.

AMANDA. You gargle? Really?

THE PROPRIETOR (*who is now completely tame, lights up with a smile*). No, not really, but then, I'm not really dumb. My gargle is a tomato with bubbly before every meal. Four times a day. I have to be careful. My grandfather was an alcoholic.

AMANDA. Why wouldn't you answer me before?

THE PROPRIETOR. I was suspicious. I hadn't spoken to you before so I didn't know you.

AMANDA. And now?

THE PROPRIETOR. Now that we've spoken, I know you.

He adds, after a pause.

Of course, if I'm offered it, I drink one in the mornings. Despite the grandfather.

AMANDA. One what?

THE PROPRIETOR. One tomato.

AMANDA. What's a tomato?

THE PROPRIETOR. It's blackberry syrup with bubbly.

AMANDA. And what's bubbly?

THE PROPRIETOR. It's the tomato without the blackberry syrup. So is it two tomatoes?

AMANDA. Yes, two, but I hope the memory of your grandfather won't keep you from drinking mine. I'm not thirsty this morning.

THE PROPRIETOR. No, when it's a lady who's asking me, I bend the rules.

He goes into the inn and comes back with two glasses.

Are you from Dinard?

AMANDA. Yes.

THE PROPRIETOR. And you wandered into the park without noticing. It happens a lot in the summer. People take this for a real inn and it lets me do a little business on the side.

AMANDA. This isn't a real inn?

THE PROPRIETOR. No, no. It's a long story. The owner is a prince, a real prince. He had all these places built in the park to remember some woman. An eccentric, know what I mean? But I think it's a cover and it's something to do with the Jesuits and the Freemasons. But it's none of my business and I keep my mouth shut.

AMANDA. Is this where they met?

THE PROPRIETOR. Who?

AMANDA. The prince and the young woman.

THE PROPRIETOR. So they say.

AMANDA (*surprised*). Don't you remember?

THE PROPRIETOR (*who is on to his second tomato*). No . . . it's a long story. The real proprietors had been here for seventeen years. They didn't want to see their place demolished and rebuilt in a park, so they retired and left me in charge.

AMANDA. What happens when the prince asks you questions?

THE PROPRIETOR. They primed me and when I'm asked to

describe how they arrived in a taxi, how they ordered a lemonade, all the details, I tell them. It's as if I'd been there myself and when I get going, I invent. The prince doesn't even notice. Sometimes I wonder if he was there himself.

He goes back into the inn, delighted by his effect.

AMANDA (*calls him back*). Sir! Sir!

THE PROPRIETOR (*reappearing on the threshold*). What is it?

AMANDA. I like you very much.

THE PROPRIETOR (*worried*). Why?

AMANDA. You've just given me a wonderful present.

THE PROPRIETOR. Ah? (*He looks at her suspiciously.*) You have to pay for the tomatoes. That'll be three francs fifty.

AMANDA. Yes, thank you.

The PRINCE, *awake now, comes out of the nightclub, shivering and with his collar pulled up.*

AMANDA (*to the* PROPRIETOR *who is still puzzled*). Go now, quickly.

She gets up and stands in front of the PRINCE, *smiling, but still a little frightened.*

THE PRINCE (*suddenly sees her*). You're here?

AMANDA. Yes, I'm here.

THE PRINCE. I'm sorry I was so violent earlier.

AMANDA. Don't mention it.

THE PRINCE (*tired, echoes*). No.

He shivers.

AMANDA. You're shivering.

THE PRINCE. I'm always a little cold in the morning.

AMANDA. Why don't you come and sit in the sun where it's warm?

The PRINCE *moves forward and looks at the inn.*

THE PRINCE. We met again at this inn. We sat inside, next to that little window with the red curtains. It was cold.

AMANDA. Let's sit on the terrace. It's such a lovely morning.

The prince *comes back, bumping into the chairs.*

THE PRINCE. Yes . . . of course . . . if you want to. I keep bumping into the chairs, I'm very clumsy and still half asleep.

AMANDA. Don't you ever rise early?

THE PRINCE. I usually go to bed at dawn. But I fell asleep in the nightclub and it was too late to go to bed. Now it's too early. (*He shivers.*) It's so cold in the mornings.

AMANDA. No. It's almost hot. Listen to the bees. They wouldn't talk that way if it was cold.

THE PRINCE. They must be right then.

He sees that AMANDA *is looking at him, smiling.*

Why are you smiling?

AMANDA. You seemed frightening earlier. Not any more.

THE PRINCE (*who is still shivering*). I'm not really frightening.

The PROPRIETOR *comes out, surprised and suspicious and goes to the* PRINCE.

THE PROPRIETOR. Shall I serve the lemonade inside, as usual, or here?

AMANDA. Don't give us any lemonade. Can't you see his Lordship is cold? Bring us two white coffees. Very hot.

THE PROPRIETOR (*shattered*). White coffees . . . I said lemonade because it's usually lemonade, but if it's coffee that's wanted, I can make coffee.

AMANDA (*shouts as he goes off*). In big cups, with bread and butter.

THE PROPRIETOR (*repeats, sick*). Big cups, with bread and butter.

He goes, muttering.

I should have known, little schemer.

AMANDA. You don't mind if we have breakfast together?

THE PRINCE. No, I don't mind . . .

He chases the bees away.

Ugh, these insects . . .

AMANDA. Don't chase them away.

THE PRINCE. I suppose you'd like to see them eat me alive.

AMANDA. I promise they won't eat you.

THE PRINCE. Are they friends of yours?

AMANDA. Yes.

THE PRINCE. You seem so at home in the morning.

AMANDA. I can welcome you here . . . to my trees, my bees, my sun.

THE PRINCE (*looks at her and murmurs*). You're the frightening one.

AMANDA. Really?

THE PRINCE. You're like a little ogre, all pink and flourishing.

The PROPRIETOR *brings the white coffees in big blue cups, and bread and butter.*

THE PROPRIETOR. Your coffees. Shall I bring the lemonade as well?

AMANDA. No.

THE PROPRIETOR. No. No. That's a bit much. No.

He leaves, grumbling.

THE PRINCE (*looking at* AMANDA *buttering her bread*). Are you going to eat all that bread and butter?

AMANDA. Don't look at me like that, it won't work. I'm not ashamed this morning and I'm hungry.

THE PRINCE. A happy little ogre. So sure of herself. Without a trace of pain or shame. You frighten me. Who are you?

AMANDA. Just a young girl in a white dress who is eating bread and butter in the sun.

THE PRINCE. Didn't I see you the other evening standing next to a pillar?

AMANDA. Yes. I asked you the way to the sea.

THE PRINCE. Three days ago?

AMANDA. Yes. The next day we met again in your aunt's house and then we rented a boat and went upriver to Dinan. Last night, after a long afternoon lying next to each other in the sun, we went to the Blue Danube, you know, the most pretentious and silly place with that false Viennese music, always the same. Lalalala.

THE PRINCE (*sings softly with her*). Lalalala.

AMANDA. Lalala.

The orchestra takes the waltz up, plays with it and lets it die.

Now it's morning and we're having breakfast together in this little inn you wanted to show me. It's nice in the sun.

THE PRINCE (*suddenly shouts, distressed*). But it's the last day!

AMANDA (*calmly*). Why the last day? It's the third day and it's only begun.

THE PRINCE (*asks again*). But tonight?

AMANDA. Tonight, we'll go wherever you choose.

THE PRINCE. And tomorrow morning?

AMANDA. We'll be together as we are this morning and it'll be the beginning of the fourth day.

Silence. The PRINCE *shivers.* AMANDA *takes his arm.*

You're cold. Let's go in.

They enter the inn and the PRINCE *goes straight to the little table near the window.*

AMANDA (*pulls him away*), No, that one's in the shade. Let's sit here in the sun.

THE PRINCE. I don't want to.

AMANDA. Why not? You've also known me for three days, and you also love me.

THE PRINCE (*shouts*). I don't love you!

AMANDA (*gently*). If you didn't love me, you wouldn't have to shout it so loud. Oh please, stop struggling with those vanishing dreams. Look: it's morning now and the world is full of real things, flowers that can be smelled, grass that can be held in the hand.

She is facing him and says, suddenly, in one breath.

Put both of your hands on my waist please and see how easy it is.

THE PRINCE. I'm afraid.

AMANDA. Why? You have such ordinary hands. They wouldn't say no or refuse to forget. Hands love and then one morning they become strangers and can only be used for a greeting or to pat a cheek. And that's as it should be. Hold me, please.

THE PRINCE. If I touch you, Amanda, I know I will love you. But I don't want to touch you.

AMANDA (*with a fresh and tender little laugh*). You don't frighten me any more. Yesterday you were a prince for me, but now you're a little fish trying to swim against the current as so many others have tried before you.

THE PRINCE (*can't help sighing*). Léocadia . . .

AMANDA (*gently, as if this was to her*). Yes, my love. Put your hands on my waist.

Silence. The PRINCE *suddenly puts his hands around her and doesn't move. She shuts her eyes and murmurs.*

AMANDA. You don't say anything. And now, I'm afraid.

THE PRINCE (*in a hoarse voice*). How simple it is, yes, how certain and easy.

He kisses her. The wall of the little inn closes in on them. The DUCHESS *and* HECTOR *enter, their guns lowered. The* GAME KEEPER *walks behind them, ceremoniously carrying a bulging game bag.*

THE DUCHESS. It was you. I know it was you.

HECTOR. It couldn't have been.

THE DUCHESS. You're so clumsy, I knew you'd hit a bird

one of these days.

HECTOR. I saw you take aim. I'll go to the stake for it.

THE DUCHESS. To the stake, to the stake. You don't think I'd waste all my firewood just to make you confess you shot a heron, do you?

THE GAME KEEPER. It's not a heron, your Grace. It's not a flamingo either. It's a wild sort of bird that's never been seen in these parts before. Strange kind of flier: its feathers are too long, it catches itself on everything. Its legs are so high it doesn't know where to put itself and the colour makes it a target a mile off. And that cry. Did you hear that cry, your Grace, when you shot it? It's not like any bird I've ever seen.

HECTOR. You see, you shot it. Germain said so.

THE DUCHESS. Very well. I shot it. Are you pleased now? You can go, Germain, and take the bird away.

THE GAME KEEPER. What shall I do with it? It's not any good to eat, a bird like that.

THE DUCHESS. Bury it.

THE GAME KEEPER. Very well, your Grace.

He bows and is about to leave. The DUCHESS *calls him back.*

THE DUCHESS. Germain?

THE GAME KEEPER. Yes, your Grace.

THE DUCHESS. Bury it in my rose garden.

He bows again and goes out. Silence. The DUCHESS *and* HECTOR *sit side by side on the bench. They're dreaming.*

THE DUCHESS (*abruptly*). What are you thinking, Hector?

HECTOR (*starts*). It's funny, I was thinking of . . .

THE DUCHESS. So was I. It's odd. Poor Léocadia. She was reduced to strangling herself with her own scarf and now we've killed her a second time in his memory. But I had to save my little Albert. And if it's the young Amandas of this world who save the little Alberts then long live the young Amandas. But however useless, misplaced and frivolous Léocadia was, one can't help shedding a tear for her.

HECTOR (*moved*). No, my dear friend.

THE DUCHESS (*looks at him with scorn and says severely*). I wasn't talking to you.

She points to the sky.

I was talking to Gaston.

She goes. HECTOR, *baffled, saunters behind her as the curtain falls to a tune that is not quite sad.*

ANTIGONE

translated by
Barbara Bray

Characters

PROLOGUE
CHORUS
CREON, *king of Thebes*
ANTIGONE, *his niece*
ISMENE, *sister of Antigone*
HAEMON, *son of Creon*
NURSE
MESSENGER
JONAS, *1st Guard*
BINNS, *2nd Guard*
SNOUT, *3rd Guard*

Scene One

Set without historical or geographical implications. Three identical doors. At curtain rise all the characters are onstage, chatting, knitting, playing cards, and so on. The PROLOGUE *emerges from the rest and comes forward to speak.*

PROLOGUE. The people gathered here are about to act the story of Antigone. The one who's going to play the lead is the thin girl sitting there silent. Staring in front of her. Thinking. She's thinking that soon she's going to be Antigone. That she'll suddenly stop being the thin dark girl whose family didn't take her seriously, and rise up alone against everyone. Against Creon, her uncle . . . the king. She's thinking she's going to die . . . though she's still young, and like everyone else would have preferred to live.

But there's nothing to be done. Her name is Antigone, and she's going to have to play her part right through to the end.

Ever since the play started she has felt herself hurtling further and further away from her sister Ismene. (That's her, chatting and laughing with a young man over there.) Further and further away from all the rest of us, who are just here to watch, and haven't got to die in a few hours' time.

The young man talking to Ismene – fair-haired, beautiful, happy Ismene – is Haemon, son of Creon. He is Antigone's fiancé. Everything combined to attract him to Ismene – his love of dancing and sport, of happiness and success. His senses too, for Ismene is much prettier than Antigone. And then one evening, when there was a ball and he'd been dancing every dance with Ismene, dazzling in a new gown, he went and sought out Antigone where she sat dreaming in a corner, as she is now, with her arms clasped round her knees. And he asked her to be his wife. She looked up at him with those sober eyes of hers, unsurprised, smiled a sad little smile . . . and said 'yes'. The orchestra struck up again, Ismene was there across the room, in peals of laughter among the young men . . . and now he, Haemon, was going to be Antigone's husband. He didn't know that never in this world would there be such a person as Antigone's husband. That all this princely title conferred on him was the right to die.

The vigorous grey-haired man deep in thought, his young page beside him, is Creon, the king. He is wrinkled, tired. He is playing a difficult game: he has become a leader of men. Before, in the reign of Oedipus, when Creon was only the most influential man at court, he loved music and fine buildings, would spend hours prowling round Thebes's little antique shops. But Oedipus and his sons are dead. And Creon, forsaking his books and his collector's pieces, has rolled up his sleeves and taken their place. Sometimes, in the evening, when he's worn out, he wonders whether it's not pointless, being a leader of men. Whether it's not a sordid business that ought to be left to others less . . . sensitive than himself. Then, next morning, he's faced with particular problems to be solved, and he just gets up without more ado, like a labourer starting a day's work.

The old woman winding wool by the fireplace is the Nurse who brought up the two girls, and the elderly lady beside her, busy with her knitting, is Eurydice, Creon's wife. She'll go on knitting right through the tragedy, until it's her turn to stand up and die. She is kind, dignified, loving. She is of no help to Creon. He is alone. Alone with his little page who is too small and can't be of any help to him either.

The pale youth alone on the other side of the room, leaning pensively against the wall, is the Messenger. He's the one who will in due course come and tell of Haemon's death. That's why he doesn't feel like talking and laughing with the others. He knows . . .

Lastly, those three red-faced fellows playing cards, with their caps pushed back on their heads – they're the guards. Not bad chaps. They've got wives . . . children . . . little worries the same as everyone else. But before long they'll be collaring the accused without turning a hair. They smell of garlic and leather and red wine, and are completely devoid of imagination. They are the agents – eternally innocent, eternally complacent – of justice. For the time being the justice they serve is the justice of Creon . . . until the day comes when Thebes designates Creon's successor, and they are ordered to arrest Creon himself.

And now that you know them all they can act out their story. It begins when Oedipus's two sons, who were supposed to rule Thebes alternately, each for one year turn and turn about, fought and slew each other outside the city walls because Eteocles, the elder, refused to give way to his brother Polynices after his first year in power. Seven great foreign princes whom Polynices had won over to his case were defeated also at the city's seven gates. Now Thebes is safe, the two rival brothers are dead, and Creon the king has decreed that Eteocles, the virtuous brother, will be given an elaborate funeral, while Polynices, the good-for-nothing, the rebel, will be left unburied and unwept, a prey to ravens and jackals. Anyone affording him proper burial rites will be mercilessly punished, with death.

While the PROLOGUE *was speaking the other characters have left the stage one by one. Then the* PROLOGUE *too disappears. The light, meanwhile, has turned to that of a grey dawn in a sleeping house.* ANTIGONE *quietly opens the door and tiptoes in from outside, carrying her shoes in her hand. She stands still and listens. The* NURSE *appears.*

NURSE. Where have you been?

ANTIGONE. Just out for a walk. It was all grey. Beautiful. But now everything's turned pink and yellow and green. Like a postcard. You'll have to get up earlier, Nan, if you want to see a world without colours.

She makes as if to go.

NURSE. Not so fast! I was up while it was still pitch dark! I went to your room to make sure you hadn't thrown the blankets off in your sleep . . . and the bed was empty!

ANTIGONE. The garden was still asleep. I caught it unawares. A garden that hasn't yet begun to think about people. Beautiful.

NURSE. I soon saw you'd gone out – you'd left the back door open.

ANTIGONE. The fields were all wet. Waiting. Everything was waiting. I made a terrific noise all by myself on the road, and I felt awkward because I knew the waiting wasn't for me. So I took my sandals off and melted into the landscape . . .

NURSE. You're going to have to wash those feet before you get back into bed.

ANTIGONE. I'm not going back to bed.

NURSE. Four o'clock. It wasn't even four o'clock yet! I get

up to make sure she's still properly covered up, and there's her bed cold, and nobody in it!

ANTIGONE. Do you think it would be like that every morning, being the first girl out?

NURSE. Morning! Middle of the night, you mean! And are you trying to tell me you were only out for a walk? Story-teller! Where've you been?

ANTIGONE (*with a strange smile*). You're right. It was still night. I was the only one out there who thought it was morning. The first person today to believe in the light.

NURSE. Go on then – play the fool. I'm up to all your tricks – I was young once myself, and I was a handful too. Now tell me where you've been, you naughty girl!

ANTIGONE (*suddenly serious*). I wasn't doing anything wrong.

NURSE. You had a rendezvous, I suppose – don't tell me you hadn't!

ANTIGONE (*quietly*). Yes, I had a rendezvous.

NURSE. You mean you've got a sweetheart?

Pause.

ANTIGONE (*strangely*). Yes . . . Poor thing.

NURSE (*angry*). A nice thing for a king's daughter, I must say! You half kill yourself to bring them up, but they're all the same . . . And yet you used not to be like the others, preening in front of the glass and putting rouge on their lips and trying to attract attention. The times I've said to myself, 'My goodness, this child isn't vain enough! For ever in the same dress, with her hair all over the place – the lads'll all be after Ismene with her curls and her ribbons, and this one'll be left on my hands!' And all the time you were just like your sister –

worse, you little hypocrite! . . . Who is it? Some young layabout, I suppose? A boy you can't even introduce to your family as the one you love and want to marry? That's it, isn't it? . . . Isn't it? Answer me, you brazen hussy!

Pause.

ANTIGONE (*with a faint smile again*). Yes, Nurse. That's it.

NURSE. 'Yes', she says! Heaven help us! I've had her since she was a tiny tot, I promised her mother I'd make a respectable young woman of her – and now look! But you haven't heard the last of this, my girl! I may only be your nurse, and you may treat me like an old fool, but your uncle Creon's going to find out about this I can tell you!

ANTIGONE (*suddenly weary*). Yes, Nan. I know. Leave me alone now.

NURSE. And do you know what he's going to say when he hears about you getting up in the middle of the night? And what about Haemon, your fiancé? She's engaged, and she gets up at four in the morning to gad about with someone else! And then she wants to be left alone – her highness doesn't want anyone to say anything about it! Do you know what I ought to do? I ought to give you a good spanking, like when you were a little girl.

ANTIGONE. Don't make a fuss, Nan. You oughtn't to be too cross this morning.

NURSE. Not make a fuss! When I think how I promised her mother . . .! What would she say if she were here? 'You silly old fool,' she'd say – 'so you couldn't keep my little girl virtuous for me! For ever fussing over them with cardigans so they shan't catch cold and egg custards to build up their strength. But at four in the morning, when you're really needed, you're sleeping like a log, you who claim you never get a wink all night, so you let them slip out of the house as easy as pie, and when you get there the bed's stone cold!' That's what your mother'll say to me up there, when I go. And I'll be so ashamed I could die, if I wasn't dead already, and all I'll be able to do is hang my head and say, 'Yes, Lady Jocasta – you're absolutely right.'

ANTIGONE. Stop crying, Nan. You'll be able to look her straight in the eye, and she'll thank you for taking such good care of me. She knows why I went out this morning.

NURSE. You haven't got a sweetheart?

ANTIGONE. No.

NURSE. So you've been making fun of me? I suppose it's because I'm old. You were always my favourite. And though your sister was easier to manage, I thought it was you who loved me best, too. But if you did love me you'd have told me the truth. Why was the bed empty when I came to tuck you in?

ANTIGONE. Please don't cry. (*She kisses her.*) Come along, my little old red apple. Do you remember when I used to rub your cheeks till they shone? Don't fill all these little furrows with tears for nothing. I am virtuous, I swear I have no other sweetheart than Haemon. If you like, I'll swear I never shall. Save your tears – you may have need of them. When you cry I feel like a little girl again. And I mustn't be little today.

Enter ISMENE.

ISMENE. Up already, Antigone? I went to your room and –

ANTIGONE. Yes. I'm up already.

NURSE. So do the pair of you mean to start getting up in

the morning before the servants? What sort of behaviour is that for princesses? Strolling about before breakfast . . . not even properly dressed. You'll both be catching colds on me again before –

ANTIGONE. It's summer now, Nan – we shall be all right. Go and make us some coffee, won't you? (*She sits down, tired suddenly.*) I could do with a cup.

NURSE. My dove! There she is, light-headed for want of something to eat, and I stand here like a fool . . .

She hurries off.

ISMENE. Don't you feel well?

ANTIGONE. It's nothing. Just a bit tired. (*Smiling.*) That comes of getting up so early.

ISMENE. I couldn't sleep either.

ANTIGONE (*smiling*). But you must, or you won't be so pretty in the morning.

ISMENE. Don't make fun.

ANTIGONE. I'm not. It's a comfort to me this morning, your being pretty. Do you remember how miserable it used to make me when I was little? How I used to daub you with mud and put worms down your neck? And once I tied you to a tree and cut off your hair! (*Stroking* ISMENE'*s hair.*) Such beautiful hair . . . How easy it must be not to have foolish thoughts, with all these lovely sleek locks hanging round your head!

ISMENE (*abruptly*). Why have you changed the subject?

ANTIGONE (*gently, still stroking* ISMENE'*s hair*). I haven't . . .

ISMENE. Listen, Antigone. I've been thinking . . .

ANTIGONE. Yes . . . ?

ISMENE. Turning it over in my mind all night . . . You're mad.

ANTIGONE. That's right.

ISMENE. We can't do it!

Pause.

ANTIGONE (*in her usual quiet voice*). Why not?

ISMENE. They'll kill us!

ANTIGONE. Of course they will. Everyone has his part to play. Creon has to have us put to death, and we have to go and bury our brother. That's how the cast-list was drawn up. What can we do about it?

ISMENE. I don't want to die!

ANTIGONE (*quietly*). I'd have preferred not to.

ISMENE. Listen. I'm older than you, and not so impulsive. You do the first thing that comes into your head, never mind whether it's sensible or stupid. But I'm more level-headed. I think.

ANTIGONE. Sometimes it's best not to think too much.

ISMENE. I disagree. It's a horrible business, of course, and I feel sorry for Polynices too. But I do see Creon's point of view.

ANTIGONE. I don't want to see it.

ISMENE. He's the king. He has to set an example.

ANTIGONE. But I'm not the king, and I don't! Antigone, self-willed little beast, does the first thing that comes into her head! So then she's stood in the corner or locked up in the dark. And serve her right! She should do as she's told!

ISMENE. That's right! Scowl! Glare! Hold forth without letting anyone else get a word in edgeways! But listen to what I say. I'm right more often than you are.

ANTIGONE. I don't want to be right!

ISMENE . At least try to understand!

ANTIGONE. Understand! You've always been on at me about that, all of you, ever since I was little. I was supposed to understand I mustn't play with water – beautiful, cool, elusive water – because it made the floor wet. Or with earth, because it dirtied my clothes. I was supposed to understand you mustn't eat your cake before you've finished your bread and butter, or give all your pocket-money away to a beggar, or run in the wind till you drop, or drink when you're hot, or go swimming just when you feel like it. Understand, understand, always understand! I don't want to understand! I can do that when I'm old. (*Softly*.) If I ever am.

ISMENE . He's the king, Antigone. He's stronger than we are. And everyone agrees with him. The streets of Thebes are full of them.

ANTIGONE. I'm not listening.

ISMENE . They'll hiss and boo. They'll seize us in their thousand arms, surround us with their thousand faces and their one expression, spit at us. And we'll have to ride in the tumbril through their hatred, through their smell and their laughter to our execution. The guards will be waiting there, with their stupid faces all red from their stiff collars, their great clean hypocrites' hands, their loutish stare. You can shout till you're hoarse, trying to explain – they'll do exactly as they're told, slavishly, without knowing or caring whether it's right or wrong. And the suffering, have you thought of that? We'll have to suffer, feel the pain increasing, mounting up till it's no longer bearable, It has to stop, but it goes on, climbing higher and higher like an ear-splitting shriek . . . I can't! I can't!

ANTIGONE. That's what thinking does for you!

ISMENE . Haven't you thought about it?

ANTIGONE. Yes, of course.

ISMENE . But I'm not brave.

ANTIGONE (*quietly*). Neither am I. What's that got to do with it?

Pause.

ISMENE . Don't you want to live then?

ANTIGONE (*low*). Not want to live . . . (*Lower still if that's possible.*) Who used to be up first in the morning just to feel the chill air on her bare skin? Who used to go to bed last, and then only when she was ready to drop, just so as to live a little bit more of the night? Who used to cry, as a child, because there were so many insects and plants in the fields that it was impossible to collect them all?

ISMENE (*suddenly drawn to her*). Antigone . . . my pet . . .

ANTIGONE (*pulling herself together, crying out*). No! Leave me alone! Now's not the time to be whimpering and putting our arms round one another! You say you've thought things over? And you've come to the conclusion that it's too much – to have the whole city howling for your blood, the pain, the fear of dying?

ISMENE (*hanging her head low*). Yes.

ANTIGONE. Excuses! You can make use of them if you like.

ISMENE (*throwing herself at* ANTIGONE). Antigone! Please! It's all right for men to die for their ideas. But you're a girl.

ANTIGONE (*through clenched teeth*). Only a girl! The tears

I've shed because of it!

ISMENE. Your happiness is within your grasp – you've only to stretch out your hand and take it . . . You're engaged, you're young, you're beautiful . . .

ANTIGONE (*dully*). No – not beautiful.

ISMENE. Yes, in your own way! You know very well it's you the boys turn to look at in the street, you the little girls stare at speechless till you disappear round the corner . . .

ANTIGONE (*faint smile*). Boys in the street . . . Little girls . . .

Pause.

ISMENE. And Haemon? What about Haemon, Antigone?

ANTIGONE (*expressionless*). I'll be talking to him. I'll soon settle him.

ISMENE. You're out of your mind.

ANTIGONE (*smiling*). You've always said that about everything I've ever done . . . Go back to bed, Ismene. It's getting light – look! – and there's nothing I can do. My dead brother's surrounded by guards now, just as if he'd managed to make himself king. Go back to bed. You're pale from lack of sleep.

ISMENE. Aren't you coming?

ANTIGONE. I don't feel like sleeping. But I promise I'll stay here until you wake up. Nurse will bring me something to eat. You go now – you can hardly keep your eyes open.

ISMENE. You will let me talk to you again? Try to make you see . . . ?

ANTIGONE (*with a tinge of weariness*). Yes, yes . . . I'll let you talk to me. I'll let you all talk to me. Go to bed now, please, or you won't be so pretty tomorrow.

She smiles sadly as she watches ISMENE *go, then, suddenly weary, collapses on a chair. Pause.*

Poor Ismene!

Enter NURSE.

NURSE. Here's a nice cup of coffee and some toast, my pigeon. Eat it all up now.

ANTIGONE. I'm not very hungry.

NURSE. I buttered the toast with my own hands, just the way you like it!

ANTIGONE. Thank you, Nan . . . I'll just sip some coffee . . .

Pause.

NURSE. You're not well, my love. Where does it hurt?

ANTIGONE. Nowhere, Nan. But cuddle me and keep me warm just the same, like you used to when I was ill . . . Dear old Nan – stronger than fever or nightmares, stronger than the shadow of the wardrobe, grinning and changing shape on the wall. Stronger than all the insects gnawing away at something in the dark. Stronger than the dark itself, full of crazy shrieks that no one listens to. Stronger than death. Hold my hand, like when you used to come and sit by my bed.

NURSE. What's the matter, my little dove?

ANTIGONE. Nothing, Nan. Just that I'm still a bit small for it all.

NURSE. A bit small for what, my sparrow?

ANTIGONE. Nothing. Anyway, you're here, I'm holding the rough hand that's always kept me safe from everything. Perhaps it will keep me safe still.

NURSE. What can I do for you, my turtle dove?

ANTIGONE. Just rest your hand on my cheek – like this. (*She keeps her eyes closed for a moment.*) There, I'm not afraid any more. Not of the wicked ogre, nor of the bogey man, nor of the Pied Piper. (*Pause. Change of tone.*) Nurse, you know Floss . . . ?

NURSE. Don't talk to me about that blessed dog. Pawmarks over everything. Oughtn't to be allowed in the house.

ANTIGONE. Promise you won't grumble at her any more. Even if she leaves pawmarks everywhere.

NURSE. You mean I'm to let her ruin everything and not say a word?

ANTIGONE. Yes.

NURSE. No, that's too much – !

ANTIGONE. You're quite fond of her really. And you enjoy polishing and scrubbing – you wouldn't like it if everything was always spick and span . . .

NURSE. What if she wets my carpets?

ANTIGONE. Promise not to scold her even then. Please, Nan.

NURSE. You know how to get round people, don't you?

ANTIGONE. And I want you to talk to her too.

NURSE (*shrugging*). Talk to brute beasts!

ANTIGONE. Not as if she's a brute beast! As I do . . . As if she were a real person.

NURSE. Play the fool like that at my age? But why?

ANTIGONE (*gently*). Well, if for some reason or other I couldn't talk to her myself any more.

NURSE (*not understanding*). What do you mean? Why not?

ANTIGONE (*first looking away, then in a harsher voice*). But if she's too miserable . . . if she keeps waiting with her nose glued to the door like when I go out without her – then perhaps it would be best to have her put to sleep.

NURSE. Have Floss put to sleep? Whatever's the matter with you this morning?

Enter HAEMON.

ANTIGONE. Here's Haemon. Leave us, Nan. And don't forget what you promised.

Exit NURSE.

ANTIGONE (*running over to* HAEMON). Forgive me for quarrelling yesterday evening, Haemon. And for everything. It was my fault. Please forgive me.

HAEMON. You know I'd forgiven you as soon as you'd gone out and slammed the door! The perfume you were wearing was still in the air, and I'd forgiven you already. (*He takes her in his arms, smiles, looks at her.*) Who did you steal it from, that scent?

ANTIGONE. Ismene.

HAEMON. And the lipstick, the powder, the pretty dress?

ANTIGONE. Ismene.

HAEMON. And what was it all in aid of?

ANTIGONE. I'll tell you presently. (*She nestles closer to him*). Oh, my darling, how stupid I've been! A whole beautiful evening wasted.

HAEMON. There'll be others.

ANTIGONE. Will there?

HAEMON. Other quarrels too. Happiness is full of them.

ANTIGONE. Happiness . . . Listen, Haemon.

HAEMON. Yes, Antigone.

ANTIGONE. Don't laugh this morning. Be serious.

HAEMON. I am serious.

ANTIGONE. And hold me tight. Tighter than ever before. Give me all your strength.

HAEMON. There . . . All my strength . . .

ANTIGONE. Ah . . . (*They remain silent for a moment.*) Haemon, you know the little boy we would have had . . . ?

HAEMON. Yes.

ANTIGONE. You know I'd have shielded him against everything?

HAEMON. Yes.

ANTIGONE. I'd have held him so tight he'd never have been afraid – not of the creeping dark, nor of the unmoving sun, nor of the shadows. He'd have had an unkempt, skinny little mother, but one who was safer than all the real mothers put together, with their real bosoms and their nice big aprons! You believe me, don't you?

HAEMON. Yes, my love.

ANTIGONE. And you do believe you'd have had a real wife?

HAEMON (*holding her*). I've got one already.

ANTIGONE. Oh Haemon, you did love me that evening, didn't you?

HAEMON (*gently*). Which evening?

ANTIGONE. You are sure, aren't you, that when you came and found me at the dance, you didn't pick the wrong girl? You're sure you've never regretted it, never thought – even deep down, even once – that you ought really to have asked Ismene?

HAEMON. Don't be silly!

ANTIGONE. You do love me, don't you? Your arms don't lie, nor the smell of you, nor this heavenly warmth, nor the confidence that fills me when I lean my head on your shoulder?

HAEMON. Yes, Antigone. I love you.

ANTIGONE. I'm so dark and thin. Ismene's pink and gold like an apricot.

HAEMON (*low*). Antigone . . .

ANTIGONE. Oh, I'm making myself blush. But this morning I must know. When you think how I'm going to be yours, do you feel a great void growing inside you, as if something were dying?

HAEMON. Yes.

ANTIGONE. So do I. And I want you to know I'd have been proud to be your wife, the one whose shoulder you'd have patted absent-mindedly as you sat down in the evening, as if you were patting something that was truly yours. (*She moves away from him and speaks in a different tone of voice.*) So. Now two things. And when you've heard them you must go away without asking any questions. Even if they seem strange. Even if they give you pain.

HAEMON. But what can they be?

ANTIGONE. Promise you'll go without even a backward glance. If you love me, promise. (*She looks at his shocked, pitiful expression.*) It's the last foolishness you'll have to forgive me.

Pause.

HAEMON. I promise.

ANTIGONE. Thank you. Well, to go back to yesterday first. You asked me just now why I was wearing Ismene's dress, her perfume and make-up. Well, I was a fool – I wasn't sure it was me you really wanted, and I was trying to make you want me by being more like the other girls.

HAEMON. So that was it!

ANTIGONE. Yes. And you laughed, and we quarrelled. My bad temper got the better of me and I flounced off. (*Pause. Lower.*) But I really came to see you yesterday evening so that you might make love to me – so that I might be your wife already. Before . . . (*He draws back and is about to speak, but she cries out.*) You promised not to ask! (*Humbly.*) Please . . . (*Turning away; harshly.*) Anyway, let me explain. I wanted to become your wife because that's how I love you . . . And because – forgive me for hurting you, my darling – because I can never marry you.

He is dumbfounded. She runs over to the window and cries out.

Haemon, you promised! Go now. If you speak, or take one step towards me I'll jump out of this window. I swear it on the head of the son we had in our dreams. The only son I'll ever have. Go now, quickly. You'll understand tomorrow. Soon. (*She sounds so despairing that* HAEMON*does as she says.*) That's right, Haemon, leave me. It's the only thing you can do now to show that you love me.

HAEMON *has gone.* ANTIGONE *stands still, with her back to the audience, then shuts the window and goes and sits on a little chair in the middle of the stage. When she speaks she sounds strangely at peace.*

There, Antigone. How Haemon's over and done with.

Enter ISMENE.

ISMENE (*calling*). Oh, you're still here!

ANTIGONE (*not moving*). Why aren't you asleep?

ISMENE. I couldn't sleep. I was so afraid you might go and bury him, even in the light. (*Close.*) Antigone . . . little sister . . . here we all are – Haemon, Nurse, me . . . Floss . . . We love you, we're alive, and we need you! Polynices is dead, and he didn't love you. He was always more a stranger to us than a brother. Forget him, Antigone, as he forgot us! Let Polynices' harsh ghost wander for ever unburied, since that's what Creon decrees. Don't attempt what's beyond your strength. You like to hurl defiance at the whole world, but you're only one small person. Stay with us. Don't go near the place. Please.

ANTIGONE *stands up, faintly smiling. She goes over to the door, and there, on the threshold, speaks.*

ANTIGONE (*quietly*). It's too late. This morning, when you saw me, I'd just come back from there.

Exit ANTIGONE. ISMENE *runs after her.*

ISMENE. Antigone!

As soon as ISMENE *disappears,* CREON *and his* PAGE *enter through another door.*

CREON. A guard, you say? One of the sentries keeping watch over the body? Have him brought in.

The GUARD *enters. A rough diamond. At present he is green with fear.*

JONAS (*coming to attention*). Jonas, your honour. B Company.

CREON. Well?

JONAS. Well, sir, we drew lots to see who was to come, and it turned out to be me. We thought it was best for just one of us to come and explain. We couldn't all come. There's three of us on duty, sir, guarding the body.

CREON. Well, what have you got to tell me?

JONAS. I'm not the only one, you see. There's Snout as well, and Lance-Corporal Binns.

CREON. Why didn't he come?

JONAS. Just what I said! It ought to have been him. When there isn't an NCO, the Lance-Corp's responsible. But the others both said no, we must draw lots. Shall I go and fetch the Lance-Corp, sir?

CREON. No. You'll do, since you're here.

JONAS. I've got a very good record, sir. Seventeen years service. Enlisted as a volunteer. One medal. Two mentions in dispatches. A stickler for the rules. Orders are sacred. The officers all say 'You can rely on Jonas.'

CREON. Right. Speak . . . What are you afraid of?

JONAS. By rights it ought to have been Binns, sir. I'm up for a stripe but I haven't got it yet . . . I was supposed to get it in June.

CREON. Will you stop babbling and say what you have to say! If anything's happened all three of you are responsible. Never mind who ought to have come.

JONAS. Right, sir . . . Well . . . it was the body . . . We did stay awake, you know! And ours was the two o'clock watch, the worst of the lot. You know what it's like, your honour, when the night's nearly over – the weight between your eyes, the ache at the back of your neck . . . The shadows all shifting about . . . And the mist rising . . . They picked the right moment, and no mistake! There we were, chatting, stamping our feet to keep warm – but we weren't asleep, sir . . . I guarantee none of us shut our eyes for a second . . . It was much too cold anyway. Well, all of a sudden I take a look at the body. It was only a couple of yards away, but I took a look at it every so often all the same. Thorough, sir, that's me. That's why all the officers say 'You can rely on –' (CREON *interrupts him with a gesture. He suddenly shouts out.*) I was the first to notice, sir! The others'll tell you the same – it was me who raised the alarm.

CREON. What do you mean – alarm? What for?

JONAS. The body, sir. Someone had covered it up. Oh, nothing much. They didn't have time with us there. Just a sprinkling of earth . . . Enough to hide it from the vultures.

CREON (*going over to him*). Are you sure it wasn't some animal scratching up the soil nearby?

JONAS. No, sir! That's what we hoped at first, too. Some animal. But no – the earth had been scattered over the body deliberately, according to the rites. By someone who knew what they were doing.

CREON. Who dared? Who was mad enough to flout my orders? Did you find any footprints?

JONAS. No, sir. Only one, lighter than a bird would make. A bit later on, further away, we found a spade, a little old child's spade, all rusty. We didn't reckon a child could have done it, but the Corp kept the spade as evidence, just in case.

CREON (*pause*). A child . . . The opposition may be crushed, but it's already working away underground. Polynices' friends, with their gold all frozen in Thebes . . . The leaders of the plebs, reeking of garlic, suddenly in alliance with the princess . . . The priests, trying to fish up something for themselves out of these murky waters . . . A child . . . Yes, they must have thought that would make it more touching, more pathetic. I can just see them and their 'child' – a hired assassin, more like, with his toy spade hidden under his coat. Unless they talked a real child into doing it. What a bonus to have innocence on their side! A genuine little white-faced brat ready to spit down the barrel of my guns! My hands stained with fresh young blood! (*He goes over to* JONAS.) But they must have had accomplices. Perhaps among my guards . . . Here, you –

JONAS. Sir, we did all we were supposed to do! Snout may have sat down for half an hour because his feet hurt, but I stayed standing up the whole time! The Corp'll back me up, sir!

CREON. Who've you told about this?

JONAS. No one, sir. We drew lots right away and I came straight here.

CREON. Now listen to me. Your watch is doubled. Send the relief away when it comes. I don't want anyone else but you three near that body. And not a word to anyone! You and your mates are already guilty of negligence and will be punished for that anyway – but if you talk, and the rumour gets about that someone's covered up Polynices' corpse, all three of you will die.

JONAS (*bawling out*). We haven't said a word, sir, I swear! But . . . I've been here all this time, and perhaps by now the others have said something to the next watch.

(*Getting more and more panic-stricken.*) Sir, I've got two kids! One of them's only a baby. You'll give evidence to the court-martial that I was here, won't you? Here, with you! I've got a witness! If anyone's blabbed it was the others, not me! I've got a witness!

CREON. Clear out. If no one finds out, you'll live.

JONAS *runs out.* CREON *remains silent a moment, then suddenly says to himself.*

CREON. A child . . .

He takes the PAGE *by the shoulder.*

CREON. Come, boy. We must go and make this known . . . And then the trouble will start . . . Would you die for me? Would you go along with your little spade?

The PAGE *stares at him.* CREON *strokes the boy's hair as they go out.*

Yes, of course you would, without a moment's hesitation. You too. (*He can be heard sighing as he goes.*) A child . . .

They are gone. Enter the CHORUS.

CHORUS. So. Now the spring is wound. The tale will unfold all of itself. That's the convenient thing about tragedy – you can start it off with a flick of the finger: a glance at a girl going past with uplifted arms in the street; a sudden hunger for fame when you wake up one day – as if it were something to eat; asking yourself one question too many some evening . . . That's all it takes. And afterwards, no need to do anything. It does itself. Like clockwork set going since the beginning of time.

Death, treachery, despair – all there ready and waiting . . . And noise, and storms, and every kind of silence. The silence when the executioner lifts his arm at the end. The silence at the beginning, when the two lovers are naked together for the first time, and at first, in the dark, don't dare to move. The silence when the shouts of the crowd rise up around the victor – like a film with the sound-track stuck . . . all those open mouths with nothing coming out of them, all that clamour no more than an image. And the victor already vanquished, there in the midst of his silence.

Nice and neat, tragedy. Restful, too. In a drama, with its traitors, its desperate villains, its innocent victims, avengers, devoted followers and glimmers of hope, death becomes something terrible, a kind of accident. You might have arrived in time with the police. But tragedy's so peaceful! For one thing, everybody's on a par. All innocent! It doesn't matter if one person kills and the other is killed – it's just a matter of casting . . . And above all, tragedy's restful, because you know there's no lousy hope left. You know you're caught, caught at last like a rat in a trap, with all heaven against you. And the only thing left to do is shout – not moan, or complain, but yell out at the top of your voice whatever it was you had to say. What you've never said before. What perhaps you didn't even know till now . . . And to no purpose – just so as to tell it to yourself . . . to learn it, yourself. In drama you struggle, because you hope you're going to survive. It's utilitarian – sordid. But tragedy is gratuitous. Pointless, irremediable. Fit for a king!

Enter ANTIGONE, *hustled in by* GUARDS.

Now it's beginning. Little Antigone has been caught – and handcuffed. She can be herself at last.

Exit CHORUS *as the* GUARDS *push* ANTIGONE *on to the stage.*

JONAS (*quite self-assured again*). Come on now, miss – no nonsense! You can explain it all to the boss. I only obey orders. I don't want to know what you were doing. Everybody has some excuse. Everybody has something to say for himself. A fine pickle we'd be in if we had to try to understand them all! Hold on tight, the rest of you! She's a slippery customer! Fat lot I care what she has to say!

ANTIGONE. Tell them to take their filthy hands off. They're hurting me.

JONAS. Filthy hands? You might at least be polite, miss. I am.

ANTIGONE. Tell them to let go of me. I am Oedipus's daughter – Antigone. I shan't run away.

JONAS. Oedipus's daughter, eh? The tarts we pick up on the beat always tell us to watch out because they're the police chief's girlfriends!

GUARDS *laugh*.

ANTIGONE. I don't care about dying – but I won't have them touch me!

JONAS. Oh? But you're not afraid of touching earth, or corpses? You talk about dirty hands – what about your own. (ANTIGONE *looks at her hands, in their handcuffs, and smiles. They are covered with earth.*) They took away your spade, so the second time you did it with youre bare hands! The cheek! I turn my back for a minute to get a chew of tobacco, and before I can stick it in my gob and say thanks, there she is clawing up the earth with her nails like a blooming hyena! And in broad daylight! And the fight she puts up when I try to arrest her! Tries to scratch my eyes out! Shouts and bawls about having to finish the job. Potty, if you ask me.

BINNS. I arrested one just as barmy the other day – showing everyone her backside.

JONAS. Anyway, we'll have a good party to celebrate this. Any ideas, Binns?

BINNS. The Crown. Best vino in town.

SNOUT. We're off duty Sunday. Shall we take the wives?

JONAS. No, it's more fun on our own – the women always complicate things and the kids keep wanting to go to the lav. (*Pause.*) Didn't think we'd be planning celebrations a while ago, did we?

BINNS. Perhaps there'll be a reward.

JONAS. If it's something really important . . .

SNOUT. Chap in C Company got double pay last month for catching an arsonist.

BINNS. If we get that let's go to the Arab Palace!

JONAS. Are you crazy? The wine's twice the price there. If you mean for the girls though, okay. (*Pause.*) Tell you what, why don't we go to the Crown first and get a skinful, then go on to the Palace? Hey, Binns – remember the fat one?

BINNS. You really did get blotto that time!

SNOUT. But if we get double pay the wives'll find out. There might be a public ceremony.

JONAS. Let's wait and see, then. We can go on the spree whatever happens. But if there's a special parade the wives and kids'll be there and the whole lot'll have to go to the Crown.

BINNS. We'll have to order in advance.

ANTIGONE (*small voice*). I'd like to sit down, please.

Pause.

JONAS. All right. Give her a chair. But don't let go of her!

Enter CREON.

JONAS (*loudly and at once*). Attenshun everybody!

CREON (*stopping, surprised*). What's this? Let go of that young lady at once! What do you think you're doing?

JONAS. We're the guard, sir. I brought my mates.

CREON. Who's watching the body, then?

JONAS. We sent for the relief.

CREON. I told you not to send them away! I told you not to tell anyone!

JONAS. We haven't, sir. But when we arrested this girl we thought we'd better bring her along. We didn't draw lots this time. We thought it was best if we all came.

CREON. Fools! (*To* ANTIGONE.) Where were you when they arrested you, Antigone?

JONAS. Right by the body, sir.

CREON. What were you doing there? You knew I'd forbidden anyone to go near it.

JONAS. You want to know what she was doing? That's why we brought her here. She was scrabbling in the earth with her hands. Covering it up again.

CREON. Do you realise what you're saying, man?

JONAS. Ask the others, sir, if you don't believe me. When I got back on duty after seeing you the first time, we uncovered the body, took the earth away. But the sun was getting hot and it was starting to smell, so we went and stood a little way away, on a mound, in the wind. We thought that'd be perfectly safe, in the daytime. To make sure, we decided one of us would keep an eye on the body all the time. But my midday, what with the heat right out there in the sun . . . And the wind had dropped, so the smell was worse . . . Well, it just knocked you out! No matter how hard I strained my eyes everything shook like a jelly – you couldn't see properly at all. I just went and asked one of my mates for a quid of tobacco to keep me awake . . . and before I have time to say thank you and turn round, there she is, grabbing away with her bare hands. In broad daylight!

She must have known we'd be bound to see her. And when I came running, do you think she stopped or tried to run off? Not a bit of it! She just scrabbled away as fast as she could, still, as if she hadn't even seen me. Even when I grabbed her she fought like a tiger and kept on trying to dig. Kept yelling at me to let her go, the body wasn't properly covered up yet . . .

CREON. Is this true, Antigone?

ANTIGONE. Yes.

JONAS. We went ahead and uncovered the body again, handed over to the next watch without saying anything, and brought here here to you, sir.

CREON. And during the night, Antigone? . . . the first time? . . . was that you too?

ANTIGONE. Yes. I used the little tin spade we used to make sandcastles with on the beach in the summer. It belonged to Polynices – he'd scratched his name on the handle. That's why I left it near him. But they took it away. So the second time I had to use my hands.

JONAS. Just like a little animal! In fact, with the air so

hazy, that's what one of my mates took her for at first. 'It's some animal,' he says, but I say, 'No it's not – it's too neat for an animal . . . It's a girl!'

CREON. Right. You may be asked for a report later . . . For the moment, leave your prisoner alone with me. Take off her handcuffs before you go. (*To* PAGE.) Take these men away, boy, and see they're kept incommunicado till I come.

Exit GUARDS, *following the* PAGE.

CREON. Did you tell anyone what you were going to do?

ANTIGONE. No.

CREON. Did you meet anyone on the way?

ANTIGONE. No.

CREON. Are you sure?

ANTIGONE. Yes.

CREON. Listen, then. Go back to your room, go to bed, and say you're ill and haven't been out since yesterday. Get your nurse to say the same. I'll get rid of those three men.

ANTIGONE. What's the point? They know I'll do it again.

Silence. They look at each other.

CREON. Why did you try to bury your brother?

ANTIGONE. I had to.

CREON. I'd forbidden it.

ANTIGONE (*quietly*). I had to just the same. People who aren't buried wander for ever in search of rest. If my brother had come home tired after a day's hunting I'd have taken off his boots, given him something to eat and got his bed ready. Polynices has done with hunting now. He's going home, to where Mother and Father, and Eteocles too, are waiting for him. He's entitled to some rest.

CREON. He was a rebel and a traitor and you know it.

ANTIGONE. He was my brother.

CREON. You heard my edict proclaimed at every cros-sroads? You saw the posters on every wall?

ANTIGONE. Yes.

CREON. So you knew what was to become of anyone who dared give him burial?

ANTIGONE. Yes.

CREON. Maybe you thought that as the daughter of Oedipus, of Oedipus's pride, you were above the law?

ANTIGONE. No. I didn't think that.

CREON. The law is meant especially for you, Antigone – it's meant especially for the daughters of kings!

ANTIGONE. If I'd been a servant girl up to the elbows in dishwater when I heard the edict, I'd have dried my hands and gone out in my apron to bury my brother.

CREON. No, you wouldn't. If you'd been a servant girl you'd have known you'd die for it – so you'd have stayed at home and mourned your brother there. But you thought that because you belonged to the royal family – because you were my niece and my son's fiancé – I wouldn't dare have you put to death whatever you did.

ANTIGONE. You're wrong. I was sure you would have put me to death.

CREON *looks at her, then bursts out suddenly, as if to himself.*

CREON. The pride of Oedipus. You're its living image.

And now I see it again in your eyes, I believe you. You thought I would have you put to death, and that struck you, in your vanity, as a very suitable end for you. For your father, too, ordinary human misery – there was no question of happiness! – wasn't enough. In your family, what's human only cramps your style – you have to have a private confrontation with destiny and death. You have to kill your father and sleep with your mother, and then find out about it later on, and drink it all in word by word. Some drink, eh, the words of doom? And how greedily you swig them down if your name's Oedipus – or Antigone. The next thing to do, of course, is to put your own eyes out and trail around with your children, begging. Well, all that's over and done with – times have changed in Thebes. What Thebes needs now is an ordinary king with no fuss. My name's only Creon, thank God. I've got both feet on the ground and both hands in my pockets. I'm not so ambitious as your father was, and all I aim at now I'm king is to try to see the world's a bit more sensibly run. There's nothing very heroic about it – just an everyday job, and, like the rest of them, not always very amusing. But since that's what I'm here for, that's what I'm going to do. And if some scruffy messenger comes down from the mountains tomorrow and tells me he's none too sure about my parentage, I'll just send him packing. I shan't go comparing dates and looking askance at my aunt. Kings have other things to do besides souping up their own woes. (*Goes over and takes her by the arm.*) Now listen carefully. You may be Antigone, Oedipus's daughter – but you're only twenty. It isn't long since all this would have been sorted out with bread and water and a box on the ears. (*Smiling.*) Have you put to death! You can't have looked at yourself in the glass, you little sparrow! You're too thin. You want to fatten yourself up a bit and give Haemon a nice sturdy son! You'd do Thebes more good that way than by dying, believe me. Now you go straight back to your room, do as I told you and say nothing. I'll see everyone else keeps quiet. Go along. And don't glare like that. You think I'm a brute, of course, and horribly unpoetic. But, handful that you are, I'm fond of you. Don't forget it was I gave you your first doll, and not very long ago either!

ANTIGONE *doesn't answer. She makes as if to leave.* CREON *stops her.*

Antigone! That's not the way to your room. Where are you going?

ANTIGONE (*stopping, and answering him quietly, without bravado*). You know very well.

Silence. Again they stand looking at each other.

CREON (*low, as if to himself*). What are you playing at?

ANTIGONE. I'm not playing.

CREON. Don't you realise that if anyone other than those three louts gets to know what you've tried to do, I shall have to have you killed? If you'll only keep quiet now and give up this foolishness there's a chance I may be able to save you. But in five minutes' time it will be too late. Do you understand?

ANTIGONE. They have uncovered my brother's body. I must go and bury him.

CREON. You really would make that senseless gesture a third time? There's another set of guards watching over Polynices' body now, and you know very well that even if you did manage to cover it up they'd only uncover it again. What else can you do but scrape more skin off your fingers and get yourself caught again?

ANTIGONE. Nothing else. But at least I can do that. And one must do what one can.

CREON. Do you really believe in this burial business? Is your brother's ghost really doomed to wander for ever if a handful of earth isn't thrown on the corpse accompanied by some ecclesiastical rigmarole? Have you ever heard the priests of Thebes at it? Ever seen them scrambling through it like overworked clerks, gabbling the words, skimping the movements, getting the deceased out of the way as fast as they can so they can botch another one before lunch?

ANTIGONE. Yes, I've seen them.

CREON. And haven't you ever thought that if it was someone you really loved lying there in that box, you'd let out a shriek and tell them to shut up and go away?

ANTIGONE. Yes. I've thought that.

CREON. Yet now you risk death because I've denied your brother that piffling passport, that mass-produced mumbo-jumbo you'd have been the first to be shamed and hurt by if it had actually been performed. It's ridiculous.

ANTIGONE. Yes. Ridiculous.

CREON. Why are you acting like this, then? To impress other people, those who do believe in it? To set them against me?

ANTIGONE. No.

CREON. Not for other people? And not for your brother himself? For whom, then?

ANTIGONE. No one. Myself.

CREON (*looks at her in silence*). You really want to die then? You look like a little hare, caught already.

ANTIGONE. Don't feel sorry for me. Be like me – do what you have to do. But if you want to be humane, do it quickly – that's all I ask. I can't be brave for ever.

CREON (*moving closer*). I want to save you, Antigone.

ANTIGONE. You're the king – you can do anything . . . But not that.

CREON. You think not?

ANTIGONE. You can't save me, and you can't force me to do what you want.

CREON. Proud Antigone! Pocket Oedipus!

ANTIGONE. All you can do is have me put to death.

CREON. And what if I have you tortured?

ANTIGONE. What for? To make me cry and beg for mercy? To make me swear to anything, and then do the same thing all over again when the pain stops?

CREON (*gripping her arm*). Now just listen. All right – I've got the villain's part and you're cast as the heroine. You're well aware of that. But don't try to push it too far, you little nuisance. If I were just an ordinary brute of a tyrant you'd have had your tongue torn out long ago, or been taken apart with red-hot pincers, or thrown into a dungeon. But you can see something in my eyes that hesitates. You can see I let you speak instead of sending for my soldiers. So you taunt and defy me to the top of your bent. What are you after, you little Fury?

ANTIGONE. Let go. You're hurting my arm.

CREON (*gripping more tightly*). No – I'm the strong one now. It's my turn to take advantage.

ANTIGONE. Ow!

CREON (*a twinkle in his eye*). Perhaps that's the answer! Perhaps I ought just to twist your wrist and pull your hair, as boys do when they play with the girls. (*He looks at her. Serious again. Close.*) I may be your uncle, but we're rather severe on each other in our family. So doesn't it strike you as strange – I, a king, set at naught by you yet listening patiently . . . an old man who's all-powerful, who's seen plenty of other people killed, just as appealing as you – and here am I taking all this trouble to try and keep you from dying?

Pause.

ANTIGONE. You're twisting too hard now. It doesn't even hurt. I just can't feel my arm.

CREON *looks at her and lets go of her, smiling.*

CREON (*low*). Heaven knows I've got other demands on my time today, but I'm going to spend however long it takes to save you, you little pest.

He makes her sit on a chair in the middle of the room, then takes off his jacket and advances on her in his shirtsleeves, heavy, powerful.

There are plenty of urgent matters to attend to after a failed revolution, you know. But they can wait. I don't want you to die mixed up in a political scandal. You deserve better than that. Because it is only a political scandal, you know – this brother of yours, this forlorn ghost, this body decomposing as the guards watch over it . . . All this pathos you get so worked up about. I may not be soft, but I am particular – I like things to be clean, neat, wholesome. Don't you think I'm as revolted as you are by that flesh rotting in the sun? You can smell it in the palace already, at night when the wind blows from the sea. It makes me feel quite sick. But I shan't even shut my window. The whole business is not only horrible, but also – between ourselves – abysmally stupid. But it's necessary that Thebes should smell the body for a while. I myself would have preferred to have your brother buried, just for reasons of hygiene. But to make those clods I govern understand what's what, the city has to stink of Polynices' corpse for a month.

ANTIGONE. You're loathsome.

CREON. Yes, child. It's my job. Whether that job should or shouldn't be done is a matter for discussion. But if it is done, it has to be done like this.

ANTIGONE. Why do you have to do it?

CREON. One morning I woke up King of Thebes. Though heaven knows there were things in life I loved better than power.

ANTIGONE. Then you should have said no!

CREON. I might have. But suddenly I felt like a workman refusing a job. It didn't seem right. I said yes.

ANTIGONE. That's your look-out. I didn't say yes! What do I care about your politics and what you 'have' to do and all your paltry affairs! I can still say no to anything I don't like, and I alone am the judge. You, with your crown and your guards and your paraphernalia – all you can do, because you said yes, is have me put to death.

CREON. Listen –

ANTIGONE. I needn't if I don't want to. There's nothing more you can tell me. But you drink in every word I say. If you don't summon your guards it's because you want to hear me out.

CREON. Huh!

ANTIGONE. You're not amused – you're afraid. That's why

you're trying to save me. It would suit you best to keep me here in the palace, alive but silent. You're too sensitive to be a tyrant. But just the same, as you know very well, you're going to have me put to death presently. And that's why you're afraid. Not a pretty sight, a man who's afraid.

CREON (*dully*). All right – I am afraid. Afraid you won't change your mind and I'll have to have you killed. And I don't want to.

ANTIGONE. I don't have to do what I don't want to! Perhaps you'd rather not have refused my brother a grave either? . . . Well?

CREON. I've told you already.

ANTIGONE. But you did it just the same! And now, though you'd rather not, you're going to have me put to death. Is that what it means to be a king?

CREON. Yes!

ANTIGONE. Poor Creon. And I, with my broken nails, and the bruises your guards have made on my arms, and my stomach all knotted up with fear – I'm a queen.

CREON. Have pity on me, then, and live. Your brother's body rotting under my windows is a high enough price to pay for law and order. My son loves you. I've paid enough. Don't force me to pay with you too.

ANTIGONE. No. You said yes. You'll never stop paying!

CREON (*suddenly shaking her, beside himself*). For God's sake! Try to understand for a minute, you little fool! I've tried hard enough to understand you! Someone has to say yes. Someone has to steer the ship. It's letting in water on all sides. It's full of crime and stupidity and suffering. The rudder's adrift. The crew won't obey orders – all they're interested in is looting the cargo. The officers are busy building a comfortable raft for themselves and cornering all the fresh water. But the mast's split, the wind's howling, the sails will soon be in shreds, and the whole lot of them will die together because they think of nothing but their own skins and their own petty concerns. And do you really think this is the moment for fine distinctions? Do you think there's time to debate whether you say yes or no, to wonder whether some day the price isn't going to be too high, whether afterwards you're going to be able to call yourself a man again? No! You grab the tiller, you stand up to the mountains of water, you shout an order – and if you're attacked you shoot the first comer. The first comer! He hasn't got a name. He's like the wave that's just broken over the deck, like the wind tearing at your limbs. He may be the man who smiled at you and gave you a light yesterday. He hasn't got a name any more. And neither have you, as you hang on desperately to the tiller. The only things that have got a name now are the ship and the storm. Do you understand?

ANTIGONE (*shaking her head*). I don't want to. It's all very well for you, but I'm not here to understand. I'm here to say no to you, and to die.

CREON. It's easy to say no!

ANTIGONE. Not always.

CREON. To say yes you have to sweat, roll up your sleeves, grab hold of life, plunge in up to the neck. It's easy to say no, even if it means dying. All you have to do is keep still and wait. Wait to live. Wait to die, even. It's feeble! – something human beings have thought up for themselves. Can you imagine a world where trees have said no to the sap? Where the animals have said no to the instincts of hunting and love? Brute beasts at least are good and natural and tough. They all jostle each other bravely along the same path. If any fall, others trample them. No matter how many die there'll always be one of every species left to reproduce and follow the same path with the same courage.

ANTIGONE. What a dream for a king! To be like an animal! Wouldn't that make life easy!

Pause. CREON *looks at her.*

CREON. You despise me, don't you? (*She doesn't answer. He goes on as if to himself.*) Funny. I've often imagined having this conversation . . . with a pale young man who's tried to kill me . . . from whom I can extract nothing but scorn. But I never thought it would be with you, Antigone, and over something so foolish . . . (*He buries his head in his hands. We realise he is at the end of his tether.*) Listen to me for the last time. I'm cast as the villain, and I'm going to have you put to death. But before I do I want you to be sure of your role. Do you know why you're going to die, Antigone? Do you realise what a squalid story it is you're going to put your poor little bloodstained name to – for ever?

Pause.

ANTIGONE. What do you mean?

CREON. The story of your brothers, Eteocles and Polynices. You think you know it, but you don't. No one in Thebes knows except me. But I think that this morning you too have the right to know. (*He meditates for a moment, his head in his hands, his elbows resting on his knees. As if to himself.*) It's not pretty. (*Dully, not looking at* ANTIGONE.) To start with, what do you remember about your brothers? You probably remember two boys who looked down on you and wouldn't let you play with them . . . who broke your dolls and were always whispering secrets together to make you jealous . . . ?

ANTIGONE. They were older than I was . . .

CREON. Later on, I suppose, you were impressed by their first cigarettes and their first long trousers. Then they started to go out in the evenings, to act like men, not to take any notice of you . . . ?

ANTIGONE. I was only a girl . . .

CREON. You saw your mother weep, your father get angry. You heard your brothers slam the door when they came home, and guffaw all along the corridors. They'd lurk past making feeble jokes and reeking of wine . . .

ANTIGONE. Once I hid behind the door. We'd just got up, and they'd just come home. Polynices saw me. He was pale, with shining eyes – so handsome in his evening clothes! He gave me a big paper flower he'd brought home with him from the party.

CREON. And you kept it, didn't you? And last night, before you went out, you opened the drawer and looked at it, to help you summon up your courage?

ANTIGONE (*with a start*). Who told you?

CREON. Poor Antigone! You and your paper flower! Do you know what your brother was really like?

ANTIGONE. I knew you'd say horrible things about him!

CREON. A brainless roisterer, a cruel, soulless little thug whose only distinction was driving faster than his cronies and spending more money in bars! I was there once when your father refused to pay his gambling debts. He turned pale, let out an oath, clenched his fist –

ANTIGONE. I don't believe it!

CREON. And drove his loutish paw right in your father's face! It was pitiful. Your father just sat at his desk with his face in his hands, his nose streaming with blood. Weeping. And Polynices stood sneering in a corner, lighting a cigarette.

ANTIGONE (*almost imploring now*). It isn't true!

CREON. You were only twelve at the time. You didn't see him for years after that. Did you?

ANTIGONE (*dully*). No.

CREON. He went away after the quarrel. Your father wouldn't bring any charges. Polynices joined the Argive army. As soon as he did they started to hunt your father down – an old man who wouldn't conveniently die and hand over his crown. There was one murder attempt after another, and whenever we caught the assassins they ended up confessing they were in the pay of Polynices. But it wasn't only him. I want you to know all the inns and outs, all the plots that were cooked up, all the machinations behind the drama you're so eager to play a part in. Yesterday I gave Eteocles an elaborate funeral. Thebes regards him now as a saint and a hero. The whole population was there. The schoolchildren pooled their pocket-money to buy wreathes. Old men pretended to be overcome with emotion and made quavering speeches in praise of the virtuous prince, the loyal brother, Oedipus's dutiful son. I made a speech too. And all the priests of Thebes were there, putting on suitable expressions. Eteocles was given military honours. I had no choice – I couldn't afford to have a scoundrel in both camps!

But now I'm going to tell you something . . . something terrible . . . that no one else knows but me.

Eteocles, that paragon of virtue, was no better than Polynices. The dutiful son had tried to murder his father, too. The loyal prince, too, was ready to sell Thebes to the highest bidder. I have proof that Eteocles was prepared to commit the same treachery as that for which Polynices' body now lies mouldering in the sun – Eteocles, sleeping peacefully in his marble tomb. It was a mere chance that Polynices pulled it off first. They were just two common crooks, cheating one another at the same time as they cheated us, cutting one another's throats like a couple of second-rate gangsters settling scores.

But it was necessary for me to make a hero of one of them. So I had my men seek out their bodies. They found them in one another's arms – for the first time in their lives, probably. They'd run one another through, then the Argive cavalry had ridden over the bodies and made mincemeat of them. They were both unrecognisable, Antigone. I gave orders for whichever corpse was least damaged to be scraped together for my national obsequies. And for the other to be left to rot. I don't even know which was which. And I assure you I don't care.

Long pause. They don't speak, or look at each other.

ANTIGONE (*quietly*). Why have you told me all this?

CREON *gets up, putts on his jacket.*

CREON. Would it have been better to let you die as part of it?

ANTIGONE. Perhaps. I believed in it.

Pause. CREON *goes over to her.*

CREON. What are you going to do now?

ANTIGONE (*getting up, like a sleepwalker*). Go to my room.

CREON. Don't stay on your own. Go and see Haemon. Get married as soon as you can.

ANTIGONE (*intake of breath*). Yes.

CREON. You've got your whole life before you. All this talk's beside the point. You still have a future.

ANTIGONE. Yes.

CREON. Nothing else matters. And you were going to waste that treasure! I can understand – I'd have done the same when I was twenty. That's why I listened to you so closely. I could hear the distant echo of a young Creon as thin and pale as you, dreaming, like you, of sacrificing everything . . . Get married quickly, Antigone, and be happy. Life's not what you think. It's like water – the young let it slip through their fingers without thinking. Shut your hands, Antigone, shut them tight and hold it back. You'll see – it'll turn into something small and hard that you can sit and munch in the sun. People will tell you different, because they need your energy and strength. Don't listen. Don't listen to me when I make my next speech over Eteocles' grave. It won't be the truth. Nothing is true but what is never said. You'll find that out for yourself . . . when it's too late.

Life's a book you enjoy, a child playing round your feet, a tool that fits into your hand, a bench outside your house to rest on in the evening. (*Pause.*) You'll despise me more than ever for saying this, but finding it out, as you'll see, is some sort of consolation for growing old: life is probably nothing other than happiness.

ANTIGONE (*a murmur, staring into space*). Happiness . . .

CREON (*suddenly rather ashamed*). Just a word, eh?

ANTIGONE (*softly*). And what will my happiness be like? What kind of a happy woman will Antigone grow into? What base things will she have to do, day after day, in order to snatch her own little scrap of happiness? Tell me – who will she have to lie to? Smile at? Sell herself to? Who will she have to avert her eyes from, and leave to die?

CREON (*exasperated*). That's enough. You're crazy.

ANTIGONE. I won't be quiet! I want to know what I have to do to be happy! Now, right away, because now is when I have to choose. You say life's so wonderful. I want to know what I have to do to live.

CREON. Do you love Haemon?

ANTIGONE. I love a Haemon who's tough and young . . . A Haemon who's demanding and loyal, like me. But if that life of yours, that happiness of yours, are going to pass over him and erode him – if he's not going to turn pale any more when I turn pale – if he won't think I must be dead if I'm five minutes late – if he doesn't feel alone in the world and hate me if I laugh and he doesn't know why – if he's going to become just a conventional spouse and learn to say yes like the rest – then no, I don't love Haemon any more!

CREON. That'll do. You don't know what you're saying.

ANTIGONE. I know what I'm saying, all right! It's just that you don't understand. I'm speaking to you from too far away now – from a country you can't enter any more, with your wrinkles, your wisdom and your belly. (*Laughs.*) I suddenly see you as you were when you were fifteen! Helpless, but thinking you're important. All life has added are those furrows in your face, that fat around your waist!

CREON (*shaking her*). Will you shut up!

ANTIGONE. Why do you want to shut me up? Because you know I'm right? Don't you think I can see it in your eyes? You know I'm right, but you'll never admit it because you're trying to defend that happiness of yours – like a dog crouching over a bone.

CREON. Your happiness as well as mine, you fool!

ANTIGONE. You disgust me, all of you, you and your happiness! And your life, that has to be loved at any price. You're like dogs fawning on everyone they come across. With just a little hope left every day – if you don't expect too much. But I want everything, now! And to the full! Or else I decline the offer, lock, stock and barrel! I don't want to be sensible, and satisfied with a scrap – if I behave myself! I want to be sure of having everything, now, this very day, and it has to be as wonderful as it was when I was little. Otherwise I prefer to die.

CREON. There you go – just like your father!

ANTIGONE. Exactly! Neither of us ever stops asking questions! Right up to the moment when there's not a spark of hope left to stifle. We're the sort who jump right on your precious, lousy hope!

CREON. If you could see how ugly you look, shouting!

ANTIGONE. Very vulgar, isn't it? Father was only beautiful afterwards – when he knew for certain that he'd killed his father and slept with his mother, and that nothing, now, could save him. He grew suddenly silent. Smiled. He was beautiful. It was all over. He had only to shut his eyes not to see you any more – all you craven candidates for happiness! It's you who are ugly, even the handsomest of you! There's something ugly about the corners of your eyes and mouths. You used the right words for it just now, Creon, when you talked about cooking up plots. You all look like cooks, with your fat faces. Cooks! Scullions!

CREON (*twisting her arm*). I order you to be silent!

ANTIGONE. You order me, scullion? Do you imagine you can give me orders?

CREON. The ante-room's full of people. They'll hear you. Do you want to destroy yourself?

ANTIGONE. Open the door! Let them hear!

CREON (*putting his hand over her mouth*). Quiet, for God's sake.

ANTIGONE (*struggling*). Quick! Quick, scullion! Call your guards!

The door opens. Enter ISMENE.

ISMENE. Antigone!

ANTIGONE. You as well? What do you want with me, then?

ISMENE. Creon! Creon! If you kill her, you'll have to kill me too! (*To* ANTIGONE.) Forgive me, Antigone. But I am brave now. I'll go with you.

ANTIGONE. Oh no! Not now! I'm on my own now. Don't you think you can just muscle in and die with me now! It'd be too easy!

ISMENE. But I don't want to live if you die! I don't want to stay on without you!

ANTIGONE. You've chosen life. I've chosen death. Leave me alone, you and your lamentations. What you ought to have done was go this morning, on all fours, in the dark . . . grub up the earth with your nails, under the noses of the guards . . . be grabbed by them like a thief.

That's what you ought to have done!

ISMENE. All right, Antigone – all right! I'll go tomorrow!

ANTIGONE. Hear that, Creon? Her too! And how do you know it won't spread to others when they hear me? What are you waiting for? Why don't you call your guards to silence me? Come on now, Creon, be brave – it won't take long! Come on, scullion! You have no choice – get it over with!

CREON (*sudden shout*). Guards!

The GUARDS *appear immediately.*

Take her away!

ANTIGONE (*crying out: relieved*). At last, Creon! At last!

BINNS (*roughly*). Come on! This way!

The GUARDS *seize her and take her off.* ISMENE *follows, crying out.*

ISMENE. Antigone! Antigone!

Enter CHORUS.

CHORUS. You're mad, Creon. What have you done?

CREON (*staring ahead of him*). She had to die.

CHORUS. Don't let her die, Creon! We'll all bear the scar for thousands of years!

CREON. It was her choice. She wanted to die! None of us was strong enough to persuade her to live. I understand now. She was born to die. She may not have known it herself, but Polynices was only an excuse. And when that excuse wouldn't work any more she chose another. All that mattered to her was to refuse everything and to die.

CHORUS. She's only a child, Creon.

CREON. What do you want me to do? Condemn her to live?

Enter HAEMON, *shouting.*

HAEMON. Father!

CREON (*hurrying over and embracing him*). Forget her, Haemon. Forget her, my boy!

HAEMON. You must be mad! Let go!

CREON (*holding on tighter*). I tried everything I could think of to save her. Everything, I swear. She doesn't love you – if she did she could have lived. She preferred her own folly, and death.

HAEMON (*struggling to escape*). But they're taking her away! Father! Tell the guards to bring her back!

CREON. She has spoken now. All Thebes knows what she's done. I must have her put to death.

HAEMON (*tearing himself free*). Let me go!

Pause. They stand facing one another.

CHORUS (*approaching*). Can't you think of something – say she's mad, have her shut up?

CREON. They'll say it isn't true. That I'm sparing her because she was going to marry my son. I can't.

CHORUS. Can't you try to gain time, and have her escape, tomorrow?

CREON. The mob knows already. They're all round the palace, yelling. I can't turn back.

HAEMON. The mob! What does it matter? You're the master!

CREON. Under the law. Not against it.

HAEMON. But I'm your son – you can't let them take her away from me!

CREON. Yes, my boy – I can. Come now – courage! Antigone can't go on living. She's already left us.

HAEMON. And do you think I can go on living, without her? Do you think I'm going to accept that life you talk about? Every day, morn till night, without her? All your bustle and blather, all your emptiness . . . without her?

CREON. You'll have to. To every man there comes a day, soon or late, sad or happy, when at last he has to accept that he's a man. For you that day's today. For the last time you stand in front of me as my little son . . . your eyes brimming, pain in your heart. In a moment, when you turn away and go through that door, it will be over.

HAEMON (*drawing back; low*). It's over already.

CREON. Don't judge me, Haemon. Don't you judge me too.

HAEMON (*looking at him, then in a sudden outburst*). That great strength and courage . . . that giant-god who used to gather me up in his arms and save me from ghosts – was that you? The thrilling smell, the delicious bread in the lamplight, the evenings when you used to take me into your study and show me your books – was that really you, do you think?

CREON (*humbly*). Yes.

HAEMON. And all that trouble, that pride, those books – were they only leading up to this? To becoming a man, as you call it – a man who's supposed to consider himself lucky just to be alive?

CREON. Yes.

HAEMON (*crying out like a child, throwing himself into* CREON*'s arms*). Oh, Father, it isn't true, it isn't you, it isn't happening! We're not both driven into a corner where we can only say yes! You're still strong, like when I was small. I beg you, let me admire you still! I'm too alone, the world's too empty, if I have to stop looking up to you.

CREON (*putting him away*). We are alone. The world is empty. And you've looked up to your father too long. Look me straight in the eyes. That's what it means to be a man.

HAEMON (*looks at him, then recoils, and bursts out*). Antigone! Antigone! Help!

HAEMON *runs out.*

CHORUS (*going over to* CREON). Creon, he's like a madman.

CREON (*standing motionless, staring into space*). Yes. Poor boy. He loves her.

CHORUS. Creon, you must do something.

CREON. I can do nothing.

CHORUS. Haemon's wounded. Mortally.

CREON. We all are.

Enter ANTIGONE, *hustled in by the* GUARDS *who then put their backs against the door. The mob can be heard howling in the distance.*

JONAS. Sir, they've broken into the palace!

ANTIGONE. Creon . . . keep them away! I don't want to see their faces any more, or hear their shouting. I don't want to see anyone! You've got my death – that's enough. Don't let me have to see anyone else till it's all over.

CREON (*going: shouting to* GUARDS). Jonas, you stay here with her! The rest of you, come with me and throw the mob out!

The other two GUARDS *go out, followed by the* CHORUS. ANTIGONE *is left with the first* GUARD. *She looks at him.*

ANTIGONE. So it's to be you.

JONAS. What do you mean?

ANTIGONE. Yours is the last human face I shall see.

JONAS. Looks like it.

ANTIGONE. Let me look at you.

JONAS (*moving away; embarrassed*). No . . . no . . . stop it . . .

ANTIGONE. Aren't you the one who arrested me just now?

JONAS. Yes.

ANTIGONE. You hurt me. There was no need. Did I look as if I'd try to run away?

JONAS. Now then, no nonsense! It was either you or me.

ANTIGONE. How old are you?

Pause.

JONAS. Thirty-nine.

ANTIGONE. Any children?

JONAS. Two.

ANTIGONE. Are you fond of them?

JONAS. Mind your own business.

He starts pacing to and fro. For a while the only sound is that of his footsteps.

ANTIGONE (*more humbly*). Have you been in the guards long?

JONAS. Since the end of the war. I was a sergeant. I signed on again.

ANTIGONE. Do you have to be a sergeant to join the guards?

JONAS. In theory. A sergeant or a special. But if you're a sergeant you lose your rank when you join the guards. So if, for the sake of argument, I meet an army recruit, he might not salute me.

ANTIGONE. Really?

JONAS. Of course they generally do. They know you're really an NCO. As for the pay, you get ordinary guard's pay, plus, as a bonus for the first six months, the extra you used to get as a sergeant. But of course there are other advantages. Living quarters, heating, family allowances. All in all a married guard can earn more than a sergeant in the regular army.

ANTIGONE. Really?

JONAS. Yes. That's why there's such rivalry. As you may have noticed, sergeants pretend to look down on guards. Because of the promotion, mainly. They're right, in a way. It's much slower and more difficult in the guards. But you mustn't forget that a lance-sergeant in the guards is more important than a quarter-master-sergeant in the army . . .

ANTIGONE (*suddenly*). Listen.

JONAS. I'm listening.

ANTIGONE. I'm going to die very soon.

He doesn't answer. Pause. He goes on pacing. Then:

JONAS. Of course, people look up more to a guard. He's a sort of official as well as a soldier . . .

ANTIGONE. Do you think it hurts?

JONAS. What?

ANTIGONE. Dying. Does it hurt?

JONAS. Couldn't say. I know it hurt during the war, when men were wounded in the stomach. But I was never wounded myself . . . Maybe that's what's stood in the way of my promotion . . .

ANTIGONE. How will they do it?

JONAS. I believe I heard they were going to wall you up, so as not to stain the city with your blood.

ANTIGONE. Wall me up? Alive?

JONAS. At first.

Silence. The GUARD *makes himself a quid of tobacco.*

ANTIGONE. Hail, then, my grave, my marriage bed, my underground home! (*She looks very small in the middle of that big base room. She looks cold. She wraps her arms around herself. Then, as if to herself.*) But all on my own . . . !

JONAS (*finishing his quid*). It'll be in the caves of Hades, outside the city gates. Right out in the sun. Another lousy job for whoever's on sentry duty. The last I heard it was going to be the guards again. They put everything on us!

ANTIGONE (*low, weary*). Two animals . . .

JONAS. What about them?

ANTIGONE. Two animals would huddle together for warmth. I'm all on my own.

JONAS. I can call somebody if you need anything.

ANTIGONE. No. I'd just like you to deliver a letter after I'm dead.

JONAS. What letter?

ANTIGONE. I'm just going to write it.

JONAS. Oh no! None of that! Letter indeed! It'd be more than my life's worth . . .

ANTIGONE. I'd give you this ring.

JONAS. Is it gold?

ANTIGONE. Yes.

JONAS. If they search me I'll be courtmartialled. You realise that, don't you? Fat lot you care . . . (*Looks at the ring again.*) Tell you what I could do . . . I could write what you want to say down in my notebook and tear the page out. It wouldn't be the same if it was in my writing . . .

ANTIGONE (*eyes closed, with an attempt at a laugh*). Your writing . . . ! (*Then she shudders.*) Oh, it's all too horrible!

JONAS (*offended, pretending to give the ring back*). All right, if you've changed your mind. It's all the same to me.

ANTIGONE. No – keep the ring, and write down what I say . . . But quickly – there isn't much time. Put: 'My darling . . .'

JONAS (*he has got out his notebook and is sucking the lead of his pencil*). Is it for your boyfriend?

ANTIGONE. 'My darling. I've chosen to die. And perhaps you'll stop loving me . . .

JONAS *mumbles the words after her as he writes.*

And Creon was right: it's awful, but here, with this man

beside me, I don't know any more what I'm dying for . . . I'm afraid . . . (JONAS *mumbles some more.*) Oh, Haemon! It's only now I realise how easy it was to live . . .'

JONAS (*stops writing*). Hey, you're going much too fast! It takes time, you know!

ANTIGONE. How far have you got?

JONAS (*reading what he's written*). '. . . here, with this man beside me . . .'

ANTIGONE. 'I don't know any more what I'm dying for . . .'

JONAS (*mumbling as he writes, then*). 'I don't know any more what I'm dying for . . .' People never do know what they're dying for . . .

ANTIGONE. 'I'm afraid . . .' (*She stops, straightens up.*) No, cross all that out! It's better no one should ever know. It'd be as if they were to see me naked, touch me, after I was dead. Just put, 'I'm sorry.'

JONAS. You mean cross out that last bit and put 'I'm sorry' instead?

ANTIGONE. 'I'm sorry, my darling. It would have been nice and peaceful for you all without me. I love you . . .'

JONAS *mumbles and writes as before. Pause.*

JONAS. Is that the lot?

ANTIGONE. Yes.

JONAS. Funny sort of a letter.

ANTIGONE. Yes. It is.

JONAS. And who's it for?

The door bursts open. The other GUARDS *enter.*

ANTIGONE stands up, looks at them, then at JONAS, now standing behind her. He pockets the ring and puts away his notebook, self-important. He sees ANTIGONE's look, and starts to shout to keep himself in countenance.

JONAS. Come on, you! No nonsense!

Effort at a smile from ANTIGONE. Then she bows her head and goes over without a word to the other GUARDS. They all go out. Enter CHORUS, suddenly.

CHORUS. So. It's all over for Antigone. Soon it will be Creon's turn. Everyone's turn will come in the end.

Door bursts open; enter MESSENGER.

MESSENGER (*shouting*). The queen! Where's the queen?

CHORUS. What do you want with her? What news do you bring?

MESSENGER. Terrible news! They'd just put Antigone in the cave. They hadn't finished rolling the last blocks of stone into place when Creon and all those around him heard cries suddenly issuing from the tomb. Everyone stopped and listened: it wasn't Antigone's voice. They all looked at Creon. And he was the first to guess. He suddenly shrieked like a madman? 'Take away the stones! Take away the stones!' The slaves hurled themselves on the heaped-up rocks, and the king fell on them too, digging with his bare hands until they bled. At last some of the rocks shifted and the thinnest person there squeezed through the opening. Antigone was in the depths of the cave, hanged with her own girdle. The blue and green and red strands looked like a child's necklace. And there was Haemon, on his knees, groaning, holding her in his arms, his face buried in her robe. They removed another rock, and Creon was able to get through at last. You could see his grey hair in the darkness of the cave. He tried to raise Haemon up, implored him, but he wouldn't listen. Then suddenly Haemon stood up. Never had he looked so much like the boy he once was. He stared at his father, his eyes black with passion, then suddenly spat in his face and drew his sword. Creon leapt out of reach. Haemon looked at him, his youthful eyes full of contempt – a look Creon could not avoid, sharper than the sword itself. Haemon stared at the trembling old man, and without a word plunged the sword into his own belly. Then he lay down beside Antigone, embracing her in a vast red pool of blood.

Enter CREON, *with his* PAGE.

CREON. I have had them laid side by side at last. They are washed now; rested. Pale, but peaceful. Two lovers after their first night. For them it's over.

CHORUS. But not for you, Creon. You still have something to learn. The poor of Thebes will go cold this winter, Creon. When Eurydice, the queen, your wife, heard of her son's death she was knitting for the poor, as usual. She quietly finished her row and laid down her needles – calmly, as she did everything . . . perhaps even a little more calmly than usual. Then she went into her room, her lavender-scented room with all the little embroidered mats and plush frames – and she cut her throat. Now she lies on one of the old-fashioned twin beds, just where you saw her lying one night when she was a girl, wearing the same smile, only sadder. If it wasn't for the red on the draperies round her throat you might think she was sleeping.

Pause.

CREON. Her too. They are all asleep now. Good. It's been a hard day. (*Pause. Dully.*) It must be good to sleep.

CHORUS. You are all alone now, Creon.

CREON. Yes . . . (*Pause. He lays his hand on the* PAGE*'s shoulder.*) Boy . . .

PAGE. Sir?

CREON. I'm going to tell you something the others don't know. There you are, face to face with what's to be done. You can't just fold your arms and do nothing. They say it's dirty work. But if you don't do it, who will?

PAGE. . . . I don't know, sir.

CREON. Of course you don't – you're lucky! And it's best never to find out. Are you looking forward to growing up?

PAGE. Oh yes!

CREON. You're mad, boy! It'd be best never to grow up, either. (*Clock strikes in the distance. He speaks as if to himself.*) Five o'clock. What've we got at five?

PAGE. Privy Council, sir.

CREON. In that case we'd better go. Come . . .

They go out. CREON *leaning on the* PAGE.

CHORUS (*coming forward*). So. Antigone was right – it would have been nice and peaceful for us all without her. But now it's over. It's nice and peaceful anyway. Everyone who had to die is dead: those who believed in one thing, those who believed in the opposite . . . even those who didn't believe in anything, but were caught up in the story without knowing what was going on. All dead: quite stiff, quite useless, quite rotten. And those who are still alive are quietly beginning to forget them and get their names mixed up. It's over. Antigone's quiet now, cured of a fever whose name we shall never know. Her work is done. A great, sad peace descends on Thebes, and on the empty palace where Creon will begin to wait for death. (*As he speaks, the* GUARDS *have entered, sat down on a bench with their caps pushed back and a bottle of wine within reach, and begun a game of cards.*) Only the guards are left. All that has happened is a matter of indifference to them. None of their business. They go on with their game of cards.

The curtain falls quickly as the GUARDS *slam down their trumps.*

THE WALTZ OF THE TOREADORS

translated by
Lucienne Hill

This play was first produced at the Arts Theatre, London, on 24 February 1956, with the following cast of characters in the order of their appearance:

Characters

GENERAL ST PE	Hugh Griffith
EMILY, *his wife*	Beatrix Lehmann
GASTON, *his secretary*	Trader Faulkner
ESTELLE } *his daughters*	Anne Bishop
SIDONIA } *his daughters*	Hilda Braid
DOCTOR BONFANTI	Walter Hudd
MLLE GHISLAINE DE STE-EUVERTE	Brenda Bruce
EUGENIE, *a maid*	Susan Richards
MME DUPONT-FREDAINE	Mary Savidge
FATHER AMBROSE	Roderick Cook
PAMELA, *a maid*	Juliet Duncombe

Directed by Peter Hall
Settings by Paul Mayo
Music composed by John Hotchkis

Act One

The GENERAL*'s study, opening on to his wife's room: exotic souvenirs, weapons, wall hangings. The communicating door is open. The* GENERAL *is at his desk, writing. A voice shrieks from next door.*

VOICE. *Leon!*

EMILY (*off*). Leon!

GENERAL. Yes?

EMILY. What are you doing?

GENERAL. Working.

EMILY. Liar! You are thinking. I can hear you. What are you thinking about?

GENERAL. You, my love.

EMILY. Liar! You are thinking about women being beautiful and good to touch, and then you don't feel alone in the world for a while, you told me so once.

GENERAL. I haven't the faintest recollection of it. Go to sleep, my love. You will be tired later.

EMILY. I am only tired, only ill, because of you. Ill with thinking, always thinking of all the things I know you are doing.

GENERAL. Come now, my love, you exaggerate, as usual. All the time you have been ill – and that makes years now – I haven't left this room, with my hams glued to this chair dictating my memoirs, or pacing about like a bear in a cage, and well you know it.

EMILY. I fell ill with thinking of all the things you are busy doing in your head while you pretend to comfort me. Admit it, hypocrite. Where were you just now in your head? With what woman? In which kitchen, tumbling Heaven knows what drab that scrubs away there on all fours? Leon, you make me sick.

GENERAL. By Hades, madam, you are dreaming. I am sitting at my desk, writing to M. Poincaré.

EMILY. He's a good scapegoat – M. Poincaré. Have you no shame, man, no refinement? Stop it, Leon.

GENERAL. Will you let me finish my letter in peace?

EMILY (*whimpering*). But inside! Inside your head! Why won't you let me inside your head, just once – just for a minute?

GENERAL. Confound it, madam, my head is out of bounds. It's the one spot where I can have a bit of peace; I want it to myself.

EMILY. I shall get into it one day. I shall come upon you there when you least expect it and I shall kill you.

GENERAL. All right. In the meantime – you've brought it on yourself – I shall take Dr Bonfant's advice and shut the door.

EMILY. Leon, I forbid you! Leon, I shall have an attack!

Despite his wife's shrieks the GENERAL *has shut the door. The* SECRETARY *has come in during this punitive expedition.*

GENERAL. Implacable! I have shut her door. By Hades, she needn't think I'm going to put up with her whims for ever.

Enter GASTON.

Good morning, my boy.

GASTON. Good morning, sir.

GENERAL. Have you got a wife, young man? A little girlfriend, eh? It's the old, old story – you meet her by chance, you take her under the apple trees and ten minutes later you are married and living with her poor old mother.

GASTON. I am too young.

GENERAL. Yes, and in a flash you'll be too old. You'll be sitting at your desk dictating your memoirs. And between the two, pouff – a game of dice. You must feel the urge, though, sometimes, I hope.

GASTON. No, sir. I have not long left the seminary. I am still chaste.

GENERAL. Good. Sad, though. Life without women, my boy, what a purge. There's another problem M. Poincaré will never solve. Now then, to work. Where were we?

GASTON. We'd finished chapter thirty. Do you wish me to read it back to you, sir?

GENERAL. Not now. I'm feeling in form. I managed to slip away for ten minutes earlier on for a turn around the garden. The air was heavy with the scent of rhododendrons – I wandered down a path, it was cool, my limbs were as sprightly as a two-year-old's – nobody called me – it was extraordinary. I fancied I was a widower. Chapter thirty-one. My African Campaigns. Paragraph One. Morocco. Until eighteen ninety-eight, the policy of the French Government in Morocco was a policy of presence. Since the ill-starred treaty of Frankfurt, however, another factor was coming to have a dangerous bearing on Moroccan policy, the creation of the German Empire whose intrigues and promises were to induce the Sultan to stiffen his attitude towards ourselves. An incident, to all outward appearances insignificant, was to set a light to the powder.

ESTELLE *and* SIDONIA, *the* GENERAL'S *daughters, enter down the stairs. They are plain, lanky women of rising twenty, still childish, ringleted, kiss-curled and wearing ridiculous little-girl dresses.*

SIDONIA. Papa.

GENERAL. Yes?

SIDONIA. What are we going to do about Corpus Christi?

GENERAL. Nothing! We'll say we forgot. Anyway, all those sheets hanging out of the windows with roses pinned on them are quite disgusting. They give children ideas.

ESTELLE. But, Papa, Father Ambrose wants me and Sidonia in white, he said so again yesterday. And we haven't anything to wear.

GENERAL. Then wear nothing. It will be fifty times more jolly. Now then, my boy, where were we?

GASTON. Relations between the Sultan and the Government.

ESTELLE. Papa! We are carrying the first banner in the procession directly behind the altar boys! We are your daughters and if we don't look as nice as all the other girls, people will talk.

GENERAL. People will talk, anyway. Wear your last year's dresses.

SIDONIA. They're too short. We've grown.

GENERAL. What, again? Hell's bells and little fishes, when are you going to stop? Look at me – have I grown?

ESTELLE. People go on growing until the age of twenty-five.

GENERAL. They do in theory. But if they have a scrap of tact they leave off sooner. Go and put on your last year's dresses and let me see them.

SIDONIA.
ESTELLE. } (*together*). Yes, Papa.

They go out. The GENERAL *watches them go.*

GENERAL. My God, aren't they ugly? To think that I, with such a soft spot for a pretty face, could have brought *that* into the world.

GASTON. The Mesdemoiselles St Pé are full of the finest moral qualities.

GENERAL. Yes – of sorts, but not the right sort. Heigh-ho – where were we?

GASTON. Relations between the Sultan and the Government.

GENERAL. Well then, they weren't going so well, either. One day, the black bastard makes off with a couple of our missionaries. He has a spot of fun with them first and then sends them back, dead as mutton, trussed up like sausages with their balls between their teeth. It was an insult to the flag. The Dubreuil expedition is decided on. Ah, my boy, what a campaign! (*He moves above the desk.*) We got our money's worth for our two priests. By Jingo, we ran through some Arabs! With good clean steel, too, and no nonsense. We ransacked their quarters at first light and slaughtered the lot – father, mother, uncle, aunt; and then, my boy – the little girls of twelve, the way they grow 'em in those parts – wonderful! There she is, terror-stricken, crouching naked in a corner, a little creature that knows it will be forced, and that desires it almost. Two young beasts, tender as fawns, and cruppers, me lad! And eyes! And you the soldier, the conqueror, the master. Your sword still steaming in your hand – you have killed – you are all-powerful – she knows it and you know it too – it is hot and dark inside the tent, and there you stand, face to face, in silence . . .

GASTON (*flushed and panting*). And then, sir?

GENERAL (*simply*). Well, dammit! We're not savages. We turned them over to the Sisters of Mercy at Rabat.

Enter DOCTOR BONFANT.

Ah, here's Dr Bonfant come to see his patient. (*To* GASTON.) Leave us for a while, my boy. I shall call for you.

GASTON (*rising*). Yes, sir. (*He picks up his papers.*)

GENERAL. Good morning, Doctor.

DOCTOR. Good day to you, General.

GASTON *goes out. The* GENERAL *watches him go.*

GENERAL. Fine-looking young chap, isn't he? Would have cut quite a dash as a dragoon but for his vocation as a virgin. Superb handwriting, though, and no fool. The Curé found him for me. He's a parish child one of his colleagues brought up.

DOCTOR. Now, tell me – how is the invalid today?

GENERAL. The same as yesterday, the same as tomorrow, no doubt. And how is medical science progressing, Doctor?

DOCTOR. No further. We have found other terms far less vague than the old ones to designate the same complaints. Oh, yes, it's a great advance linguistically. Tell me, no scenes today?

GENERAL (*moving*). A small one, on the usual theme. However, I took your advice and shut the door.

DOCTOR. Excellent! And did that silence her?

GENERAL. She may have gone on on the other side, but at least I couldn't hear her.

DOCTOR. Well, as I say, this paralysis of the lower limbs is of a purely nervous origin, like all the rest. The mental process is quite simple – we won't walk any more so as to arouse his pity and make it impossible for him to leave us. You must have led her quite a dance, General, to bring her to that.

GENERAL. Not to that extent, Doctor, not to that extent. I loved my wife very much at first, of course. Yes, it seems as odd to me now as my craze over a stamp collection at fifteen. But it's a fact, we had a few happy years – well, when I say happy . . . (*He sits in the armchair.*) Before lapsing into bigotry and fruit-bottling, Emily had quite an amorous disposition. My wife was an opera singer, you know. She bellowed her way through Wagner as a Valkyrie. I married her and made her give up the theatre, to my eternal cost. She was to go on acting for myself alone. A performance at one's own expense, lasting for more than twenty years, tends to wear a man out. So I set about finding my fun elsewhere, naturally. Chambermaids, waitresses – whatever hole and corner capers a man dares to indulge in, who is very closely watched. And so I grew old, little by little. First a shade too much stomach, then the paunch advancing as the hair recedes, and the sleeve wound round with more and more gold string. And beneath this fancy dress the heart of an aged youngster still waiting for a chance to give his all. But who's to recognise me underneath the mask? That, my dear Doctor, is what they call a fine career.

DOCTOR. What would you say if I told you more or less the same tale, General?

GENERAL. It wouldn't be the slightest consolation. At least your lady wife didn't choose to fall madly in love with you at the eleventh hour and die of unrequited passion.

DOCTOR. No, no, she spared me that ordeal. But she makes up for it in other ways. Well now, I shall go and take my patient's blood pressure. That won't do her any harm. It's always normal, anyway. Tell me, does she eat at all?

GENERAL. Like you or me. I won't come with you. I shall make the most of your visit and take a little stroll around the garden, like any carefree bachelor. Don't tell her, she would accuse me of playing false with a geranium.

The DOCTOR *goes into the wife's room, the* GENERAL *goes out the other way. The stage is empty for a moment. The* SECRETARY *is heard outside singing an Italian love song. Then the* MAID *shows in* GHISLAINE, *much befeathered and swamped in travelling veils.*

MAID. It's very early, Madame. I think the master is taking his morning stroll around the garden.

GHISLAINE. Is that he singing? It sounds like his voice.

MAID. Oh, no, Madame. The master doesn't sing that kind of song. That's the Secretary. I'll go and ask the master if he will receive you, Madame. (*She turns to go.*)

GHISLAINE. Mademoiselle.

MAID (*stopping and turning*). I beg your pardon, Mademoiselle. What name shall I say?

GHISLAINE. Mademoiselle de Ste-Euverte.

MAID. Very good, Mademoiselle.

MAID *goes out.* MLLE DE STE-EUVRTE *moves around the room, touching things here and there with her sunshade.*

GHISLAINE (*looking around*). Nothing has changed in this house. (*She runs her finger over the desk.*) Still as much dust as ever. The poor darling needs someone badly. (*She listens to* GASTON'*s song. In a murmur.*) Strange – that sounds so like his voice.

GASTON *stops singing. The* GENERAL *enters and stops, dumbfounded.*

GENERAL. Ghislaine!

GHISLAINE. Leon!

GENERAL. You here?

GHISLAINE. Yes. And with head high.

GENERAL. There'll be the devil of a row.

GHISLAINE. I came so that it might take place.

GENERAL (*terrified*). Careful. She's in that room.

GHISLAINE. Alone?

GENERAL. The doctor is with her.

GHISLAINE (*with a short laugh*). I thought as much. I'll explain in a minute. First, let me look at you, Leon!

GENERAL (*crossing*). Ghislaine! You!

GHISLAINE. Myself.

GENERAL. As intrepid as an Amazon.

GHISLAINE. I took the night express. I found myself alone in the compartment with a fellow of sinister aspect who was pretending to read a newspaper.

GENERAL (*anxiously*). Ghislaine . . .

GHISLAINE. At one point he asked me the time.

GENERAL. The swine!

GHISLAINE. But I gave him such a look that he took the hint immediately. He even said 'thank you' as if I really had told him the time. He folded his newspaper and fell asleep. Or perhaps he was only pretending. But I was perfectly calm – I was armed. See, this little revolver with the mother-of-pearl handle which you may remember, Leon.

GENERAL. Ghislaine, you have it still?

GHISLAINE. Had he made one false move, had he so much as touched the hem of my dress I would have slain him first and myself afterwards – I had to get to you intact.

GENERAL (*bowing*). Thank you, Ghislaine.

GHISLAINE. He got out at Marmande. At Castlenaudry I hired a brake. Hidden as I was beneath my veils the driver never even saw my face, and here I am.

GENERAL. You know it's impossible, Ghislaine.

GHISLAINE. Everything is possible, now. I have the proof of it here in my reticule. Our long years of waiting will not have been in vain, Leon.

GENERAL. Seventeen years . . .

GHISLAINE. Seventeen years since the Garrison Ball at Saumur.

GENERAL. The Chinese lanterns, Ghislaine, the gypsy orchestra – the Colonel thought it too daring but I stood my ground. I had them sent out specially from Paris.

GHISLAINE. Oh, the strange enchantment of that waltz, Leon.

GENERAL. *The Waltz of the Toreadors*.

The music of 'The Waltz of the Toreadors' is heard.

(*He sings.*) Tra la la la . . .

GHISLAINE (*singing*). Tra la la, la la la . . .

GENERAL (*with a step and a bow*). Mademoiselle, may I have the pleasure?

GHISLAINE. But, sir, you are not on my card.

GENERAL. I will inscribe myself on it officially. Major St Pé. We have not been introduced, Mademoiselle, but I feel that I have known you all my life.

The music fades.

GHISLAINE (*coyly*). Why, Major, how bold you are. (*She rises.*) Then you took me by the waist and all at once your hand burned me right through your glove and my dress. From the moment your hand touched my back I no longer heard the music. Everything whirled.

GENERAL. The waltz! Tra la la – Tra la la . . .

The GENERAL *takes* GHISLAINE *in his arms and waltzes a little.*

GHISLAINE (*swooning*). It was love! Tra la la la . . .

ESTELLE *and* SIDONIA *appear in the doorway in their too-short dresses and veils.*

SIDONIA. Papa, we have come about the dresses.

GENERAL. Ten thousand demons, can't you see I'm busy? This lady is my teacher. I am having a dancing lesson.

ESTELLE. Is there going to be a ball, then, Papa?

GENERAL (*improvising wildly*). I'm arranging one. For Corpus Christi, strangely enough. (*To* GHISLAINE.) My daughters.

GHISLAINE. Is it possible? Those darling little babies!

GENERAL (*shrugging*). There we are!

GHISLAINE. But it was only yesterday . . .

GENERAL. They shot up very fast. You see, they've already grown out of their dresses. This lady is an old friend who saw you when you were tiny. As for the dresses, it's perfectly clear you both want new ones. Granted. Run along to Madame Dupont-Fredaine, choose the stuff –

ESTELLE. Oh, thank you, Papa, darling Papa.

GENERAL. – and tell her to come for a first fitting no later than this afternoon.

SIDONIA (*clapping her hands*). We'll look lovely after all, Papa, thanks to you.

GENERAL. Well, we'll have a shot at it, anyhow.

ESTELLE *and* SIDONIA *run out, hand in hand.*

What a pair of silly geese! Did you ever see anything so ugly? We're in a nice mess. Heaven knows what tales they're going to spread.

GHISLAINE (*in a strangely altered voice*). But why are they so big? Leon, can I have aged as well?

GENERAL. You are still the same Ghislaine, the same sweet tuber rose wafting her night-time fragrance over the gardens of Saumaur.

GHISLAINE. But I was eighteen years old at that ball.

GENERAL. It never does to start adding up. (*He takes her hand.*) Your hand! Your tiny hand imprisoned in its glove. Do you remember that meringue at *Rumpel-meyers* seven years ago?

GHISLAINE. No. You're wrong. The whole of nineteen hundred and four we couldn't meet at all. It was the beginning of her attacks. The meringue was nineteen hundred and three.

GENERAL. I ate the little bits from off your fingers.

GHISLAINE. You were as bolt as brass even then. Yet we had only known each other a few years.

GENERAL. Why count the years? It was a week ago. Your fingers still smell of meringue.

Enter the MAID.

MAID. Excuse me, sir.

GENERAL (*starting and releasing* GHISLAINE). Yes – what?

EUGENIE. The new one's come, sir.

GENERAL. The new what?

EUGENIE. The new girl to replace Justine.

GENERAL. Suffering catfish! Can't you see I'm busy? I haven't time to go on choosing chambermaids. Engage her. On second thoughts – what does she look like? She's not a freak, I hope?

EUGENIE. Far from it. A fine-looking girl, sir, red-haired and a little on the plump side.

GENERAL (*dreamily*). A little on the plump side . . . Engage her .

EUGENIE *exits*.

GHISLAINE. Leon, I wish you would let me help you. This is no job for a man. You don't know what you may be getting.

GENERAL. Thank you, Ghislaine, but there's no need. From what I hear she's sure to be very nice. Besides, we have decisions to make. Your presence here is unthinkable, my love, you know that.

GHISLAINE. This time, though, I am quite determined to stay.

GENERAL. What did you say?

GHISLAINE (*solemnly*). Leon, I have waited for so long in silence, keeping myself for you. If I were to bring you positive proof of the unworthiness of her for whom we sacrificed ourselves, what would you do?

GENERAL. Unworthiness? Emily unworthy? Alas! You must be dreaming, Ghislaine.

GHISLAINE. Yes, Leon, I am dreaming, dreaming that I am about to live at last. In this reticule I hold clasped to my heart I have two letters, and my little revolver with the mother-of-pearl handle, loaded. Two letters signed by her hand. Two love-letters to a man.

GENERAL. Thundering cannonballs, it can't be true!

GHISLAINE. We are free, Leon!

GENERAL. Who is it? I demand to know his name!

GHISLAINE. Doctor Bonfant.

The DOCTOR *enters, beaming.*

DOCTOR (*moving above the desk*). General, I am happy to be able to tell you that she seems very much better today. We chatted for a while and that seemed to soothe her. You see how wrong you are to poke fun at doctoring. It all depends on the doctor, and the way he sets about it.

GENERAL (*icily*). Don't labour the point, sir. There is a lady present.

The DOCTOR *turns to* GHISLAINE *in mild surprise.*

DOCTOR. I do beg your pardon. (*He bows.*) Madame.

GHISLAINE (*with infinite nobility*). Mademoiselle. But not for very long now.

The DOCTOR *straightens, astonished.*

Curtain.

Act Two

The same scene. When the curtain rises, the DOCTOR *is seated. The* GENERAL *is pacing feverishly about the room.*

GENERAL. What do you say to swords, sir?

DOCTOR. General, I say you are quite wrong.

GENERAL. Blood must be shed, sir. I shall listen to your explanations afterwards.

DOCTOR. It may be a trifle late by then.

GENERAL. I can't help that. Blood to begin with, sir.

DOCTOR. So I would advise, incidentally, with the present state of your arteries. How about a little cut with the lancet, first? I have my bag here.

GENERAL. Your sawbones humour is uncalled for, sir.

DOCTOR. I am quite serious. Blood pressure is our triumph. It is one of the few chances we have of being accurate, thanks to our little gadget here. That is why we take it on every conceivable occasion. The last time yours was up on two hundred and fifty. That's very high, you know.

GENERAL. I don't care, sir. I shall consult one of your colleagues. It is a question of honour at the moment. (*After a pause.*) Two hundred and fifty – is that high?

DOCTOR. Very.

GENERAL (*after a pause*). Did you or did you not receive those letters?

DOCTOR. I tell you I never did. If I had, how could they come to be in your possession?

GENERAL. True enough. You've read them, though – they aren't forgeries.

DOCTOR. Apparently not.

GENERAL. Therefore, sir, the fact is this: my wife is in love with you.

DOCTOR. So she writes.

GENERAL. And does that appear to you to be perfectly normal?

DOCTOR. What can I do about it?

GENERAL. God bless my soul, sir, what are you? Has the Medical Corps no honour? Any cadet – what am I saying – any regular N.C.O. would already have replied: 'At your service'. Explanations would have followed later. How would you like it if I slapped your face?

DOCTOR. I should promptly slap yours back, sir. And there I should have the advantage of you. I am Acting President of the Sports Club of which you are merely the Hon. Sec. I do an hour's exercise every morning. You spoke of your paunch just now. We are the same age. Just look at mine. (*He lets his trousers down.*)

GENERAL (*grudgingly*). You're pulling it in.

DOCTOR. No. It's perfectly natural. Feel. Now look at yours.

The GENERAL *undoes his own trousers and examines his figure.*

GENERAL. Holy Moses!

DOCTOR. Go on, feel. Feel mine. Now feel yours.

GHISLAINE *appears in the doorway.*

GHISLAINE (*as she enters*). I entreat you, don't do anything foolish.

The DOCTOR *and the* GENERAL *hastily pull up their trousers.*

Oh, my God, you're wounded.

GENERAL. No, no, of course not. Go back into the morning room, and don't come out whatever you do. We will call you when it's all over.

GHISLAINE *goes out.*

What a business!

DOCTOR. I am all at sea, I must confess. Who is this young woman?

GENERAL. Young girl, sir – a friend of mine, and I forbid you to jump to any conclusions.

DOCTOR. If I cannot even form a supposition I shall be more at sea than ever. Who is she?

GENERAL. Mademoiselle de Ste-Euverte – a lady descended from one of the noblest houses of Lorraine – is the love of my life, Doctor, and I am hers. We met at the Annual Ball of the Eighth Dragoons at Saumur in eighteen ninety-three. She was a girl of the best society, I was a married man. Anything between us was quite out of the question. At the time, owing to my career and the children, I dared not contemplate divorce. And yet we could not give up our love. Seventeen years that's been going on. Mademoiselle de Ste-Euverte is still a maiden and I am still a prisoner.

DOCTOR. But dammit, General, your career is established, your daughters are grown up, what in heaven's name are you waiting for?

GENERAL. I'll tell you a secret, Doctor, a miserable secret. I am a coward.

DOCTOR. Stuff and nonsense, General! You wanted to run me through just now. And what about your oak leaves and your eighteen wounds?

GENERAL (*simply*). Those were done to me. It's not the same thing. Besides, in battle it's merely a matter of not imagining yourself dead. Life is a different thing. (*He pauses. Dully.*) I can't make people suffer.

DOCTOR (*gently*). Then you are going to make them suffer a great deal, my friend, and you will suffer a great deal yourself.

GENERAL. I fear so.

DOCTOR. Let us sum up the situation, shall we? I want to help you out of this dilemma. You are in love with this young woman.

GENERAL. Young girl, sir.

DOCTOR. Young girl, if you prefer it. She loves you. She has spent years waiting for you. She sacrificed her youth in vain anticipation of a happiness which you once promised her. You owe her that happiness now.

GENERAL. I know. I know. Not a minute has gone by during those seventeen years that has not been poisoned by the thought of it. What is she doing? She is alone, playing the piano in the deserted drawing room of her big house, doing her embroidery, eating alone at her vast table in the chilly dining room where my place is always laid and always vacant. I know it, sir. I know it all. Time and again I have seized my service revolver – I'm not afraid of death – he's an old comrade – bang-bang, all over. For me, not for her. I had no right to do it.

DOCTOR. Leave your revolver, with your sword, up on its rack, General. Among all your military equipment, did you never think of your kitbag?

GENERAL. My kitbag?

DOCTOR. Two shirts, three pairs of pants, six handkerchiefs, hey presto and Mademoiselle de Ste-Euverte is no longer – a young girl.

GENERAL. And my wife, sir?

DOCTOR. Do you love her?

GENERAL. Lord, no. But she loves me. She'll die of it.

DOCTOR. Hum, I wonder. Women have unexpected reserves. I understand she wrote to say she was in love with me.

GENERAL. Upon my soul, sir, how dare you! Two of my friends will call on two of yours at first light tomorrow morning. To the death, sir, to the death!

DOCTOR. Now, come, come, General, we must try to understand each other. Do you want to kill me, or do you want to live?

GENERAL. I want to kill you for a start, sir! After that we'll see.

DOCTOR. See what, pray? Having given your wife this handsome token of your love, I can't see you anywhere near to leaving her. You say she makes a scene if you so much as step into the garden, although she knows full well that you no longer love her. If you kill a man for her sake I challenge you after that to retire to the bathroom on your own. You really must be logical, General.

GENERAL. Can you swear that you are not her lover?

DOCTOR. On the head of Madame Bonfant.

GENERAL. You don't catch me that way. On your own.

DOCTOR. On my own, then.

GENERAL. That's better. Anyway, she's ugly – nothing but a bag of bones.

DOCTOR. No, she's not ugly.

GENERAL. What do you mean, she's not ugly. What are you insinuating now?

DOCTOR. Come, come, General, your wife was never what one would call a beauty, but when you came to live here fifteen years ago, I don't mind telling you, my dear fellow, that she created quite a stir. Not in me, sir, not in me – particularly. But her personality, her clothes, her talent! Very attractive woman, sir, was your wife – and then, coming from Paris as she did . . .

GENERAL. She comes from Carpentras.

DOCTOR. She had just come from Paris, none the less, and from the Opera. You know what they are in the provinces. I personally am acquainted with two who at all events cherished secret hopes.

GENERAL (*turning; awful in his anger*). Their names?

DOCTOR. What is the use, now, General? One of them is in a wheel chair through sacrificing overmuch to Venus. The other is dead.

GENERAL. Too late. Always too late.

DOCTOR. Exactly. You know, General, the more I think over your case the more disturbed I am by it. This constant living in the past. Your jealousy of Madame de St Pé was fine in the old tooth and claw days. What on earth can it possibly matter to you now? Your love for Mademoiselle de Ste-Euverte was for Mademoiselle de Ste-Euverte at eighteen, the night of the Garrison Ball. That girl has been dead these many years. Neither you nor she herself can so much as recall what she once was.

GENERAL (*with a disarming smile*). Oh, yes, Doctor, dear me, yes.

DOCTOR. A tender memory. The memory of a girl who is dead. And Major St Pé is dead, too. He was a young officer you once knew, venturesome, romantic, in love – soft-hearted, too, and crammed full of scruples. God rest his soul. Why don't you forget all about him and turn your attention to your rose trees? You haven't so very much longer, you know.

GENERAL. Never!

DOCTOR. Then I am going to talk to you like a sawbones. How many wild oats, how many sicknesses, between you and that young Major while Mademoiselle de Ste-Euverte was waiting?

GENERAL. The heart has stayed the same, sir, under the ironmongery. (*He springs to attention.*) Lieutenant St Pé. Graduated second from Saumur. No money, but plenty of courage. Ready to give his all for France, for honour, for a woman. A real woman, sweet and loving and faithful and pure; not that third-rate prima donna. I am thirty years old, I swear I am! And I found that woman. I found her last night, at the Annual Ball at Saumur. I am ready.

DOCTOR. Then you'd better make haste, General. (*He rises and moves above the desk.*) One good honest explanation. Cut to the quick before gangrene sets in. Hurt if you must but do it without flinching. And then start again afresh. Crossing the threshold of that door seems like flying to the moon, but in fact all it requires is one step.

GENERAL. You're a fine one! You don't love your wife, either. Did you manage to decamp, yourself?

DOCTOR. No, but then I never met a student nurse at the Medical School Ball. That's the difference between us.

GHISLAINE *appears in the doorway.*

GHISLAINE. I can't stand it! I must know.

GENERAL (*going to her slightly on edge*). Dammit all, Ghislaine, you've waited seventeen years, surely you can contain yourself for another ten minutes.

GHISLAINE. No, I can't, not even for ten minutes. Those seventeen years were nothing. But since I brought you those letters every second's delay is a century. I cannot bear it any longer.

GENERAL. I must have time to make her confess, and inform her of my irrevocable decision. She is an invalid, dammit. I owe her some consideration. Don't you be cruel, too.

GHISLAINE. I bore her cruelty, and respected her love so long as I believed her faithful to you. But now I know that she dared to betray you I shall know no pity, Leon, and no patience. Either way, should you be capable of hesitating still – I have a little revolver with a mother-of-pearl handle here in my handbag. I shall end this life within the hour, without ever having known more of love than your vain promises, Leon.

GENERAL. Give me strength! All I ask is a moment to set my life in order. Go back into the morning room, my love, and be patient. There are some magazines on the table.

GHISLAINE. Magazines! Like at the dentist's. You have wounded me for the first time, my dear.

GENERAL. Who said anything about a dentist? I was merely suggesting you should read to pass the time away. Anyhow, it's not you who is going to have the tooth out. I adore you! Just one moment.

The GENERAL *pushes* GHISLAINE *gently but firmly out of the room and comes back.*

Time is getting on. Suppose you spoke to her first, Doctor?

DOCTOR. Mightn't that prove to be a little awkward, considering those letters? Suppose she flung herself into my arms? There'll be no end of explaining to do then.

GENERAL. True enough. Stay here, though, will you, and if I call for help, come in.

The GENERAL *runs out of the room and comes back almost at once, distractedly waving a letter.*

Doctor, she's not in her room!

DOCTOR. What! Is there another way out?

GENERAL. Through the window, by hanging on to the wistaria.

DOCTOR. Don't talk nonsense! In her condition . . .

GENERAL. She left this note on her dressing-table. (*He reads.*) 'I heard everything. Men are all cowards. Whatever they may have said to you, Leon, I have never loved anyone but you. I was lying. I can walk when I want to. I am going. You will never hear of me again. Emily.' Good God! Do you think she means to kill herself?

DOCTOR (*looking at his watch*). The level crossing! She spoke of it! It's two minutes to, the train goes by at five past!

GENERAL. The pond! You go one way – I'll go the other.

They run out. GHISLAINE *enters almost immediately.*

GHISLAINE (*crossing to the desk*). I, too, heard everything.

(*She sits at the desk.*) There is only one way out. You love her still, Leon. (*She picks up a pen and writes rapidly, calm but dabbing away a tear through her veil. Murmuring.*) Leon, here is my last letter . . . But I was always so alone . . . (*Her voice trails away as she continues to write.*)

GASTON, *off, is heard singing his Italian love song. The ditty continues throughout the writing of the letter. When she has finished* GHISLAINE *puts the letter in a prominent position on the desk. The singing continues.*

There. On his papers. That's all.

She rises, unhurriedly, opens her reticule, draws out the revolver, presses it to her heart and pulls the trigger. Nothing happens. She looks at the gun in surprise, pulls out a catch, pushes another, blows in the barrel and fires again. Still nothing happens. She sighs.

It too has been waiting seventeen years. (*She throws the gun into the waste-paper basket, looks at her fob-watch and mutters.*) Too late for the train. The pond! (*She runs, stops and turns.*) No. Not in the same place as her, for heaven's sake. (*She darts a quick look round the room.*) The window. (*She runs to the window.*) With a little luck . . .

She swings her legs over the window-sill and jumps out, disappearing from view. The singing ends abruptly in a loud hiccup. The stage is empty for a moment, then GASTON *enters, carrying a senseless* GHISLAINE. *The* MAID *follows them on.*

MAID. My goodness gracious, sir, whatever's the matter? You hiccupped fit to wake the dead.

GASTON *lays* GHISLAINE *on the sofa and kneels beside her.*

GASTON. I was quietly reading the paper in the hammock

when this lady comes tumbling down on my head.

MAID. Well, fancy that! Maybe she wanted to kill you.

GASTON. Herself, more likely. Besides, I don't know her from Adam.

GHISLAINE *moans.*

She's fainted.

MAID. And the Doctor just this minute left. The man as good as lives here half the time, and the one day we have a suicide, he's out.

GASTON (*slapping* GHISLAINE*'s face.*) For God's sake go and fetch something.

MAID. What?

GASTON. Well, *I* don't know – ointment, smelling salts – iodine – anything.

MAID. I'll make her a nice strong cup of coffee.

The MAID *goes out.*

GASTON. No blood, anyway. (*He feels* GHISLAINE *all over.*) No bones broken, apparently. No bumps. Madame. Madame.

GHISLAINE (*weakly*). Mademoiselle.

GASTON (*rising*). Mademoiselle – I beg your pardon. (*He bends over her.*) Are you feeling better?

GHISLAINE (*sitting up; murmuring*). Leave your hands where they are, Leon.

GASTON (*turning away in embarrassment*). Excuse me, but you are making a mistake.

GHISLAINE (*crying out*). Leave your hands, Leon – all over me – or I feel I shall go off again – your hands, quickly – I'm going . . .

GASTON (*panicking*). My hands?

GASTON. Oh, dear, I can't very well let her faint away again.

GHISLAINE *leans against him and sighs contentedly.*

Not that it's at all unpleasant, and I am such a lonely young man. Besides, I'll mention it when I go to confession.

GHISLAINE. Oh, how good it feels. You are touching me at last, Leon. You thought me strong – and I was strong – I had to be, but oh, how long they were, all those nights on my own. Before I met you I was alone too, but I never knew it. It was on the morrow of the Saumur Ball that my bed suddenly grew big. That next night and all the nights for seventeen years. And all the wicked thoughts – you don't know. I shall never tell you. I struggled alone. No one was to touch me until you finally came. Your arms are strong and gentle your hands, gentler even than at the Saumur Ball. Kiss me, Leon, now that you know I am going to die. What are you waiting for, Leon, my death?

GASTON. The lady is obviously making a mistake, but seeing that she may be going to die . . . (*He kisses her.*)

GHISLAINE (*she has the time to sigh*). At last.

A long kiss. Enter the GENERAL, *carrying an unconscious* EMILY *over his shoulder. He stops dead when he sees* GHISLAINE *and* GASTON.

GENERAL. What the devil do you think you're doing?

GASTON (*breaking away from* GHISLAINE *and rising in terror*). But, sir, the lady is delirious.

GENERAL (*bawling*). Ten thousand demons, I can well believe it! But what about you?

GASTON. She fell on top of me, sir, and ordered me to kiss her.

GENERAL. Hell's bells, has everyone around here gone mad this morning? What's the matter? What happened?

GASTON. She threw herself out of the window, sir.

GENERAL. Out of the window! Holy Moses, they're insane, the lot of them. My beloved! Here, my boy, take my wife, will you?

He hands EMILY *to* GASTON *and rushes over to* GHISLAINE.

Ghislaine! Beloved! Why did you want to die?

GHISLAINE (*sitting up*). Who is this touching me? I do not know those hands.

GENERAL. It's I, Leon. Your Leon.

GHISLAINE (*pushing him away*). Go away. You aren't Leon. I don't recognise your hands. (*The* GENERAL *kisses her*.) Nor your mouth. I forbid you to touch me. No one may touch me but him. You know perfectly well. I am keeping myself.

EMILY (*coming to in* GASTON'*s arms*). Leon!

GENERAL (*picking* GHISLAINE *up in his arms*). That's done it. The other one's coming to. She mustn't see her here. She'd kill herself a second time.

EMILY (*clinging to* GASTON'*s neck and screeching*). Leon, hold me. Kiss me, Leon. You can see I'm dying. Kiss me quickly before I'm quite dead.

GASTON (*in a panic; yelling*). This one wants to be kissed before she dies, as well! What am I going to do?

GENERAL. Can't you see they're both delirious. Put Madame de St Pé down in her room. I am taking this young lady next door.

They both go out, carrying their unconscious burdens as the curtain falls.

Act Three

The same scene. Before the curtain rises, the music is heard of 'The Waltz of the Toreadors'. The GENERAL *is alone. He appears to be waiting. The* DOCTOR *enters the small sitting room.*

GENERAL. Well?

DOCTOR. They are both resting. I have given them a sedative, a good dose of gardenal. The trouble is, they'll eventually wake up.

GENERAL. We're so peaceful as we are. It's most odd, for an hour now there hasn't been a sound. I was even on the point of gathering a few ideas. You know, science ought to find a way of putting women permanently to sleep. We could wake them up for a while at night and they could go back to sleep again.

DOCTOR. Ah, General, if we only could. But what about the housework? You should see the performance if I have to fry myself an egg. And that's nothing, there's the washing up afterwards.

GENERAL. We might try it and see. If the worst came to the worst we wouldn't put the maids to sleep. Have you seen the latest little one? With all these upsets I haven't even had a chance to say hello to her. A bosom, my dear chap! (*He sighs.*) Dear Lord, how simple it all could be. Why do we complicate life so?

DOCTOR. Because we have a soul, General. You take an old free-thinker's word for it. That's what makes life hell for us. The maid's petticoats are very pleasant at the time, but afterwards – without any love, without any real desire – what a vacuum. So then the soul flows back into this vacuum, your mouth is full of it, it streams out through your nose – very nasty.

GENERAL. I know that feeling. But it's not nasty, far from it. Afterwards, why – you think of higher things. The idealist in you comes out, that's all. It's a kind of sensuous joy, you know, to feel one's soul. The afternoon drifts on, very tastefully – one reads a good book, takes a little stroll, and smells the flowers; one muses on the nature of the world, one walks on air, light-hearted – quite the artist. You eat a first-class dinner, and then later in the evening, when you've built up your strength, out in the passage, mum's the word, and nobody's any the wiser. A moment's shame is sweet to take. There aren't so many to be had, either, with all the scruples a man invents for himself. And after that what happens? Down goes the sinner, up comes the idealist and you go to bed, thanks to that little interlude, brimful of good resolutions. It's a pity that women have never grasped this ingenious system of balance. They dramatise everything.

DOCTOR. That's because they haven't our particular conception of selfishness, that's all. We have decided that everything under the sun is food for us and we sit back and draw it all towards our hungry little egos. But women don't sit back; not they. They swoop on to the world and mould it to their image. That's their way of expressing themselves. And heaven help the man they have singled out to be their other self. The poor wretch keeps his big moustaches, his top hat, his social position and his job, but – before he has time to turn round the trick's been played. All that is no more than a false front. She has turned him into a lady's jack-a-dandy; for love, money, power, revenge – for everything. And he's happy, what's more, the poor simpleton, at least in the beginning. Milady loves him.

GENERAL. God preserve us from the love of women. If they at least went about their gruesome little task with a smile – but not on your life. The fact is they suffer agonies in the process of devouring us. Forever tearful and moaning and in pain. Do you think there are so many grounds for suffering in this world?

DOCTOR. No.

GENERAL. Nor do I. And when for a wonder they stop being hurt themselves, there is no respite, they start hurting you.

DOCTOR. I'll tell you a secret, General. We have stayed little boys. Only the little girls grow up.

GENERAL. I'm lying. (*He looks towards the door.*) There is one, though, who never hurt me, who never once complained. True, I never lived with her. Oh, if you could have seen her at the Saumur Ball. I bet you don't believe that I really do love that girl, having waited all these years.

DOCTOR. My good man, one must never judge the courage or the love of others. No one can say who loves or is afraid.

GENERAL. There's my life story, Doctor, in a nutshell. The shell is handsome. They have painted the oakleaves on to it, and Lord knows how many decorations. I am in Poincaré's pocket – let Germany so much as make a move and I know I'll be recalled – he told me so. I have a lovely house, splendid whiskers, the easy wenches in these parts refuse me nothing. When I go by on my black mare of a morning, in my corsets, I'll even wager that I make the little virgins at the High School dream of me, as they peep behind their curtains. I make a noise; I curse and swear; I utter enormities when the fancy takes me and everyone turns a blind eye, even the priest, because I have a way with me. I thump my chest like a gorilla – and the world says, 'What a man!' Well, my friend, the shell is empty. There's nobody inside. I am alone, and I'm afraid.

DOCTOR. Afraid of what?

GENERAL. I dunno. Of my loneliness, I suppose.

DOCTOR. My poor old friend.

GENERAL. Yes, I'm letting my hair down, Doctor. My bits of fun, even, do you think they amuse me? They bore me to death. It is my terror of living which sends me scampering after them. When you see them swinging by with their buttocks and their breasts under their dresses you feel I don't know what wild hope surge up inside you. But once the dress is off and you have to get down to it . . . The only thing about all these philanderings is that you get to my age realising that you have never in your life made love. It's wrong of me to make fun of my secretary. I am an old virgin, Doctor.

DOCTOR. No, General, you have the sickness, that's all.

GENERAL. Which one? I've had the lot. I've been peppered God knows how often.

DOCTOR. Those sicknesses are nothing. They can be treated. We have a soul, General. I long denied the phenomenon. I belonged to the old school; we did not bother with that subject in my day, at the Sorbonne. I wanted to stick to abscesses and cancers. But now I know. In nine cases out of ten it's there the trouble lies.

GENERAL. But, dammit, everyone has a soul. There's no

reason for being scared out of one's wits a whole life long.

DOCTOR. It is, General. Souls are rare. And when, by ill luck, you happen to possess one, if you don't make your peace with it, it's war.

GENERAL. Peace, peace? But what brand of peace does it want, damn its eyes? It surely doesn't expect me to take Holy Orders, does it?

DOCTOR. No. If it were as simple as that you would have done it years ago.

GENERAL. Then what *does* the jade want? The only time I feel slightly at peace is when I look at something beautiful. Dammit, I can't turn myself into a painter or sculptor, can I? I don't know the first thing about it. What then – scuttling from art gallery to museum like a halfwit, brandishing a Kodak? No, by Heaven! Beauty's a thing one should be able to fashion for onself. It takes a simple simon to go through life gawping at shop windows.

DOCTOR. What about Mademoiselle de Ste-Euverte, General?

GENERAL (*after a pause*). Well, yes, there it is. For seventeen years I've been telling myself that. You know, it's an extraordinary thing what happened to me at Saumur – I had asked a young woman to dance; a girl like any other; the colour of her dress and hair had caught my eye . . . And all of a sudden I ceased to be afraid. It was an enchanted moment, Doctor.

'The Waltz of the Toreadors' is heard.

(*He sings.*) Tra la la la . . . I introduce myself, ask her for the dance, take her by the waist and all of a sudden I say to myself – 'How good I feel. What's happening to me? It was my soul piping down for a bit.

DOCTOR. And did it happen again?

GENERAL. Every time. Every time, at all our pathetic little meetings, and every time came the miracle – I stopped being afraid.

DOCTOR. Then in Heaven's name why didn't you make her your wife at once then, or your mistress?

GENERAL. My mistress? To tell you the truth, I could have. But I didn't want to break the spell; I wanted to wait until I was free, and love could take its rightful place in the normal life of everyday.

DOCTOR. That was wise of you. But then, why did you wait so long?

GENERAL. It's easy to talk. You don't know the old bitch – I refer to my soul. When she comes face to face with my wife, she bawls with disgust and fright; but when I make Emily cry, when she starts to whimper in her wheel-chair – where I know she only sits in order to annoy me – when I am at last on the point of throttling her – don't laugh – it has crossed my mind – and take my cap off the hall-stand and decamp for good and all; do you know what she does then, the great goop – my soul, that is – she cuts off my legs, and fills me with pity – mean, ignoble pity, and old memories of love from the days before everything became dried up and stale between us. She roots me to the spot. So I hang my cap back on its peg again and take my soul on a little jaunt to the brothel to see if I can't cheer her up a bit. Have you got a soul, Doctor?

DOCTOR. Yes, but she's extremely shy and fairly modest in her demands.

GENERAL. Well, don't let her get out of hand. Rule her with a rod of iron, or by Heaven, she'll have your skin. (*He murmurs dreamily.*) Dear Ghislaine! Dear sweet, patient Ghislaine. Dear little soldier on half pay. Dear widow. (*With a shout.*) Lieutenant St Pé! Graduated second from Saumur. I am thirty years of age, I swear I am! (*Turning to the* DOCTOR.) Give her a little less gardenal, than the other one, will you, Doctor? I should so like to console her.

DOCTOR (*smiling*). Very well. You know I am very fond of you, General. And to think that we nearly murdered each other over that letter business.

GENERAL (*thumping his breast with clenched fist*). God in Heaven, what a fool I am. Suppose I thought of myself a little for a change. When I held an Arab at the point of my sword did I stop to ask myself so many questions, dammit! Suppose I gave up trying to understand others for a while? How good it would be. What do you say, Doctor?

DOCTOR. The best thing you could do, General, if you can bring yourself to do it.

GENERAL. Then it's all settled. Inspection over. Dis-miss! Carry on! What's that? No broom, you say? Too bad. I don't want to hear any more about it.

GASTON *enters.*

GENERAL. Ah, there you are, my boy. You're in luck! I'm in a rollicking mood. We are going to mop up the chapter on Morocco in two shakes of a lamb's tail, and we'll postpone the next one until ten years from now. I'll show them what I'm made of.

DOCTOR (*rising*). I'll leave you, General. My wife will think I'm here far too often. I don't have to tell you what reproaches are, eh? I shall look in to see them both this evening. In the meantime, you should take advantage of the gardenal to rehearse your lines for the big scene.

GENERAL. I'm bearing them in mind. But it's so good to talk about something else for a bit. I shall take a little stroll around Morocco and come straight home again.

GASTON. Good-bye, sir.

DOCTOR. Good-bye.

The DOCTOR *goes out.*

GENERAL (*turning to his secretary*). Now, let's get back to our two sky pilots. As I was saying, there they were, minus their goolies. Write down: 'A fearful mutilation, the details of which one hesitates to enlarge upon, perpetrated on the persons of two saintly churchmen, placed us under the sorry obligation of shedding blood ourselves.'

Enter SIDONIA *and* ESTELLE *in their new dresses, followed by a handsome dressmaker,* MME DUPONT-FREDAINE.

SIDONIA. Papa, we've come about the dresses.

GENERAL. Pipe down, will you? I've other fish to fry just now. We go into the attack first thing tomorrow morning. (*Seeing her.*) Why, Madame Dupont-Fredaine! How delightful to see you. (*Kissing her hand.*) Lovely and tempting and swish-swishing as ever. By Jove, what a figure. What allure! Madame Dupont-Fredaine, you are the loveliest woman in the neighbourhood.

MME FREDAINE. Now General, that's all over and done with. We must think of the young ones now. You gave us very little notice, you know – we had to perform miracles to make beauties out of these two girlies.

GENERAL. A miracle. How right you are.

MME FREDAINE (*giving him a little slap*). Naughty! What do you say to this little frill at the bottom, hinted at again in the sleeves? I think it's a dream.

GENERAL. Enchanting! Enchanting! Your own dress is delightful, too. What is this splendid material?

MME FREDAINE (*sliding away*). General! Look at your daughters. Their material is very much finer.

GENERAL. Lovely, lovely! Is it going to cost a lot?

MME FREDAINE. Now, General, you know I'm very reasonable . . .

GENERAL (*close to her*). Oh, Emma, how I wish you were.

MME FREDAINE. Now, now! Let's not talk about the price. The young ladies wanted to make sure of pleasing you – and Monsieur Gaston, too, I fancy.

GASTON (*blushing*). I'm not qualified to judge. I have so little experience of young ladies.

MME FREDAINE. When one is twenty years of age and handsome one is always qualified, young man. Why, he's blushing! He's adorable, this secretary of yours, General.

GENERAL. Ten thousand demons, madam. I forbid you to adore him!

MME FREDAINE. Walk around the room, will you, young ladies? The gentlemen will give us their verdict.

While SIDONIA *and* ESTELLE *parade about, the* GENERAL *moves closer to* MME DUPONT-FREDAINE.

GENERAL. These repeated refusals of yours are quite absurd, you know, Emma.

MME FREDAINE. Stop it now! You are a wicked wolf. Dupont-Fredaine is a friend of yours.

GENERAL. Exactly. Nobody would take the slightest exception. Charming! Charming! I really must have a serious talk with you about the cost of these fal-lals, dear lady. Will you take a little stroll around the garden? I shall present you with a rose. Carry on, girls. Gaston, I leave them in your care.

MME DUPONT-FREDAINE *goes out with the* GENERAL. SIDONIA *and* ESTELLE *hurl themselves upon* GASTON.

SIDONIA. Aren't you ashamed, letting her say you're adorable?

ESTELLE. An old fly-by-night like her! Doesn't it mean anything to you that we are pining away?

GASTON. But, my dear young ladies, how could I help it?

ESTELLE. And the other one this morning, I suppose you couldn't help her, either? Why did you kiss her on the mouth?

SIDONIA. It's shameful! Everybody saw you.

GASTON. I was alone.

ESTELLE. You don't suppose we ever leave you alone, do you? We never let you out of our sight. We were outside on the stairs.

GASTON. She had fallen on top of me. She was dying. What else could I do?

ESTELLE. You swore, Gaston.

SIDONIA. You swore. One or the other.

GASTON. My dear young ladies, I love you both.

ESTELLE. Yet it's a third you kiss. A nice thing!

SIDONIA. Ah, my dear – men! Does it surprise you? What a child you are.

ESTELLE. You never even kiss us.

GASTON. But you are young ladies. Besides, there are always two of you.

SIDONIA. Ooh!

ESTELLE *and* SIDONIA *turn to each other in a fury.*

ESTELLE. You see!

SIDONIA. You see!

ESTELLE. You never let me see him alone.

SIDONIA. No, it's you!

ESTELLE. 'Tisn't! It's you!

SIDONIA. 'Tisn't! It's you! You skinny lizard! You great big lamp post! You beanpole!

ESTELLE. You bag of lard! You suet pudding! You soppy sausage, you!

They fight. GASTON, *distracted, hops ineffectually around trying to separate them.*

GASTON. Ladies! Ladies! Help! Help! They're going to kill each other. Help!

MME DUPONT-FREDAINE *and the* GENERAL, *very red in the face, come flying in.*

MME FREDAINE. Young ladies! Your dresses!

GENERAL (*in the teeth*). Lord, they gave me a fright. I thought they'd seen us. (*He shouts.*) Holy suffering catfish, have you finished? Where did I get such a pair of misbegotten frumps? What happened? Explain yourselves.

SIDONIA. She started it.

ESTELLE. I didn't! She did!

GENERAL (*to* GASTON). Devil take it, man, I leave them in your charge and you can't even stop them fighting.

MME FREDAINE (*kneeling to repair the damage*). Oh, your dresses! Your dresses! Little vandals!

GENERAL. Answer me. What were they fighting about?

GASTON (*crimson*). I can't tell you, sir.

GENERAL. Can't tell me, eh? Ye Gods and little fishes, who is making a monkey out of who? Now then, you two, what were you fighting about?

Silence.

ESTELLE (*blurting it out*). Papa! We love him to distraction.

SIDONIA. Both of us.

GENERAL. Whom?

ESTELLE }
SIDONIA } (*together; sobbing*). Him.

GENERAL. This is the rampaging limit!

ESTELLE. But, Papa, you don't know what it's like to be in love.

MME FREDAINE. Young ladies! You're weeping on to your dresses.

GENERAL. Blood and giblets, that's a good one. That emasculated greenhorn?

MME FREDAINE. General!

GENERAL. Sorry, it slipped out. That zany? That trashy little pen-pusher?

ESTELLE. Papa, what's a greenhorn?

GENERAL. Suffering Jehosophat, leave the room this instant. Madame Dupont-Fredaine, be so good as to take them away, and leave me alone with this young feller-me-lad here. I don't know what's going on in this house, but things are beginning to get out of hand.

MME FREDAINE (*going out with the girls*). It's love, General.

GENERAL. Love! That's a good one. Love isn't an excuse for everything.

MME FREDAINE. Naughty fibber. (*Giving him a surreptitious little slap.*) You just told me the exact opposite. Good-bye for the moment.

GENERAL (*winking*). See you later, Emma.

They go. The GENERAL *turns to* GASTON *and gives him a long look.*

Well, what have you got to say for yourself, young man?

GASTON (*rising*). I don't know, sir. I am quite overcome.

GENERAL. Exactly. You were recommended to me by a venerable ecclesiastic, who vouched for your morals and your handwriting. I had up till now testified to the excellence of both. I am beginning to change my tune, my friend.

GASTON. I swear to you, sir, that nothing in my behaviour could have incited the young ladies to . . .

GENERAL. Don't drown the salmon, sir. Nothing in your behaviour could have incited you to kiss Mademoiselle de Ste-Euverte on the mouth this morning, either, I suppose?

GASTON. She mistook me for somebody else, sir.

GENERAL. That makes it worse. You are an impostor, sir.

GASTON. And that's not all, general. What happened is far more serious than that.

GENERAL (*terrified*). By God, sir! Don't think I'm going to make light of this for ever! You mean you didn't draw the line at kissing her?

GASTON. Oh but I did! What else could I have done?

GENERAL (*reassured*). Well, I dunno . . . Take her hands . . .

GASTON. I took her hands as well. But that's not it. The terrifying thing is that while I held her in my arms I quite thought that it was me she loved.

GENERAL. She wasn't properly conscious, my boy.

GASTON. Oh, I know. She kept calling me Leon.

GENERAL (*easily*). Leon? What a coincidence. The name of her intended, no doubt.

GASTON. All the same, it was to me she said it. I just know, something inside me tells me so. And ever since, General – and I'm prepared to take the consequences of this fearsome, this marvellous event – I do believe that I love her myself.

The GENERAL *bursts out laughing.*

GENERAL. Ha, ha, ha, ha, there's a good one. That's a very good one. So you think one falls in love like that, do you? At first sight and for always? Fiddlesticks! You must gorge yourself on tuppeny novelettes.

GASTON. No, sir, on the classics, exclusively. But the course of events is frequently quite similar. (*With dignity.*) In any case I am prepared to confess my fault to this lady when she is once more herself, and offer to make amends.

GENERAL. Confess? Confess what? You will do no such thing. I will not have you confuse the wits of this poor unfortunate girl. God bless my soul, am I going to have to teach you, by soundly boxing your ears, just what a young girl's honour means? I've seen you already, my lad, with that last little tweenie we had here.

GASTON. General!

GENERAL. Don't deny it. I saw you, I tell you.

GASTON. It was she who pursued me, sir, I avoided her. She was always coming up behind me in the passages . . .

GENERAL. Oh, the little bitch! I mean, the boldness of the girl.

GASTON. She said she was fed to the teeth with this dump – I quote, of course – and that she absolutely had to have a young one.

GENERAL (*interrupting in a voice of thunder*). Young man! You are on the threshold of life. You appear to me to be completely devoid of principles. You were put into my care – I could be your father – and it is my duty to instil those principles into you. Quiet! You will speak when your turn comes and not before. Firstly, one point about which it is forbidden to make light. Honour. Do you know what I mean by honour?

GASTON. Yes, sir.

GENERAL. I should hope so. You have been bred on the classics, you say. I do not therefore have to teach you that ancient fable of the Spartan youth who, having stolen a fox and hidden it beneath his tunic, preferred to have his stomach gnawed away rather than confess his theft. This admirable fable contains a moral. Will you kindly tell me what that moral is?

GASTON (*after a moment's hesitation*). Never confess.

GENERAL. No, sir, wrong answer.

GASTON. Never steal a fox.

GENERAL. Wrong again. He did steal, but having stolen, what remained for our Spartan youth to do then?

GASTON. Give back the fox and take his punishment.

GENERAL. That's better. By confessing and returning the fruits of his felony, our Spartan youth would have given proof of good citizenship. But in allowing his stomach to be gnawed away without a murmur he did better. He showed he had honour. Draw the moral, now that I have put you on the right track.

GASTON. When one does something contrary to honour, honour consists in never owning up to it.

GENERAL. No, sir. That is pride, which is an insufferable fault.

GASTON. I give up, sir.

GENERAL. Ha! You give up, do you? I can see your sense of honour is choking you. A fine bunch, I must say, the younger generation. The meaning of this fable, sir, is perfectly simple. Honour bids me not to steal. Right. I do steal – well, if one is not a born fool one sidesteps the rules and regulations now and then. But one thing is certain, I am not capable of forfeiting my honour. Therein lies the principle. I have been caught. Am I, a young Spartan, going to admit that I have been found wanting in honour? No. I cannot be found wanting in honour. Hence there is no fox under my tunic. You get it?

GASTON. No, sir.

GENERAL. Never mind. You'll understand when you grow

up. Simply retain from all this that it is essential to keep up appearances. Let us take a more familiar instance. You are sleeping with the maid.

GASTON (*indignantly*). General!

GENERAL. Don't have a fit. You were on the point of doing so, you young Pecksniff. And if you weren't a born ass you would have. To resume, honour is willing, but the flesh is weak. Do you for all that go and pinch her bottom at table in the very middle of lunch?

GASTON (*blushing*). Oh, no, sir.

GENERAL. No, you simply say, 'Leontine, please bring some bread.' And yet you know damn well it isn't a bread roll you're after. But you have learnt how to master your passions, that's the important thing. Lunch runs its course, impeccably, and after the coffee you proceed to the pantry where you do whatever you fancy.

GASTON. Yes, sir.

GENERAL. Life, my dear Gaston, is one long family lunch, tiresome like all family meals, but necessary. Firstly, because one has to eat, and secondly, because it has to be done – in accordance with a long established ritual, with initialled napkin rings, embroidered table mats, forks of different shapes and sizes and a bell-push under the table. But wait a minute. Those are the appearances. It is a game we have agreed to play. So therefore we must play it according to the rules; answer the children's questions, divide the plum tart into equal slices, scold the youngest when he dribbles, fold one's napkin nicely and put it back into its ring – until the coffee. But the coffee once drunk, down the back stairs and the best of luck. The law of the jungle comes into its own. Dammit, there's no need to be a complete fool.

GENERAL. Wait a minute! I haven't finished yet. I can see the way your mind's working. You are young, you want the moon – you are going to say – 'There's middle-class hypocrisy – what about ideals? Where does the ideal come in?' The ideal, my boy, is doing very nicely, thank you. The ideal, my friend, is the lifebuoy. You're in the ocean, splashing about, doing your damnedest not to drown, in spite of whirlwinds and cross currents; the main thing to remember is to do the regulation breast stroke, and if you are not a clod, never to let the lifebuoy out of your sight. Nobody asks any more than that of you. Now if you choose to piss in the water now and then, that's your affair. The ocean is big enough, and if the top half of your body is still doing the breast stroke, nobody will say a word.

GASTON. But, General, does one ever reach the lifebuoy?

GENERAL. Never. But if your heart's in the right place, you never lose sight of it, either. The few fanatics who try a faster stroke to reach it at all costs deluge everybody else and always finish up by drowning, generally dragging down God knows how many other poor devils with them, who could otherwise have gone on quietly floundering about and minding their own business. Do you see what I mean?

GASTON. No, sir. Might I say something, though?

GENERAL. Carry on, my boy, carry on. Your turn to speak now.

GASTON. I'm twenty years of age, General. I'd rather try to go fast and drown.

GENERAL (*after a pause; gently*). Quite right, my boy, quite right. It's a sorry business, growing old, and understanding. (*With a sudden shout.*) Lieutenant St Pé. Graduated second from Saumur. Volunteer! Wait for me. I'm done for, anyway – here goes, I'd rather drown. I only said all that because one has to say it. Try all the same, my boy, not to drown others, even in a good cause. That's what weighs heavy on a man, hurting other people, always, no matter what one does. I have got used to everything, but not to that.

EMILY (*calling*). Leon!

GENERAL (*calling*). Yes?

EMILY. Where are you?

GENERAL (*wearily*). I'm here. I'm here, for heaven's sake. I'm always here.

EMILY. Come and sit with me. Goodness only knows what you're playing at while you think I'm asleep.

GENERAL (*looking at* GASTON *with a smile*). Playing the fool, my dear, with a young spark who wasn't even listening and quite right he was, too, damn him. (*Tapping his shoulder.*) You young stripling, you. You lucky little brand new devil of a greenhorn. Wait a bit, my boy. There's no almighty hurry after all, even if they do make fun of you. Wait until the right girl comes along and with her you will miraculously cease to be afraid. But when you find her, by Hades, don't wait seventeen years.

GASTON. I won't, sir.

GENERAL. At once! Remember my advice! Immediately! And make for the lifebuoy, side by side – the only proper way to swim is two by two. Wish me luck. I'm going in myself. But it's on the cards that one of us may drown en route.

EMILY (*off; calling*). Leon!

GENERAL. Here I am, madam. At your service for the last time.

The GENERAL *goes out, shutting the door behind him.*

GASTON. At once! That's all I'll keep of his advice.

GASTON *takes his courage in both hands and makes for the little sitting room.* GHISLAINE *is heard murmuring through the half-open door.*

GHISLAINE (*off*). Leon! Leon, you've come back. Can it be true, then? Will I really never be alone again? Oh, Leon!

There is a pause. The stage remains empty. Then GASTON *reappears, beetroot red.*

GASTON. Another case of mistaken identity. And yet, despite the effect of the medication, something tells me that she isn't altogether taken in. How interesting it is, living! The Reverend Fathers never told me. Let's screw up our courage a bit, and this time let's confess, with a certain circumspection, that it's us.

GASTON *screws up his courage and goes back into the room.*

Curtain.

Act Four

Same set, but the partition screening off the GENERAL'S WIFE*'s bedroom has been removed. It is towards the end of the day. The shutters in the* GENERAL*'s room are closed, as they are in this one. Darkness and silence. The* GENERAL'S WIFE, *in a nightcap and bedjacket, is sitting up against her pillows on her monumental, quilted bed. The* GENERAL *is on his feet.*

GENERAL. We must thrash this matter out, madam, once and for all.

EMILY. I tried to kill myself, you monster, isn't that enough for you?

GENERAL. You were stretched out on the sleepers – an awkward position but quite safe. The train had already passed.

EMILY. I didn't know. I was waiting for it.

GENERAL. On that branch line you could reckon on a good twenty-four hours of it. You'd have had pins and needles before then.

EMILY. Is nothing sacred to you? You brute! I might have died of cold during the night.

GENERAL. We are well into April, madam, and spring is early this year. We are dying of heat.

EMILY. Of sunstroke, then – starvation, I don't know – of sorrow – yes, that's it – quite simply of sorrow, in my state of health.

GENERAL. Sorrow you can die of in your bed, madam, at leisure. No need to make us rick our ankles merely to stumble upon you over a mile away, in equilibrium across two rails. It was absurd, like everything else you do.

EMILY. I am seriously ill. How often has the doctor told you that my condition gives cause for the gravest alarm! I did truly mean to kill myself and that alone should make you fall sobbing at my feet, if you didn't have a heart of granite.

GENERAL. My heart is not made of granite, madam, but I am thrifty with my tears. I am getting old.

EMILY. I sacrificed my youth for you. (*She screams.*) Murderer!

GENERAL. Be quiet, damn you, or I'll leave the room. Let us talk things over calmly.

EMILY. I'm too unhappy. You aren't unhappy, not you. You have your health and strength, you have. You get up and dress each morning, you go riding your horse, you walk around the garden, you go drinking with your friends. You live. You jeer at me, on your two legs, while I sit glued to my bathchair. Aren't you ashamed of being well?

GENERAL. Rubbish! You are glued to your bathchair for no reason other than because you want to be. We know that now.

EMILY. Are you saying that I'm not ill? Are you telling me that I haven't lost two stone in weight?

GENERAL. How do you know? You refuse to weigh yourself.

EMILY. *I know* that I have lost two stone. I don't need your weighted scales, yours and Doctor Bonfant's.

GENERAL. You eat as much as anybody else.

EMILY. I? Eat? Are you daring to suggest that I eat, you monster? I told Eugenie to show you at each meal what

I leave on my tray and you have the audacity to say I eat. That woman hates me. She takes advantage of my helplessness, and my poor ailing legs. When I ask for my jewellery she gives me playing cards. No one in this whole house cares whether I live or die.

GENERAL. You ring for her a hundred times a day. As for your poor ailing legs, thank God we'll hear no more about those for a while. They helped you mighty well to keep your balance down the wistaria and over to the railway line this morning. I strongly suspect you of stretching them here in your room every night.

EMILY. It was the last spasm of the stricken beast who longs for death – a superhuman effort towards nothingness and oblivion. Call your accomplice Doctor Bonfant with his rubber mallet; let him test my reflexes.

GENERAL. Death and damnation, madam, that's too easy. I won't walk any more just to spite you. On second thoughts, yes, just to spite you I will walk, and then, just to spite you a bit more, I won't walk at all.

EMILY. It's my nerves, my poor nerves which you have torn to pieces torturing me for twenty years. Look at your handiwork, you devil, and blame no one but yourself.

GENERAL. I tell you, madam, that's too easy.

EMILY. Too easy for you, no doubt. What have you got to complain about? While I lie here, racked with pain, you can wander fancy free on your great fat legs. Where do you go to, eh?

GENERAL. From my study to the garden, at your beck and call every ten minutes of the day.

EMILY. What is there in the garden? Answer me that, you pig, you satyr, you lascivious goat.

GENERAL. Well, I dunno – roses . . .

EMILY (*cackling*). Roses! There's Madam Tardieu on the other side of the privet hedge, that dreadful woman who shows you her bodice as she leans over the flower beds. They're a household word hereabouts, Ma Tardieu's breasts. Rubber, whalebone, steel probably – she's propped up like a tumbledown barn.

GENERAL. All right, all right, all right. After all, I haven't been to look.

EMILY. You dream of nothing else. You'll be mighty disillusioned when the great day comes. But at the bottom of the garden, on the other side of the railings, along the school path, at midday and at four, there are younger ones, aren't there? The little convent girls. You centaur. One of these days the parents are going to complain.

GENERAL. You're wandering, madam. They say good morning to me, and I say good morning back.

EMILY. And what about Prize-giving Day, when you always manage to officiate, you old faun – when you kiss them, red as a lobster in your uniform?

GENERAL. It's the custom.

EMILY. What you're thinking isn't the custom, and you know it. You tickle their bosoms with your decorations when you lean over them. Don't say you don't. I've seen you.

GENERAL. Well, if nothing worse happens to them when they grow up we'll make May Queens out of them.

EMILY. Queens of the May! You've always managed to officiate on May Day, too. Last year's one, that hussy, when you bent over her and kissed her you whispered something in her ear. It was reported to me.

GENERAL (*chaffingly*). I whispered something? You don't say so?

EMILY. You arranged to meet her, I know. Besides, I've seen her since. She's pregnant.

GENERAL. Nonsense, she's put on weight, that's all.

EMILY. My maids are putting on weight, too, one after the other.

GENERAL. Let's change the subject, madam. I have something very serious to talk to you about. You are untrue to me, madam, that's the long and short of it. You wrote to Dr Bonfant that you were in love with him. I have proof of it here in my wallet, down in black and white with two spelling mistakes which identify your hand. Yes, for you have always accused me of being a clodhopper, too lumpish to appreciate Baudelaire or Wagner, but when I took you you were nothing but a nobody, and as for your idea of grammar you can't tell a conjunction from a carrot. You never had a day's schooling in your life.

EMILY. How shabby you are. I wish you could hear yourself. To come to my death-bed and throw my unhappy childhood in my face. Anyway, you're wrong, you silly old fool. For over a year I was a boarder with the daughters of consuls and ambassadors in one of the most select ladies' colleges in Paris.

GENERAL. Where your mother went to do the household mending and they took you in and fed you out of charity.

EMILY. My poor mother and I may have suffered a great deal, I have no doubt. When have I ever denied it? Driven as we were from pillar to post after the tragic death of my father, I had to go on the stage at the age of fifteen and my education as such may perhaps have suffered. But natural instinct, in people of breeding, makes up for much. Please to remember that my mother was a woman of infinite distinction, not a little provincial housewife like yours.

GENERAL. One trade is as good as another, but your mother, madam, was a dresser at the Opera.

EMILY. She accepted the post at the earnest request of the Director, solely for love of music.

GENERAL. You and your mother were folk of small account when I committed the signal folly of proposing to you.

EMILY. My mother – of small account? A woman whose hand was kissed by Monsieur Gounod at a gala matinée for charity? Ah, in my youth with her I knew another world than yours, my poor Leon.

GENERAL. Have it your way then, if it amuses you. But let us get back to those letters. Did you or did you not write them? Do you or do you not address him as 'Armand'? Do you tell him, yes or no, that his hair smells of vanilla as he sounds your chest, and that you pretend to have a belly ache so he can come and feel it for you? It's down in black and white with two spelling mistakes and I'll not budge from that.

EMILY. How could you stoop so low as to come poking about in my correspondence?

GENERAL. I did not poke about in your correspondence. I obtained possession of those letters. How? That's none of your business.

EMILY. Oh, isn't it? None of my business? Those letters were in my bedside table in a drawer where I keep my curlers and other objects of an intimate nature. You tell me they are in your wallet. And you dare to cross-question *me*? It's past belief. I did think you were still a gentleman.

GENERAL. Dammit, madam, will you stick to the point?

EMILY. So you ransack a lady's drawers, do you, my lad? You try to dishonour her, you a senior officer. Very well then, I shall tell. I shall tell everybody. I shall get up. I'll recover, for a day, the use of my poor ailing legs, and on the night of the reception at the Annual Tattoo, in front of all the high-ranking military personnel, I shall make a sensational entrance and I shall tell all.

GENERAL. Madam, I repeat I have not ransacked your drawers.

EMILY. Have you got those letters?

GENERAL. I have.

EMILY. Show them to me.

GENERAL. Ha, ha! Not on your life.

EMILY. Very well. If you really have those letters in your wallet, there can be nothing more between us, but an ocean of contempt. You may go. I am sleepy, I'm asleep. (*She lies back with her eyes closed.*)

GENERAL. No, madam, you are not asleep. That would be too easy again. Open your eyes. Open your eyes, this instant, or I'll open them for you. (*He shakes her.*) Emily! Do as I say. Open your eyes. (*He shakes her, slaps her, forces her eyelids up from their white eyeballs, then begins to panic.*) Come to your senses, damn you. What new game are you up to now?

EMILY (*weakly*). My heart!

GENERAL. What about your heart?

EMILY. It's shrinking. It's getting smaller and smaller; it's the size of a jinglebell now. Good-bye, Leon. I never loved anyone but you.

GENERAL. Oh, no, not your heart attack. We haven't even raised our voices. Your heart attack is for after the big scenes, madam. Come to, will you? You're warm, your pulse is all right. I'm not falling for that. (*He shakes her.*) Wake up, Emily. Good God, you can't be as rigid as that. You're doing it on purpose. I'll give you your drops. (*He rummages about among the bottles in the medicine chest.*) Holy Moses, what a collection. It would take a qualified dispenser to make head or tail of this lot. There's enough here to upset the constitution of a cart-horse. Needless to say, no dropper. Where the devil did Eugenie put the thing? Oh, well, here goes. One drop more, one drop less, the way things are at the moment . . . Emily, drink this, and if that doesn't do the trick I'll get the Doctor. Unclench your teeth, my love – unclench your teeth, damn you, it's dripping all over your woolly. Give me strength, what's the matter with you? Your pulse is all right. I'll give you your injection.

EMILY (*feebly*). You're still rummaging, Leon. Suspicious of me even on my death-bed.

GENERAL. I'm not rummaging, I'm looking for your capsules.

EMILY. Too late. Call the children.

GENERAL. What are you raving about, my love? You aren't dying. You're weak, that's all. I'll get the Doctor.

EMILY. Too late. I implore you, don't move. Hold my hand as you used to in the old days, when I was first ill. You took care of me then, you were patient with me. You used to bathe my temples with eau de cologne and murmur sweet nothings in my ear.

GENERAL (*grunting as he looks for the cologne*). I can still dab you with a bit of cologne.

EMILY. But no sweet nothings. That's what's killing me – you murderer.

The GENERAL *bathes* EMILY'*s forehead.*

GENERAL (*kneeling by her*). There now, Emily. That will revive you.

EMILY. It frightens you, eh, to hear me say it? Leon, I'm dying for want of your love.

GENERAL. No, no, no, don't talk nonsense. To begin with, you're not dying at all, and you know that I am always full of attentions for you.

EMILY. Attentions! What do I want with attentions? I want you to love me the way you used to. When you used to take me in your arms and call me your little girl, and bite me all over. Aren't I your little girl any more, to be carried naked to her bath?

GENERAL (*uncomfortably*). We all have to grow up sometime, Emily.

EMILY (*plaintively*). Why don't you bite me all over like a young terrier any more?

GENERAL (*more and more embarrassed*). Dammit, young terriers grow into old ones, after twenty years. Besides, I've lost my teeth.

EMILY *sits up with astonishing vigour, considering her heart attack.*

EMILY. You've got teeth enough for others, you mealy-mouthed old fraud. You talk about my letters which were never even sent. I have evidence of another kind, in a trinket box under my mattress, letters both sent and received, in which there's no question of your having lost your teeth. Where you play the young man for another's benefit – and there you flatter yourself, incidentally, my poor Leon – for, apart from your summary prowess with the maids, you aren't up to much in that line, either.

GENERAL. Be quiet, damn you. What do you know about it?

EMILY. I know as much as any woman knows who's left unsatisfied. Learn first to satisfy one woman, to be a man in her bed, before you go scampering off into the beds of others.

GENERAL. So I haven't been a man in your bed, madam, is that it?

EMILY. Soon weary, my friend, soon asleep, and when for a wonder you had a little energy, soon replete. A woman, my good sir, belongs to whoever takes and keeps her.

GENERAL. Stay lovely and desirable yourselves, then, and we'll see. Allow me to inform you, madam, it took all my imagination to do what was expected of me in your bed of an evening.

EMILY. Do you think it took me any less imagination not to be continually disappointed? You don't think, do you, that it was you I thought about?

GENERAL. How vulgar you are, madam – vulgar and shameless. However, if that was so, why the reproaches, why the scenes, why so many tears for so long?

EMILY. Because you belong to me, Leon. You are mine like my house, mine like my jewels, mine like my furniture, mine like your name.

She stands upon the bed, a nightmarish figure in her nightgown.

GENERAL. And is that what you understand by love?

EMILY (*in a great and fearful cry*). Yes!

GENERAL. Death and damnation, I do not belong to you, madam.

EMILY. To whom, then?

GENERAL. To no one. To myself, perhaps.

EMILY. No. Not any longer. I am your wife. Your wife before God and before the law.

GENERAL. Hell's bells, madam, I'll escape you.

EMILY. Never!

GENERAL. I'll pretend not to know you.

EMILY. I'll scream, I'll cause a riot. I'll break things, I'll run up debts to ruin you – I'll buy myself things in the shops.

GENERAL. I tell you I'll take the train and disappear into thin air. You won't know where I've gone.

EMILY. You'd never dare, and if you did, I'd follow you to the far ends of the earth.

GENERAL. And when I die, hell's teeth! Will you make that journey, too?

EMILY. When you die, I shall cry out loud – 'I was his wife.' I shall put on widow's weeds and I, and I alone, will have the right, and I shall come and visit your grave on All Soul's Day. I'll have my name engraved on your tombstone and when my turn comes to die I shall come and lie beside you for eternity and unknown people will pass and read that I was your wife, on the stone.

GENERAL. By God, I hate you, madam.

EMILY. What difference does that make? I am your wife.

GENERAL. I hate the sight and sound of you. And I'll tell you something else that's stronger even than my hatred and disgust. I am dying of boredom, madam, by your side.

EMILY. You bore me, too, but I am your wife just the same, and about that you can do nothing.

GENERAL. But devil take it, you hate me just as much.

EMILY. Yes, I hate you. You ruined my career. I had a superb voice, a dazzling future – you forced me to give up the stage. Everything that was brilliant in me you crushed underfoot. Other men worshipped me; you frightened them away with your great sword. You created a desert around me with your stupid jealousy, you made me unlearn how to be beautiful – unlearn how to love and be loved. You forced me to keep house for you like a servant, feed your sickly children, I, whose breasts were famous throughout Paris.

GENERAL. Your breasts famous? Don't make me laugh. Where did you exhibit them, anyway? In *Lohengrin*?

EMILY. At festivals of Art. Before people whose refinement and luxurious living your petty tradesman's world could never guess at.

GENERAL. Death and damnation, that is ancient history, madam. This time I am determined to sue for a divorce.

EMILY. A divorce! You could never live alone – you'd be much too frightened. And whom do you think would have you, you poor fool!

GENERAL. I've found someone who will have me.

EMILY. She must be very old and very ugly – or very poor to be reduced to that.

GENERAL. It's a lie. She is young and beautiful. She's true to me. She is waiting for me.

EMILY. Since when?

GENERAL. Seventeen years.

EMILY. You must be joking! Seventeen years. And you think she loves you? And you love her? And they've been waiting seventeen years, poor lambs.

GENERAL. Yes, madam, and because of you.

EMILY. Oh, if I weren't so ill, I'd laugh. I'd laugh like a mad thing. It's too silly – really too silly. Seventeen years. Why, if you really loved her, you poor imbecile, you would have left me long ago.

GENERAL. I stayed out of respect for your grief and pity for your illness, madam, which I long took to be genuine.

EMILY (*sitting up*). What a fool you are. Do you think I couldn't dance if I wanted to? Look! You see how well I can stand. Come and dance with me. Come. Tra-la-la-la.

EMILY *sings and dances a few steps*.

GENERAL. Let me go! You're mad. Get back to bed.

EMILY. No. You are my true love and I want to dance with you. Like at the Garrison Ball at Saumur, the one of 'ninety-three – seventeen years ago, funnily enough. Do you remember?

GENERAL. Confound you, why?

EMILY. Because you were so handsome and scintillating and sure of yourself with the women at that ball. 'Major St Pé!' And you clicked your heels, German fashion, when you introduced yourself. How fetchingly you smoothed your whiskers, how prettily you kissed their hands. I shall never forget that ball. I was still in love with you then, and I had stayed faithful, fool that I was, in spite of your lady friends, whom you forced me to invite to dinner. But on the night of that ball I suddenly had enough, all at once, in the space of a second. You were dancing a waltz with a great ninny of a girl – I saw you whisper in her ear and she simpered and made eyes at you.

'The Waltz of the Toreadors' is heard.

(*She hums and sways to the music.*) 'The Waltz of the Toreadors' I even remember the title. Tra-la-la-la. I was too wretched. I had to get out of that ball room. I went out into the lobby to order my carriage. There was a man there, younger and handsomer than you, and he helped me. And when he found our brougham among the other carrieges he said I couldn't possibly go home alone and he got in and escorted me.

The volume of the music increases.

GENERAL. Well?

EMILY. Well, you were still waltzing, my poor dear, with your superb half turns and your airs and graces. What do you think women are made of? He became my lover.

GENERAL. You have had a lover, madam, and it was at that Saumur ball that you made his acquaintance? A man who had merely helped you find our carriage, a complete stranger – I won't even ask his rank! How horrible! But I hope that you had a few doubts, dear God, a few misgivings, before taking such a step. I fondly hope you at least waited a little while?

EMILY. Of course, my dear. I was a respectable woman. I waited.

GENERAL. How long?

EMILY. Three days.

GENERAL (*exploding*). Holy suffering bloodstained rattlesnakes, I waited seventeen years, madam, and I'm waiting still.

EMILY. And when that one was posted, I forgot where, to

the devil – to the Fast East, I took another and another, and another, and so on until I grew too old and there was only you left who would have me.

GENERAL. But, dammit, if you were untrue to me, why the tears and reproaches – why the immense heartaches and the torment – why this illness?

EMILY. To keep you, Leon. To keep you for always because I am your wife. For I do love you, Leon. Yes, you must wear my love along with your horns. I hate you for all the harm you did to me, but I love you – not tenderly, not with seventeen years of waiting and letter-writing – not for the bliss of being in your arms at night – we have never made love and you know it – not for your conversation – you bore me – not for your rank, either, or your wealth – I've been offered more – I love you because you are mine – my thing, my object, my hold-all, my garbage bin . . .

GENERAL (*backing away*). No!

EMILY. Yes, and you know it. And whatever you may promise others you know you will never be anything but that.

GENERAL. No!

EMILY. Yes. You will never be able to bring yourself to hurt me, you're too cowardly. You know it, and you know I know it, too.

GENERAL. No!

EMILY. Yes! Come, darling. Dance with me. *The Waltz of the Toreadors*, the last waltz. With me this time.

GENERAL. No!

EMILY. Yes. I want you to. And you want whatever I want. Come, dance with your chronic invalid – come dance with your bag of bones. Come dance with your remorse. Come dance with your love!

GENERAL (*running away*). No! Don't touch me! Pity's sake don't touch me. Lieutenant St. Pé! Save me! (*He cringes away, then suddenly stretches out his arms, grabs her throat, and yells*). Phantasmagoria!

EMILY *struggles in her voluminous nightgown, trying to tear his hands away from her throat.*

Curtain.

Act Five

The same scene. Evening.

The setting is now as Act One. When the curtain rises, the GENERAL *is alone, prowling about like a caged bear, a shadow in the gathering darkness. All of a sudden he stops and cries out.*

GENERAL. Lieutenant St Pé! Graduated second from Saumur. Forward march, damn you.

The DOCTOR *comes out of* EMILY*'s room. The* GENERAL *turns and looks at him in silence.*

DOCTOR. I have just taken her blood pressure. She's as right as a trivet. She had a bad fright, that's all.

GENERAL. So did I.

DOCTOR. So did I, my friend. That would have been a very nasty ending to the story, I must say. The moment your maid came and said to come at once, the mistress was choking, I guessed. We were drinking soup. I spat out the lot. Madame Bonfant will have a good fortnight of it moaning over her tablecloth.

GENERAL. What did she say?

DOCTOR. Who? Madame Bonfant?

GENERAL. My wife.

DOCTOR. My poor old friend, she seems to think it quite in order that you should want to do away with her. Murder is the regular concomitant of passion at the Opera. She submits gracefully, biding her time, no doubt, and feeling vaguely flattered; she is more than ever con vinced that you are a pair of sublime and starcrossed lovers.

GENERAL. Oh, the idiocy of it! Will she never understand that she quite simply bores me?

DOCTOR. I'm afraid you will have to face it, General. Never.

GENERAL. But, dear God, that can't be all there is to life. Why did no one ever warn me? What are they all talking about then in their books, those writer johnnies? Everybody looks happy round about me, and content. How do they do it, damn them – how do they manage not to suffer? What is their password? Let them tell it me at once. I've no more time to wait now.

DOCTOR. My dear old friend, that is a question one must ask oneself when one is very much younger.

GENERAL (*yelling*). I *am* young. Lieutenant St Pé! I decline all other rank. I see it now. It's nothing but a booby-trap. Doctor, has medicine not discovered anything to put the clock back seventeen years?

DOCTOR. Nothing so far.

GENERAL. Are you sure?

DOCTOR. It would surely have been mentioned in certain – specialist publications.

GENERAL. I'm in no mood for levity. Are you aware what's going on? Mademoiselle de Ste-Euverte and my secretary have gone out for a walk. They've been away nearly two hours.

DOCTOR. Nothing very odd about that. You were closeted with your wife; your explanations looked as if they were going on for ever. I expect they simply decided to go for a walk while they were waiting.

GENERAL. A curious misunderstanding arose between the

two of them this morning. They left, with their little fingers linked, so the maid tells me. Does that strike you as normal, too? As for my daughters – who were enamoured of our hero – they have gone, as well – (*he takes a letter from his pocket.*) leaving this letter on their dressing-table, together with their tupenny-ha'-penny jewellery wrapped up in tissue paper. (*He reads.*) 'We are too unhappy. He is in love with another. We prefer to die.' Two more of them, it's all the rage in this house. (*He reads.*) 'Tell Madame Dupont-Fredaine not to go on with our dresses.' Among other primordial virtues their mother has imbued them with a solid notion of economy.

DOCTOR. Good heavens, and haven't they come home yet?

GENERAL. I sent the gardener in search of them. They must be dabbling their feet in the pond. They are far too plain to kill themselves. Everything is tumbling about my ears. Dear God, how will it all end?

DOCTOR. As in real life, or in the theatre, in the days when plays *were* plays – a contrived dénouement, not too gloomy on the face of it, and which doesn't really fool a soul, and then a little later – curtain. I speak for you as well as myself. Your blood pressure's up to two hundred and fifty and my gall-bladder is a bag of stones. Make way for the young – and may they commit the self-same follies and die of the same diseases.

GENERAL. But I love her, Doctor, and I am young.

DOCTOR. I don't now why, but it suddenly strikes me as being rather late.

GENERAL (*misunderstanding him*). Nine o'clock. If that was a genuine walk, they should be back by now.

DOCTOR. I wasn't meaning that, General.

The MAID *enters with a lamp which she sets on the table.*

MAID. Will you please say if I am to serve dinner, sir? If we wait much longer, the devilled mushrooms won't be devilled mushrooms any more.

GENERAL. Oh, shut up about your mushrooms. We'll call them something else, then.

MAID. And there's Father Ambrose drinking white wine in the pantry. He says he'll wait as long as you please for you to receive him, sir, but what he has to tell you is too important to put off until tomorrow.

GENERAL. Feed him the devilled mushrooms. He gets on my nerves, that fellow. What does he want, today of all days?

MAID. I already suggested he should eat something. He won't. He says the excitement of what he has to tell you has quite spoilt his appetite. But, my word, he's catching up on the white wine. If you don't see him soon, whatever it is he has to tell you is going to be pretty muddled. He says it's Providence, and we must have some Masses said in thanksgiving.

GENERAL. Why, what's Providence been up to this time?

MAID. He says he can tell no-one but yourself, sir, it's that important. It's a secret between Providence and him.

GENERAL. Well, tell them both to wait.

MAID (*grumbling*). There's no call to go insulting them – (*she crosses herself and turns to go.*) especially as one of them has the wherewithal to get Its own back.

GENERAL. Something tells me that's been done already.

The MAID *goes out.*

My reason is tottering, I can feel it. I can't have lost her so stupidly after all these years, the way one loses a dog in the street. With her lost to me, there's nothing left but a ludicrous old pantaloon, who never saw a single one of his gestures through to its conclusion. I have the impression that Lieutenant St Pé is lying bloodless on a field of battle, not even wounded in the fight – some idiot's rifle blew up in his back a few minutes before zero hour – but that all the same he is going to die. Doctor, if I've lost her . . .

DOCTOR. No, you have not lost her. (*He turns from the window.*) Here she is, with her ravisher, all rosy from the evening air.

There is a pause. The GENERAL *and the* DOCTOR *look up.* GASTON, *tomato red, and* GHISLAINE, *eyes downcast, have appeared in the doorway.*

GENERAL (*rushing foward in relief*). Ghislaine – this unaccountable stroll – I nearly died of fright. Now, will you please explain.

GHISLAINE (*in her usual slightly solemn manner*). My dear, will you ask the doctor to leave us for a moment? Gaston, leave us, too, please.

GASTON (*very self-assured, and a little sombre*). Very well. But only for a moment.

GENERAL. Only for a moment? Only for a moment! What's come over the young pup? He never dared to speak to anyone like that in his life before.

DOCTOR. Courage, Lieutenant. Something tells me this is going to be your last campaign.

GENERAL (*grumpily*). With your Arab fellah it was different. He knew what he wanted and so did I.

The DOCTOR *and* GASTON, *with one last dark look, have at last gone.*

(*Timidly*.) Are you going to explain, Ghislaine?

GHISLAINE. Yes, my dear, I'll tell you. It's quite simple. I love that young man.

GENERAL. You're joking! And it isn't funny, Ghislaine. Why, thundering Hades, two hours ago you'd never even seen the fellow.

GHISLAINE. Had I seen you before the Saumur Ball? And yet the very second when you took me by the waist I fell in love with you. Those seventeen years took nothing away, but added nothing, either, to my love. Did I ever tell you that, my dear?

GENERAL. Yes, my dearest; yes, Ghislaine, and that wonderful mad gift of yourself in one moment is something I have always understood and loved you for. But this isn't the same thing at all.

GHISLAINE (*transparently*). Why isn't it, Leon?

GENERAL. Well because – at Saumur – it was me.

GHISLAINE (*gently*). Well?

GENERAL. Well, dammit all, it's not for me to say so, but I was brilliant, I was witty, I was young. And I desired you madly – that counts for something, too. But him!

GHISLAINE. He is retiring – or he was – a little naïve, perhaps, but you see, my dear – how can I put it – for a woman those are opposing qualities, but equally appealing. We love everything. It's like having to choose at a fitting, between a green silk and a pink one. I might add that he is young, younger even than you were at Saumur, and that he desires me, too.

GENERAL (*spluttering with laughter*). Him? That nonentity? That mooncalf? That lilyboy?

GHISLAINE. Leon, I forbid you to insult him.

GENERAL (*beside himself*). Try and stop me! So he desires you, does he? Do you expect me to believe that when he saw you his anaemic blood gave one leap? Don't make me laugh. It's something you can't possibly know anything about, Ghislaine. Forgive me, this is partly my fault. The respect in which I held you for so long while I waited for my situation to become a little clearer, could scarcely make a real woman out of you. Say he was speechless with adoration, if you like – say he knelt at your feet, as those kids do at that age, recited poetry *perhaps* – but don't tell me the boy desires you – it's grotesque.

GHISLAINE. But he proved it, my dear.

GENERAL. Get along with you. How? How could he have proved it? Vows exchanged in a moment's exaltation by the pond, maybe, wedding rings made out of rushes and slipped on to each other's fingers as keepers for the real ones – adolescent fiddle-faddle. We've all been through it. Let a real man, worthy of that title, take you in his arms tonight – and it will be tonight, my dearest, I swear it – let a real man once make love to you, God dammit and all the rest will disappear like so much smoke.

GHISLAINE (*superbly.*) I know. It *is* all so much smoke. Because at long last, someone has made love to me. I'll shout it to the world, I'm not ashamed. What words do you need, then, to make you understand? I belong to him.

GENERAL. He dared, that two-faced, vice-ridden little villain? That brute? Took you by force, did he? I'll kill him!

GHISLAINE. No, no, my dear, not by force. He took me, and I gave myself, and I am his now, for always.

The GENERAL, *stricken, holds out his hands to her, suddenly humble.*

GENERAL. Ghislaine, it's all a nightmare. I'll help you to forget it . . .

GHISLAINE (*drawing away*). No, Leon, you must not touch me any more, only he may touch me now. And you should know how faithful I can be.

GENERAL. But when he touched you, you were asleep, you had fallen on your head, you were pumped full of gardenal, you didn't even know who was touching you. You thought that it was me.

GHISLAINE. The first few times, yes. But afterwards I knew quite well.

GENERAL. No!

GHISLAINE. Oh, we could stay such good friends, Leon. Why will you not understand?

GENERAL. Never. I shall never understand. It's absolutely unthinkable.

GHISLAINE. He touched me, he really touched me. And all of a sudden I was no longer sad and lonely and forever drifting with the tide, I found my footing on the shore at last and I shall never be alone again – at meals, in church, in my over-large bed. Don't you see what a wonderful adventure it is? You would be a tiny bit glad, too, if you really loved me, Leon.

GENERAL. I do love you, Ghislaine.

GHISLAINE. Then why not share my joy and let everyone be happy? (*With a happy sigh.*) I am not alone any more. You so often wished it for me. You used to say I should have a companion . . .

GENERAL. Yes, but a female . . .

GHISLAINE. I have a male companion now, it's so much better. Besides, we saw so little of each other, nothing or next to nothing will be changed. We'll meet from time to time just as we used to do. He said he would permit it. Although, between ourselves, my dear, I rather doubt it. He's insanely jealous, do you know that? He says he won't let me out of his sight. Oh, how good it feels. I shall not have to shrink away into my shell any more when men pass me, or make myself ugly always or invisible, but beautiful now, to flatter him, and hurt him a tiny bit at the same time – since he will be with me, and he will protect me from them. Oh, my dear, I am so happy. I am no longer a dog without a collar, I have a little cord around my neck with my owner's name on it. And you seem quite astonished at my happiness? Why, then, you are the one who knows nothing about women. He does.

GENERAL. Lieutenant St Pé! Don't leave me. What is happening!

GHISLAINE (*heedless of the interruption*). You say he has no wit. Not with others, perhaps, not with you, but what does that matter to me? To me he says the prettiest things. He told me that we must swim abreast towards the ideal as if towards a lifebuoy, and that the only proper way to swim is two by two.

GENERAL. I might have known it. Did he also tell you that life was one long family lunch with napkin rings, forks of different shapes and sizes and a bell-push under the table?

GHISLAINE. What are you suggesting, spiteful? He says poetic things. He says life is but a holiday, a ball.

GENERAL (*with an involuntary cry of pain*). A ball!

GHISLAINE. Yes, isn't that a sweet idea? A ball of a night, and we must make haste, he says, before the lamps go out. I loved him from the very first, I told you so. But I had got so into the way of thinking love was nothing but one endless vigil, that when he asked me to be his, I wanted to cry – 'Later. Tomorrow.' Do you know what he said?

GENERAL (*in a strangled voice*). No.

GHISLAINE (*triumphantly*). He said, 'At once. At once, my darling.' Now who but he would say a thing like that? At once! It's wonderful. I never guessed that one could have something at once. And do you know what he whispered as he held me in his arms?

The GENERAL *sits at his desk, a humble old man now before her rediscovered youth.*

GENERAL. No, I don't know anything today. I have everything to learn.

GHISLAINE (*stopping short in charming confusion*). No, my dear, I really can't tell you that. I'm afraid that it might hurt you.

GENERAL. Thank you. But it's a bit late in the day.

GASTON *enters, his suspicions aroused but resolved to stand no nonsense.*

GASTON. The moment is up, Ghislaine.

GHISLAINE (*flustered*). I'm sorry, Gaston.

GENERAL (*bearing down on him*). 'I'm sorry, Gaston!' So there you are, Casanova. The pretty turtle-doves. Just look at them, will you? It's enough to make a cat laugh. What the devil do you take me for, the pair of you? Death and damnation! I'll soon show you what you're up against.

The DOCTOR *is in the doorway.*

Come in, Doctor, come in. You're just in time. Do you know what they've just told me, these two starry-eyed cherubs here? They're in love with each other, if you please. Yes, sir, since two hours ago. And they haven't wasted any time, what's more. Some folk have a scruple or two, some folk wait a little while – not they, oh, dear me, no. In the woods, anyhow, like animals. And they expect my blessing into the bargain. God Almighty, have they completely lost every scrap of critical and moral sense?

DOCTOR (*gently*). Lieutenant St Pé.

GENERAL (*thundering*). General! Please to address me by my proper rank! By Jove, I'll show them what I'm made of. I am going to put on my full-dress uniform and all my decorations. No, it'll take too long. (*He turns to* GASTON.) Aha, so you seduce young girls, do you, eh? Steal another man's wife, would you, me hearty? Play cock of the roost, sir, would you? Well, me young jacko, when you've got guts you must show 'em, and otherwise than with the ladies – and that may not prove quite so funny. But virility cannot be pigeon-holed – I'm sorry. (*He yells.*) Fetch me two swords, someone. Those two up there, on the wall. God dammit, I'll get them myself. (*He climbs on the chair and tries to unhook the swords from the wall.*) And no need for seconds, either. The Doctor can stand by with his clobber.

GHISLAINE. Oh, my God, he wants blood! He wants blood, I feel it. He's a cannibal!

DOCTOR. General, you aren't going to start all that nonsense again?

GENERAL. And you down there, you hold your tongue, too, sir. I haven't forgotten that business of the letters. Don't remind me of it.

GHISLAINE (*clasping the* GENERAL'*s legs*). Leon! I love him. And if you love me, as you say, you won't hurt him.

GENERAL. The hell I will! I'll cut his ears off, madam. Just because I do love you. I'll kill him.

DOCTOR. General, get down from that chair.

GASTON (*with great nobility*). Though I have never held a sword, if the General insists, I am prepared to fight.

GHISLAINE. Gaston, not you. Not you. Let him fight by himself!

DOCTOR. General, it would be murder. He's a mere child.

GENERAL (*still struggling to get the sword down*). There are no children any more. If he's a child, let him leave grown-ups alone and go and play with his hoop. If he wants to play at anything else, by Hades, let him take the consequences. Holy suffering blood-stained billicans who's the double-dyed blockhead who put up these swords! (*He calls unthinkingly.*) Gaston!

GASTON (*moving quickly*). Yes, sir?

GENERAL. Give me a hand, my boy.

GASTON (*keenly*). Yes, sir. (*He jumps on the armchair.*)

GENERAL. What the devil are you doing there, sir? Get off that chair. Doctor, come and help me, will you?

DOCTOR. General, I refuse to be a party any longer to this tragic tomfoolery. You have no right to provoke this lad.

GENERAL. Did he or did he not consider himself old enough to take the woman I love?

GHISLAINE. But you never would take her at all!

GENERAL. I know my manners. Besides, I was going to. (*He changes his mind and gives a gleeful smile.*) Why, what a fool I am! It's so much simpler than that. Come to think of it, he *is* a child. (*Paternally, still up on his chair.*) How old are you exactly, my boy?

GASTON. Twenty in strawberry time, sir. The twenty-third of May.

GENERAL. Twenty in strawberry time, splendid. In order to marry then, unless I'm much mistaken, you need your parents' consent, do you not?

GASTON. Why recall in her presence the painful circumstances attendant on my birth? I have no parents, sir, as you well know. I am a foundling.

GENERAL (*climbing down from the chair*). True. But you have a guardian, have you not, a venerable churchman. Father Lambert, I think I'm right in saying? We'll see if Father Lambert will consent to the marriage when I've told him a thing or two.

GHISLAINE. Gaston, his dishonesty frightens me.

GENERAL (*calling*). Eugenie!

MAID (*off; calling*). Yes, sir.

GENERAL (*calling*). The curé. The curé, quickly. Send his reverence up here at the double. She's quite right, it *is* Providence that brings the fellow here, for once. I'll bet my braces Father Lambert will never let you marry an adventuress.

GHISLAINE. Oh, Leon! How could you?

FATHER AMBROSE *enters*.

GENERAL. Ah, there you are, Father.

FATHER AMBROSE. General, at last!

GENERAL. You take the words out of my mouth.

GENERAL } (*together*). { a matter of the utmost importance . . .
FATHER AMBROSE } { A revelation of the utmost interest . . .

GENERAL / FATHER AMBROSE (*together*).
GENERAL: The peace and honour of the family. A watchful firmness . . .
FATHER AMBROSE: The joy and sanctification of the home. A sacred duty . . .

GENERAL. After you.

FATHER AMBROSE. After you, General. No, on second thoughts, me first. It's too serious. General, may I speak freely before everyone?

GENERAL. If you like. But make haste. I'm in a hurry.

FATHER AMBROSE (*sitting in the armchair*). But we are all friends here, I see – friends who will soon be as deeply moved as I . . .

GASTON. If I am in the way, General, I can withdraw.

FATHER AMBROSE (*mysteriously*). No, my son, you are not in the way. Far from it. General, it is with deep emotion that I recognise in this the hand of Providence.

GENERAL. No preambles, Father. Come to the point, come to the point. I want to talk to you about this young rascal here.

FATHER AMBROSE. So do I. When I brought Gaston to you for the post of secretary, I had indeed no inkling . . .

GENERAL. Come to the point, I say. I'm an old soldier. In a couple of words.

FATHER AMBROSE. Heaven has nevertheless willed it, in its infinite mansuetude and the exquisite delicacy of its Grace . . .

FATHER AMBROSE. Very well. You have asked for it, General, but it may sound a little crude. Montauban. Lea.

GENERAL. What do you mean, Montauban Lea? What's that, an address?

FATHER AMBROSE. You see how difficult it is in a couple of words? Allow me to amplify a little. There lived in eighteen ninety at Montauban, where the Eighth Dragoons were on manœuvres, a young dressmaker by the name of Lea.

GENERAL (*racking his brains*). Lea? Lea? Holy codfish, Lea! Well, what about her? You don't know what army life can be, your reverence. I could recite you a whole almanack on those lines.

FATHER AMBROSE. There was also a dashing captain, dashing, alas, but very fickle, very careless of a young girl's honour. This captain, the whole while the manœuvres lasted, gave young Lea to believe he loved her. Perhaps indeed he did.

GENERAL. My dear fellow, why, of course. Lea! A ravishing girl, Doctor. A sonsy dark-haired filly with eyes a man could drown in – reserved, prudish, almost, but in bed of a night time – oh, my dear fellow . . . (*He inadvertently takes* FATHER AMBROSE'*s arm.*) I beg your pardon, Father. Have you had news of this young girl then?

FATHER AMBROSE. To begin with, she was not exactly a young girl, General, by this time; and she has just yielded up the ghost after a very honourable marriage, releasing by her death Father Lambert of a secret.

GENERAL. Fancy. Twenty years ago already.

FATHER AMBROSE. Twenty years. The exact age of this young man here, less nine months.

GENERAL. What!

FATHER AMBROSE. A child was born, unbeknownst to you, of this guilty and transient union. A child entrusted to

Father Lambert who in turn entrusted him to me. Gaston, kiss your father.

GENERAL. Well, I'll be . . . !

GASTON, *sobbing with emotion, crosses and throws himself into the* GENERAL'*s arms.*

GASTON. Papa! My dear little Papa!

GENERAL. Don't choke me, you great oaf. Just because he tells you I'm your father, there's no call to . . . And look at the size of him!

DOCTOR. Yes, General. One thing to sow a wild oat, and see, what should spring up but a young tree.

GHISLAINE (*rapturous*). Why, then, everything is quite simple, now. You are the man I have loved all along. It's you, Leon, you. Young and free, and even handsomer than your own self. I knew those hands reminded me of someone.

GENERAL. Don't overdo it, it's becoming indecent.

GHISLAINE (*flying into* GASTON'*s arms*). Gaston, we are free to love each other.

GASTON. Thank you, Father.

GENERAL (*mimicking* GASTON). Thank you, Father. Simple as pie, isn't it? Thank you, Father. Ha, so I'm your father, am I? Right. I refuse to give my consent.

GHISLAINE. What?

GENERAL. Do not protest, madam. I do not want my son to form an alliance with just anybody. I shall make the necessary enquiries.

GHISLAINE. Leon! After all this time that you've known me . . .

GASTON. Father! Dearest Father. It's so good to have a father.

FATHER AMBROSE. General! When Providence itself went to such trouble.

DOCTOR (*the last*). Lieutenant St Pé!

GENERAL. All right. My part in this is growing more and more ridiculous. I give up. Death and damnation, let them marry, then, and never let me hear any more about anything.

SIDONIA *and* ESTELLE *enter, soaking wet, wrapped in blankets, and crying.*

(*He rises.*) Oh, Lord, what is it now? Will this charade never end?

ESTELLE. We really did jump in the lake, Papa, and we swam right out to the middle.

SIDONIA. Until we could swim no longer.

GENERAL. Then what?

ESTELLE. Then we came back.

GENERAL. Quite right. You can always die some other time. He's your brother, you sillies. So you see there wasn't any need to go and drown yourselves.

SIDONIA }
ESTELLE } (*together*). Our brother!

GENERAL. Yes. I have just this minute heard the news.

GASTON (*embarrassed*). So that simplifies everything, young ladies. Now I can love you both.

GHISLAINE (*jealously*). Gaston, I forbid you! (*To the others. In seventh heaven.*) What a man! Isn't he dreadful?

SIDONIA. Our brother? But, Papa, how can that be?

ESTELLE. Why wasn't mother in the know?

GENERAL. I haven't the time to explain. Ask Father

Ambrose. He did the trick with the help of Providence. He'll explain it all to you in Sunday School.

ESTELLE. Papa, if this lady is to be married, won't we need new dresses for the wedding?

GENERAL (*acidly*). Naturally.

ESTELLE. I want to be in duck-egg blue.

SIDONIA. And I want to be in yellow.

GENERAL. As you please, you look ravishing in anything. Run along to Madame Dupont-Fredaine and tell her to call in and see me about terms.

SIDONIA }
ESTELLE } (*together*). Yes, Papa.

FATHER AMBROSE. One moment, my children. I feel that Providence has more than shown today that its bounty extends over us all. The parish chapel is close by. What do you say to a little prayer, all together, by way of thanksgiving? Won't you join us, General? Once won't make a habit of it. Besides, I'm sure that deep down you believe in Providence.

GENERAL. I shall have to, now that it's beginning to take notice of me. But as to saying 'thank you', my heart wouldn't be in it. Tomorrow, Father, tomorrow.

SIDONIA, ESTELLE, FATHER AMBROSE, GASTON and GHISLAINE go out. The GENERAL is alone with the DOCTOR.

What a farce! It's lugubrious.

DOCTOR. Yes, General. Darkness is falling. We must sound the curfew. (*He sings, a little flat.*) Da da! Da da! Da di di da di di da . . .

GENERAL. Stop that! What do you take me for? That's the Infantry Lights Out!

DOCTOR (*making conversation*). I beg your pardon. Eh – how does it go exactly – in the Cavalry?

GENERAL (*in a racked voice*). Da di! Da di! Da . . . I haven't the heart for it. It's too silly. (*Softly*.) Lieutenant St Pé. I want to live. I want to love. I want to give my heart as well, dear God.

DOCTOR. General, nobody wants it any more. Let it unswell quietly, that old over-tender sponge. You should have sown fewer wild oats and had the courage to hurt while there was still time. Life should be led like a cavalry charge, General. They ought to have told you that at Saumur. My poor old friend, shall I tell you the moral of this story? One must never understand one's enemy or one's wife. One must never understand anyone for that matter or one will die of it. Heigh-ho, I must go home to Madame Bonfant and her scenes. I think you will do very nicely on your own. (*He pats the* GENERAL *on the shoulder*.) See you very soon.

GENERAL (*motionless*). Yes, yes.

The DOCTOR *exits. Silence. Then* EMILY *shrieks suddenly from next door.*

EMILY (*off*). Leon!

GENERAL. Yes.

EMILY (*off*). Are you there?

GENERAL. Yes.

EMILY (*off*). Good. I'm going to have a little nap. Don't do anything in the meantime.

GENERAL. No. (*He shudders and cries suddenly*.) Lieutenant St Pé. Graduated second from Saumur. Take aim, steady! Fire! (*He stands quite still for a second*.)

PAMELA, *the new maid, enters carrying a broom.*

PAMELA. Did you call, sir?

GENERAL (*staring*). Eh? What? No, I didn't call. Who are you?

PAMELA. I'm the new girl, sir. The new chambermaid you engaged this morning.

GENERAL (*looking absently at her, then stroking his moustache*). Ah, yes, of course, by Jove, yes, yes. And what is your name, my dear?

PAMELA. Pamela, sir.

GENERAL. Pamela. Fancy that, now. Pamela. And the prettiest little bosom in the world, too. What is all this nonsense about a soul? Do you believe in it? He's a fool, that doctor. Put your broom down, my child. It's a bit late to be sweeping up now. And there is never enough dust on things, anyway. We must let it settle. You know, you'll find this an easy sort of place. I'm an old youngster and I don't ask for very much – provided folk are nice to me. You haven't seen my roses, have you? Come, I'll show you round the garden, and if you're a good girl I'll give you one, just like a real lady. It doesn't bother you, does it, Pamela – (*He puts his arm around her waist.*) if I put my arm round your waist?

PAMELA (*coyly*). No, sir, but what will madam say?

GENERAL. Madam will say nothing so long as you don't tell her. That's a good girl. It's nicer like this, don't you think? Not that it means anything, but still, one feels less lonely, in the dark.

The GENERAL *and* PAMELA, *an absurd couple, turn and exit as 'Lights Out', the Cavalry's this time, is heard in the distance, played by a distant bugle from the barracks in the town – and the curtain falls.*

THE LARK

translated by
Christopher Fry

This play was first presented at The Lyric Theatre, Hammersmith, on 11 May 1955, with the following cast, in the order of their appearance:

BEAUCHAMP, *Earl of Warwick*	Richard Johnson
CAUCHON, *Bishop of Beauvais*	Laurence Naismith
JOAN,	Dorothy Tutin
HER FATHER	Peter Duguid
HER MOTHER	Alexis France
HER BROTHER	Barry MacGregor
THE PROMOTER	Leo McKern
THE INQUISITOR	Michael Goodliffe
BROTHER LADVENU	Michael David
ROBERT DE BEAUDRICOURT *Squire of Vaucouleurs*	David Bird
BOUDOUSSE, *a guard*	Churton Fairman
AGNES SOREL	Hazel Penwarden
THE YOUNG QUEEN	Catherine Feller
CHARLES, *the Dauphin*	Donald Pleasence
QUEEN YOLANDE	Lucienne Hill
ARCHBISHOP OF RHEIMS	John Gill
M. DE LA TREMOUILLE	Peter Cellier
PAGE TO THE DAUPHIN	David Spenser
CAPTAIN LA HIRE	George Murcell
THE HANGMAN	Gareth Jones
AN ENGLISH SOLDIER	Norman Scace

Directed by Peter Brook
Scenery and costumes based on designs by
Jean-Denis Malclès

PART ONE

A simple, neutral setting. The stage is empty at first; then the characters enter by twos and threes. The costumes are plain. JOAN *wears man's clothes throughout the play.* WARWICK *is the last to enter.*

WARWICK. Well now; is everyone here? If so, let's have the trial and be done with it. The sooner she is found guilty and burned the better for all concerned.

CAUCHON. But, my lord, before we do that we have the whole story to play: Domremy, the Voices, Vaucouleurs, Chinon, the Coronation.

WARWICK. Theatrical poppycock! You can tell that story to the children: the beautiful white armour, the fluttering standard, the gentle and implacable warrior maid. The statues of her can tell that story, later on, when policies have changed. We might even put up a statue ourselves in London, though I know at the moment that sounds wildly improbable: but you never know, in a few hundred years it might suit His Majesty's Government for some reason or other. But, as for now, I am Beauchamp, Earl of Warwick; and I've got my grubby little witch lying on the straw in the dungeon at Rouen, and a fine packet of trouble she has been, and a pretty sum she has cost us; but the money's been paid, and the next thing is to put her on trial and burn her.

CAUCHON. Not immediately. Before we come to that, there's the whole of her life to go through. It won't take very long, my lord.

WARWICK (*going to a corner resignedly*). Well, if you insist. An Englishman knows how to wait. (*Anxiously.*) I hope you're not expecting me to stand by while you go through that monstrous farce of a coronation again. And all the battles as well—Orleans, Patay, Beaugency?—I may as well tell you now, I should find that in very poor taste.

CAUCHON (*smiling*). Put your mind at rest, my lord. There are too few of us here to stage the battles.

WARWICK. Good.

CAUCHON. Joan.

She looks up.

You may begin.

JOAN. May I begin wherever I like?

CAUCHON. Yes.

JOAN. I like remembering the beginning: at home, in the fields, when I was still a little girl looking after the sheep, the first time I heard the Voices, that is what I like to remember. . . . It is after the evening Angelus. I am very small and my hair is still in pigtails. I am sitting in the field, thinking of nothing at all. God is good and keeps me safe and happy, close to my mother and my father and my brother, in the quiet countryside of Domremy, while the English soldiers are looting and burning villages up and down the land. My big sheep-dog is lying with his head in my lap; and suddenly I feel his body ripple and tremble, and a hand seems to have touched my shoulder, though I know no one has touched me, and the voice says——

SOMEONE IN THE CROWD. Who is going to be the voice?

JOAN. I am, of course. I turned to look. A great light was filling the shadows behind me. The voice was gentle and grave. I had never heard it before, and all it said to me was: "Be a good and sensible child, and go often to church." But I *was* good, and I *did* go to church often, and I showed I was sensible by running away to safety. That was all that happened the first time. And I didn't say anything about it when I got home; but after supper I went back. The moon was rising; it shone on the white sheep; and that was all the light there was. And then came the second time; the bells were ringing for the noonday Angelus. The light came again, in bright sunlight, but brighter than the sun, and that time I saw him.

CAUCHON. You saw whom?

JOAN. A man in a white robe, with two white wings reaching from the sky to the ground. He didn't tell me his name that day, but later on I found out that he was the blessed St. Michael.

WARWICK. Is it absolutely necessary to have her telling these absurdities all over again?

CAUCHON. Absolutely necessary, my lord.

WARWICK *goes back to his corner in silence, and smells the rose he has in his hand.*

JOAN (*in the deep voice of the Archangel*).—Joan, go to the help of the King of France, and give him back his kingdom. (*She replies in her own voice.*) Oh sir, you haven't looked at me; I am only a young peasant girl, not a great captain who can lead an army.—You will go and search out Robert de Beaudricourt, the Governor of Vaucouleurs. He will give you a suit of clothes to dress you like a man, and he will take you to the Dauphin. St. Catherine and St. Margaret will protect you. (*She suddenly drops to the floor sobbing with fear.*) —Please, please pity me, holy sir! I'm a little girl; I'm happy here alone in the fields. I've never had to be responsible for anything, except my sheep. The Kingdom of France is far beyond anything I can do. If you will only look at me you will see I am small, and ignorant. The realm of France is too heavy sir. But the King of France has famous Captains, as strong as you could need and they're used to doing these things. If they lose a battle they sleep as soundly as ever. They simply say the snow or the wind was against them; and they just cross all the dead men off their roll. But I should always remember I had killed them. Please have pity on me! . . . No such thing. No pity. He had gone already, and there I was, with France on my shoulders. Not to mention the work on the farm, and father, who wasn't easy.

Her FATHER, *who has been wandering around her* MOTHER, *suddenly speaks.*

FATHER. Where has that girl got to?

MOTHER (*going on with her knitting*). She is out in the fields.

FATHER. Well, I was out in the fields, and I'm back home again. It's six o'clock. She's no business to be out in the fields.

BROTHER. She's sitting under the Fairy Tree, staring at nothing. I saw her when I went to fetch in the bull.

PROMOTER (*from among the crowd*). The Fairy Tree! Note that, gentlemen, if you will. Note the superstition. The beginning of witchcraft already. The Fairy Tree! I ask you to note that!

CAUCHON. There are Fairy Trees all over France, my Lord Promoter. It's in our own interest not to refuse the fairies to these little girls.

PROMOTER (*primly*). We have our saints. That should be sufficient.

CAUCHON (*conciliating him*). Later on, certainly. But I mean while they are still very young; as Joan was; not yet fifteen.

PROMOTER. By fifteen they know everything: they're as old as Eve.

CAUCHON. Not Joan: Joan at that time was very simple and innocent. It will be another matter when we come to the trial; I shan't spare her Voices then. But a little girl shall keep her fairies. (*Firmly.*) And these discussions are under my charge.

The PROMOTER *bows, and retires, unmollified.*

FATHER (*bursting out afresh, to the* BROTHER). So that's where you say she is? And what does she think she's doing there, sitting under the tree?

BROTHER. Try and find out! She's just staring in front of her as if she was expecting something. And it isn't the first time either.

FATHER. Well, why didn't you tell me when you saw her before, then? Aren't you old enough to know what trouble there is with girls of her age, you little fool? What do you think she was expecting, eh? Somebody, not something, idiot! She's got a lover, and you know it! Give me my stick!

MOTHER (*gently, still knitting*). You know quite well, Joan's as innocent as a baby.

FATHER. Maybe she is. And girls as innocent as babies can come to you one evening and hold up their faces to be kissed, and the next morning, though you've kept them locked in their room all night, what has happened? You can't see into their eyes at all: they're avoiding you, and lying to you. They're the devil, all at once.

PROMOTER (*raising a finger*). The word has been said, my lords, and by her father!

MOTHER. How do you know that? The day I married you I was as innocent as Joan, and I daresay you could look into my eyes just as well next morning.

FATHER (*muttering*). That's nothing to do with it.

MOTHER. Who are these other girls you've known, then, that you've never told me about?

FATHER (*thundering to cover his embarrassment*). I tell you it's got nothing to do with it! We're not talking about other girls, we're talking about Joan! Hand me that stick. I'm going to look for her, and if she's been meeting somebody on the quiet I'll skin them alive!

JOAN (*smiling gently*). I was meeting someone on the quiet, and his solemn voice was saying: "Joan! Joan! What are you waiting for? There's a great sorrow in the realm of France."—"Holy Sir of Heaven, I'm so afraid, I'm only a young village girl; surely you've made a mistake?"—"Does God make mistakes, Joan?" (*She turns to her Judges.*) How could I have answered Yes?

PROMOTER (*shrugging*). You should have made the sign of the cross.

JOAN. I did, and the Archangel made it, too, all the time keeping his eyes carefully on mine, and the church clock sounded.

PROMOTER. You should have cried: Vade retro Satanus!

JOAN. I don't know Latin, my Lord.

PROMOTER. Don't be an idiot! The devil understands French. You should have cried: Get thee behind me, foul Satan, and don't tempt me again.

JOAN. But, my Lord, it was St. Michael.

PROMOTER (*sneering*). So he told you. And you were fool enough to believe him.

JOAN. Yes, I believed him. He couldn't have been the devil. He shone with light; he was beautiful.

PROMOTER (*losing his temper*). So is the devil, so is the devil, I tell you!

JOAN (*scandalised*). Oh, my Lord!

CAUCHON (*calming the* PROMOTER *with a gesture*). These subtle theological points, my lord Promoter, are proper for debating between ourselves, but they're beyond the understanding of this poor girl. No good is served by shocking her.

JOAN (*to the* PROMOTER). You're telling a lie, Canon! I haven't any of your learning, but I know the devil is ugly, and all that's beautiful is the work of God.

PROMOTER (*sneering*). Very charming, simple and stupid! Do you think the devil is stupid? He's a thousand times more intelligent than you and I put together. Do you think when he comes to snare a soul he would come like a horror of the flesh, with black ploughed skin and a snouting tusk like a rhinoceros? If he did, souls would fly to virtue at the sight of him. I tell you he chooses a moonlit summer night, and comes with coaxing hands, with eyes that receive you into them like water that drowns you, with naked women's flesh, transparent, white . . . beautiful——

CAUCHON (*stopping him sternly*). Canon! You are losing your way! This is very far from Joan's devil, if she has seen one. I beg you not to confuse your devil with hers.

PROMOTER (*flushed and confused in front of the smiling crowd*). I beg your pardon, my lord; there is only one devil.

CAUCHON. Go on, Joan.

JOAN (*still troubled*). If the devil is beautiful, how can we know him?

PROMOTER. By asking your parish priest.

JOAN. Can we never know by ourselves?

PROMOTER. No. That is why there is no salvation outside the church.

JOAN. Only rich people have a parish priest always at hand. It's hard for the poor.

PROMOTER. It is hard for everyone to escape damnation.

CAUCHON. My lord Promoter, let her talk with her Voices in peace and quiet. It is the beginning of the story. We mustn't reproach her with them yet.

JOAN (*continuing*). Another time it was St. Catherine and St. Margaret who came to me. (*She turns to the* PROMOTER *with a slightly mischievous defiance.*) They were beautiful, too.

PROMOTER (*blushing, but unable to prevent himself*). Did they appear to you naked?

JOAN (*smiling*). Oh, my lord! Do you imagine that God can't afford clothes for the saints in heaven?

The CROWD *chuckles at this answer, and the* PROMOTER *sits down confused.*

CAUCHON. You see, you make us all smile with your questions, my lord Promoter. Be wise enough to keep your interruptions until we come to the serious heart of this business. And when we do so, particularly when we come to judge her, remember that the soul in this little arrogant body is in our care. Aren't you risking very much confusion in her mind, to suggest to her that good and evil are no more than a question of clothes? It is true certainly, that our saints are traditionally represented as clothed; yet, on the other hand——

JOAN (*to the* PROMOTER). Our Lord is naked on the cross.

CAUCHON (*turning to her*). I was going to say so, Joan, if you had not prevented me. It isn't for you to correct the reverend Canon. You forget who you are; you forget that we are your priests, your masters and your judges. Beware of your pride, Joan. If the devil one day wins you for his own, that is the way he will come to you.

JOAN. I know I am proud. But if God didn't mean me to be proud, why did He send an Archangel to see me, and saints with the light of heaven on them to speak to me? Why did He promise I should persuade all the people I have persuaded—men as learned and as wise as you—and say I should ride in white armour, with a bright sword given me by the King, to lead France into battle: and it has been so. He had only to leave me looking after the sheep, and I don't think pride would ever have entered my head.

CAUCHON. Weigh your words, Joan; weigh your thoughts. It is your Saviour you are accusing now.

JOAN (*crossing herself*). God guide me. His will be done, if His will is to make me proud and damned. That is His right, as well.

PROMOTER (*unable to contain himself*). Terrible! What she says is terrible! God's will to damn a soul? And you all listen to this without a murmur, my lords? I see here the seed of a fearful heresy which will one day tear the Church apart.

The INQUISITOR *has risen. He is an intelligent looking man, spare and hard, speaking with great quietness.*

INQUISITOR. Listen carefully to what I am going to ask you, Joan. Do you think you are in a state of grace at this moment?

JOAN (*firmly*). At what moment, my lord? Is it the beginning, when I hear my Voices, or the end, when my King and all my friends have deserted me, when I doubt and recant and the Church receives me again?

INQUISITOR. Don't evade my question. Do you think you are in a state of grace?

All the PRIESTS *are watching her in silence; it seems a dangerous question.*

LADVENU (*rising*). My lord Inquisitor, it is a formidable question for a simple girl who believes in all sincerity that God has called her. I ask that her reply shall not be held against her: she is risking quite unwittingly——

INQUISITOR. Quiet, Brother Ladvenu! I ask what I consider good to ask. Let her answer my question. Do you think you are in a state of grace, Joan?

JOAN. If I am not, may God in His goodness set me there. If I am, may God in His goodness keep me so.

The PRIESTS *murmur. The* INQUISITOR *sits again, inscrutable.*

LADVENU (*quietly*). Well answered, Joan.

PROMOTER (*muttering, annoyed by* JOAN'S *success*). What of it? The devil has cunning, or he wouldn't be the devil. It isn't the first time he has been asked that question. We know what he is; he has his answers all ready.

WARWICK (*bored, to* CAUCHON). No doubt this is all very interesting, my lord, but if you go on at this rate we shall never get to the trial, never have her burnt, never get anywhere. I said she could take us over the old ground again, if you thought it so necessary, but let her get on with it. And let us come to the essentials. His Majesty's Government have to discredit this wretched little Charles Valois, at once; it's imperative that we should let

Christendom know that the Coronation was all a humbug, the performance of a witch, a heretic, an army's whore.

CAUCHON. My lord, we're trying her only for heresy.

WARWICK. I know that; but I have to make more of it for the sake of the troops. The findings of your trial, I'm afraid, will be too rarefied for my soldiers. Propaganda, my lord Archbishop, is black or white. The main thing is to say something pretty staggering, and repeat it often enough until you turn it into a truth. It's a new idea, but believe me, it will make its way. The essential thing, so far as I am concerned, is that the girl should be a nonentity, whatever she is in fact. And what she is in fact is of no particular importance to His Majesty's Government. Personally, I must admit, I find the girl attractive. The way she takes the wind out of your sails gives me a lot of pleasure; and her seat on a horse is very good: that's rare in a woman. If the circumstances had been different, and she had belonged to my own set, I should have enjoyed a day's hunting with her. But unfortunately there's been this damned Coronation, and that was nobody's notion but hers in the first place. Really, my lords, what impudence! To have himself crowned King of France right under our noses: a Valois, King of France! and to do it at Rheims, our territory! To dare to pick France out of our pockets, and pilfer the English heritage! Luckily, God is on the side of England, as he satisfactorily proved at Agincourt. God and our right. Two ideas completely synonymous. And moreover, inscribed on our coat-of-arms. So rattle her through the rest of it, and have her burned, and not so much talk. Earlier on I was joking. I give it ten years, and this whole incident will have been forgotten.

CAUCHON (*sighing*). God grant so, my lord.

WARWICK. Where had we got to?

FATHER (*coming forward with his stick*). To where I was going out to find her, sitting under her tree, waiting to get herself into trouble, the little bitch. And I can tell you she'll be sorry she ever began it! (*He drags* JOAN *up by the wrists.*) What are you doing here, eh? Tell me what you're waiting about here for, when you know you ought to be indoors, eating your supper!

JOAN (*stammering, shy at being surprised, raising her arm to protect her face*). I didn't know it was so late. I had lost count of the time.

FATHER. That's it, you lost count of the time! And what else have you lost that you daren't tell me? (*He shakes her abominably.*) Who made you forget it was so late? I heard you as I came along, calling out goodbye to somebody. Well, who was it?

JOAN. St. Michael, father.

FATHER (*giving her a resounding slap on the face*). You make fun at your father, you'll be sorry! I won't have any girl of mine sitting out in the fields waiting for any man who wants to find her. You'll marry the decent fellow we choose for you, or I'll break every bone in your body!

JOAN. I've done nothing wrong, father: truthfully it was the blessed St. Michael who spoke to me.

FATHER. And when you can't hide your sinning any longer, and every day it grows bigger in you for all to see, and you've killed your mother with grief, and your brothers have to join the army to get away from the scandal in the village, it will be the Holy Ghost who brought it on us, I suppose? I'll tell the priest: not content with whoring, you have to blaspheme: and you'll be shut up in a convent on bread and water, my girl.

JOAN (*kneeling before him*). Father, stop shouting, you can't hear what I say. I promise you, by our Saviour, I'm telling you the truth. They've been coming for a long time now to ask things of me. It is always at the mid-day Angelus or the evening Angelus; always when I'm praying, when I am least sinful and nearest to God. Above all doubt, surely it must be true. St. Michael has appeared to me, and St. Margaret, and St. Catherine. They speak to me, and they answer when I question them, and each one says the same as the others.

FATHER (*pulling her about*). Why should St. Michael speak to you, you little idiot? Does he speak to me? Natural enough, if he had something to say to us, he'd say it to me, the head of the family. Does he speak to our priest?

JOAN. Father, as well as shaking me and shouting at me, try to understand what I'm saying. I'm so alone, and they want me to do so much. For three years I've been trying not to believe them, but all that time they've been saying the same thing. These voices I hear: I can't go on fighting them all by myself. I've got to do what they say.

FATHER. The voices you hear? Do you want to drive me mad?

JOAN. They say it can't wait any longer; the time has come when I have to say yes.

FATHER. What can't wait any longer, idiot? What are they telling you to do, what you call these Voices? Voices! Well, it's better than being deaf!

JOAN. They tell me to go and save the realm of France which is in grave danger of being destroyed. Is it true?

FATHER. Heavens above! Of course the realm of France is in danger of being destroyed. It isn't the first time, and it won't be the last: and she always gets out of it. Leave it in God's hands; there's nothing you can do about it, you poor girl. Even a man can't do anything about it, unless he's a soldier.

JOAN. But I can. My voices have said so.

FATHER (*laughing*). Oh, you can, can you? Dear me! You're sharper than all our great captains, of course, who can't do anything these days except be beaten every time they fight?

JOAN. Yes, father.

FATHER. Yes, father! Perhaps you're not a bad girl, but worse. You're a mad, idiot girl. What do you think you can do then, poor idiot?

JOAN. What my Voices tell me. I can ask the Squire of Beaudricourt for an armed escort. And when I've got my escort, I can go straight to the Dauphin at Chinon, to tell him that he's the rightful King; and I can lead him out at the head of the soldiers to save Orleans; and then I can persuade him to be consecrated with holy oil by the Archbishop, and then we can hurl the English into the sea.

FATHER (*suddenly understanding*). Now you're explaining yourself, at last, you filthy little slut! You want to go off with the soldiers, like the lowest of the low?

JOAN (*smiling mysteriously*). No, father, like the highest under God, riding first into the battle, and not looking back until I have saved France. (*Suddenly sad.*) And after that is done, what happens is God's will.

FATHER. I've heard enough shameless lying! I won't stand any more of it! I'll teach you what happens to girls who go chasing after soldiers, pretending to save France!

He savagely and unmercifully beats and kicks her.

JOAN (*crying*). Stop, father, stop! stop!

The FATHER *has taken off his belt, and starts to leather her, gasping with effort.*

LADVENU (*rising, very pale*). This must be stopped! He means to injure her.

CAUCHON (*gently*). We can do nothing, Brother Ladvenu. At this part of the story we have never met Joan; we don't get to know her until the trial. We can only act our parts, each his own, good or bad, as they are written, and in his turn. And later on, you know, we shall do worse things than this to her. (*He turns to* WARWICK.) This domestic scene is not very pleasant to witness, my lord?

WARWICK (*with a gesture*). Why not? We're firm believers in corporal punishment in England; it forms the character. I myself have been flogged many times as a boy; and I took it extremely well.

The FATHER, *at last too exhausted to go on, wipes the sweat off his forehead, and shouts at* JOAN, *lying crumpled at his feet.*

FATHER. There! you carrion! Do you still want to save France? (*He turns to the others, rather ashamed of himself.*) Well, sirs, what would you have done in my place if your daughter had said that to you?

MOTHER (*coming forward*). Have you killed her?

FATHER. Not this time. But if she talks any more about going off with the soldiers, I'll drown that girl of yours in the river with my own hands, do you hear me? And if I'm nowhere about, I give her brother full permission to do it for me. (*He strides off.*)

The MOTHER *bends over* JOAN *and dries her face.*

MOTHER. Joan, my little Joan, my little Joan. Did he hurt you?

JOAN (*giving a pathetic smile when she recognises her* MOTHER). Yes. He meant me to feel it.

MOTHER. He's your father, Joan; you must bear it patiently.

JOAN (*in a small voice*). I do bear it, mother. I prayed while he beat me: prayed that our heavenly Father would forgive him.

MOTHER (*shocked*). Our heavenly Father doesn't have to forgive fathers for beating their daughters. It's their right.

JOAN. And I prayed for him to understand.

MOTHER (*fondling her*). Understand what, my silly one? Why did you have to tell him all this nonsense?

JOAN (*in agony*). Someone has to understand; otherwise I'm by myself, and I have to face them alone!

MOTHER (*rocking her in her arms*). Now, now, now, you don't have to upset yourself. You remember when you were little, we would rock away your nightmares together. But now you're nearly a woman: nearly too big to hold in my arms any more, and I can tell you it's no good breaking your heart to make men understand anything. All you can do is say " yes " to whatever they think, and wait till they've gone out to the fields. Then you can be mistress in your own house again. Your father's a good man; but if I didn't trick him sometimes for his own good I don't know where we should be. Who is it, Joan? You can tell your mother. Don't you even know his name, perhaps? And yet I don't know but it must be someone in the village. Why, your father might even agree to him; he's not against a good marriage for you. We might even be able to persuade him he chose the boy himself, the poor old stupid. You know what men are: roar a lot, and lay down the law, and bang you about; but, the same as with a bull, you can lead them by the nose.

JOAN. It isn't marriage that I have to think of, mother. The blessed St. Michael has told me I should leave the village, put on a man's clothes, and go and find his highness the Dauphin, to save the realm of France.

MOTHER (*severely*). Joan, I speak nicely and gently to you, but I won't have you talking wickedness. And I won't have you put on a man's clothes, not if you beg at my grave. Have my daughter a man! You let me catch you, my goodness!

JOAN. But, mother, I should have to, if I'm to ride horseback with the soldiers. It's the blessed St. Michael who says so.

MOTHER. I don't care what the blessed St. Michael says. you shall never go off on a horse. Joan of Arc on a horse! It would be the talk of the village.

JOAN. But the lady of Vaucouleurs rides a horse to hawking.

MOTHER. You will not ride a horse, never! It isn't the station of life you were born to. Such grand ideas, indeed!

JOAN. But if I don't ride a horse, how can I lead the soldiers?

MOTHER. And you won't go with the soldiers, either, you wicked girl! I'd rather see you cold and dead. You see, how you make me talk the same as your father. There are some things we feel the same about. A daughter spins, and scrubs, and stays at home. Your grandmother never left this village, and neither have I, and neither will you, and when you have a daughter of your own, neither will she. (*She suddenly bursts into tears*). Going off with the soldiers! Do you want to kill me?

JOAN (*throwing herself into her mother's arms, crying too*). No, mother!

MOTHER. You do: I can see you do. And you'll destroy yourself in the end if you don't soon get these thoughts out of your head. (*Exit.*)

JOAN *straightens herself up, still in tears, while her* MOTHER *goes back to the* CROWD.

JOAN. You see, St. Michael, it isn't possible; they won't ever understand. No one will. It is better that I should give up at once. Our Lord has said that we have to obey our father and mother. (*She speaks with the voice of the Archangel.*)

——But, first, Joan, you have to obey God.

——But if God commands the impossible?

——Then you have to attempt the impossible, calmly and quietly. It is a cause for pride, Joan, that God gives you something of His burden to carry.

After a pause.

——My Lord, do you think our Saviour can want a daughter to make her parents weep, and leave them alone to break their hearts, perhaps to die? That's hard to understand.

——He has said, I come to bring not peace, but a sword. I am come to set the brother against the sister and the son against the father. God came to bring struggle, Joan; not to make the way easy, but to make the way harder. He doesn't ask the impossible of everybody, but He does ask it of you. That is all. (JOAN *looks up, and says simply.*)—Well, I will go.

A VOICE (*from somewhere out of the shadows behind*). Proud and arrogant!

JOAN (*disturbed*). Who is calling me proud and arrogant?

(*After a pause, in the voice of the Archangel.*)

——It was you, Joan. And when you begin to do what God is asking, it will be what the world calls you. But if you give yourself humbly into the hands of God, you can bear this blame of pride.

——It is heavy to bear, my Lord!

——Yes, it is heavy. But God knows that you are strong.

A silence. She looks straight in front of her, and suddenly becomes a little girl again, happy and decided.

All right, then. It's all decided. I shall go and find my Uncle Durand. With him I always get my own way. He's easy to manage as a tame sparrow. I shall kiss him on both cheeks, and on the top of his head, and sit on his lap, and he will say "Oh Lord, Oh Lord," and take me to Vaucouleurs!

BROTHER. You're a silly donkey! Why did you have to go and tell the old people all that stuff? Next time, if you give me a ha'penny, I won't say a word about where I saw you.

JOAN (*leaping cheerfully at him*). Oh, so it was you who told them, you beastly little pig? Sneak, sneak, I'll give you a tweak! Tell tales out of school, duck him in a muddy pool! There's your halfpenny, lardy-head. Tell-tale-tit, your tongue shall be split, and all the children in the town shall have a little bit!

They fight like urchins. She chases straight across the stage towards BEAUDRICOURT *who has come forward to take the centre of the stage.*

BEAUDRICOURT. Well, what is it? What does she want? What is it you want, you infernal nuisance? What's this nonsensical story I hear——

JOAN *collides head first with* BEAUDRICOURT'S *great paunch. He is half winded, gives a yell of pain, grabs her by the arm and lifts her level with his nose, apoplectic with rage.*

What the devil do you want, you horrible mosquito? What the devil do you mean, playing the fool outside my gates for three days on end? What the devil are these tales you've been telling the guards until their eyes pop out as far as their noses?

JOAN (*breathless with her running and poised on tip-toe in the arms of the giant*). I want a horse, my lord, a man's clothes, and an escort, to go to Chinon to see his highness the Dauphin.

BEAUDRICOURT. And my boot, you want that, too, of course?

JOAN. If you like, my lord, and a good clout, as long as I get the horse as well.

BEAUDRICOURT (*still holding her*). You know about me and you know what I want; the village girls have told you all about it, haven't they? They come along to see me, usually to beg for the life of a brother, or their old father who's been caught poaching on my lands. If the girl is pretty, I always hook him down off the gallows, being amiable at heart. If she's ugly, I hang the old chap, to make an example of him. But it's always the pretty ones who come; they manage to dig up one in the family somehow; with the admirable result that I have a fine reputation for benevolence in the neighbourhood. So now you know the rate of exchange, and we can come to terms.

JOAN (*simply*). I don't know what you're trying to say, my lord. The blessed St. Michael sent me to you.

BEAUDRICOURT (*crossing himself anxiously with his free hand*). You don't have to bring the saints into this. That was all right for the guards, to get you in to see me. But now you're here, and you can leave the saints in their proper places. And I wouldn't be surprised if you get your horse. An old jade for a young maid; it's a reasonable bargain. Are you a virgin?

JOAN. Yes, my lord.

BEAUDRICOURT (*looking at her all the time*). I agree to the horse.

JOAN. That isn't all I want, my lord.

BEAUDRICOURT. A greedy child, I see! Well, go on; you're amusing me. If I pay well for my pleasures it helps me to believe I really want them. You understand where this conversation is leading?

JOAN (*frankly*). No, my lord.

BEAUDRICOURT. Splendid. The bed's no place for brains. What else do you want beside the horse? The taxes are coming in very well this autumn; I don't mind being generous.

JOAN. An escort of men-at-arms, my lord, to accompany me to Chinon.

BEAUDRICOURT (*freeing her, changing his tone*). Now listen to me, if we're to get on together: I may be easygoing, but I won't stand any impudence. I'm the master here and you're using up my patience fast. I can just as well have you whipped for forcing your way in here, and send you home with nothing except the marks on your backside. So behave yourself. Why do you want to go to Chinon?

JOAN. To find his highness the Dauphin.

BEAUDRICOURT. Well, well, you mean to get on! Why not the Duke of Burgundy while you're about it? In theory, you might have a sporting chance with him: the Duke's as hot as a buck rabbit. Whereas, as you probably know, the Dauphin when it comes to war and women . . . I don't know what you expect to get from him.

JOAN. An army, my lord, which I can lead to Orleans.

BEAUDRICOURT. Ah: if you're mad it's another thing altogether. I'm not getting involved in any scandal. (*He turns to the crowd upstage.*) Hey, there, Boudousse!

A GUARD *comes forward.*

Take her away and give her a ducking, and then lock her up. You can send her back to her father tomorrow evening. But no beating, I don't want any trouble; the girl's mad.

JOAN (*calmly, held by the* GUARD). You can lock me up. my lord: I don't mind that; but when they let me out tomorrow evening I shall come back again. So it would be simpler if you let me talk to you now.

BEAUDRICOURT. Ten million thunders! Don't I frighten you?

JOAN. No, my lord. Not at all.

BEAUDRICOURT (*to the* GUARD). Get back to your post! you don't need to stand about, listening to this.

The GUARD *goes, and when he has gone* BEAUDRICOURT *asks uneasily.*

And why don't I frighten you? I frighten everybody.

JOAN (*quietly*). You are very good, my lord.

BEAUDRICOURT. Good? Good? I've told you, that depends on the price.

JOAN. And what's more, very intelligent. There are many people I will have to convince before I can do everything my Voices want; so its lucky the first person I have to deal with, the one everything really depends on, should turn out to be the most intelligent.

BEAUDRICOURT (*slightly puzzled, asks in a casual voice while he pours himself some wine*). You're an odd girl, in your way. How did you come to notice that I'm intelligent?

JOAN. Because you're very handsome, my lord.

BEAUDRICOURT (*with a furtive glance into the metal mirror beside him*). Oh, tush! I suppose, twenty years ago, I might say that I pleased the ladies; and I've taken care of myself, not let myself get too old too soon; that's all it is.—It's quite peculiar and unsettling to have a conversation like this with a farm girl I've never heard of, who happens to drop in like a stray kitten. (*He sighs.*) On the whole I vegetate here. My lieutenants are a poor bunch: hardly a brain between them. And while we're on the subject, what's this connection you find between intellect and beauty? I've usually heard quite the opposite: handsome people are always stupid; that's the general opinion.

JOAN. That's the opinion of the plain people, who like to believe God can't manage both things at once.

BEAUDRICOURT (*flattered*). Ah, well, you've made a point there. But then, take myself for example. I know, as you so kindly say, I'm not one of the plain people; but I wonder sometimes, am I, after all, very intelligent? No no, don't protest. It's a question I have to ask now and again. I can tell you this, between ourselves, as you're not anyone in particular. Obviously I'm more intelligent than my lieutenants, that's only natural, being officer in command. If that wasn't an established fact there wouldn't be an army at all. But even so, I sometimes meet with problems which I find very troublesome. They ask me to decide something, some tactical or administrative point, and quite suddenly, I don't know why, my mind is a blank. There it is, nothing but a sort of fog. Mark you, nobody knows that. I get out of it, without my face showing any change of expression; I make a decision all right. And that's the essential thing when you're in command, of course: make a decision, whatever it is. Until you've had some experience you're apt to get flustered: but you realise after a bit, it all amounts to the same thing, whatever you decide. Still, I should like to see myself doing better. Vaucouleurs, as you see, is of no great size. I'm looking forward to the day when I make a really important decision: one of those momentous decisions, of great consequence to the nation: not a question of somebody who hasn't paid his taxes, or half a dozen prisoners to be hanged: but something a bit exceptional, which would get me noticed and talked about higher up. (*He stops dreaming, and looks at her.*) I don't know what in the world I'm doing telling you all this. You can't do anything about it, and God help you, you're half crazy into the bargain.

JOAN (*smiling gently*). I know why. I knew it would happen, because they told me so. Listen, Robert——

BEAUDRICOURT (*startled*). What are you doing calling me by my Christian name?

JOAN. It's God's name for you, Robert. Now listen, Robert, and don't bluster again, because it isn't any use. What is the important decision, which will get you noticed and talked about higher up? I can tell you, Robert. It's me.

BEAUDRICOURT. What are you talking about?

JOAN (*coming to him*). I'll tell you, if you'll listen. First of all, you have to stop thinking of me as a girl, that's what is getting you confused. And I don't mean much to you anyway, do I?

He hesitates, afraid of being cheated; she flares up.

Robert, if you want to help yourself, you have to help me, too! When I tell you the truth, acknowledge it and say Yes: otherwise we shall never get anywhere.

BEAUDRICOURT (*muttering, rather shamefaced*). Well, no . . .

JOAN (*severely*). What do you mean, no?

BEAUDRICOURT. I mean, yes, it's true. I'm not particular about you. (*Adding politely.*) Though, mind you, you're a pretty enough little thing. . . .

JOAN. All right, you don't have to think you've upset me. I'm very happy the point is cleared up. And now you can imagine you have already given me the suit of clothes I asked for, and we can discuss things together, sensibly and calmly, as man to man.

BEAUDRICOURT (*still suspicious*). Discuss what?

JOAN (*sitting on the edge of the table, finishing the dregs in the wine glass*). Your own important decision, my splendid Robert. Your great achievement which will make everyone take notice of you. Think of all of them, there at Bourges. They don't know whether they're praying or cursing, or which saint to turn to next. The English are everywhere. And you know the French army. Good boys, who have still got fight in them, but they're discouraged. They've got it into their heads that the English will always be the strongest, and there's nothing to be done. Dunois the Bastard; he's a good captain; intelligent, which is rare in the army, but no one listens to him any more, and he's getting tired of it. So he spends his days having a high old time with the women in the camp (and that's something else I shall have to deal with): and he's far too cock-a-hoop, like all bastards. "The affairs of France aren't his concern: let that milksop Charles get his country out of the tangle for himself." Then there's La Hire, and there's Xantrailles: prize angry bulls: they always want to charge in head first, slashing and thrusting like old heroes in the chronicles. They belong among the champions of single combat, who don't understand how to use their cannons, and always get killed to no purpose whatever, the way they did at Agincourt. They're wonderful at getting killed, but it isn't any help. That's true, isn't it, Robert. You can't treat war like a tournament. You have to win. You have to be cunning. (*She touches her forehead.*) You have to wage it here. With all your intelligence, Robert, you know that better than I do.

BEAUDRICOURT. I've always said so. Nowadays we don't think enough. Take my lieutenants: always spoiling for a fight, and that's all they can think of. And the men who know how to think get overlooked; nobody dreams of using them.

JOAN. Nobody. So they have to think for themselves. It's a lucky thing you have had such a tremendous idea. It's certain to alter everything.

BEAUDRICOURT (*uneasily*). I have an idea?

JOAN. Don't question it, Robert; be very proud of it. Your brain is working at great speed, clearly and concisely. It's a sad thing to think that, in the whole of France at this moment, no one sees things clearly, except you.

BEAUDRICOURT. You believe so?

JOAN. I tell you so.

BEADRICOURT. And what is it I see?

JOAN. You see simply that the people of France have to be given a spirit and a faith. And it so happens that you have with you at this moment a young country girl. St. Michael has appeared to her, and St. Catherine and St. Margaret, or at least she says they have. You are not so sure about it, but for the time being it's not important. And this is where you show yourself to be so remarkable. You say to yourself: Here's a little peasant girl, of no consequence at all; all right. If by any chance she really has been sent by God, then nothing could stop her, and it can't be proved one way or the other whether God sent her or not. She certainly got in to see me, without my permission, and I've been listening to her for half an hour; nobody could deny that. And then, like a sword of lightning, the idea strikes home to you. You say to yourself: If she has the power to convince me, why shouldn't she convince the Dauphin and Dunois and the Archbishop? They're men, just as I'm a man; as a matter of fact, between ourselves, rather less intelligent. Moreover, why shouldn't she convince our soldiers that the English in the main are exactly like themselves, half courage and half a wish to save their skins; pummel them hard enough at the right moment, and you send them staggering out of Orleans. It's magnificent how you marshal the whole situation in your mind. What our fellows need, you are saying to yourself: what they need is someone to rouse their spirit and prove to them that God is still with them. This is where you show yourself a born leader, Robert.

BEAUDRICOURT (*pitifully*). You think that?

JOAN. I know it. And very soon so will everyone else. Like all great politicians, you're a realist, Robert. You say to yourself: I, Beaudricourt, have my doubts about her coming from God, but I'll send her off to them, and if they think she is, it will have the same effect whether it's true or false. By a stroke of good luck my courier is leaving for Bourges tomorrow morning——

BEAUDRICOURT. Who told you that? It's a secret.

JOAN. I found it out. (*She continues.*) I pick half a dozen strong men for an escort, give her a horse and send her off with the courier. At Chinon, as far as I can see, she will work things out for herself. (*She looks at him admiringly.*) My word, my word, Robert!

BEAUDRICOURT. What?

JOAN. You have a marvellous intelligence to think of all that.

BEAUDRICOURT (*wiping his forehead, worn out*). Yes.

JOAN. Only, please give me a quiet horse, because I don't know how to ride one yet.

BEAUDRICOURT (*delighted*). You're going to break your neck, my girl!

JOAN. I don't think so. St. Michael will hold me on. I tell you what, Robert: I'll have a wager with you. I'll bet you a suit of clothes—the man's clothes which you still haven't said you'll give me—against a punch on the nose. Bring two horses into the courtyard and we'll gallop them together. If I fall off, you can lose faith in me. Is that fair? (*She offers him her hand.*) Agreed? And whoever doesn't pay up is a man of mud!

BEAUDRICOURT (*getting up*). Agreed! I need to move about a bit. I wouldn't have believed how tiring it is to think so much. (*He calls.*) Boudousse!

Enter the GUARD.

GUARD. Do I take her away and give her a ducking, sir?

BEAUDRICOURT. No, you idiot! You fetch her some breeches, and bring us a couple of horses. We're taking a gallop together.

GUARD. What about the Council, sir? It's four o'clock.

BEAUDRICOURT. It can wait till tomorrow. Today I've used my brains quite enough.

He goes. JOAN *passes the astonished* GUARD *and sticks out her tongue. They lose themselves in the crowd up stage.*

WARWICK (*to* CAUCHON). I can see this girl had quality. Very entertaining, to watch her playing the old fish, didn't you think so?

CAUCHON. Rather too crude for my taste, my lord. Something subtler than that will be needed when she comes to deal with Charles.

WARWICK. My lord Bishop, the tricks that you and I use in our way of business aren't so remarkably different from hers. Whether we're ruling the world with a mace or a crozier, in the long run, we do it by persuading fools that what we make them think is their own opinion. No need for any intervention of God in that. Which is why I found it so entertaining. (*He bows politely towards the* BISHOP.) Entertaining, at least, if one isn't professionally concerned, of course, as you are. Have you faith yourself, my lord Bishop? Forgive my bluntness; but between ourselves. I'm interested to know.

CAUCHON (*simply*). A child's faith, my lord. And that is why I shall make problems for you during the trial, and why we shall go as far as ever we can to save Joan, even though we have been sincere collaborators with the English rule, which seemed to us then the only reasonable solution to chaos. It was very easy for those who were at Bourges to call us traitors, when they had the protection of the French army. We were in occupied Rouen.

WARWICK. I don't like the word "occupied": You forget the Treaty of Troyes. You were quite simply on His Majesty's territory.

CAUCHON. In the midst of His Majesty's army, and the execution of His Majesty's hostages; submitting to the curfew, and the condescension of His Majesty's food-supplies. We were men, with the frailty of men, who wanted to go on living, and yet at the same time to save Joan if we could. It was not in any way a happy part that we were called upon to fill.

WARWICK (*smiling*). There was nothing to stop you becoming martyrs, my dear fellow, if that would have made it more inspiring for you. My eight hundred soldiers were quite ready.

CAUCHON. We knew it. They took great pleasure in shouting their insults at us, hammering on the door with the butts of their halberds, to remind us they were there. We temporised for nine months before we would deliver Joan up to you; this little girl, forsaken by everyone; nine months to make her say Yes. Future times will be pleased to say we were barbarous. But I fancy, for all their fine principles, they will take to expediency faster than we did; in every camp.

WARWICK. Nine months, that's quite true. What a difficult confinement this trial has been. Our Holy Mother Church takes her time, when she's asked to give birth to a small matter of policy. But the nightmare is over. The mother and child are both doing well.

CAUCHON. I have pondered deeply over these things, my lord. The health of the mother, as you put it, is our one concern. And that is why, when we saw there could be no alternative, we sacrificed the child in good faith. Ever since that day of Joan's arrest, God has been dead to us. Neither she, whatever she may imagine, nor we, certainly, have heard Him any more. We have gone on, following our daily custom; our pre-eminent duty, to defend the old house, this great and wise human building which is all that remains to us in the absence of God. From the time we were fifteen years old, we were taught how to defend it. Joan had no such help, and yet, though her faith fell on dreadful days, when she was left alone by men and by God, she also has gone on, recovering at once after the single moment when she weakened, bearing herself with her curious mixture of humility and insolence, of grandeur and good sense, even up to execution and death. We weren't able to understand it then; we had our eyes buried in our mother's skirts, like children grown old. And yet, precisely in this loneliness, in the desert of a vanished God, in the privation and misery of the animal, the man is indeed great who continues to lift his head. Greatly alone.

WARWICK. Yes, well, no doubt. But if our business is politics we can't afford to brood about such men. We seem fated, as a rule, to meet them among the people we condemn to execution.

CAUCHON (*quietly, after a pause*). It is a consolation to me sometimes to think of those old priests who, though they were deeply offended by her insolent answers, nevertheless, even with English swords at their back, tried for nine months not to commit the irreparable.

WARWICK. Enough of fine phrases, Bishop. Nothing is irreparable in politics. I tell you we shall raise a handsome statue to her in London one day, when the right time comes.

He turns towards the people of Chinon, who have been putting up a small palace set during this conversation.

But now let's come to Chinon, my lord. I've got a profound disrespect for that lounging little idler, Charles, but he's a character who never fails to amuse me.

CHARLES *is with the two Queens and* AGNES SOREL.

AGNES. But Charles, it's impossible! You can't let me appear at the ball looking such a frump. Your mistress in one of last year's steeple-hats.

QUEEN. And your Queen, Charles! The Queen of France! What would they say?

CHARLES (*playing cup-and-ball, dropping into his throne*). They would say the King of France isn't worth a farthing. Which is quite right.

QUEEN. And think how the English court would laugh! The Duchess of Bedford, and Gloucester's wife, to say nothing of the Cardinal of Winchester's mistress! Now there's someone who knows how to dress.

AGNES. Imagine, Charles, if they're wearing our newest fashions over there before we are!

CHARLES. At least they pay for them. Fashion is practically the only thing we can sell them: our fashions and our cooking. They are the only things which still give us some prestige with the foreigners.

YOLANDE. We have to defend this prestige. The girls aren't altogether wrong, Charles. It's most important there should be no question at this ball that ladies of the court of France are the best dressed women in the world. No one has ever been able to decide, remember, exactly where triviality begins. A steeple-hat the English have never seen before might be as good as a great victory.

CHARLES (*with a dry laugh*). A victory which isn't going to stop them making off with Orleans, mother-in-law! According to the latest reports, Orleans is lost. And you think we should counter-attack with a new fashion.

AGNES. Certainly. You've no idea what a dangerous blow it will be to their confidence. If you want a victory, Charles, here is one you can have for nothing.

CHARLES. For nothing? You make me laugh! How much did you say these steeple-hats would come to?

AGNES. Six thousand francs, my darling. That's next to nothing, when you remember they're completely embroidered with pearls. And the pearls are a good investment. When the steeple-hat isn't fashionable any more you can always sell the pearls at a profit and put it towards the army's back pay.

CHARLES. Six thousand francs! But where do you think I can find six thousand francs, you poor little fool?

QUEEN (*softly*). Twelve thousand francs, Charles, because there are two of us, remember. You wouldn't want your mistress to be better dressed than your wife.

CHARLES (*raising his hands to heaven*). Twelve thousand francs! They've gone out of their minds!

AGNES. Of course there's a simpler model, but I wouldn't advise it. You would forfeit the moral effect we should have on the stupid English. And that, after all, is the effect we're after.

CHARLES. Twelve thousand francs! Enough to pay three-quarters of Dunois's army. I don't understand how you can encourage them, mother-in-law, a woman of your good judgment.

YOLANDE. It's because I'm a woman of good judgment that I support them, Charles. Have you ever found me opposing anything that might be for your good or the dignity of the throne? I am the mother of your Queen, and yet it was I who introduced you to Agnes when I saw clearly how it might help you.

QUEEN. Please, mother, don't brag about it!

YOLANDE. Daughter, Agnes is a very charming girl who perfectly knows her place. It was quite as important to you as to me, that Charles should decide to become a man. And the kingdom had even more need of it than we had. A little more pride, dear girl; at the moment you have thoughts like a tradesman's wife! Before Charles could become a man he had to be given a woman.

QUEEN (*acidly*). I was a woman, it seems to me, and his wife, what is more.

YOLANDE. I don't want to wound you, my dearest girl: but only slightly a woman. I can say this to you, because I was very much the same. Good sense, intelligence—more than you have—but that was all. Which is why I was always willing that the King, your father, should have his mistresses. Be his Queen, run his house, give him a son and heir and leave the rest to other people. We can't do everything. And anyway, love is scarcely an honest woman's concern. We don't do well at it. Besides, you will thank me later on: one sleeps so much better alone. And Charles is far more manly since he knew Agnes. You are more manly, aren't you, Charles?

CHARLES. Yesterday I said "No" to the Archbishop. He tried to scare me, he sent La Tremouille in first to roar at me, and then he threatened to excommunicate me. All the old tricks. But I held firm.

AGNES. And thanks to whom?

CHARLES. Thanks to Agnes! We had rehearsed the whole scene in bed.

YOLANDE. What did the Archbishop want? You didn't tell me.

CHARLES (*caressing* AGNES *absent-mindedly*). I can't remember. To give up Paris to the Duke of Burgundy, or something of the sort, in return for a year's truce. I might say it wouldn't really have meant anything at all. The Duke's in Paris already. But it was a matter of principle: Paris is France, and France is mine. At least I encourage myself to believe it is. So I said " No ". The Archbishop made such a great fuss about it, the Duke must have promised him a pretty good sum.

AGNES. And what would have happened, Charles dear, if you had said " yes " in spite of me?

CHARLES. You would have had a headache for a week, and although, I suppose, if I had to, I could do without Paris, I couldn't do without you.

AGNES. Well, then, my darling, if I have helped you to save Paris, you can surely buy me the new steeple-hat, and one for your little Queen, too, because you have said some very hurtful things to her, without noticing it, as usual, you bad boy. You don't want me to be ill for a whole week, do you? You wouldn't know what to do with yourself.

CHARLES. All right, then, order your steeple-hats. I always have to say "yes" to somebody, if it isn't the Archbishop, it's you. But I may as well tell you, I haven't the least idea how I'm going to pay for them.

AGNES. You're going to sign a draft on the Treasury Charles, and we will see what happens later. Come along, little Majesty, we will try them on together. Would you rather have this rose-coloured one, or the sky-blue? I think myself the rose is the one which will suit you best.

CHARLES. What do you mean? Have you got them already?

AGNES. You're very slow at understanding, my dearest! Surely you can see, if we were to have them in time for the ball we had to order them a month ago? But we were so sure you would say " yes ", weren't we, Your Majesty? You shall see what a sensation this causes in London! It's a great victory for France, you know, Charles!

They take to their heels.

CHARLES (*sitting back on his throne again*). There's nothing you can do but laugh, the way they harp on victories. La Tremouille, Dunois, they're all the same! There is always going to be a great victory. But everything has to be paid for, including great victories, these days. And suppose I can't afford a great victory? Suppose France is above my means? (*He takes his writing desk, muttering.*) Ah well, we shall see! I can always sign a draft on the Treasury. Let's hope it will please the tradesmen. The Treasury is empty, but there's nothing on this paper to say so. (*He turns towards the* QUEEN YOLANDE.) You wouldn't like a steeple-hat too, while I'm doing it? You needn't mind saying so. My signature isn't worth the ink it's written in.

YOLANDE (*coming to him*). I'm past the age for steeple-hats, Charles. I want something else.

CHARLES (*wearily*). To make me a great King, I know! It gets very boring in the end, everybody wants to make me a great King. Even Agnes. Even in bed. Imagine how jolly that is. I wish you would all try and get it into your heads, I'm an unimportant, insignificant Valois, and to make a King of me would need a miracle. I know my grandfather Charles was a great king; but he lived before the war when everything was much cheaper. Besides, he was rich. But my father and mother spent it all, so whether you like it or not, I can't afford to be a great king; I haven't got the money, and I haven't got the courage; you all know I haven't. Courage is far too dangerous in a world full of bullying brutes. That fat pig La Tremouille was in a raging temper the other day, and drew his sword on me. We were alone together: nobody there to defend me. He was quite prepared to give me a jab with it, the beastly hooligan! I only just had time to dodge behind the throne. So you see what we've come to. Drawing his sword on the King! I should have sent for the constable to arrest him, except that unfortunately he is the constable, and I'm not sure that I am the King. That's why they treat me like this; they know that I may be only a bastard.

YOLANDE. It's nobody but yourself, Charles, who is always saying so.

CHARLES. When I look at the legitimate faces all round me I hope I am a bastard. It's a charming day and age to live in, when a man isn't considered anybody unless he can brandish an eight-pound sword, and stroll about in a suit of armour which would sink a galleon. When they put it on me, I'm welded into the ground; a great help to my dignity. And I don't like fighting. I don't like hitting, and I don't like being hit. And what's more, if you want to know, I'm frightened of it. (*He turns towards her crossly.*) What other impossibilities do you want me to do?

YOLANDE. I want you to receive this girl from Vaucouleurs. She says God sent her; and furthermore she says she has come to deliver Orleans. The people can think and talk of nothing else, and they're only waiting now to hear that you agree to receive her.

CHARLES. Then they're going to find I'm not as ridiculous

as they think I am. Give audience to an eccentric peasant girl? Really, mother-in-law, for a woman of good sense you disappoint me.

YOLANDE. I've given you Agnes, because I thought it was for your good, Charles, though against my interest as a mother. Now I tell you to accept this girl from Domremy. She seems to possess some exceptional power, or so everybody says, which is a point to be considered.

CHARLES (*bored*). I don't like virgins. I know, you're going to tell me again that I'm not virile enough. But they frighten me. And, anyway, I have Agnes, who still pleases me quite well enough. Don't think I'm reproaching you, but for someone who is a queen and my mother-in-law, you have a very remarkable vocation.

YOLANDE (*smiles*). You don't understand me, Charles, or else you're pretending not to. I'm asking you to take this peasant girl into your counsel, not into your bed.

CHARLES. In that case, in spite of all the respect I owe you, I have to tell you you're absolutely mad. Into my council, with the Archbishop, and La Tremouille, who believes that he sprang from Jupiter's thigh? Do you want them to knock my head off?

YOLANDE (*gently*). I think a peasant in your counsels is exactly what you all need. The nobility governs the kingdom, which is as it should be; God has entrusted it into their hands. But, without presuming to criticise the wisdom of providence, I wonder sometimes that he hasn't given them what he gives so generously to humbler men, a better measure of simplicity and common sense.

CHARLES (*ironically*). And courage!

YOLANDE (*gently*). And courage, Charles.

CHARLES. As far as I can understand you, you recommend turning the government over to the people? To the good people who have all the virtues. You've read the history of tyrants, I suppose?

YOLANDE. No, Charles. In my day, knowledge was not encouraged in young women.

CHARLES. But I've read it: the endless procession of horrors and scandals; and I amuse myself sometimes by imagining how the procession will go on in the future. They will certainly try what you recommend. They'll try everything. Men of the people will become masters of the kingdoms, maybe for centuries, the time it takes for a meteor to cross the sky; and that will be the time for massacres and the most monstrous errors. And what will they find, at the great account, when all is done? They'll find that not even the most vile, capricious, and cruel of the princes have cost the world as much as one of these virtuous men. Give France a powerful man of action, born of the people, whose ambition is to make the people happy, whatever it may entail, and see how they'll come to wish to God they had their poor lazy Charles back again, with his everlasting game of cup-and-ball. At least I've no theories about organizing the happy life. A negative virtue, perhaps, but more valuable than they realise yet.

YOLANDE. You should give up this cup-and-ball game, Charles, and this habit of sitting upside down on your throne. It's no behaviour for a king.

CHARLES. You would be sensible to let me be as I am. When the ball misses the cup, it drops on to my nose and nobody else's. But sit me on the throne the right way up, with the orb in one hand and the sceptre in the other, then whenever I make a mistake the ball will drop on everybody's nose.

Enter the ARCHBISHOP *and* LA TREMOUILLE. *He sits like a king on his throne.*

CHARLES. Archbishop, Constable, you've come at the perfect moment. I am starting to govern. You see I have here the orb and the sceptre.

ARCHBISHOP (*taking his eye-glass*). It's a cup-and-ball!

CHARLES. Unimportant. Archbishop; symbolism, after all. That isn't something I have to teach a prince of the Church. Your announced visit to me, my lord, must mean you wish for an audience.

ARCHBISHOP. I haven't come to be playful, Sire I know very well the minority opinion, which cares to intrigue and agitate on every possible occasion, is trying to persuade you to see this notorious peasant girl you have heard of. The Constable and I are here, Sire, to say it is not our intention to admit her.

CHARLES (*to* QUEEN YOLANDE). What did I tell you?—— I have taken note of what you recommend, my lord, and I shall consider what course to follow. Now you may go; the audience is over.

ARCHBISHOP. I will remind you, Sire, we are not here for your amusement.

CHARLES. Whenever I talk like a king for a moment, they always think I'm amusing myself. (*He lies back on his throne with the cup and ball.*) Very well, then; leave me to amuse myself in peace.

ARCHBISHOP. This girl's miraculous reputation is spreading across the country ahead of her; it was here before she arrived; it's already causing excitement in beseiged Orleans. God has taken her by the hand and leads her: this is the story. God has decided that she shall save France and drive the English back across the sea; and other such nonsense. God will expect you to receive her into the royal presence, and nothing is going to prevent her. I don't know why they're so anxious that God should concern Himself in their affairs. And naturally she has performed miracles; it would have surprised me more if she hadn't. A soldier called her I don't know what when she arrived at Chinon. She told him that he was wrong to swear, because soon he would be standing before his Redeemer. And an hour later this boorish fellow missed his footing, and fell into the well in the servants' yard, and drowned himself. That blundering step of a drunkard has done more for the girl's reputation than a great victory ever did for Dunois. Apparently the opinion is unanimous, from the lowest kennel-boy to the highest lady in your court: only this wretched girl can save us. A preposterous infatuation!——I speak to you, sir, of the gravest matters of the realm, and you play at cup-and-ball.

CHARLES. My lord, let us be clear about this. Do you want me to play at cup-and-ball, or do you want me to govern? (*He sits up.*) Do you want me to govern?

ARCHBISHOP (*disturbed*). Sir, we don't ask you to go as far as that. We wish you to notice and appreciate the efforts we are making . . .

CHARLES. I assure you, I notice them; I appreciate them; and I find them quite useless, my lord. Everyone expects me to see this girl, isn't it so?

ARCHBISHOP. I haven't said that!

CHARLES. Well, I'm not at all curious to see her. I'm not fond of new faces; we have to know too many people as it is. And messengers from God aren't usually very enlivening. But I want to be a good king, and content my people. I shall see this peasant girl, if only to take the wind out of her sails. Have you spoken to her yourself, Archbishop?

ARCHBISHOP. I have other things to do, sir, when you consider that I carry the whole burden of the Kingdom's affairs.

CHARLES. Quite so. And I have nothing else to do except play at cup-and-ball. So I shall see her to save you the trouble: and I shall tell you frankly what I think of her. You can trust me to do that, my lord. I know you don't easily credit me with any qualities worth having, but at least you will agree that I'm a frivolous man: a quite useful condition for this interview. I'm very soon bored by anyone who takes himself seriously. I am going to receive this girl, and if she can make me want to listen to her talking about the welfare of the kingdom, which no one has ever done yet without making me yawn, then there's no doubt about her performing miracles.

ARCHBISHOP (*muttering*). A peasant girl in the presence of the king!

CHARLES (*simply*). You will remember, I think, that some of all kinds have been admitted to my presence. I don't mean M. de la Tremouille, who springs, of course, direct from Jupiter's thigh. But, for instance, yourself, my lord: —I think I remember being told you were the grandson of a wine merchant. There is no reproach in that. What could be more natural? You have carried the wine from your cellars to the altar. And as for myself, as you frequently have told me, it's a moot point whether I'm the son of a king. So we'd better not play the ancestry game, my lord, or we shall be making ourselves altogether ridiculous. (*To* QUEEN YOLANDE.) Come with me, and help me get ready for her. I've thought of a very amusing joke. We can disguise one of the pages in a royal doublet, if we can find one that isn't too shabby; sit him on the throne, which I am sure he will manage better than I can, and I shall hide myself in the crowd. Then we can listen to a solemn harangue from the messenger of God to a page-boy! It ought to be irresistible, don't you think so?

They go out.

ARCHBISHOP (*to* LA TREMOUILLE). Do we let him do it? It's a game to him, like everything else. It shouldn't be dangerous. And once he has seen her, the people may very well calm down again. In a fortnight they will have found some other messenger of God to infatuate them, and the girl will be forgotten.

LA TREMOUILLE. I command the army, Archbishop, and I can only tell you, the official doctor of the nation has nothing more to say. We're now entirely in the hands of the bone-setters, the faith-healers, the quacks. In other words, what you call messengers from God. What do we risk?

ARCHBISHOP (*anxiously*). Constable, wherever God concerns himself everything is a risk. If the unlikely should be true, and He really has sent this girl to us: if, in fact, He means to take our part, then our troubles are only beginning. We shall be shaken out of all custom and orthodoxy, contrive to win four or five battles, and then will come the problems, the complications. Long experience as a man, both in the church and in government, teaches me that never, never must we draw God's attention to us. It is better to remain very small, Constable, very small and unnoticed.

The COURTIERS *take their places with the* QUEENS; *a* PAGE *sits on the throne;* CHARLES *slips into the crowd. The* ARCHBISHOP *concludes in an undertone. Everybody is grouped round the throne where the little* PAGE *sits;* CHARLES *is in the crowd.* JOAN *enters alone, looking very small and simple among the armour and the court fashions. They make a way for her to pass to the throne. She is about to kneel, hesitates, blushes, looking at the* PAGE.

YOLANDE (*whispering in her ear*). You must kneel, child, before the king.

JOAN *turns towards her, puzzled; then suddenly she looks at all the silent people who are watching her, and advances silently in the crowd, who make way for her. She goes towards* CHARLES, *who tries to hide from her. When he sees that she is about to reach him, he almost runs to hide behind the others, but she follows him, almost running, too. She finds him in a corner and falls on her knees.*

CHARLES (*embarrassed in the silence*). What do you want with me?

JOAN. Gentle Dauphin, I am called Joan the Maid. God has brought me to you, to tell you that you will be anointed and crowned in the city of Rheims. You will be viceroy of the King of Heaven, who is King of France.

CHARLES (*awkwardly*). Well, that is very nice. But Rheims belongs to the English, I understand. How would I get there?

JOAN (*still on her knees*). By your own strength, gentle Dauphin; by beating them. We will start with Orleans, and then we can go to Rheims.

LA TREMOUILLE (*coming up*). Little lunatic! Isn't that what all the army commanders have been trying to do for months? I am the head of them; I know something about it. And they haven't got there.

JOAN (*getting up*). I will get there.

LA TREMOUILLE. Will you indeed? And how will you get there?

JOAN. With the help of God Who sends me.

LA TREMOUILLE. I see. So God has arranged for us to retake Orleans?

JOAN. Yes, my lord; and to hunt the English out of France.

LA TREMOUILLE (*jeering*). A very beautiful thought! But God can't convey His own messages Himself? He has to have you to do it for Him?

JOAN. Yes, my lord.

ARCHBISHOP (*approaching her*). Young woman . . .

JOAN *sees him, kneels and kisses the hem of his robe. He gives her his ring to kiss, and motions her to rise.*

You say that God wishes to deliver the kingdom of France. If such is indeed His will, He has no need of armies, or you to lead them.

JOAN. Oh, my lord, does God care for those who have no care? First the soldiers must fight, and then He will give the victory.

CHARLES. How did you recognise me without my crown?

JOAN. Gentle Dauphin, it was a good joke to put your crown on this boy, it doesn't take much to see that he's really a little nobody.

CHARLES. You're mistaken. The boy is the son of a great lord.

JOAN. Great lords are not the king.

CHARLES (*troubled*). Who told you I was the king? I don't look like a king.

JOAN. God told me, gentle Dauphin: Who appointed you from the beginning of time, through your father and your grandfather and all the line of kings, to be viceroy of His kingdom.

The ARCHBISHOP *and* LA TREMOUILLE *exchange a look of annoyance.*

ARCHBISHOP. Sire. The girl's answers are interesting: they show a remarkable good sense. But in a matter as delicate as this you cannot surround yourself with precautions too strict or thorough. A commission of learned theologians must question and examine her very closely. We will then discuss their report in Council, and decide if it is timely for you to give this girl a longer hearing. There's no need for her to importune you any further today. First of all I shall interrogate her myself. Come here, my daughter.

CHARLES. Not at all. (*He stops* JOAN.) Stay where you are. (*He turns to the* ARCHBISHOP, *taking* JOAN'S *hand to give himself courage.*) I was the one she recognised. I was the one she spoke to. I wish you to leave me alone with her: all of you.

ARCHBISHOP. This blunt dismissal, sir: it is quite extraordinary, it is improper! Apart from all else, you should at least think of your own security . . .

CHARLES (*fearful for a moment, but he looks at* JOAN *and pulls himself together*). I am the only judge of that. (*He recites*:) Through my father, my grandfather, and all the line of kings . . . (*He winks at* JOAN.) Isn't that right? (*He turns to the others, imperturbable.*) Leave us, my lords, when the king commands it.

They ALL *bow, and go.*

CHARLES *keeps his regal pose for a moment, and then explodes with laughter.*

They've gone, they've gone! Did I do that, or did you? It's the first time in my life I have ever made myself obeyed. (*He looks at her, suddenly anxious.*) I hope there is nothing in what the Archbishop was trying to suggest. You haven't come here to kill me? There isn't a knife hidden about you somewhere?

He looks at her, and she smiles gravely.

No. You reassure me. I had forgotten, among all these pirates in my court, how reassuring a smile could be. Are there many of you in my kingdom with such honest faces?

JOAN (*still smiling gravely*). Yes, sir, very many.

CHARLES. But I never see you. Only ruffians, hypocrites, and whores: my entourage. Though of course there's my little queen, who has a certain amount of charm but not many brains. (*He goes back to his throne, his feet on the rail, and sighs*). Well, there you are. I suppose now you have to start boring me. You're going to tell me to become a great king.

JOAN (*gently*). Yes, Charles.

CHARLES. Don't let's bother. We shall have to stay shut up here together for an hour at least, to impress them. If you talk to me about God and the kingdom of France for an hour, I shall never last out. I propose instead we talk about something quite different. Do you play cards?

JOAN (*opening her eyes wide*). I don't know what it is.

CHARLES. It's an amusing game they invented for Papa, to distract him during his illness. You'll see, I shall teach you. I've played so often now I've got tired of it, but I think you may like it if you've never played before. (*He goes to rummage about in a chest.*) I hope they haven't stolen them from me. They steal everything here. And a pack of cards, you know, costs a lot of money. Only the royal princes have them. Mine were left to me by my father. I shall never have enough money to buy myself another pack. If those devils have stolen them . . . No, here they are. (*He returns with the cards.*) You knew Papa was mad, did you? Sometimes I hope I'm really his son, so that I can be sure I'm the true king; and then, at other times I hope I'm a bastard, so that I don't have to dread going mad before I'm thirty.

JOAN (*gently*). And which of the two would you prefer, Charles?

CHARLES (*turning in surprise*). Good heavens, are you calling me Charles? This is turning out to be a most surprising day. I believe I'm not going to be bored, for once; it's marvellous.

JOAN. Not now, Charles, or ever again.

CHARLES. Extraordinary.—Which of the two would I prefer? Well, I suppose on the days when I have some courage I would rather take the risk of going mad, and be the true king; and on the days when I haven't I would rather let everything go, and retire on my twopence-ha'penny to somewhere abroad, and live in peace. Have you met Agnes?

JOAN. No.

CHARLES (*shuffling the cards*). No, of course you haven't. Retiring wouldn't do for her. And I couldn't afford her then. She is always wanting me to buy her things.

JOAN (*suddenly grave*). And today: are you feeling brave today, Charles?

CHARLES. Today? (*He ponders a moment.*) Yes, it seems to me I feel fairly brave. Not very, but fairly. Well, you saw how I packed off the Archbishop.

JOAN. How would you like to be brave all the time, from today onwards?

CHARLES (*leaning forward, interested*). Do you mean you know the secret?

JOAN. Yes.

CHARLES. Are you some sort of a witch? You needn't be afraid to tell me; it isn't something I object to. I promise you I won't repeat it. Those executions horrify me. I was taken once to see them burn a heretic. I was sick all night.

JOAN (*smiling*). No, I'm not a witch, Charles. But I know the secret.

CHARLES. Would you sell it to me, without letting the others know about it? I'm not very well off, but I could make you a draft on the Treasury.

JOAN. I will give it to you, Charles.

CHARLES (*suspiciously*). For nothing?

JOAN. Yes.

CHARLES. Then I'm not interested. A secret is either no good, or far beyond my means. Disinterested people are too rare, at any price. (*He shuffles the cards.*) I've taken to behaving like a fool, so that I shall be left in peace, but I know more than you think I know. I'm not so easily gulled.

JOAN. You know too much.

CHARLES. Too much? You can never know too much.

JOAN. Sometimes; it is possible.

CHARLES. I have to defend myself. You would soon see, if you were here in my position! If you were alone, among a lot of brutes whose one idea is to stab you when you are least expecting it, and if you've been born a weak sort of fellow, as I was, you would soon realise the only way to steer safely through it is by being more clever than they are. And I am; much more clever. Which is why I more or less hang on to my throne.

JOAN (*puts her hand on his arm*). I shall be with you now, defending you.

CHARLES. Do you think you will?

JOAN. And I'm strong. I'm not afraid of anything.

CHARLES (*sighing*). You're very lucky! (*He deals the cards.*) Sit down on the cushion; I'm going to teach you to play cards.

JOAN (*smiling, sitting close to the throne*). All right. And then I'll teach you something.

CHARLES. What?

JOAN. Not to be afraid. And not to know too much.

CHARLES. Now pay attention. You see the cards, and these pictures on them? There's something of everything here: knaves, queens, kings: the same as in the world: and here are the commoners: spades, hearts, clubs, diamonds. Those are the troops. There are plenty of them, you can lose as many as you like. You deal the cards without looking at them, and fate either gives you a good hand, or a bad hand, and then the battle begins. The higher cards can capture the lower cards. Which do you think is the strongest?

JOAN. The king is.

CHARLES. Well, he is almost the strongest, but there's one stronger still. This card here, for instance, the single heart. Do you know what it's called?

JOAN. God, of course: because He's the only one who commands kings.

CHARLES (*annoyed*). No, it isn't at all. For goodness sake let God alone for five minutes. For the time being we're playing cards. It's called the ace.

JOAN. Then the game of cards is ridiculous. What can be stronger than a king, except God?

CHARLES. The ace, in fact. The ace, or God if you like; but there's one in each camp. You see: ace of hearts, ace of spades, ace of clubs, ace of diamonds. One for each of them. You're not so intelligent as I thought you were. Do you think the English don't say their prayers, as well as us? And, what's more, to a God who protects them, and gives them victories over us. And my cousin, the Duke of Burgundy, he has a God for Burgundy, in just the same way: a smallish one, maybe, but a bold one, a cunning one, who gets my cousin out of difficulties very well. God is with everybody, my girl. He marks the points, and keeps the score. But, in the long run, He plumps for the people who have the most money and the biggest armies. So why do you imagine He should be with France, now that France has got nothing at all?

JOAN. Perhaps for that reason: because she has nothing at all, Charles.

CHARLES (*shrugging his shoulders*). You don't know Him!

JOAN. I do. God isn't with the strongest; He is with the bravest. There's the difference. God hasn't any love for cowards.

CHARLES. Then He doesn't love me. And if He doesn't love me, why do you expect me to love Him? All He had to do was to give me some courage. I don't ask for anything better.

JOAN (*severely*). Do you think He's your nurse, with no one else to think about but you? Why can't you make the best of what you have got; I know He has made you weak in the legs. . . .

CHARLES. You've noticed that? He ought to have managed better than that. Particularly with the present fashions. It's because of my legs that Agnes can't bring herself to love me. If He had only an eye for proportion, and hadn't given me my big knees as well. . . .

JOAN. Well, I grant you that. He didn't go to much trouble over your knees. But there was something else that more concerned Him; His eye was on your head and your heart, Charles, where you most resemble Him. And there it is He makes you free, to be whatever you will. You can use them to play cards, or to outmanœuvre the Archbishop for a time, though in the end you have to pay for it; or else you can use them to make the house of Valois glorious again, and remake the kingdom. Your little queen gave you a son, Charles. What are you going to leave the boy when you die? This wretched scrap of France, nibbled by the English? If so, when he grows up, the boy will be able to say, as you did just now, that God hasn't any interest in him. You are God, Charles, to your little son; and you have to take care of him.

CHARLES (*groans*). But I keep telling you, everything frightens me.

JOAN (*coming nearer to him*). You shall have the secret now, Charles. But don't give me away when I tell you first that everything frightens me, too. Do you know why M. de la Tremouille isn't afraid of anything?

CHARLES. Because he is strong.

JOAN. No. Because he is stupid. He never imagines anything. Wild boars, and bulls, and barrel-headed oxen are never afraid of anything, either. And I tell you this: it has been even more complicated for me to get to you than it will be for you to get to Orleans and refashion your kingdom. I had to explain to my father, and that was a bad enough beginning. He wouldn't believe I wanted anything, except to go dragging off after the soldiers; and so he beat me, and, my goodness, the English don't hit any harder than he does. And then I had to make my mother cry; there was nothing worse than that; and then to convince Beaudricourt, who didn't want to think of anything except adding one more to his list of sins. Don't think I haven't been afraid. I was afraid all the time, from the very beginning.

CHARLES. Then how have you done it?

JOAN. Just as I should have done without the fear. That's all the difficulty there is, Charles. Try it once, and see. You say: one thing is obvious, I'm frightened, which is nobody's business but mine, and now on I go. And on you go. And if you see something ahead which nothing can overcome . . .

CHARLES. Like Tremouille enjoying one of his rages—

JOAN. Yes, if you like. Or the unshakable English facing Orleans in their fortress built like rocks. You say: Here it is—they outnumber us, their walls are as thick as the length of a giant's arm, their cannons out-thunder thunder, their arrows out-rain the rain. So be it. I'm frightened. Now I've realised how frightening it is, on we go.—And the English are so astonished, they begin to be frightened themselves, and you get through! You get through because you think deeper, imagine more, and get your fear over first. That's the secret of it.

CHARLES. But is it always so successful?

JOAN. Always. As long as you turn and face what frightens you. But the first step has to be yours; He waits for that.

CHARLES (*after a pause*). You think we could try your secret?

JOAN. We have to try it.

CHARLES (*suddenly frightened by his temerity*). Tomorrow, perhaps. By tomorrow I shall have had time to prepare for it.

JOAN. No, Charles; now; you're ready now.

CHARLES. Do you mean that I'm ready to call the Archbishop and La Tremouille? That I'm ready to tell them that I've given you command of the army, and then sit calmly back and watch their faces?

JOAN. Absolutely ready.

CHARLES. I'm scared out of my life.

JOAN. Then the worst is over. One thing is essential: you mustn't be still frightened after you've called them. Are you sure you are as frightened as you possibly can be?

CHARLES (*his hand on his belly*). Oh yes, I agree with you.

JOAN. Wonderful! That's an enormous advantage. When they start to be frightened, you will have got over it already. The whole scheme is to be afraid first, before the battle begins. You'll soon see. I'll call them. (*She calls offstage.*) My Lord Archbishop, M. de la Tremouille! M. le Dauphin wishes to speak to you.

CHARLES (*taken by panic*). Oh dear, I'm so frightened! Goodness, goodness, I'm so frightened.

JOAN. That's it, that's right Charles; more frightened still!

CHARLES (*his teeth chattering*). I can't be more frightened: it's impossible!

JOAN. Then we have the victory! God has joined you; He says "Charles is afraid, but still he calls them." In eight hours we shall hold Orleans!

(*Enter the* ARCHBISHOP *and* LA TREMOUILLE, *surprised.*)

ARCHBISHOP. You called us, your Highness?

CHARLES (*suddenly, after a last look at* JOAN). Yes: I've come to a decision, my lord, and it also concerns you, M. de la Tremouille. I am giving the command of my royal army to this Maid here. (*He suddenly shouts.*) If you don't agree, M. de la Tremouille, I must ask you to surrender your sword to me. You are under arrest!

(LA TREMOUILLE *and the* ARCHBISHOP *stand petrified.*)

JOAN (*clapping her hands*). Well done! Now you know how simple it is! Do you see their faces, Charles? Look at them: do look at them! Who is frightened now, Charles?

She bursts out laughing; CHARLES *begins to laugh as well: they rock with laughter, unable to stop; and the* ARCHBISHOP *and* LA TREMOUILLE *seem turned to stone.*

(JOAN *drops suddenly on to her knees, crying*) Thank you, God!

CHARLES (*also kneeling*). On your knees, M. de la Tremouille, on to your knees! And give us your blessing, Archbishop: no hesitating: give us your blessing! Now that we've all been thoroughly frightened, we must make straight for Orleans!

LA TREMOUILLE *is on his knees, stupefied by the blow.*

The ARCHBISHOP, *bewildered, mechanically gives his blessing.*

PART TWO

WARWICK (*laughing and coming forward with* CAUCHON). In point of fact, that wasn't exactly how it happened. They called a meeting of the Council, and discussed the matter for hours. In the end they agreed to use Joan as a sort of flagpole to nail their colours to: an attractive little mascot, well qualified to charm the general public into letting themselves be killed. The best we could do to restore the balance was to treble the men's drink ration before they went into action, though it had nothing like as good an effect. We started being beaten from that time on, against all the laws of strategy. I know some people have said there was nothing miraculous about that. They maintain that our system of isolated forts around Orleans was ludicrous, and all the enemy had to do was attack: which is what Joan made them agree to try. But that's not true. Sir John Talbot was no fool. He knew his job thoroughly well; as he has proved again and again, both before this regrettable business, and since. His system of fortification was theoretically impregnable. No: we must have the grace to admit there was more in it than that: a strong element of the imponderable—or God, as you might say, my Lord Bishop—which the rules of strategy don't provide for. Without question, it was Joan: singing like a lark in the sky over the heads of your French armies on the march. I am very fond of France, my Lord: which is why I should be most unhappy if we lost her. This lark singing in the sky, while we all take aim to shoot her down: that seems very like France to me. Or at least like the best of her. In her time she has had plenty of fools, rogues and blunderers; but every now and then a lark sings in her sky, and the fools and the rogues can be forgotten. I am very fond of France.

CAUCHON (*gently*). But still you take aim and shoot her down.

WARWICK. A man is a mass of contradictions, my lord Bishop. It isn't unusual in him to kill what he loves. I love animals, but I hunt them, too.

He suddenly gets up, looking stern. He raps with his stick on his boot, and makes a sign to TWO SOLDIERS *who come forward.*

Come along now: the lark has been caught. The cage of Compiègne has shut her in. The singing is over; and Charles and his court are leaving her there, without a second glance. They're going back to their old political methods, now that their little mascot isn't bringing them luck any more.

Indeed, CHARLES, LA TREMOUILLE, *and the* ARCHBISHOP *have slyly got up and edged away from* JOAN, *who is on her knees, praying. She starts up astonished to be alone, and sees* CHARLES *deserting her. The* GUARDS *begin to drag her away.*

CAUCHON. Your king has left you, Joan! There's no reason now to go on defending him. Yesterday we read you the letter he has sent to every town, telling them to say he repudiates you.

JOAN (*after a pause, quietly*). He is my king.

CHARLES (*in a low voice to the* ARCHBISHOP). That letter is going to be thrown in our teeth for a long time yet.

ARCHBISHOP (*also aside*). It had to be, sir: it was absolutely necessary. At this juncture, the cause of France cannot be linked in any way with Joan's.

CAUCHON. Joan: listen carefully, and try to understand what I'm saying. Your king is not our king. A treaty in rightful and due form has made Henry the Sixth of Lancaster King of France and England. Your trial is not a political trial. We are simply trying with all our power and with all our faith to lead a lost sheep back into the fold of our Holy Mother Church. But as men, Joan, we consider ourselves to be faithful subjects of His Majesty King Henry. We have as great and sincere a love of France as you: and because of that we recognise him as our sovereign: so that France can rise up again out of her ruins, dress her wounds, and be free of this appalling, interminable war which has drained all her strength. The useless resistance of the man you call your king, and his absurd pretensions to a throne which isn't his, appear to us to be acts of rebellion and terrorism against a peace which was almost assured. The puppet who you served is not our master, be certain of that.

JOAN. Say what you like, you can't alter the truth. This is the king God gave you. Thin as he is, with his long legs and his big, bony knees.

CHARLES (*to the* ARCHBISHOP). This is really most disagreeable.

ARCHBISHOP. For a little while we have to have patience; but they mean to hurry through the trial and burn her, and after that we shall not be disturbed. You must surely admit, sir, the English have done us a good turn, making themselves responsible for her arrest and execution. If they hadn't done it, we ourselves should have had to, some day or other. She was becoming impossible!

They withdraw, unnoticed.

CAUCHON. We know by many of your answers, insolent though they were, that you're not slow of understanding, Joan. Put yourself for a moment in our place. How can you suppose that we, men with most earnest human convictions, can agree that God has sent you to oppose the cause we defend? How can you think, only because you say voices have spoken to you, that we should believe God to be against us?

JOAN. You will know when we have beaten you.

CAUCHON (*shrugging*). You are answering like a self-willed, obstinate child. Considering the question now as priests and defenders of our Holy Mother Church, have we any better reason to put faith in what you tell us? Do you think you are the first who has heard Voices?

JOAN. No, of course not.

CAUCHON. Neither the first, nor the last, Joan. Now, do you believe that each time a little girl goes to her village priest and says: I have seen some saint, or the Blessed Virgin, I have heard Voices which have told me to do one thing or another—that her priest should believe and encourage her: and how long then would the Church still remain?

JOAN. I don't know.

CAUCHON. You don't know; but you are full of good sense, and that is why I am trying to lead you to reason with me. Have you not been in command in battle, Joan?

JOAN. Yes, I was in command of hundreds of good soldiers who followed me, and believed me.

CAUCHON. You were in command. And if on the morning of some attack one of your soldiers had heard voices persuading him to attack by another gate than the one you had chosen, or not to attack at all, what would you have done?

JOAN (*speechless for a moment, before she suddenly bursts out laughing*). My lord Bishop, it's easy to see you're a priest! It's clear you don't know much about our men. They can drink and swear and fight, but they're not ones for hearing Voices!

CAUCHON. A joke is no answer, Joan. But you gave your answer before you spoke, in the second of hesitation when you were held and disarmed by what I said to you. And you see it is true: that the Church militant is an army in a world still overrun by infidels and the powers of evil. The Church owes obedience to our Holy Father the Pope and his bishops, as your soldiers owed obedience to you and your lieutenants. If a soldier says on the morning of attack that Voices have told him not to advance, in yours or any army in the world he would be silenced. And far more brutally than this effort of ours to reason with you.

JOAN (*gathering herself together, on the defensive*). You have a right to hit at me with all your power. And my right is to say No, and go on believing.

CAUCHON. Don't make yourself a prisoner of your own pride, Joan. You can surely see that we have no possible reason, either as men or as priests, to believe that your mission is divinely inspired. You alone have a reason to believe so; encouraged by the fiend who means to damn you, and also, as long as you were useful to them, by those whom you served. You served them; and yet the way they behaved before your capture, and their explicit repudiation since, certainly proves that the most intelligent of them never believed you. No one believes you, Joan, any longer, except the common people, who believe everything, and tomorrow they will believe half a dozen others. You are quite alone.

JOAN *makes no reply, sitting small and quiet among them all.*

I beg you not to imagine that your strong will and your stubborn resistance to us is a sign that God is upholding you. The devil has also got intelligence and a tough hide. His mind had the flash of a star among the angels before he rebelled.

JOAN (*after a pause*). I am not intelligent, my lord. I am a peasant girl, the same as any other in my village. But when something is black I cannot say it is white, that is all.

Another pause.

PROMOTER (*suddenly rising up behind her*). What was the sign you gave to the man you are calling your king, to make him trust you with his army?

JOAN. I don't know what you mean: what sign I gave.

PROMOTER. Did you make him sip mandragora, to be a protection against harm?

JOAN. I don't know what you mean by mandragora.

PROMOTER. Your secret has a name, whether it's a potion or a formula, and we mean to know it. What did you give him at Chinon to make him so heroic all of a sudden? A Hebrew name? The devil speaks all languages, but he delights in Hebrew.

JOAN (*smiling*). No, my lord: it has a French name. I gave him courage.

CAUCHON. And so you think that God, or at least the power you believe to be God, took no part in this.

JOAN. He always takes part, my lord Bishop. When a girl speaks two words of good sense and someone listens, there He is. But He is thrifty; when those two words of good sense will do, He isn't likely to throw away a miracle.

LADVENU (*quietly*). The answer's a good one, in all humility, my lord: it can't be held against her.

PROMOTER (*with venom, to* JOAN). I see, I see! So you don't believe in such miracles as we are shown in the gospels? You deny what was done by Our Lord Jesus at the marriage of Cana? You deny that He raised Lazarus from the dead?

JOAN. No, my lord. What is written in Holy Scripture was surely done. He changed the water into wine just as easily as He created them. And it was no more extraordinary for Him, the Master of life and death, to make Lazarus live again, than for me to thread a needle.

PROMOTER (*yelping*). Listen to that! Listen to that! She says there is no such thing as a miracle!

JOAN. No, my lord. I say that a true miracle is not done with a magic wand or incantation. The gypsies on our village green can do miracles of that sort. The true miracle is done by men themselves, with the mind and the courage which God has given to them.

CAUCHON. Are you measuring the gravity of your words, Joan? You seem to be telling us quite calmly that God's true miracle on earth is man, who is nothing but sin and error, blindness and futility. . . .

JOAN. And strength, too, and courage, and light sometimes when he is deepest in sin. I have seen men during the battles. . . .

LADVENU. My lord, Joan is talking to us in her rough and ready language about things which come instinctively from her heart, which may be wrong but are surely simple and genuine. Her thoughts are not so schooled that she can shape them to our way of argument. Perhaps by pressing her with questions we run the risk of making her say more than she meant, or something different from her belief.

CAUCHON. Brother Ladvenu, we shall try and estimate as fairly as we can what part lack of skill plays in her answers. But our duty is to question her to the last point of doubt. We are not perfectly sure, remember, that our concern now is *only* the question of Joan. So then, Joan, you excuse man all his faults, and think him one of God's greatest miracles, even the only one?

JOAN. Yes, my lord.

PROMOTER (*yelping, beside himself*). It's blasphemy! Man is filth, lust, a nightmare of obscenity!

JOAN. Yes, my lord. He sins; he is evil enough. And then something happens: it may be he is coming out of a brothel, roaring out his bawdy songs in praise of a good time, and suddenly he has thrown himself at the reins of a runaway horse to save some child he has never seen before; his bones broken, he dies at peace.

PROMOTER. But he dies like an animal, without a priest, in the full damnation of sin.

JOAN. No, my lord; he dies in the light which was lighted within him when the world began. He behaved as a man, both in doing evil and doing good, and God created him in that contradiction to make his difficult way.

A storm of indignation from the PRIESTS *when they hear this said. The* INQUISITOR *quietens them, and suddenly rises.*

INQUISITOR (*calmly*). Joan. I have let you speak throughout this trial, with scarcely a question to you. I wanted you to find your way clearly to your position. It has taken some time. The Promoter could see only the Devil, the Bishop only the pride of a young girl intoxicated with success; I waited for something else to show itself. Now it has happened—I represent the Holy Inquisition. My Lord the Bishop told you just now, with great humanity, how his human feelings linked him with the English cause, which he considers just; and how they were confounded by his sentiments as priest and bishop, charged with the defence of our Mother Church. But I have come from the heart of Spain. This is the first time I have been sent to France. I know nothing of either the Armagnac faction, or of the English. It is indifferent to me who shall rule France, whether your prince or Henry of Lancaster. As for that strict discipline of our Mother Church which will not tolerate those who play a lone hand, however well-intentioned, but directs them back into the fold: I'll not say that is indifferent to me; but it is perhaps a secondary task, which the Inquisition leaves to the Bishops and the parish priests. The Holy Inquisition has something higher and more secret to defend than the temporal integrity of the Church. She wrestles on an invisible ground, inwardly, with an enemy only she knows how to detect, of whom only she can estimate the danger. It has been her care sometimes to take up arms against an Emperor; at other times the same solemnity, the same vigilance, the same fixity of purpose have been deployed against some old apparently inoffensive scholar, or a herdsman buried away in a mountain village, or a young girl. The princes of the earth laugh very heartily to see the Inquisition give itself such endless care, when for them a piece of rope or a sergeant's signature on a death warrant would be enough. The Inquisition lets them laugh. It knows how to recognise the enemy; it knows better than to under-estimate him wherever he may be found. And its enemy is not the devil, not the devil with the cloven hooves, the chastener of troublesome children, whom my lord Promoter sees on every side. His enemy, you yourself spoke his name, when at last you came into the open: his only enemy, is man. Stand up, Joan, and answer me. I am your interrogator now.

JOAN *rises and turns towards him. He asks in an expressionless voice:*

Are you a Christian?

JOAN. Yes, my lord.

INQUISITOR. You were baptized, and in your earliest years you lived in the shadow of the church whose walls touched the walls of your home. The church bells ruled over your day, your playtime, your work, and your prayers. The emissaries we sent to your village have all come back with the same story: you were a little girl full of piety. Sometimes, instead of playing and running about with other children, though you were not a solemn child, you delighted to play, yet you would slip away into the church, and for a long time you would be there alone, kneeling, not even praying, but gazing at the coloured glass of the window.

JOAN. Yes. I was happy.

INQUISITOR. You had a friend you loved very dearly, a little girl called Haumette.

JOAN. Yes, my lord.

INQUISITOR. And when you made up your mind to leave for Vaucouleurs, already believing that you would never go back, you said goodbye to all your other friends, but you passed her house by.

JOAN. Yes. I was afraid to be too unhappy.

INQUISITOR. But you cared for more than only those you loved most. You cared for old people in sickness, children in poverty. And later on, when you fought in your first battle, you stood among the wounded and cried very bitterly.

JOAN. French blood was being shed; it was hard to bear.

INQUISITOR. Not only because it was French blood. A bully who had captured two English soldiers in a skirmish outside Orleans, knocked one of them down because he didn't move fast enough for him. You jumped off your horse, took the man's head on your knee, wiped the blood from his mouth, and helped him in his dying, calling him your little son, and promising him Heaven.

JOAN. How is it you can know that, my lord?

INQUISITOR. The Holy Inquisition knows everything, Joan. It weighed your human tenderness in the scales before it sent me to judge you.

LADVENU (*rising*). My Lord Inquisitor, I am happy to hear you recalling all these details which until now have been passed over in silence. Yes, indeed, everything we know of Joan since her earliest years has been gentleness, humility, and Christian charity.

INQUISITOR (*turning upon him, suddenly stern*). Silence, Brother Ladvenu! I ask you to remember that I stand here for the Holy Inquisition, alone qualified to make the distinction between Charity, the theological virtue, and the uncommendable, graceless, cloudy drink of the milk of human kindness. (*He passes his eye over them all.*) Ah, my Masters! How quickly your hearts can be melted. The accused has only to be a little girl, looking at you with a pair of wide-open eyes, and with a ha'porth of simple kindness, and you're all ready to fall over yourselves to absolve her. Very good guardians of the faith we have here! I see that the Holy Inquisition has enough to occupy it still: and still so much has to be cut away, cut, cut, always the dead wood to be cut away: and after us, others will go on, still pruning, hacking away without mercy, clearing the ranks of unruliness, so that the forest will be sound from root to branch.

A pause, and then LADVENU *replies.*

LADVENU. Our Saviour also loved with this loving-kindness, my lord. He said: Suffer the little children to come unto me. He put His hand on the shoulder of the woman taken in adultery, and said to her: Go in peace.

INQUISITOR. I tell you to be silent, Brother Ladvenu! Otherwise I shall have to investigate your case as well as Joan's. Lessons from the Gospels are read to the congregations, and we ask the parish priests to explain them. But we have not translated them into the vulgar tongue, or put them into every hand to make of them what they will. How mischievous that would be, to leave untutored souls to let their imaginations play with the texts which only we should interpret. (*He quietens down.*) You are young, Brother Ladvenu, and you have a young man's generosity. But you must not suppose that youth and generosity find grace in the eyes of the faith's defenders. Those are transitory ills which experience will cure. I see that we should have considered your age, and not your learning which I believe is remarkable, before we invited you to join us here. Experience will soon make plain to you that youth, generosity, human tenderness are names of the enemy. At least, I trust it may. Surely you can see, if we were so unwise as to put these words you have spoken into the hands of simple people, they would draw from them a love of Man. And love of Man excludes the love of God.

LADVENU (*quietly*). And yet He chose to become a man . . .

INQUISITOR (*turning suddenly to* CAUCHON, *curtly*). My lord Bishop, in virtue of your discretionary power as president of these debates, I ask you to dispense for today with the collaboration of your young assessor. I shall inform you, when the sesssion is over, what conclusions will be entered against him, if needs be. (*He suddenly thunders.*) Against him or against whomsoever! For no one is of too great importance to be put out of our care: understand so! I would denounce myself, if God should allow me to be misled. (*He gravely crosses himself and ends.*) May He mercifully watch over me!

A breath of fear whispers through the tribunal. CAUCHON *says simply, with a gesture of distress to* BROTHER LADVENU.

CAUCHON. Leave us, Brother Ladvenu.

LADVENU (*before he moves off*). My lord Inquisitor, I owe you obedience, as I do my Reverend Lord Bishop. I will go, saying no more: except that my prayers must be to our Lord Jesus that He shall lead you to remember the fragility of your small enemy who faces you now.

INQUISITOR (*not answering until he has gone, and then speaking quietly*). Small, fragile, tender, pure: and therefore formidable. (*He turns to* JOAN *and says in his neutral tone.*) The first time you heard your Voices you were not yet fifteen. On that occasion they simply said to you: "Be a good and sensible child, and go often to church." In fact you were a happy and contented little girl. And the unhappiness of France was only old men's talk. And yet one day you felt you should leave the village.

JOAN. My Voices told me that I must.

INQUISITOR. One day you felt that you must take upon yourself the unhappiness of others around you. And you knew even then everything that would come of it: how glorious your ride would be, how soon it would come to an end, and once your King had been anointed, how you would find yourself where you are now, surrounded and alone, the faggots heaped up in the market place, waiting to be set alight. You know this is——

JOAN. My Voices told me that I should be captured, and then delivered.

INQUISITOR. Delivered! They very well might use that word: and you guessed in what way it might be taken, how ambiguously as a word from heaven. Death is a deliverance, certainly. And you set off all the same, in spite of your father and mother, and in spite of all the grave difficulties ahead of you.

JOAN. Yes, my lord; it had to be. If I had been the daughter of a hundred mothers and a hundred fathers: still it would have had to be.

INQUISITOR. So that you could help your fellow men to keep possession of the soil where they were born, which they fondly imagine belongs to them.

JOAN. Our Lord couldn't want the English to pillage, and kill and overrule us in our own country. When they have gone back across the sea, they can be God's children then in their own land. I shall pick no quarrel with them then.

PROMOTER. Presumption! Pride! Don't you think you would have done better to go on with your sewing and spinning beside your mother?

JOAN. I had something else to do, my lord. There have always been plenty of women to do women's work.

INQUISITOR. When you found yourself in such direct communication with heaven did it never occur to you to consecrate your life to prayer, supplicating that heaven itself should expel the English from France?

JOAN. God likes to see action first, my lord. Prayer is extra. It was simpler to explain to Charles that he ought to attack, and he believed me, and gentle Dunois believed me, too. And so did La Hire and Xantrailles, my fine couple of angry bulls! We had some joyful battles, all of us together. It was good to face every new day with friends, ready to turn on the English, ready to rescue France, ready to——

PROMOTER. Kill, Joan? Ready to kill? And does Our Lord tell us to kill for what we want, as though we had fangs and claws?

(JOAN *does not reply.*)

CAUCHON (*gently*). You loved the war, Joan . . .

JOAN (*simply*). Yes. It is one of the sins which I have most need of God's forgiveness for. Though in the evening I would look across the battlefield and cry to see that the joyous beginning to the morning had gone down in a heap of dead.

PROMOTER. And the next day, you began again?

JOAN. God wished it. While there remained one Englishman in France. It isn't difficult to understand. There was work to be done first, that was all. You are learned, and you think too much. You can't understand the simple things, but the dullest of my soldiers understands them. Isn't that true, La Hire?

LA HIRE *strides forward, in huge armour, gay and alarming.*

LA HIRE. You bet it's true.

Everybody finds himself pushed into the shade: this one figure is clear. A vague music of the fife is heard. JOAN *goes quietly up to him, incredulous, and touches him with her finger.*

JOAN. La Hire . . .

LA HIRE (*taking up again the comradeship of the battle mornings*). Well, Miss, we've had the bit of praying we agreed to have: what's the next thing? Do we take a bash at them this morning?

JOAN (*throwing herself into his arms*). It is La Hire, my dear, fat La Hire! You smell so good!

LA HIRE (*embarrassed*). A glass of wine and an onion. It's my usual morning meal. Excuse me, Miss: I know you don't like it, but I did my praying beforehand so that God shouldn't take against my breath. Don't come too near: I know I stink in a way.

JOAN (*pressed against him*). No: it's good.

LA HIRE. You don't want to make me feel awkward. Usually you tell me I stink and it's a shame for a Christian. Usually you say that if the wind carries in that direction I shall give us away to the goddams, I stink so much; and we shall ruin our ambush because of me. One quite small onion and two tots of red wine, no more. Of course, let's be honest, no water with it.

JOAN. Well, I was a fool if I said so. If an onion has a right to stink why shouldn't you?

LA HIRE. It's what war does for you. Be a clerk, or a priest, or a linen draper: no smell. But be a captain, you're bound to sweat. As for washing, up in the line: a man doesn't see the interest in it. There was no need to add the onion, I suppose: I ought to do with a bit of garlic sausage like the other fellows: it's better behaved when you come to conversation. But, look here, you wouldn't call it a sin, would you, eating the onion?

JOAN (*smiling*). No, La Hire: not a sin.

LA HIRE. You never know with you, you know.

JOAN. Have I pestered you with sins, La Hire? I was silly to tease you so much: it's odd, but there you are, a great bear smelling of sweat and onions and red wine, and you kill, and swear, and think of nothing except the girls. . . .

LA HIRE (*very astonished*). Who, me?

JOAN. You. Yes. Look astonished, you old rogue. And yet you shine in the hand of God as bright as a new penny.

LA HIRE. Is that a fact? I should have thought I'd bitched my chance of paradise years ago. But you think if I keep on praying as arranged, a bit every day, I might still get there?

JOAN. They're expecting you. I know that God's paradise must be full of ruffians like you.

LA HIRE. Is that a fact? It would make all the difference to feel that there were a few kindred spirits around. I wasn't much looking forward to being in a crowd of saints and bishops looking like Heaven's village idiot.

JOAN (*gaily thumping him*). Great Jackass! Of course Heaven's full of dunces. Hasn't our Lord said so? It may even be they're the only ones who get in: the others have had so many brains to sin with, they never get past the door.

LA HIRE (*uneasily*). You don't think, between ourselves, we'll get bored to death, do you, always on our best behaviour? Any fighting at all, do you imagine?

JOAN. All the day long.

LA HIRE (*respectfully*). Wait, now. Only when God isn't looking at us.

JOAN. But He's looking at you all the time, crackpot! He sees everything. And what's more, He is going to enjoy watching you at it. "Go it, La Hire," He'll say: "Bash the stuffing out of old Xantraille! Pitch into him, now! Show him what you're made of!"

LA HIRE. Is that a fact?

JOAN. Not in those words perhaps, but in His own way.

LA HIRE. By God Almighty. (*Enthusiastically.*)

JOAN (*suddenly stern*). La Hire!

LA HIRE (*hanging his head*). Sorry, miss.

JOAN (*pitilessly*). If you swear He will throw you out.

LA HIRE (*stammering*). I was feeling pleased, you see: had to thank Him somehow.

JOAN. So He thought. But don't do it again! We've talked quite enough for one morning. Let's get up on horseback and take a look at the day.

LA HIRE. It's dead country this morning. Not a soul to see.

They ride imaginary horses side by side.

JOAN. Look, we've got France all to ourselves—shall we ever see the world to better advantage? Here on horseback side by side: this is how it will be, La Hire, when the English have gone. Smell the wet grass, La Hire, isn't this why men go fighting? To ride out together smelling the world when the light of day is just beginning to discover it.

LA HIRE. So anyone can who likes to take a walk in his garden.

JOAN. No. I think death has to be somewhere near before God will show us the world like this.

LA HIRE. Suppose we should meet some English, who might also be liking the good smells of the morning?

JOAN. We attack them, we smite them, and send them flying. That's what we're here for!

A little pause.

(*She suddenly cries.*) Stop!

They draw in their horses.

There are three English over there. They've seen us. They're running away! No! Now they've turned back again: they've seen there are only two of us. They're attacking. You're not afraid, La Hire? No use counting on me; I'm only a girl, and I've got no sword. Will you fight them alone?

LA HIRE (*brandishing his sword with a delighted roar*). Hell, yes, by God I will! (*Shouting to the sky as he charges.*) I didn't say anything, God, I didn't say anything. Pay no attention . . .

He charges into the middle of the Tribunal: they scatter as he swings his sword to left and right. He disappears still fighting.

JOAN. He didn't say anything, God. He didn't say anything! He is as good as a French loaf. So all my soldiers are, though they kill, and loot, and swear: good as your wolves are, God, whom you created innocent. I will answer for all of them!

JOAN *is deep in prayer. The Tribunal has re-formed round her: the light has come back.* JOAN *raises her head, sees them, seems to shake herself free of a dream.*

La Hire and Xantrailles! Oh, we're not at the end of things yet. You can be sure they will come and deliver me with two or three or four hundred men . . .

CAUCHON (*quietly*). They came, Joan: right up to the gates of Rouen to find out how many of the English were in the town, and then they went away again.

JOAN (*dashed*). Oh, they went away? Without fighting? (*A silence; she looks up.*) Why, they have gone to find reinforcements, of course. I myself taught them, it is no good to attack willynilly, as they did at Agincourt.

CAUCHON. They withdrew to the South of the Loire; Charles is down there, disbanding his armies. He is tired of the war, and if he can he will make a treaty, to secure at least his own small portion of France. They will never come back again, Joan.

JOAN. That isn't true! La Hire will come back, even if he hasn't a chance.

CAUCHON. La Hire is only the captain of an army of mercenaries, who sold himself and his men to another Prince as soon as he found that yours was out to make peace. He is marching at this moment towards Germany, to find another country to plunder; simply that.

JOAN. It isn't true!

CAUCHON (*rising*). Have I ever lied to you, Joan? It is true. Then why will you sacrifice yourself to defend those who have deserted you? The only men on earth who are trying to save you—paradoxical though it may seem—are ourselves, your old enemies and now your judges. Recant, Joan: your resistance helps no-one now; your friends are betraying you. Return to the arms of your Mother Church. Humble yourself, she will lift you up again. I am convinced that deep in your heart you have never ceased to be one of her daughters.

JOAN. Yes, I am a daughter of the Church!

CAUCHON. Then give yourself into the care of your mother, Joan, without question. She will weigh your burden of error, and so release you from the anguish of judging it for yourself. You needn't think of anything any more: you will do your penance, whether it be heavy or light, and at last you will be at peace. Surely you have a great need of peace.

JOAN (*after a pause*). In what concerns the Faith, I trust myself to the Church. But what I have done I shall never wish to undo.

(*A stir among the priests. The* INQUISITOR *breaks in.*)

INQUISITOR. Do you hear, my masters? Do you see Man raising up his head, like a serpent ready to strike us dead? Do you understand now what it is you have to judge? These heavenly voices have deafened you as well as the girl, on my word they have! You have been labouring to discover what devil has been behind her actions. Would it were only a question of the devil. His trial would soon be over. The devil speaks our language. In his time he was an angel, and we understand him. The sum of his blasphemies, his insults, even his hatred of God, is an act of faith. But man, calm and transparent as he seems, frightens me infinitely more. Look at him: in chains, disarmed, deserted, no longer sure even in himself (isn't that so, Joan?) that the voices which have been silent for so long have ever truly spoken. Does he throw himself down, supplicating God to hold him again in His hand? Does he at least implore his Voices to come back and give light to his path? No. He turns away, suffers the torture, suffers humiliation and beating, suffers like a dumb animal, while his eyes fasten on the invincible image of himself; (*he thunders*) himself, his only true God! That is what I fear! And he replies—repeat it, Joan; you are longing to say it again; " But what I have done . . . "

JOAN (*quietly*) . . . I shall never wish to undo.

INQUISITOR (*repeats*). ' But what I have done I shall never wish to undo! '. You hear those words? And you will hear them said on the scaffold, at the stake, in the torture chamber, wherever they come to suffer for the errors they commit. And centuries hence they will be saying it; the hunting down of Man will go on endlessly. However powerful we become one day in one shape or another, however inexorably the Idea shall dominate the world, however rigorous, precise and subtle its organisation and its police, there will always be a man who has escaped, a man to hunt, who will presently be caught, presently be killed: a man who, even so, will humiliate the Idea at the highest point of its Power, simply because he will say " No " without lowering his eyes. (*He hisses through his teeth, looking at* JOAN *with hatred.*) An insolent breed! (*He turns again towards the Tribunal.*) Do you need to question her any more? Do you need to ask her why she threw herself from the height of the tower where she was imprisoned, whether to escape, or to destroy herself against the commandments of God? Why she has left her father and mother, put on the clothes of a man, and wears them still, against the commandments of the Church? She will give you the same reply, the reply of Man: What I have done, I have done. It is mine, and my doing. No-one can take it from me; no-one can make me disown it. All that you can do is kill me, to make me cry out no matter what under the torture, but make me say " Yes ", you cannot do. (*He cries to them.*) Ah well: by some means or other he must be taught to say Yes, whatever it may cost the world. As long as one man remains who will not be broken, the Idea, even if it dominates and pervades all the rest of mankind, will be in danger of perishing. That is why I require Joan's excommunication, her rejection from the bosom of the Church and that she should be given over to the secular arm for punishment. (*He adds neutrally, reciting a formula.*) Beseeching it nevertheless to limit its sentence on this side of death and the mutilation of the limbs. (*He turns to* JOAN.) This will be a paltry victory against you, Joan, but at least it will silence you. And, up to now, we have not thought of a better. (*He sits down again in silence.*)

CAUCHON (*gently*). My Lord Inquisitor is the first to ask for your excommunication, Joan. In a moment I am afraid my Lord Promoter will ask for the same thing. Each one of us will speak his mind and then I shall have to give my decision. Before lopping the dead branch, which you have become, and casting it far from her, your Holy Mother Church, to whom the one lost sheep is more dear than all the others, remember that, entreats you now for the last time.

CAUCHON *makes a sign, and a man comes forward.*

Do you know this man, Joan?

She turns to look and gives a little shudder of fear.

It is the master hangman of Rouen. In a short while from now you will belong to him, unless you give your soul into our keeping so that we can save it. Is the stake ready, Master Hangman?

HANGMAN. Quite ready, my lord. Higher than the regulation stake, such was the orders: so that the girl can be got a good view of from all sides. The nuisance of it for her is that I shan't be able to help her at all, she will be too high up.

CAUCHON. What do you call helping her, Master Hangman?

HANGMAN. A trick of the trade, my lord: it's the custom, when there aren't any special instructions. You wait till the first flames get up, and then I climb up behind, under cover of the smoke, and strangle the party. Then it's only the corpse that burns, and it isn't so bad. But with the instructions I've had, it's too high, and I won't be able to get up there. (*He adds simply*) So, naturally, it will take longer.

CAUCHON. Do you hear that, Joan?

JOAN (*softly*). Yes.

CAUCHON. I am going to offer you once more the hand of your Mother, the great hand which opens towards you to take you back and save you. But the delay can't be for long. You hear the noise outside, as though the sea had come up to the door? That is the sound of the crowd, who already have been waiting for you since daybreak. They came early to get good places: and there they are still, eating the food they brought with them, grumbling at their children, joking and singing, and asking the soldiers how long it will be before things begin to happen. They are not bad people. They are the same men and women who would have cheered you if you had captured Rouen. But things have turned out differently, that's all, and so instead they come to see you burned. As nothing very much ever happens to them, they make their adventures out of the triumphs or the deaths of the world's great ones. You will have to forgive them, Joan. All their lives long they pay dearly for being the common people; they deserve these little distractions.

JOAN (*quietly*). I do forgive them. And I forgive you, as well, my lord.

PROMOTER. Appalling, abominable pride! My lord the Bishop troubles to talk to you like a father, in the hope of saving your miserable soul, and you have the effrontery to say that you forgive him!

JOAN. My lord talks to me gently, but I don't know whether it is to save me or to overthrow me. And since in a little while he will have to burn me anyway, I forgive him.

CAUCHON. Joan: try to understand that there is something absurd in your refusal. You are not an unbeliever. The God you claim as your own is ours also. And we are, in fact, those whom God has ordained to guide you, through the apostle Peter upon whom His Church is built. God did not say to His creatures: You will understand My will from Me. He said " Thou art Peter, and upon this rock I will build My church . . . and its priests will be your shepherds . . . ". Do you think us unworthy priests, Joan?

JOAN (*quietly*). No.

CAUCHON. Then why will you not do as God has said? Why will you not resign your fault to the Church, as you did when you were a small girl, at home in your village? Has your faith so changed?

JOAN. (*crying out in anguish*). I want to submit to the Church. I want to receive the Holy Sacrament, but you won't let me!

CAUCHON. We will give it to you after your confession, and when your penance has begun; we only wait for you to say 'Yes'. You are brave, we know that indeed: but your flesh is still frail: you are surely afraid of dying?

JOAN (*quietly*). Yes. I'm afraid. But what else can I do?

CAUCHON. I think well enough of you, Joan, to know that fear in itself is not enough to make you draw back. But you should have another, greater fear: the fear of being deceived, and of laying yourself open to eternal damnation. Now, what risk do you run, even if your voices are from God, if you perform the act of submission to the priests of His church? If we do not believe in your Voices, and if nevertheless God has really spoken to you, then it is we who have committed the monstrous sin of ignorance, presumption and pride, and we who will have to make expiation through all eternity. We will take this risk for you, Joan, and you risk nothing. Say to us: 'I submit to you', say simply 'Yes', and you will be at peace, blameless, and safe in your redemption.

JOAN (*suddenly exhausted*). Why will you torture me so gently, my lord? I would far rather you beat me.

CAUCHON (*smiling*). If I beat you, Joan, I should only add to your pride: your pride which wishes to see you persecuted and killed. I reason with you because God gifted you with reason and good sense. I beseech you, because I know you have gentle feeling. I am an old man, Joan; I have no more ambitions in this world, and, like each of us here, I have put many to death in defence of the Church, as you have put many to death in defence of your Voices. It is enough. I am tired. I wish to die without adding to those deaths the death of a little girl. Help me.

JOAN (*after a pause*). What do I have to say?

CAUCHON. First of all you must understand that by insisting that God sent you, you no longer help anything or anyone. It is only playing into the hand of the English and the Executioner. Your king himself has declared in his letters that he doesn't in any way wish to owe the possession of his crown to a divine intervention of which you were the instrument.

JOAN *turns towards* CHARLES *in distress.*

CHARLES. Put yourself in my place, Joan! If there had to be a miracle to crown me King of France, it means I wasn't naturally king at all. It means I wasn't the true son of my father, or else my coronation would have followed of its own accord. All the other kings in my family have been crowned without needing a miracle. Divine help is all very well in its way, but suspect. And it's even more suspect when it stops. Since that unhappy Paris business, we've been beaten at every step; and then you let yourself be captured at Compiegne. They've got a little verdict up their sleeve for you, to denounce you as a witch, a heretic, the devil's intermediary, all in one. I prefer people to think you were never sent by anyone, God or devil. In that way, God has neither helped me, nor thrown me over. I won because I was the strongest at the time; I am being beaten now because I am the weakest, for the moment. That is healthy politics, if you understand?

JOAN (*softly*). Yes, I understand.

CAUCHON. I'm thankful to see you're wiser at last. We have put so many questions to you, you became confused. I am going to ask you three more, three essential ones. If you answer "Yes" three times, we shall all of us be saved, you who are going to die, and we who are putting you to death.

JOAN (*quietly, after a pause*). Ask them. I will see whether I can answer them.

CAUCHON. The first question is the really important one. If you answer "yes", the other answers will take care of themselves. Listen carefully, weighing each word:

Do you humbly put yourself into the hands of the Holy Apostolic Church of Rome; of our Holy Father the Pope and his bishops, that they shall estimate your deeds and judge you? Do you surrender yourself entirely and undoubtedly, and do you ask to be received again into the bosom of the Church? " It is enough for you to answer "yes ".

JOAN *after a pause, looks around her without moving. At last she speaks.*

JOAN. Yes, but . . .

INQUISITOR (*in a level voice*). With no " but ".

JOAN. I do not wish to be made to deny what my Voices have said to me. I do not wish to be made to bear witness against my king, or to say anything which will dim the glory of his coronation which is his, irrevocably, now and for ever.

The INQUISITOR *shrugs his shoulders.*

INQUISITOR. Such is the voice of man. There is only one way of bringing him to silence.

CAUCHON (*becoming angry*). Joan, Joan, Joan, are you mad? Do you not see this man in red who is waiting for you? Realise, understand, this is my last effort to save you, after this there is nothing more I can do. The Church still wishes to believe that you are one of her daughters. She has weighed with care the form her question should take, to help you on the path, and you cavil and try to bargain. There is no bargaining with your Mother, you impudent girl! You should beg her on your knees to wrap you in her cloak of love and protect you. Our Lord suffered far more than you in the humiliation and injustice of His Passion. Did He bargain or cavil when He came to die for you? Your suffering bears no comparison with His: scourged, mocked, spat upon: crowned with thorns, and nailed in a long agony between two thieves; you can never hope to rival His suffering! And He asks, through us, only one thing of you, that you submit to the judgment of His Church, and you hesitate.

JOAN (*after a pause, tears in her eyes*). Forgive me, my lord. I hadn't thought that Our Saviour might wish it. It is true that He has surely suffered more than I. (*A short pause, again, and she says*) I submit.

CAUCHON. Do you humbly and without any restriction supplicate the Holy Catholic Church to receive you again into her bosom, and do you defer to her judgment?

JOAN. I humbly supplicate my Mother Church to receive me again into her bosom, and I surrender myself to her judgment.

CAUCHON (*with a sigh of relief*). Good, Joan; well done. The rest will be simple enough now. Do you promise never again to take up arms?

JOAN. There is still work to be done . . .

CAUCHON. The work, as you call it, will be done by others. Don't be foolish, Joan. You are in chains, a prisoner, and in great danger of being burned. So whether you say yes or no the work will not be done by you. Your part is played out. The English have you in their grasp, and they'll not let you fight again. You said to us just now that when a girl has two words of good sense God is there performing His miracle. If God is protecting you, this is the time for Him to bring you the two words of good sense. So you promise never again to take up arms?

JOAN (*groaning*). But if my King still needs me?

CHARLES (*hastily*). Oh, goodness me! If it's me you're thinking about you can say yes at once. I don't need you any more.

JOAN (*heavily*). Then, yes; yes.

CAUCHON. Do you promise never to wear again these man's clothes, which is contrary to all the rules of decency and Christian modesty?

JOAN (*tired of the question*). You have asked me that ten times. The clothes are nothing. My Voices told me to wear them.

PROMOTER. The devil told you! Who except the devil would incite a girl to overthrow decency?

JOAN (*quietly*). Common sense, my lord.

PROMOTER (*sneering*). Common sense? Common sense is your strong card! Are breeches on a girl common sense?

JOAN. Of course, my lord. I had to ride horseback with the soldiers: I had to wear what they wore so that they wouldn't think of me as a girl, but as a soldier like themselves.

PROMOTER. A worthless reply! A girl who isn't damned to begin with wouldn't wish to ride with the soldiers!

CAUCHON. Even though it may be that these clothes had their purpose during the war, why do you still refuse to dress as a woman? The fighting's over, you are in our hands; yet you still refuse.

JOAN. It is necessary.

CAUCHON. Why?

JOAN (*hesitating for a moment, blushing*). If I were in a Church prison, I wouldn't refuse then.

PROMOTER. You hear this nonsense, my lord? What hair splitting: what deliberate prevarication! Why should she agree to modesty in a Church prison, and not where she is? I don't understand it, and I don't wish to!

JOAN (*smiling sadly*). And yet it is very easy to understand, my lord. You don't have to be very wise to see it.

PROMOTER. It is very easy to understand, and I don't understand because I'm a fool, I suppose? Will you note that, my lord? She insults me, in the exercise of my public office. She treats her indecency as something to glory in, boasts of it, in fact. Takes a gross delight in it, I've no doubt! If she submits to the Church, as she apparently wants to, I may have to give up my chief accusation of heresy; but as long as she refuses to put off this diabolical dress, I shall persist in my charge of witchcraft, even though pressure is put upon me by the conspiracy to shield her which I see presides over this debate. I shall appeal, if necessary, to the Council of Basle! The devil is in this, my lord, the devil is in it! I can feel his terrible presence! He it is who is making her refuse to give up these clothes of immodesty and vice, no doubt of that.

JOAN. Put me in a Church prison, and I shall give them up.

PROMOTER. You shall not make your bargains with the Church: my lord has already told you so. You will give up this dress altogether, or you will be condemned as a witch and burnt!

CAUCHON. If you accept the principle, Joan, why don't you wish to obey us now, in the prison where you are?

JOAN. I'm not alone there.

PROMOTER. Well? you're not alone there. Well? What of that?

JOAN. The English soldiers are on guard in the cell, all through the day, and through the night.

PROMOTER. Well? (*A pause.*) Do you mean to go on? Your powers of invention have failed you already, is that it? I should have thought the devil was more ingenious! You feel that you've been caught out, my girl, and it makes you blush.

CAUCHON (*quietly*). You must answer him, Joan. I think I understand but it must be you who tells us so.

JOAN (*after a moment of hesitation*). The nights are long, my lord. I am in chains. I do my best to keep awake, but sleep sometimes is too strong for me. (*She stops*).

PROMOTER (*more and more obtuse*). Well, what then? The nights are long, you are in chains, you want to sleep. What then?

JOAN (*quietly*). I can defend myself better if I wear these clothes.

CAUCHON (*heavily*). Has this been so all the time of the trial?

JOAN. Ever since I was captured, my lord, each night; and when you send me back there in the evening, it begins again. I've got into the way of not sleeping now, which is why my answers are so sleepy and muddled when I'm brought before you in the mornings. But each night seems longer; and the soldiers are strong, and full of tricks. I should as soon wear a woman's dress on the battlefield.

CAUCHON. Why don't you call the officer, and he would defend you?

JOAN (*after a pause*). They told me they would be hanged if I called for help.

WARWICK (*to* CAUCHON). Incredible. I never heard of such a thing! Quite possible in the French army. But in the English army, no, quite ridiculous. I shall inquire into this.

CAUCHON. If you would return, Joan, back to your Mother the Church who is waiting for you: promise to change from these clothes to the dress of a girl: the Church from now on would see you had no such fears.

JOAN. Then I do promise.

CAUCHON (*giving a deep sigh*). Good. Thank you, Joan, you have helped me. I was afraid for a time we should have no power to save you. We shall read your promise to adjure your sins: the document is all ready, you have only to sign it.

JOAN. I don't know how to write.

CAUCHON. You will make a cross. My lord Inquisitor, allow me to recall Brother Ladvenu so that he may read this to the prisoner. It is Brother Ladvenu who is responsible, at my request, for drawing up this paper. And, moreover, we have all to be here now, to pronounce sentence, now that Joan has returned to us. (*He leans towards him.*) You should be gratified, my lord: Man has said 'yes'.

INQUISITOR (*a pallid smile on his thin lips*). I am waiting until the conclusion; until the conclusion.

CAUCHON *calls to the* GUARD.

CAUCHON. Recall Brother Ladvenu!

PROMOTER (*whispering*). My lord Inquisitor, you won't allow them to do this?

INQUISITOR (*with a vague gesture*). If she has said 'yes' . . .

PROMOTER. My lord Bishop has conducted the enquiry

with an indulgence towards the girl which I can't begin to understand! And yet I have reliable information that he feeds well from the English manger. Does he feed even more rapaciously from the French? That is what I ask myself.

INQUISITOR (*smiling*). It is not what I ask myself, my lord Promoter. It is not of eating, well or better, that I am thinking, but of something graver. (*He falls on to his knees, oblivious of all around him.*) O Lord! It has pleased You to grant that Man should humble himself at the eleventh hour in the person of this young girl. It has been Your will that this time he shall say 'Yes'. But why has it also pleased You to let an evident and earthly tenderness be born in the heart of this old man who was judging her? Will you never grant, O Lord, that this world should be unburdened of every trace of humanity, so that at last we may in peace consecrate it to Thy glory alone?

BROTHER LADVENU *has come forward.*

CAUCHON. She is saved, Brother Ladvenu, Joan is saved. She has agreed to return to us, and to Holy Mother Church. Read her the act of Abjuration, and she will sign it.

LADVENU. Thank you, Joan. I was praying for you, I prayed that this might be possible. (*He reads*) 'I, Joan, known as the Maid, confess to having sinned, by pride, obstinacy, and wrong-doing, in pretending to receive revelation from Our Lord God, Father of all Men, through the means of His angels and His blessed Saints. I confess to having blasphemed by wearing immodest clothing, contrary to the ruling of our Holy Mother Church; and to having, by persuasion, incited men to kill one another. I forswear and abjure all these sins; I vow upon the Holy Gospels no more to wear these clothes or to bear arms. I promise to surrender myself in humility to our Holy Mother Church, and to our Holy Father the Pope of Rome, and to his Bishops, that they shall weigh and estimate my sins and wickedness. I beseech the Church to receive me again into her bosom; and I declare myself ready to suffer the sentence which it will please her to inflict upon me. In token of which I have signed my name to this Act of Abjuration which I profess I have understood.'

JOAN (*who seems now like a shy and awkward girl*). Do I make a circle or a cross? I can't write my name.

LADVENU. I will guide your hand. (*He helps her to sign.*)

CAUCHON. There; it is done, Joan; and the Church rejoices to see her daughter safely returned: and you know she rejoices more for the one lost sheep than for the ninety-and-nine safely enfolded. Your soul is saved, and your body will not be delivered up to the executioner. We condemn you only, through the mercy and the grace of God, to live the rest of your days a prisoner, in penitence of these errors, eating the bread of sorrow, drinking the water of anguish, so that in solitary contemplation you may repent; and by these means we shall admit you free of the danger of excommunication into which you were fallen. You may go in peace. (*He makes the sign of the cross over her.*) Take her away.

The SOLDIERS *lead* JOAN *away.*

The assembly breaks up into groups, conversing among themselves.

WARWICK (*coming up to* CAUCHON). Good enough, my lord; good enough. I was wondering for a moment or so what irresponsible whim was urging you to save the girl, and whether you hadn't a slight inclination to betray your king.

CAUCHON. Which king, my lord?

WARWICK (*with a touch of frigidity*). I said your king. I imagine you have only one? Yes; very uncertain for a time whether His Majesty was going to get his money's worth, owing to this fancy of yours. But then, when I thought about it, I could see this method would discredit young Charles equally well, without the disadvantages of martyrdom, which are unpredictable, when you think of the sort of sentimental reactions we get from the public. The resolute, unshakable girl, tied to the stake and burning in the flames, would have seemed, even so, something of a triumph for the French cause. This admission of guilt, on the other hand, is properly disgraceful. Perfect.

The CHARACTERS *move away.*

The lighting changes.

JOAN *is brought on by a* GUARD. AGNES SOREL *and* QUEEN YOLANDE *slip in beside her.*

AGNES (*coming forward*). Joan, Joan, my dear; we're so very happy it has all turned out well for you. Congratulations!

YOLANDE. Dying is quite useless, my little Joan: and whatever we do in life should have a use of some kind. People may have different opinions about the way my life has been lived, but at least I've never done anything absolutely useless.

AGNES. It was all so very stupid. Usually I adore political trials, and I particularly begged Charles to get me a seat; to watch someone fighting for his life is desperately exciting, as a rule. But really I didn't feel in the least happy when I was there. All the time I kept saying to myself: This is so very stupid: this poor little tomboy: she is going to get herself killed, and all for nothing. (*She takes* CHARLES' *arm*). Being alive is much better, you know, in every way.

CHARLES. Yes, of course it is; and when you practically ruined your chances, just because of me—well, I was very touched, naturally, but I didn't know how to make you understand that you were getting everything quite wrong. In the first place, as you might expect, I had taken the precaution to disown you, on the advice of that old fox of an Archbishop; but, more than that, I don't like people being devoted to me. I don't like being loved. It creates obligations, and obligations are detestable.

JOAN *does not look at them; she hears their prattle without seeming to hear it. Then suddenly she speaks quietly.*

JOAN. Take care of Charles. I hope he keeps his courage.

AGNES. Of course he will; why shouldn't he? My way with him is not so different from yours. I don't want him to be a poor little king who is always being beaten, any more than you do; and you shall see, I shall make our Charles a great King yet, and without getting myself burnt either. (*She adds in a low voice.*) I suppose it may be rather disillusioning to say so, Joan (though, of course, the two sexes are presumably what God wanted): but I do seem to get as much out of CHARLES by my little campaigns in the bedroom as ever you did with swords and angels.

JOAN (*murmuring*). Poor Charles . . .

AGNES. Why poor? He is perfectly happy, like all egoists:

and one of these days he is going to be a great king into the bargain.

YOLANDE. We shall see that done, Joan: not your way, but ours, and effectively enough.

AGNES (*with a gesture to the little* QUEEN). Even her little Majesty will help. She has just given him a second son. It is all she can do, but she does it very well. So if the first son dies there is no feverish worry. The succession is assured. You can be quite happy, Joan, that you're leaving everything in good order at the Court of France.

CHARLES (*after a sneeze*). Are you coming, my dear? This prison atmosphere is deadly, so damp it would really be healthier to sit in the river. Goodbye, Joan, for the moment; we'll come and visit you from time to time.

JOAN. Goodbye, Charles.

CHARLES. Goodbye, goodbye . . . I might say, if ever you come back to Court, you will have to call me Sire, like anybody else. I've seen to that, since my coronation. Even La Tremouille does it. It's a great victory.

They go off, rustling their robes.

JOAN (*murmuring*). Goodbye, Sire. I am glad I got you that privilege at least.

The light changes again, as the GUARD *leads her to a three-legged stool; she is alone now in her cell.*

Blessed St Michael, blessed ladies Catherine and Margaret, are you never going to come again and speak to me? Why have you left me alone since the English captured me? You were there to see me safely to victory: but it's now, in the suffering time, that I need you most. I know it would be too simple, too easy, if God always held me by the hand: where would the merit be? I know

He took my hand at the beginning because I was still too small to be alone, and later He thought I could make my own way. But I am not very big yet, God. It was very difficult to follow clearly everything the Bishop said to me. With the Canon it was easy: I could see where he was wrong, and where he was wicked, and I was ready to give him any answer which would make him furious. But the Bishop spoke so gently, and it often seemed to me he was right. Are you sure that you meant that, God? Did you mean me to feel so afraid of suffering, when the man said he would have no chance to strangle me before the flames could reach me? Are you sure that you want me to live? (*A pause. She seems to be waiting for an answer, her eyes on the sky.*) No word for me? I shall have to answer that question for myself, as well. (*A pause. She nods.*) Perhaps I am only proud and self-willed after all? Perhaps after all, I did imagine everything?

Another pause. She suddenly bursts into tears, her head on the stool. WARWICK *comes quickly on to the stage, preceded by a* GUARD *who leaves them at once.* WARWICK *stops, and looks at* JOAN, *surprised.*

WARWICK. Are you crying?

JOAN. Yes, my lord.

WARWICK. And I came here to congratulate you! That was a very happy solution to it all, I thought, the outcome of the trial, very. I told Cauchon, I was delighted you managed to avoid an execution. Quite apart from my own personal sympathy for you, the suffering is really frightful, you know, and quite useless, and most unpleasant to watch. I'm perfectly convinced you've done right to steer clear of martyrdom; better for us all. I congratulate you most sincerely. It was astonishing, considering the peasant stock you come from, that you should behave with such distinction. A gentleman is always ready, when he must, to die for his honour or his king, but it's only the riff-raff who get themselves killed for nothing. And then I was very entertained to see you queen the Inquisitor's pawn. A sinister character, that Inquisitor fellow! I detest intellectuals more than anybody. These fleshless people, what unpleasant fossils they are—Are you really a virgin?

JOAN. Yes.

WARWICK. Well, yes, of course you are. No woman would have spoken quite in the way you did. My fiancée in England, who's a very innocent girl, reasons exactly like a boy herself, and, like you, there's no gainsaying her. There's an Indian proverb—I don't know whether you may have heard it—which says it takes a virgin to walk on water. (*He gives a little laugh.*) We shall see how long she manages that, once she becomes Lady Warwick! Being a virgin is a state of grace. We adore them, and revere them, and yet, the sad thing is, as soon as we meet one we're in the greatest possible hurry to make a woman of her: and we expect the miracle to go on as if nothing had happened. Madmen! Just as soon as ever this campaign is over—it won't be long now, I hope: your little Charles is tottering to a fall—but as soon as it is, back I go to England, to do that very same idiotic thing. Warwick Castle is a very beautiful place, a bit big, a bit severe, but very beautiful. I breed superb horses—and my fiancée rides rather well, not as well as you do, but rather well. So she ought to be very happy there. We shall go fox-hunting, of course, and entertain fairly lavishly from time to time. I'm only sorry the circumstances make it so difficult to invite you over. (*An awkward pause.*) Well, there it is, I thought I'd pay you this visit, rather like shaking hands after a match, if you know what I mean. I hope I haven't disturbed you. Are my men behaving themselves now?

JOAN. Yes.

WARWICK. I should think they will certainly transfer you to a Church prison. But in any case, until they do, if there's any sign of a lapse, don't hesitate to report it to me. I'll have the blackguard hung. It's not really possible to have a whole army of gentlemen, but we can try. (*He bows.*) Madam.

He starts to go. JOAN *calls him back.*

JOAN. My lord!

WARWICK (*returning*). Yes?

JOAN (*without looking at him*). It would have been better, wouldn't it, if I had been burned?

WARWICK. I told you, for His Majesty's Government, the admission of guilt was just as good.

JOAN. But for me?

WARWICK. Unprofitable suffering. An ugly business. No, really, it wouldn't have been better. It would have been, as I told you just now, slightly plebeian, and ill-bred, and more than slightly stupid, to insist on dying just to embarrass everybody and make a demonstration.

JOAN (*as though to herself*). But I am ill-bred, I am stupid. And then, remember, my lord, my life isn't prepared and perfected like yours, running so orderly and smoothly between war, hunting, and your beautiful bride waiting for you in England. What is left of me when I am not Joan any longer?

WARWICK. Life isn't going to be very gay for you, I agree, not at first anyway. But things will adjust themselves in time, I don't think you need have any doubt of that

JOAN. But I don't want things to adjust themselves. I don't want to live through however long this 'in time' of yours will be. (*She gets up like a sleepwalker, and stares blindly ahead.*) Do you see Joan after living through it, when things have adjusted themselves: Joan, set free, perhaps, and vegetating at the French Court on her small pension?

WARWICK (*impatient*). My dear girl, I can tell you, in six months there won't be a French Court!

JOAN (*almost laughing, though sadly*). Joan accepting everything, Joan fat and complacent, Joan doing nothing but eat. Can you see me painted and powdered, trying to look fashionable, getting entangled in her skirts, fussing over her little dog, or trailing a man at her heels: who knows, perhaps with a husband?

WARWICK. Why not? Everything has to come to an end sometime. I'm going to be married myself.

JOAN (*suddenly cries out in another voice*). But I don't want everything to come to an end! Or at least not an end like that, an end which is no end at all. Blessed St. Michael: St. Margaret: St. Catherine! You may be silent now, but I wasn't born until you first spoke to me, that day in the fields: my life truly began when I did what you told me to do, riding horseback with a sword in my hand. And that is Joan, and no other one. Certainly not one sitting placid in her convent, pasty-faced and going to pieces in comfort: continuing to live as a tolerable habit: set free, they would call it! You kept yourself silent, God, while all the priests were trying to speak at once, and everything became a confusion of words. But You told St. Michael to make it clear to me in the very beginning, that when You're silent You have then the most certain trust in us. It is the time when You let us take on everything alone. (*She draws herself up.*) Well, I take it on, O

God: I take it upon myself! I give Joan back to You: true to what she is, now and forever! Call your soldiers, Warwick; call them, call them, quickly now: for I tell you I withdraw my admission of guilt: I take back my promises: they can pile their faggots, and set up their stake: they can have their holiday after all!

WARWICK (*bored*). Now for God's sake don't let's have any such nonsense, I do implore you. I told you, I'm very satisfied with things as they are. And besides, I loathe executions. I couldn't bear to watch you going through anything of the kind.

JOAN. You have to have courage, that's all; I shall have courage. (*She looks at his pale face and puts a hand on his shoulder.*) You're a good dear fellow, in spite of your gentlemanly poker-face; but there isn't anything you can do: we belong, as you say, to different ways of life. (*She unexpectedly gives him a little kiss on the cheeks, and runs off, calling.*) Soldiers, goddams! Hey there, goddams! Fetch me the clothes I wore to fight in, and when I'm back in my breeches tell all my judges Joan is herself again!

WARWICK *remains alone, wiping his cheek.*

WARWICK. How out of place this all is. What bad form. It's impossible to get on well with these French for long.

A great clamour.

CROWD. Death to the witch! Burn the heretic! Kill her, kill her, kill her!

All the actors return quickly, grasping faggots: the EXECUTIONER *dragging* JOAN *with the help of* TWO ENGLISH SOLDIERS. LADVENU *follows, very pale. The movement is rapid and brutal. The* EXECUTIONER, *with someone's help, perhaps the* PROMOTER'S, *makes a stake with the benches from the trial scene. They make* JOAN *climb up, they tie her to the stake, and nail a defamatory inscription over her head. The* CROWD *yells.*

CROWD. To the stake with the witch! To the stake! Shave her head, the soldier's bitch! To the stake! To the stake! Burn her!

WARWICK. Stupidity! Absurd stupidity! This is something we could have done without, perfectly well.

JOAN. A cross! Let me have a cross, a cross to hold: pity me!

PROMOTER. No, No! No cross for a witch!

JOAN. Give me a cross, a cross to hold, a crucifix!

CAUCHON. Ladvenu! To the parish church! Run, Ladvenu!

LADVENU *runs off.*

PROMOTER (*to the* INQUISITOR). This is most irregular! Aren't you going to protest, my lord?

INQUISITOR (*staring at* JOAN). With or without a cross, she has to be silenced, and quickly! Look at her, defying us. Are we never going to be able to master this flaunting spirit of man?

JOAN. A cross!

An ENGLISH SOLDIER *has taken two sticks, ties them together and calls to* JOAN.

SOLDIER. Hold on, wait a bit, my girl: here you are! What are they talking about, these two priests? They make me vomit. She's got a right to a cross, like anybody else.

PROMOTER (*rushing forward*). She is a heretic! I forbid you to give it to her!

SOLDIER (*jostling him off*). You choke yourself.

He offers the improvised cross to JOAN, *who clasps it against her, and kisses it.*

PROMOTER (*rushing to* WARWICK). My lord! This man ought to be arrested as a heretic. I insist that you arrest him immediately!

WARWICK. You make me tired, sir. I have eight hundred men like that, each one more heretical than the others. They are what I use to fight the wars with.

INQUISITOR (*to the* EXECUTIONER). Will you hurry and light the fire? Let the smoke cover her quickly, and hide her away out of our sight! (*To* WARWICK.) We must make haste! In five minutes everybody will have swung to her side, they will all be for her!

WARWICK. I'm very much afraid that has already happened.

LADVENU *runs in with a cross.*

PROMOTER (*yelling*). Don't dare to give her the cross, Brother Ladvenu!

CAUCHON. Let him alone, Canon: I order you to let him alone.

PROMOTER. I shall refer this matter to the court of Rome!

CAUCHON. You can refer it to the devil, if you like: for the present moment, the orders to be obeyed here are mine.

All this is rapid, hurly-burly, improvised, like a police operation.

INQUISITOR (*running from one to the other nervously*). We must be quick! We must be quick! We must be quick!

LADVENU (*who has climbed up to the stake*). Courage, Joan. We are all praying for you.

JOAN. Thank you, little brother. But get down: the flames will catch you: you will be burnt as well.

INQUISITOR (*who can't bear it any more, to the* EXECUTIONER). Well, man, have you done it yet, have you done it?

EXECUTIONER (*climbing down*). Yes, it's done, my lord, it's alight. In two minutes, you'll see, the flames will have reached her.

INQUISITOR (*with a sigh of relief*). At last!

CAUCHON (*falling on his knees*). O God, forgive us!

They all kneel, and start the prayers for the dead. The PROMOTER, *in a fury of hatred, remains standing.*

Get down on your knees, Canon!

The PROMOTER *looks like a cornered animal: he kneels.*

INQUISITOR (*who dare not look, to* LADVENU *who is near him and holding the cross for* JOAN). Is she looking straight in front of her?

LADVENU. Yes, my lord.

INQUISITOR. Without flinching?

LADVENU. Yes, my lord.

INQUISITOR (*almost sorrowfully*). And there is almost a smile on her lips, is there not?

LADVENU. Yes, my lord.

INQUISITOR (*with bowed head, overwhelmed, heavily*). I shall never be able to master him.

LADVENU (*radiant with confidence and joy*). No, my lord!

JOAN (*murmuring, already twisted with pain*). Blessed Michael, Margaret, and Catherine, you were brighter than these flames: let your voices burn me. O Lord Jesus, let them speak to me. Speak to me. In the fields, in the heat of the sun. Noon.

AGNES (*kneeling in a corner with* CHARLES *and the* QUEEN).

Poor little Joan. It is monstrous and stupid. Do you think she is suffering already?

CHARLES (*wiping his forehead and looking away*). There is still the agony to come.

The murmur of the prayers for the dead drowns the voices. Suddenly BEAUDRICOURT *bursts on to the stage, breathless from running.*

BEAUDRICOURT. Stop! Stop! Stop!

Everyone is startled; a moment of uncertainty.

(*To* CAUCHON).

This can't be the way it goes! Grant a stay of execution, and let me have time to think! For, as I said to her when she first came to me, I don't think clearly when suddenly put to it. But one thing I do see: we haven't done what we said we'd do. We haven't performed the coronation! We said that we were going to play everything! And we haven't at all. It isn't justice to her. And she has a right to see the coronation performed: it's a part of her story.

CAUCHON (*struck by this*). We did say so, indeed; you are right to remind us. You remember, gentlemen: the whole of her life to go through, was what we said. We were in too great a hurry to bring her to an end. We were committing an injustice!

CHARLES. You see! I knew they would forget my coronation. No one here remembers my coronation. And look what it cost me.

WARWICK. Well, really! The Coronation, now! And at this time of the day, as though their little victory came last. It would be most improper for me to attend any such ceremony; I shall go away. As far as I'm concerned it is all over, and Joan is burnt. His Majesty's Government has obtained its political objective.

He goes.

CAUCHON. Unchain her! Drag away the faggots! Give her the sword and the standard again!

He goes.

Everyone joyously drags down the stake and faggots.

CAUCHON. This man is quite right the real end of Joan's story, the end which will never come to an end, which they will always tell, long after they have forgotten our names or confused them all together: it isn't the painful and miserable end of the cornered animal caught at Rouen: but the lark singing in the open sky. Joan at Rheims in all her glory. The true end of the story is a kind of joy. Joan of Arc: a story which ends happily.

They have quickly set up an altar where the stake was standing. Bells suddenly ring out proudly. A procession forms with CHARLES, JOAN *a little behind him, then the* QUEENS, LA TREMOUILLE, *etc. The procession moves towards the altar.* EVERYONE *kneels. Only* JOAN *remains standing, leaning on her standard, smiling upwards, like a statue of her. The* ARCHBISHOP *puts the crown on* CHARLES'S *head, Bells, a salute of cannon, a flight of doves, a play of light perhaps, which throws the reflection of the cathedral stained glass across the scene, transforming it. The Curtain falls slowly on this beautiful illustration from a school prize.*

This play was first presented in London at the Arts Theatre Club, on 13 November 1963 with the following cast:

BITOS, *who plays Robespierre*	Donald Pleasance
MAXIME, *who plays Saint-Just*	Charles Gray
PHILIPPE, *who plays the Jesuit Father*	Victor Winding
JULIEN, *who plays Danton*	Ronald Lewis
VULTURNE, *who plays Mirabeau*	Hugh Manning
BRASSAC, *who plays Tallien*	Terence Alexander
DESCHAMPS, *who plays Camille Desmoulins*	Patrick O'Connell
VICTOIRE, *who plays Lucille Desmoulins*	Narissa Knights
AMANDA, *who plays Madame Tallien*	Susan Clark
LILA, *who plays Marie Antoinette*	Caroline Blakiston
CHARLES, *Maxime's butler*	Michael Golden
JOSEPH, *Maxime's cook*	Gregory Warwick
DELANOUE	Martin Jarvis
CHILD ROBESPIERRE	Douglas Cann

Directed by Shirley Butler
Designed by Timothy O'Brien

ACT ONE

An immense room, vaulted and completely bare. Stone steps upstage leading up and off to an unseen street door. Downstage a big trestle table laid for several guests.

MAXIME, *dressed in a dinner jacket and carrying a lighted candelabrum, is showing* PHILIPPE *round the room. He is wearing the wig and neck linen of the French revolutionary period.* PHILIPPE *is in travelling clothes.*

MAXIME. This is the great hall. It's all that remains of the old Carmelite Priory. The local Jacobins held their meetings here in 1792. In '93 they set up the Revolutionary Tribunal here.

PHILIPPE. What are you going to do with it?

MAXIME (*shortly*). Sell it. I'm signing next week with Shell. Yes, my dear fellow, a garage. Ultra modern. Neon everywhere. With petrol pumps gleaming like graven images. They'll pour cement into it all with whoops of glee. That will teach my ancestors to let themselves be guillotined like sheep. I loathe those tales of aristocrats who mounted the scaffold smiling with contempt. Had they barricaded themselves in here and died fighting like men, I should have preserved this edifice. But they listened nice and politely to their death sentence, so – a garage!

PHILIPPE. Pity. It was lovely.

MAXIME. With neon lights it will be lovelier still. However, as occasions for enjoying oneself are rare in the provinces, I decided, since it's been left to me, to have a house-warming before I sold the place.

PHILIPPE (*grunting*). A wig party! Nobody gives those any more. It's going to be lugubrious.

MAXIME (*with a smile*). I fondly hope so.

PHILIPPE *eyes him, surprised.*

PHILIPPE. How very cheering.

MAXIME (*taking his arm*). I'd better let you into the secret. I'm hatching a vast scheme for the ruination of an upstart who annoys me. That's the real reason for tonight's festivities. You remember Bitos at school?

PHILIPPE. Bitos?

MAXIME. That boring little scholarship boy who always came top.

PHILIPPE. Oh yes, I'm with you now. The one we called 'Beastly Bitos'. What became of him?

MAXIME. Deputy public prosecutor, my dear. Now let us so much as dabble in some unsavoury affair – decadent lot that we are – and he could crush us in his iron glove. Vengeance arriving by the local bus, and on market day too, along with the pigs and chickens, with his grey knitted gloves and his mock-leather briefcase crammed full of principles.

PHILIPPE. A zealot, is he?

MAXIME. That's putting it mildly. He thinks he's Robespierre. Ever-present Justice is on the march and he is it. Our corrupt little city will have to behave itself or else. You've noticed my wig and ruffles? Do I look deadly enough? I'm supposed to be Saint-Just. The joke is, I'm told it's very like. This evening, we're back in 1793. The guests are all coming as figures of the period and they've made a thorough study of their roles. And mind, there's to be no discussing anything else all evening, that's an order. We must have our facts at our fingertips. Poor Julien, who never passed an exam in his life, has been swotting up his revolutionary history for a fortnight.

PHILLIPE. But, my dear boy, we're going to be bored to tears at your little historical evening.

MAXIME (*with a wicked smile*). No, you won't. The bill of fare includes a sentence of death and that's always fun. I've persuaded Bitos to come as Robespierre. Philippe my boy, you won't regret your evening.

PHILIPPE. You know I've always been hopeless at history. I don't know that I'm too well qualified at this short notice.

MAXIME. My dear, I've reserved you Louis 16th. You've the profile for it and it's a virtually non-speaking role. As a matter of fact, you've only one line to say. 'Is this a revolt?' 'No, Sire, it's a revolution.' Can you remember that? Come along. We're going to paint and powder you.

PHILIPPE. And you think that Bitos dressed up as Robespierre and holding forth will be enough to liven up your little surprise party, do you?

MAXIME. The fellow – I know this at first hand – the fellow can't hold his liquor. And – it's a big word and and I loathe big words – but the fact is I hate him. He won't leave my little surprise party, as you call it – alive.

He repeats, lifting a finger with a smile, suddenly strange.

Not alive.

Enter CHARLES, *the manservant, white-coated, with a period wig.*

This is Charles, whom you know but possibly don't recognize.

CHARLES. Good evening, sir.

MAXIME. Our guests will be arriving any minute, I asked them all to get here before the guinea-pig.

PHILIPPE. But suppose the guinea-pig suspects something and doesn't come at all?

MAXIME (*leading him off*). That breed are much too sure of themselves ever to suspect a thing. I asked him for nine o'clock. At one minute to nine – the breed is always early – he'll be here.

They go out. CHARLES *starts to light the candles on the table. A knock. He goes up the steps to answer the door. Two young women and a young man, all in period wigs, appear at the top of the steps.*

CHARLES (*off*). Good evening, ladies.

LILA. Good evening, Charles. How do we look?

CHARLES. Marvellous, ladies. M. Maxime will be delighted.

LILA (*who is made up as Marie Antoinette*). I've gone to no end of trouble. My little edifice is a work of art. But it won't stay perched on my head until the sweet, that's certain.

JULIEN (*who is made up as Danton*). A point of no importance, dear girl, your role is comparatively short. They cut your head off before then.

LILA (*looking around her*). Maxime has some impossible ideas! Fancy inviting people to dinner in a cellar!

JULIEN. I've seldom been bored at a party of Maxime's. He has an astonishing sense of theatre. (*He looks at* CHARLES.) Why, look at Charles; he's in it, too!

CHARLES (*smiling with faint embarassment*). A little fancy of M. Maxime's. He said I might be useful when the time came.

AMANDA. I rather fear that what Maxime wants us to do won't be very charitable.

JULIEN. My love, this evening we've come here to have fun. Charity is for tomorrow morning, after Mass. But for tonight, let Charity sleep.

VULTURNE *appears at the top of the stairs, made up as Mirabeau.*

VULTURNE. Excuse me, the door was open. Is this the right house for the conspiracy? Marie Antoinette, if memory serves?

LILA. The Count of Mirabeau?

VULTURNE (*with a mock bow*). Thank you, your Majesty. I was afraid there might be some doubt. That's why I've been very lavish with the pock marks. Do you like it? I've put them on every available inch. (*To* AMANDA.) Evening, Amanda. Dear God, aren't we pretty! Who are we exactly?

AMANDA (*reciting like a schoolgirl*). Theresa Cabarrus, known as Our Lady of Thermidor, who married Tallien, Member of the National Convention. It was because of her that Tallien brought matters to a head with Robespierre on the 8th Thermidor. It seems they cooked Robespierre's goose with a handbell.

VULTURNE. President of assassins! I demand to speak. Ting-a-ling! Ting-a-ling! I can't wait to hear our little Bitos shouting that.

JULIEN. Marvellous, that smallpox, Vulturne. I swear it's almost catching. Tell me honestly, do you think I look like Danton? Maxime picked the role out for me entirely because I spent my youth booting Bitos in the behind. He says the memory of it would help considerably to set the mood.

BRASSAC *appears. Tallien's head, feathered hat.*

BRASSAC. Good evening.

LILA (*to* BRASSAC). Brassac, who are you supposed to be? One can tell that you're supposed to be something, but it isn't clear what quite.

BRASSAC. Tallien. An excellent role for a wig party. Nobody quite knows his true face. Yes, my dear, the turncoats, the putrefied of conscience, the traitors, they're me, rolled into one.

LILA. What an ugly role. Aren't you ashamed?

BRASSAC. No. You owe the turncoats of this world an almighty lot, let me tell you. They were the ones who decided at last to put a stop to the Terror and knock Robespierre off his perch. All they were concerned with was saving their skins and their fat purses. They were more surprised than anyone, on meeting the cheering mob outside the National Assembly, to learn that they had just saved France.

AMANDA. You mean they made fortunes during the Revolution? I thought everything had been given to the people.

BRASSAC *puts his arm around her and kisses her familiarly on the neck.*

BRASSAC. Darling little Amanda. Why, my little dove, money was never made so fast as when they started bothering about the common people. It's become a veritable industry.

LILA. Bitos will be furious when he sees you here!

BRASSAC. I should hope so. What amazes me is that he should accept an invitation to dine with the forces of Capital. But he's the ambitious one, as it turns out. I was quite content to take over my papa's numerous factories. He didn't deign to carry on his mother's laundry business, not he. He got himself appointed deputy public prosecutor and started washing dirty linen on a grander scale.

JULIEN. Have you heard the latest Bitos story?

LILA. The one about the apartment he requisitioned for his sister on the same day he demanded the death penalty for the tenant on charges of collaboration? It was magnificent.

One couldn't tell in the end what he was pleading for – the man's head or the apartment.

JULIEN. No, not that. The one about the boyhood friend he had sentenced to death in a fit of righteousness. Bitos had obtained the conviction of a young member of Laval's militia, arrested a good while after the liberation. The boy had made his first communion with him and they'd been friendly, it seems, up until the war. All this was three years ago. Now whether because of red tape, indecision, forgetfulness or I don't know what, the fact is that our humanitarian régime kept this boy in the condemned cell, in leg irons, for three years, watching for the dawn. Last week, they suddenly remember him and decide to execute him after all. Visit from the wretched fellow's wife, in tears, accompanied by their little girl. Bitos, more and more the noble Roman, weeps with her – and sincerely, too, I think – but doesn't yield an inch. Anyway, the matter was out of his hands. He's included, of course, in the little early morning expedition to see his fellow communicant peppered with bullets, wondering if he'll manage to keep his breakfast down. The other fellow, in a desperate bid to raise the tone of this final minute, asks to shake Bitos by the hand before walking to the execution post. Mutual forgiveness. He cries 'Vive La France' very nicely and they allow him to shout 'Fire' himself; so they duly shoot holes in his belly and lungs, some ten years after the offence. The death shot fired, Bitos takes out his watch and says simply 'On time to the minute'. A station-master! That night, he forks out and sends the little girl a doll – as a replacement, no doubt. A very expensive doll. That's the beautiful part. Bitos is a poor man. It cost him more than half his month's salary. A doll that opens and shuts her eyes, says Mamma and Papa and does weewee. It was, in fact, a German doll; we're still executing people, but trade, of course, is well on its feet again.

LILA. You're determined to spoil our appetite, Julien my pet, that's perfectly obvious. How do you expect us to dine with Bitos after what you've told us?

JULIEN (*negligently*). My dear girl, if we had to respect all the people we dine with, there'd be no possiblity of social life at all. Besides, Bitos isn't a murderer, he's a prosecuting counsel. In principle, he was only doing his duty.

A young man appears at the top of the steps; dark suit, bewigged and made up, looking rather ill at ease.

YOUNG MAN. Excuse me. The door was open.

LILA (*in a murmur*). This dinner party is certainly producing some surprising guests. Who's he?

JULIEN (*under his breath*). No idea.

YOUNG MAN. May I introduce myself? I'm Marcel Deschamps. M. Maxime de Jaucourt invited me here tonight . . .

BRASSAC (*going to him*). I apologize for Maxime. The preparations for this little party are keeping him backstage. We haven't seen him ourselves yet. (*Introducing himself.*) My name is Brassac. Let me introduce you. Monsieur Deschamps: the Comtesse de Preuil, Mlle Amanda Forrest, Julien du Bief.

VULTURNE (*introducing himself*). Verdreuil.

DESCHAMPS (*surprised*). Are you Count Verdreuil?

VULTURNE. Yes.

DESCHAMPS. We're not quite strangers then. I'm headmaster of the local school.

VULTURNE. Really? I'm delighted to meet you; my gamekeeper's two boys are with you. Their father tells me that since you've been in charge he scarcely recognizes them. No doubt that's why he's stopped thrashing them every night.

DESCHAMPS (*smiling*). They're good boys and they've really

got down to work, now. All they needed was the right handling.

VULTURNE (*with a charming bow*). And I see you know how to do that. Are you a friend of Maxime's?

DESCHAMPS (*a little embarrassed*). I hadn't the honour of his acquaintance until recently. He came to see me a fortnight ago and invited me to this little party. Perhaps because he assumed I knew a little history. He asked me to come as Camille Desmoulins. I've done my best.

LILA (*aside to* JULIEN). This party is getting more and more mysterious.

JULIEN. Maxime is a man of dark designs.

MAXIME *walks in quickly.*

MAXIME. Are you all here? I can't apologize enough, but I was making up our dear old friend Philippe as Louis 16th. M. Deschamps, have you been introduced?

DESCHAMPS. I introduced myself.

MAXIME. You know he's our local schoolmaster, Vulturne?

VULTURNE. So he said.

MAXIME. M. Deschamps, you and André Bitos have known each other for years, I believe?

DESCHAMPS (*surprised and on his guard*). Yes, Very well. Especially as children.

MAXIME. He's coming here this evening. Yes, he picked the role of Robespierre and I asked you to come as Camille Desmoulins. In view of what happened between you – it remains your secret, don't worry – can you see any objection to your meeting?

DESCHAMPS. On the contrary, I should be delighted to be given the chance of telling André Bitos just what I think of him – under the mask of Camille Desmoulins . . .

MAXIME (*smiling*). Under the mask of Camille Desmoulins . . . I see we understand each other.

He begins to pour drinks, speaking as he does so.

I want you to take your roles seriously, all of you, and not attack Bitos with any but historical arguments, will you do that? No personal references, whatever you do. That would ruin everything.

JULIEN (*nervous, consulting his little book*). Will our history be up to it, though, that's the thing.

MAXIME. Don't worry, those fellows were great talkers. The problem was holding the floor for as long as you could. The least interruption was fatal. When they cut into your speeches they cut off your head as well. That was made very clear on the 9th Thermidor. How do you suppose they got Robespierre? By making enough noise to drown his voice. The second he couldn't talk any more, he was dead. Long live democracy, which gave us the spoken word.

JULIEN. Talking of that, have you got a handbell?

MAXIME. The murder weapon? I should think so!

He rings the bell. CHARLES *appears.*

All right, Charles, just testing. But I've something even better than that. The high spot of the evening, the deus ex machina who brings the play to a successful end. Merda, the gendarme. Angelic little Merda, who walked straight into the City Hall, asked which of them was Robespierre and then just drew his gun and shot him. So simple it was silly, but someone had to think of it.

AMANDA (*clapping her hands, delighted with her knowledge*). Why yes, that's another thing I learnt last night. It's as exciting as a thriller. Who's to play Merda?

MAXIME. A very handsome young man, my angel, who won't arrive until the dessert.

LILA. Who is he? Do we know him?

MAXIME. I don't think so.

AMANDA. But why isn't he coming earlier? Did he have a previous engagement?

MAXIME. No, poor fellow. He has very few invitations these days. But I thought that his presence at the beginning of dinner might sour the proceedings somewhat prematurely.

VULTURNE. Ah, so you do mean to sour the proceedings, do you?

MAXIME (*with a wicked smile*). Towards the end, yes. You know that moment in the theatre, when the lights change and everyone shows in their true colours.

VULTURNE. That's the moment when I always lose interest. When you start feeling sorry for the villain and the honest characters turn into an ugly pack around him.

MAXIME (*suddenly cold*). Vulturne, you can always withdraw from this dinner party if you're afraid you'll weep over Bitos.

VULTURNE (*shrugging*). No. After all, it's only a romp and Bitos is a second-rate man. And I think God will forgive everybody except the second rate.

MAXIME. Let's not be more forgiving than God, then, my dear Vulturne.

A knock.

Charles! The door! I hope to heaven it's Victoire. She absolutely must be here before he is. We can't do anything without a Lucille Desmoulins. Saved! She's here!

VICTOIRE *appears, and smiles and nods to everybody from the top of the stairs. She is wearing a period bonnet.*

VICTOIRE. Good evening. I'm the last, I'm sorry. Will you excuse me, there's something I must say to Maxime. Maxime?

She draws him aside.

MAXIME. What's the matter?

VICTORIE. Maxime, I can't stay this evening.

MAXIME. My darling Victoire, you can't ruin my party! I simply cannot do without you.

VICTOIRE. You'll see why when I tell you. Something quite unbelievable has happened. My father only told me about it just as I was leaving. Bitos came to see him this afternoon and he asked him for my hand.

MAXIME. That's splendid! Splendid! I suspected he was vaguely paying court to you. But I never dreamed I'd hit the target! (*He cries comically to the others.*) I'm a clairvoyant!

VICTOIRE. Maxime! I don't know what he can have imagined. I've seen him four times at home, when my father entertained the members of the Court. I was pleasant to him – as I was to everyone else. But for him to think for one instant that I'd even noticed him!

MAXIME (*bursting with delight*). It's too perfect! It's too, too perfect!

VICTOIRE. You know my father. He went for him, all beard and eyebrows – it must have been sheer carnage – and told him very brutally that the answer was no.

MAXIME (*dancing round her gleefully*). It's too perfect!

VICTOIRE (*freeing herself*). Maxime, stop pretending. You must see that I can't possibly join in this evening's game; it would be too cruel.

MAXIME. In the first place, my darling Victoire, one can't be too cruel to fools. Besides, I need a Lucille Desmoulins or everything will be ruined. And that is that.

VICTOIRE. If at least I'd refused him myself! But my father was very harsh. Bitos will think he's committed some dreadful social blunder. He's probably dying of shame and mortification.

MAXIME. Let him die of whatever he likes, so long as I can give my party. My darling Victoire! Must I go down on my knees to you? (*He does so.*) You who are kindness itself!
VICTOIRE. That's just why. I can't do it.
MAXIME (*pettishly*). Be kindness itself to me then, and not to him.

A knock.

Anyway, it's too late. He's here now. Charles, answer the door. Straighten your little bonnet, Lucille Desmoulins, and have no remorse. Children, on stage for Act One.

He gets to his feet, turns his back to her and goes to the others.

Julien, do you know your part? The Prairial Laws?
JULIEN. 22 Prairial '94. Intensification of the powers of the Revolutionary Tribunal.
MAXIME. Well done. Nine out of ten.
LILA (*aside to him*). What's the matter with Victoire?
MAXIME. Nothing. A slight hitch, which is a real godsend, as it turns out. (*To the others.*) Don't force the pace at first, just let it come. Then, when he's had a drink or two, launch into the argument. He'll tighten his own noose. Let's not look as though we're waiting.

BITOS *appears at the top of the stairs. He is dressed as Robespierre from head to foot, under his skimpy top-coat and bowler hat. When* CHARLES *takes his coat, he stands revealed in sky blue.*

BITOS. Good evening, ladies and –
MAXIME. My dear Bitos, you're the last! Why, what on earth have you got on?

BITOS (*already on the defensive*). What do you mean? What is this, a practical joke? You're all in dinner jackets! You told me it was fancy dress!

MAXIME (*roaring with laughter*). A wig party! My dear Bitos, you misunderstood me, or perhaps you weren't familiar with the custom. A wig party has nothing to do with a costume ball! My dear man, you only dress up your head!

Everyone laughs at BITOS'S *bewilderment.*

BITOS (*crushed*). I apologize. I must look ridiculous. I'll go home and change.

MAXIME. No, no, don't bother. You'd make us dine at an impossible hour. Anyway, sky blue suits you wonderfully. I'm sure the ladies will be enchanted to have you in blue. Now don't forget everyone, the game has begun. We aren't ourselves any more. You know nearly everyone, I think? Her majesty, our queen. The beautiful Madame Tallien. Count Mirabeau. Your good friends Danton and Camille Desmoulins. A gentle virtuous young woman whom you loved very much, I believe – Lucille Desmoulins. Tallien, whom I understand you didn't care for. I got Brassac to play him; we needed someone really rich didn't we? Have I forgotten anyone? Oh yes, of course! One always forgets him, poor thing, and nobody ever lets him speak. Gentlemen, the King!

PHILIPPE *has come in. He is greeted with exclamations: the women sink playfully into deep curtsies as he passes.*

PHILIPPE. I'm not sure that it's a very good likeness. Anyway, I put as much powder on my head as it will hold.

MAXIME. You'll get it cut off soon, so why worry? Make your bow, Bitos! And politely, too. Whatever your present feelings, in '92 you were still a monarchist, remember?

BITOS (*banteringly*). A monarchist? Even after the King's death? He voted for it, didn't he? Correct me if I'm wrong.

MAXIME. My dear fellow, that's exactly what we're here to talk about. Let's have dinner. You all have place cards.

BITOS *bows to everyone, then strolls over to* DESCHAMPS, *very much at ease, while the company find their places at the table and* CHARLES *begins to serve.*

BITOS. Deschamps, it's good to see you after all this time. But I must say I'm surprised. I would never have guessed you were a friend of Maxime's.

MAXIME. Monsieur Deschamps is the schoolmaster at the village school at Breville. Vulturne asked if he could bring him. I gather that you two were friends years ago.

BITOS (*a trifle strained*). It's always nice to meet old friends. Are you still a schoolmaster? Why have you never shown signs of life since I've been appointed to the Courts here?

DESCHAMPS (*quietly*). You know why. Do you want to hear me say it again?

MAXIME. Do come and sit down, Bitos! Your soup will get cold. And don't forget, from this moment on you are Robespierre.

BITOS (*glancing along the table as he sits down*). There's an empty place.

MAXIME. Yes. Another friend of ours who's coming later. I have reconstructed a meal of the times for you. Before the austerity laws, that is. So I want you all to enjoy your dinner. And eat a little too much as well.

A pause. They eat.

BITOS (*stiffly, as he takes the proffered dish*). I don't believe that the members of the Convention, the dedicated ones, were very interested in that kind of thing. Besides, times were terribly hard, don't forget that.

MAXIME. My dear man, in the midst of the worst catastrophes, the French have never once given up the thought of eating well. Those who could afford it, that is. I read somewhere that there was a very well-organized black market at the time.

BITOS (*already a little tight-lipped*). I'm afraid it has always been virtually impossible, no matter how stringent the laws, to prevent the rich from polluting everything with their money. Even among the revolutionaries some pleasure-seekers, the Dantons – the Talliens –

JULIEN (*ringing the bell, cries*). Easy now, Max my lad, you haven't guillotined me yet!

BRASSAC (*passing him the dish*). Help yourself while you can, then. When you're dead everything will be cold.

BITOS (*with a pale smile at the interruption*). But Robespierre, I'm sure, never took part in those banquets. He lodged with a poor cabinet-maker and broke bread with him at the family table.

MAXIME. Oh yes, but that poor cabinet-maker had a cousin in the country who sent him the odd hunk of bacon now and then. So take one of these plovers' eggs, my dear fellow, and don't think badly of yourself.

BITOS (*helping himself primly*). But I am convinced that Robespierre, determined as he was to be incorruptible, did not share in their feasting.

AMANDA. 'No, thank you,' he said, 'I'm incorruptible. No roast lamb for me. Just beans.'

BITOS (*trying to laugh*). Don't scoff, young lady! I meant that when those good folk indulged themselves, they probably took care he didn't know about it.

LILA. How horrid of them! Do you think they waited until he'd gone up to his room all by himself with his little bowl of broth?

BRASSAC. And they shouted at the children: 'Don't crunch the bones, you little idiots! Robespierre will hear you!'

BITOS (*with a jaundiced smile*). You have a very fanciful way of imagining history, my dear sir.

BRASSAC. To begin with, don't call me my dear sir. Call me citizen. And don't forget you used to address me by my Christian name. All those men who handed one another over to the executioner used to slap each other on the back and call each other by their Christian names. You called Danton Georges and Desmoulins Camille; both of whom dined with you the very evening before you clamoured for their heads in the National Assembly. You called me Jean! The man you must have hated the most.

BITOS (*pontificating*). A great band of friends they were, yes – but friends who didn't shrink from sacrificing each other along the road so that the furrow ploughed by their common love for the people should stay straight. I am amazed that you don't feel the grandeur of it, Brassac.

MAXIME (*pretending to interview him*). Monsieur Robespierre, would you say that the populace valued the grandeur of these men's sacrifice?

BITOS (*bitterly*). It isn't always those who lead them along the thorny road of happiness whom the people love.

MAXIME (*continuing the game*). I seem to detect a hint of bitterness in your words. Would you say that the people did not care for you?

BITOS (*smiling affably and joining for the first time in the game*). They feared me. That was enough. I lived amongst them. I shared their discomfort and their poverty. Apart from this blue suit, my one conceit, I lived as they did.

JULIEN (*shouting from the other end of the table*). Hypocrite! All the Duplay women where you lodged petted and pampered you!

BITOS (*bristling*). Who called me hypocrite?

JULIEN (*leaping to his feet, his mouth full*). Your old friend

Danton! Danton the Big Mouth. Wait till I swallow. I've got my mouth full of friend Tallien's plovers' eggs. For *I* loved good food, I did! I loved women, I loved life. And that's why you had me killed, you hypocrite! You thought you hated sloppiness, disorder and dirt; it was the people you hated! And do you know why? Because they frightened you and so did women – whence your purity – and so did life. You killed us all because you didn't know how to live. We paid dearly for those complexes of yours.

BITOS (*with a shrug, trying to make the others laugh*). Complexes, I ask you, in 1793!

JULIEN. You were a priest, Robespierre, that's the truth of it, a dirty little priest from Arras, all prim and proper, a nasty little snotty-nosed runt.

BITOS *has half risen, nettled. One feels that Julien bawling at him frightens him rather as it did long ago.*

BITOS. I rather think you've overstepped the mark now, my dear fellow.

MAXIME. My dear Bitos, the game may be a little bitter, but let's play it like sportsmen. I'm sure you yourself were hardly more indulgent towards Danton.

BITOS (*sitting down again, balefully*). Danton was a hog! Sprawled out all night long with whores, he'd arrive at meetings in the morning, half dressed, stinking of cheap scent and drink. And one had to discuss the Revolution with that trash!

JULIEN. *My* Revolution smelt strong! Too bad for your precious little nostrils. When it went to fetch the King in October, do you think the Revolution didn't stink of female sweat and wine on the road to Versailles?

BITOS (*shouting*). Danton loved rioting; he didn't love the Revolution!

JULIEN (*turning comically to the others*). Give me something to drink, or I'll do a murder! A murder that wouldn't even be historical! And to think I have to let them guillotine me first.

BITOS. Your verve, your audacity, your enthusiasm, let's say it, your big mouth, were all useful in their day. But there came a time when the Revolution had to rise above the sentimentality and the mob riots. That day Danton became expendable. You should have realized that and kept quiet.

JULIEN (*rising and shouting as at a trial*). Jury of murderers, you shall listen to me! You shall not stop my mouth, any of you! The Revolution is my sister and my sweetheart. I know her, none better! I've lain with her.

BITOS (*with a contemptuous shrug*). Phrases!

JULIEN. No! Cries! Real cries of men bursting from our guts, Camille's and mine. Cries of innocence which will haunt men's memories for ever!

BITOS (*stiffly*). I didn't hear anything.

JULIEN *eyes him steadily and says suddenly.*

JULIEN. Deaf, too. It wasn't enough being shortsighted. You were deaf. Stiff and clumsy. With your fingers bunched at the ends of your stiff arms, you bumped into doors, knocking over chairs as you went, stepping on people's feet and too ill at ease to apologize. A dry little bit of clockwork without grace. A tightly wound automaton. Thin lips that never smiled, never kissed anybody, hands with bitten nails that had touched nothing ever – big staring eyes that never saw a thing. Without the Revolution, I could have been a wheelwright or a shoesmith. But you – you couldn't do a thing with your hands. All you could do was talk. A nasty little lawyer. Do you remember what I said about you at the trial? The fool can't even boil himself an egg!

BITOS (*with a hollow laugh*). Phrases! You died spouting words like a ham actor. I did at least die in silence.

JULIEN (*starting to eat again*). Because they'd broken your jaw. Otherwise you'd have talked like the rest of them. One always talks.

LILA (*suddenly, in the silence which has oddly fallen*). It must have been exciting, I should think, Danton's trial.

BITOS (*shrugging*). Good Lord, madam, a trial . . .

VULTURNE (*smiling*). Breathtaking, my dear. A big star beloved of the vast public and – a rare thrill lost to the theatre since Roman times – one they were actually going to kill. All the ladies wanted tickets. The house was nearly as glittering as at the trial of the King. Of course, it was less of a grand occasion than the trial of Louis 16th, with all the women of fashion fanning themselves and eating ices in the boxes. At Danton's trial it was less dressy. In the first place, it was no longer the done thing in '93. A lot of friends had lost their heads since then. The vogue was for simple little day dresses, a light half-mourning. It had rather more the flavour of an avantgarde piece for connoisseurs. The fascinating question was how Danton was to be stopped from speaking.

AMANDA. And how did they manage it?

VULTURNE. By passing a vote excluding all the accused from the proceedings on the grounds that they were insulting to the Court. It was a master-stroke. This neat little vanishing trick permitted them to be condemned to death without a hearing. Every century or so French justice, rather backward in other respects, produces little inventions of this kind to help it out of difficult situations – deft little tricks of the trade which enable it to serve the régime, whatever it happens to be.

BITOS *has risen, ashen pale*.

BITOS. Maxime, this is going too far. I am a guest in your house and as a member of the judiciary I cannot allow –

VULTURNE (*very calmly*). Will you deny that this was the way poor old Danton was whisked off?

BITOS (*leaping up*). Whisked off! I realize that you are not a democrat, but there *was* a vote taken. A properly conducted vote. Danton's death was therefore a decision taken by France.

JULIEN. The things they get France to say with a majority of twelve votes.

BITOS (*yelping*). A vote is a vote!

JULIEN (*ironically*). Alas.

BRASSAC. And that vote, my dear Robespierre, you could only get from us! It was by leaning over to the Right that you got Danton's head.

BITOS (*shouting*). I deny this slanderous allegation! Robespierre was never in collusion with the Right!

BRASSAC. How else could he have formed a majority? He knew his political onions, the sea-green incorruptible! The 9th Thermidor, when he sensed he was doomed, he turned to us and cried: 'You, the pure of conscience! It is to you I speak!' Pure of conscience – us! He *must* have felt queasy!

BITOS. That's a lie! Everything you've put forward is a lie! You're interpreting history –

BRASSAC. It's in the encyclopedia. I learnt it all at school with you, when we were twelve.

JULIEN (*waving the book*). Pass him the little book and let him see for himself – it's all there.

MAXIME *rings the handbell and makes them all sit down again.*

MAXIME. Gentlemen, gentlemen . . . We're going much too fast. If we go at this rate we'll get to Waterloo before the coffee and I haven't even thought of a Bonaparte! Besides, I feel we're boring the ladies. With all these high politics they haven't been able to say a word. The ladies played their part, too, you know, and a very vital one it was.

He seizes a serving spoon from CHARLES *as he passes and hands it to* LILA *like a microphone.*

Your Majesty, with the passing of time, would you be kind enough to tell our listeners your personal feelings on the sad incidents which marked your reign?

LILA (*into the microphone*). Well, we were most surprised, the King and I, at the turn events were taking . . . We were a most united family. Louis was a good father, a good husband and – we were convinced of this – a good king. His concern for the well-being of his subjects was the most touching thing in the world. How many times, on coming home from a ball, did I find him, late at night, poring over his little red account book in his study, working out ways of economizing.

MAXIME (*still very much the radio interviewer*). There were some unfortunate rumours about you at the time, your Majesty. Could you tell our listeners whether there was any truth in them?

LILA. Yes and no. I was very young. I loved parties. I was very pretty. What young woman doesn't want to enjoy herself? Louis was very kind, very honest. He wasn't a very amusing man. I had friends.

MAXIME. And could one say, as was alleged, that those friends led you into doing one or two rather rash things?

LILA. What young woman isn't rash at some time in her life?

MAXIME. We won't mention the balls and parties particularly . . . (*Into the microphone*) It is important to remember, ladies and gentlemen, that the pomp and splendour of the Royal house was a real political necessity at the time. The populace would have been the first to feel mortified if their King hadn't the finest festivities, the finest palaces, the finest diamonds – the loveliest Queen.

LILA (*simpering*). Thank you.

MAXIME (*still into the microphone*). This love, which they have since transferred to popular singers, footballers and film stars, this love they bestowed in those days on their King and Queen.

LILA. They're always talking about the money I spent, but I set the simplest fashions. I used to wear muslins and cotton prints. The common people resented me for it, as a matter of fact. They detest simplicity. My extravagant follies? Combing my lambs on my little farm, milking my cow? I was the first Queen of France who took a delight in living like the humblest of her subjects. Well, really, one can't say I was ruining France by milking Roussette! . . . that was my cow.

MAXIME (*banteringly into the microphone*). Her Majesty has just let us into an amusing little secret; her cow was called Roussette.

BITOS *thrusts his face into hers. They are nose to nose, like two quarrelling children.*

BITOS. The Trianon farm cost an outrageous fortune!

LILA. Everything cost us a fortune. You could hardly expect us to haggle with the tradesmen!

BITOS. What about your friends? What about the favourites?

LILA. Have you never helped a friend, sir?

BITOS (*with a cry*). Never! –

Everyone laughs.

JULIEN. At last, a cry from the heart.

BITOS (*shouting, nettled*). Let me finish, will you? I really don't see what's so funny. Never, with the people's money –

LILA (*innocently*). Because you never had the spending of it.

BITOS (*bawling*). I did! And far more freely than you did, possibly. I never lived in a palace. All I ever had were my attendance vouchers and my salary from the Assembly. At the end, all they found in my room were fifty silver francs and I owed the Duplays four years' rent. Who else could boast a balance sheet like that? Danton, Mirabeau, Tallien even?

BRASSAC (*seriously*). My dear fellow, I was a financier. If I had had to produce accounts at any time, they would have been in order, you can be certain of that.

BITOS (*cackling*). I'm sure. And what about Mirabeau's pensions?

VULTURNE (*smiling*). I was a sincere royalist, my dear fellow. When convictions are genuine, it's somewhat specious to insist they shouldn't pay.

BITOS (*sneering*). Attractive principles.

VULTURNE (*smiling*). Pardon me. Lack of principles, which is quite a different thing.

BITOS. That's leaving the door wide open to grafters – to thieves!

VULTURNE. Possibly. But in politics France has often had occasion to note that they were less of a danger than the virtuous. It's a known fact, thieves do less killing. Blood is the price one always pays for the haste of a few men like yourself who are impatient to play their little roles.

BITOS. Your cynicism is revolting.

VULTURNE. Possibly, but it's gentle towards men, whose frailty it has accepted. Human tenderness, that lady whom you've never met, counts too.

BITOS. Human tenderness, as you call it, can consist of something other than indulgence and laxity! Remember what I shouted at the Convention when the fainthearted were talking about leniency. 'Leniency for Royalists? Mercy for villains? No! Mercy for innocence! Mercy for the weak! Mercy for the unfortunate! Mercy for mankind!'

Everyone applauds as in a public meeting, which disconcerts him a little.

VULTURNE (*retorts with a smile*). Oh, yes, and very fine it sounded, too. But I've observed that those who talk too often of mankind have a curious propensity for decimating men.

BITOS. Nature decimates, weeds out, and slaughters, too! Nature spawns and exterminates millions of creatures every day! A day in the life of the world is just one vast birth and one vast slaughter for the fulfilment of her plans.

VULTURNE. Possibly. But Nature's plan, if she can be said to have one, was certainly not born in the brain of M. de Robespierre. Faced with an earthquake, one can only bow the head, agreed. But when the earthquake has been conceived by a handful of petty intellectuals, one may be tempted to intervene –

BITOS (*shouting*). Are you preaching civil war?

VULTURNE. My dear man, I have a horror of bloodshed, but I do not, for all that, feel myself cut out to be a rabbit.

BITOS *bangs on the table, forgetting himself.*

BITOS (*screeching*). Nothing will halt the march of progress! That's what enrages you. And when it comes to defending yourselves and your property, your side aren't so economical with blood then!

VULTURNE. Kings have massacred since the dawn of the world, too. But they at least had the courage to say it was for the advancement of their affairs or for their own good pleasure. You and your like, while doing the same sort of work, lay your hands on your hearts. That's what I find repulsive in you.

BITOS (*has risen, very pale*). Sir, take that back.

VULTURNE (*filling his glass*). Too late. It's out. Some more champagne?

BITOS *has thrown down his napkin. He now affects a haughty calm and turns to* MAXIME.

BITOS. Maxime, I realized if I came to your house that I should be alone in defending my opinions. I did think this exchange of ideas would be spirited but courteous. I see I was wrong. I must ask you to excuse me. Will you kindly send for my coat?

MAXIME *has risen, too.*

MAXIME (*with a calm smile*). No.

BITOS. What do you mean, no?

MAXIME. My little party isn't over yet and you are indispensable. Charles will not give you your coat.

BITOS *smiles a superior smile and takes a step towards the cloakroom.*

BITOS. Then I'll fetch it myself.

MAXIME *and* JULIEN *bar his way.*

MAXIME (*still quietly*). You won't do that either. I assure you, Bitos, that we cannot do without you this evening.

BITOS. Is this a trap?

MAXIME (*laughing*). What a big word! It's a firm invitation.

BITOS (*looks at them and mutters*). What are you going to do to me?

MAXIME (*still calm*). Make you play your role to the end, that's all.
BITOS (*yelping*). You don't think I'm going to stand here and be your whipping boy with a good grace, do you?
MAXIME. It would be better, Bitos, if it were with a good grace.

BITOS *goes to sit on a couch, pale but calm, and folds his arms.*

BITOS. Very well. Do what you like. This town is rotten with fascists and reactionaries, I knew that. I came with no illusions, but I did think I would be protected whilst under your roof by the laws of hospitality – if not honour. I know they talk a lot about honour in your world.
MAXIME. I promise you that honour, as far as I'm concerned, will be intact.
BITOS (*with a mirthless laugh*). We know your methods. My compliments, ladies. I see the young women of your class have wholesome and innocent amusements. (*Suddenly glaring at* VICTOIRE.) Madamoiselle de Bremes, you are the only one whose presence here surprises and pains me. I suppose it was to punish me for daring to ask your father for your hand in marriage that you came here this evening.
VICTOIRE (*murmurs, very pale*). I thought it would just be a harmless joke . . .
BITOS (*cackling*). And as you see, it is not a harmless joke.

He turns to the men, very dignified but slightly absurd.

Have you decided to eliminate me? I am a deputy to the Public Prosecutor and the Republic still exists. This will cause a stir in town tomorrow.
MAXIME (*bursting into laughter*). Don't be an ass, Bitos. Nobody's going to eliminate you. We need you too much

to have fun with. Do you remember at school how we locked you in the dormitory and tossed you in a blanket? You came out of that with a few bruises and some skin off your nose. It didn't kill you.

BITOS (*bitterly*). And the reverend fathers finally admitted that you were only reviving an good old college custom – rather boisterous as amusements go – but in the great tradition, very old world, very French. Don't imagine the police and the law courts will be content to stop your chocolate money. This is an established criminal offence! (*He yelps absurdly.*) Intent to inflict bodily harm! Article 132!

MAXIME. You see what comes of knowing too much law. You dramatize everything. We haven't laid a finger on you yet. Don't tell me you're a coward?

BITOS. No.

MAXIME. No. One must be fair. I don't think you are. I'm sorry you aren't. (*He says heavily, between clenched teeth.*) I loathe you, Bitos. I've loathed you ever since I was a small boy.

BITOS (*heavily too*). I know. I tried with all my might to be your friend. I made myself your slave. I used to carry your things, so that you could be free to run about. I never ran. All I ever got from you were snubs.

MAXIME (*softly*). I didn't like you.

BITOS (*murmurs, without looking at him*). Why didn't you?

MAXIME. You lacked grace.

BITOS (*after a very slight pause*). You're the only one whose dislike ever hurt me. Everybody always hated me at school because I always came first – and because I was a washer-woman's son! That's why they took me in for nothing. She washed your sheets, you little perverts – she washed your stained sheets for twenty years! It's those washed-out stains that have made me what I am – Doctor at Law and Philosophy, Bachelor of Science, History, Letters, Mathematics, German (*He yells, unaccountably.*) – and Italian! Funny, isn't it? I passed every examination it was possible to pass. When the others went off for a beer after lectures I went up to my room and sat alone over my books. And when they came back late at night, after their evenings out with girls, I was still at it. Until the markets opened; then I went to help unload the lorries. After that I slept three hours – when I had three left. And at the first lecture, there I was again, the first in my seat, in the front row, with my stupid great eyes open wide, to catch as much as I could of that precious bourgeois knowledge that my mother's soapy arms were paying for. (*He adds, calmer now, with a curious little gesture, venomous and yet prim.*) If ever I'm entitled to a family crest like you, gentlemen, it will have my mother's two red arms upon it – crossed.

A silence follows this. Then VULTURNE *says gently.*

VULTURNE. What became of your mother, Bitos?
BITOS (*stiffly*). She's dead. The sheets got her in the end.
VULTURNE. I'm sorry. I knew her. She was a brave woman.

BITOS *bows ceremoniously, with a thin smile.*

BITOS. Thank you, your Grace, as they say in melodramas. Your mother was a fine woman, too. I know that she helped mine, when my father died.
VULTURNE (*after a pause*). I don't take back anything I said, Bitos, but I respect your courage and your integrity. I'm sorry if I hurt you. It only goes to prove that political discussion is always very difficult in France. In any event, Maxime's game could lead to no good. I think they should let you have your coat.
MAXIME. I'm sorry, but there are a few of us here – aren't

there, M. Deschamps? – for whom the memory of Bitos's mother, however touching, is not enough to wipe out certain things. Robespierre, the real one, had a mother, too, I imagine. Like all the men he sent to the guillotine, in fact.

DESCHAMPS *steps forward.*

DESCHAMPS (*quietly*). While we're on the subject of your mother, I'm going to tell my story after all. When you demanded the death penalty for Lucien – who made his first communion with us, remember? – his mother came to see you the night before the trial, with yours. Those two old women knelt at your feet and clasped your knees and begged you to relent. And your mother wept as much as Lucien's did.

BITOS (*stonily*). He was a traitor.

DESCHAMPS (*quietly*). You and I were in the same Resistance group, Bitos, and every night we used to clench our fists, both of us, and say: 'When it's all over, we'll get Lucien, we'll get him'!

BITOS (*with a malicious smile*). So you admit it?

DESCHAMPS. Yes. But I should have settled it with fists, as we did years ago, in the school yard. Not with twelve rifles pumping lead into his guts at point-blank range, ten whole years later.

BITOS. Lucien fought against us. He'd killed men.

DESCHAMPS (*in a murmur*). So had we.

BITOS (*screeching*). Are you comparing that little traitor's work with ours?

DESCHAMPS. No. We've had this argument before, the night our friendship died. All I wanted to say, since you brought up the memory of your mother, was that she pleaded with you, on her knees, for the best part of the night, and then at dawn, when she saw that her son was a true blue Roman, she got to her feet, did good old mother Bitos, and with her big red washerwoman's hand she hit our hero twice across the face, hard.

BITOS, *very pale, half touches his cheek.*

BITOS. Very delicate of you, I must say, bringing up that grotesque incident.

DESCHAMPS. Not very delicate, no. Since the war I've given up being delicate. But as you've chosen to hide behind your mother's skirts, I just wanted everyone to know exactly what *she* thought of you, too.

BITOS (*looking round at them like a trapped animal*). Beatings, always beatings – everybody's always wanted to beat me! (*He cries out.*) All right then, go on, beat me. There are six of you and I'm alone, what are you waiting for?

MAXIME (*coldly to the others – one must not know whether he means it or whether he is still only trying to frighten* BITOS). I won't keep the women here, nor anyone else who no longer finds the game amusing. Charles, you may bring coats for anyone who asks for them. Except M. Bitos.

Everybody looks at one another anxiously. PHILIPPE *steps forward, trying to make a joke of it.*

PHILIPPE. Now, now, what's this – a revolt?

MAXIME (*smiling, says coldly*). No, Sire. It is a revolution.

PHILIPPE (*more serious*). Maxime . . . I haven't said anything yet. You made me put a wig on the second I arrived, after an eight-hour drive. I haven't even had a chance to speak my one line, and I've hardly had any dinner. You've led me to expect more generous hospitality. I think you should let Bitos go if he wants to, and then you should serve us the rest of that fabulous meal of yours.

LILA (*stepping forward*). Maxime dear, we can't waste a whole evening like this. You surely aren't going to send us home at ten o'clock?

AMANDA (*taking his arm*). Maxime darling, now you're being ridiculous. You tried to make M. Bitos angry. You've succeeded. M. Bitos is angry. Now let him go home and let's finish our dinner.

MAXIME *grips her by the arm and shouts.*

MAXIME. Are you sorry for him?

AMANDA. Perhaps.

MAXIME. Women are always sorry for the wounds they haven't inflicted themselves. All right then, if you're sorry for him, kiss him.

He pushes them roughly towards each other.

AMANDA. Maxime! Are you mad?

MAXIME. Go on. Kiss him, and I'll let him go.

AMANDA. Maxime!

MAXIME. They smell good, rich women, eh, little priest? But when you ask for young girls' hands in marriage, you get thrown out of the house, and if you want to go to bed with the others, you have to make yourself attractive. So kiss her, you virgin!

The others rush forward to free them from his grip.

LILA. Maxime, you're abominable.

VULTURNE. I'm very fond of a joke, Maxime, but this one's gone far enough. We're all leaving and we're taking Bitos with us. I don't know what you were thinking of doing, but don't count on me to help you. I don't like him any more than you, but there are some things that simply aren't done, that's all.

A pause.

MAXIME. You may be sure he'll have far fewer scruples when he sends you to the firing squad. Bring the coats, Charles. M. Bitos's, too.

CHARLES has hurried out to get the coats. He comes in a moment later, comically laden with garments. Everyone on stage has remained motionless and silent.

CHARLES. Here we are . . . I hope you'll forgive me, ladies and gentlemen. I may get a little muddled up . . . (*He says nervously to himself.*) Ladies first. I think this one belongs to Mlle de Bremes. Excuse me, mademeoiselle . . . (*He hands her the coat, muttering.*) As a rule I have a system. I never allow it to form a bottleneck, but it's been so rushed with everybody leaving at once like this. This is M. le Comte's . . . (*He hands VULTURNE a coat clearly far too small for him.*) Oh no! Beg pardon, sir. Joseph, come and give me a hand. In thirty years I've never done such a thing. This is yours. No, it's not. What a muddle! I'll never sort it out on my own.

Nobody seems at all inclined to help him. He mutters. He goes out and calls. The KITCHEN BOY appears, bewildered, in his blue striped apron.

Everybody's leaving at once. It's a stampede! Look for the ladies' cloaks.

The game goes on for a moment, a comic little piece of dumb show between the two servants, until the audience can stand it no longer, and at that instant the door into the kitchens opens and a YOUNG MAN comes bursting in. He is wearing a belted raincoat and an odd two-cornered gendarme's hat of the period. He halts in the doorway and says simply.

YOUNG MAN. What about me, then?

They all turn in surprise. He goes on, a tense smile on his thin lips.

What about Merda the policeman? Forgotten him in the kitchen, have we? Isn't he needed any more?

They all look at him blankly. BITOS *instinctively steps back. He is deathly white.* MAXIME *stands frozen-faced. The* YOUNG MAN *looks at* BITOS *and says quietly.*

The 9th Thermidor – remember? Aren't we doing it now?

LILA (*crying out suddenly*). Maxime, who is this man?

YOUNG MAN (*stopping her with a gesture*). Introductions would take too long. And the only person concerned doesn't need one. Taller and a little thinner, aren't I?

BITOS (*getting the words out with difficulty*). Have you escaped?

YOUNG MAN (*smiling*). It takes a magistrate to imagine you can escape from city jails. You asked for the maximum, remember, ten years. But even so, five seemed sufficient to the court. A year awaiting trial and the rest in the cells because, thanks to the length of the inquiry, I was just old enough to be considered a man. Sentence served, with a year off for good behaviour, right? You can check up. I've done my time.

BITOS (*turning to* MAXIME). You brought this man here, didn't you?

MAXIME (*softly*). I needed a Merda. I couldn't think of anybody better for the part.

BITOS (*crying out nervously*). My conscience is clear! I only did my duty. He deserved no pity. A young thug who hadn't even the excuse of poverty. You stole a car, and you walked into a post office brandishing a gun, like a gangster in a bad film.

YOUNG MAN (*quietly*). Exactly like a bad film, yes. But it's amazing how one's artistic sense develops in jail. These few years of solitude have given me a chance to realize the poor taste of what I did. So I have to thank you for playing an important part in the neglected education of a youngster who was – am I right? – utterly unknown to you.

He stresses these last words. A pause.

BITOS (*dully*). Yes, I knew your father. Some say I owed my first promotion to him. I'm not denying it: I was his secretary at the County Court for a time. But it didn't affect the issue – just because you were the son of a former official in this town! (*He shouts vengefully, his face twisted with hate.*) Who is himself in jail as a collaborator! I wasn't in charge of you! Is it my fault if your mother let you roam the streets like a hooligan? I have nothing but loathing and contempt for little boys who hold up post offices after school, I'm sorry.

VULTURNE (*going to him*). Franz Delanoue. I remember you. Yours is an appalling story, and they made you pay dearly for your childish prank, I know. But you're a man now. Come along, we're all leaving.

He takes his arm, but the YOUNG MAN *frees himself gently.*

YOUNG MAN. Just a moment. I was supposed to play Constable Merda. They arrested me once for playing at robbers; I want to play at cops now, to rehabilitate myself. (*He smiles.*) That's all I know how to do – play. They never taught me anything else.

He starts to walk slowly over to BITOS *through the crowd.*

VULTURNE makes a move, but MAXIME holds him back, as he stands there, staring in fascination like the others, like BITOS, too, while the YOUNG MAN comes slowly forward.

. . . and Constable Merda walked through the crowd in the City Hall. He went straight up to Robespierre. 'Are you citizen Robespierre? I arrest you.'

BITOS (*murmuring as if in a dream*). You're a traitor! *I* am going to arrest *you*.

YOUNG MAN (*finishing the sentence with a thin smile*). . . . Said Robespierre. But Constable Merda, who wasn't much of a talker, saw no point in saying anything else and he drew his pistol –

The YOUNG MAN has pulled a gun from his raincoat pocket. A silly little period pistol, and he suddenly aims it at BITOS, who has been staring at him as if mesmerized. A shot. BITOS clutches his jaw. A woman screams. They all rush forward. Too late. Sudden BLACKOUT. Voices in the darkness. 'Who was he? The little hoodlum! A doctor! Get a doctor quickly! Keep calm, all of you! The gun wasn't loaded! But he's bleeding! Lie him down on the table . . .' *Over the hubbub, MAXIME's voice is heard shouting to the YOUNG MAN.*

MAXIME. You get out of here! Go on, get out, I tell you. I'll take over now.

When the lights go up again at the end of this speech the room is the same, but a strange pale daylight falls from the high window on to the table, now cleared of cutlery, where ROBESPIERRE is lying. In a corner, two men in red caps of liberty appear to be on guard. Later, but not yet, we will recognize CHARLES *and the* KITCHEN BOY. *They are playing cards on a stool. Suddenly* JOSEPH *stops playing and goes to the table where* ROBESPIERRE *is lying motionless, automatically staunching blood from his jaw from time to time.*

CHARLES. Is he dead?

JOSEPH (*coming back*). No. He's still moving. He's just wiped the blood off his mouth.

CHARLES. Have we got to stand guard over him all night?

JOSEPH. Yes, use your head, man! Four o'clock in the morning, that's no time to start guillotining people. This is the Age of Equality. They'll guillotine him at noon, like anybody else.

He stuffs a wad of tobacco in his mouth. The other lights his pipe and they go on with their game, laying down their winning cards as

THE CURTAIN FALLS

ACT TWO

The same set. The two men are still playing cards. The light has changed. One of them takes a gulp of wine from a bottle, goes to take a look at ROBESPIERRE *and comes back again.*

CHARLES (*shuffling the cards*). Is he dead?

JOSEPH. No. Still breathing.

CHARLES. If they wait till noon, they won't even be able to show him to the people. I know a dying man when I see one.

JOSEPH. They have a tougher hide than you'd think, some of them. I was turnkey over at the 'Force' in September '92 when they liquidated the prisoners. Rough day of it we had. Oh, did we sweat! A whole day, killing in the blazing sun. (*Bitterly.*) There was one I saw – he was a non-juring priest. I lift my hatchet and I bash him one full in the face. He turns round, grabs me by the throat, and he starts to throttle me – with his skull split wide open, the bastard! (*He adds indignantly.*) A priest, man! Spurting all over the place, it was. I was covered in it.

CHARLES. Your wife must have said a thing or two when you got home!

JOSEPH. She knew you couldn't keep clean killing all day. She dressed me according. But it was our little Louison, my youngest. She'd just come back from the country, from my brother's farm. When she sees me coming in like that, guess what she says? A real gem it was. 'Dada,' she says, 'you've killed the pig! Shall we have sausage for supper?'

They both laugh. He wipes away a little tear.

Parson sausage! The things they think of the little innocents. (*Carrying straight on.*) Talking of meat though, I'd say '92 was the worst year of the lot.

CHARLES. Do you reckon it's better now, then?

JOSEPH. No. It's tough. And to think that's what we stormed the Bastille for.

CHARLES. You were there, were you, at the Bastille?

JOSEPH (*after a slight pause*). N-no. Were you?

CHARLES (*equally cautious*). No. Mind you, everybody couldn't be there. And when they transferred you to the Committee, it was a step up for you, was it – after being a turnkey?

JOSEPH. In a way, yes. It was better thought of. But over at the 'Force', if you know when to look the other way, the night before executions, say, with people wanting to say good-bye to their friends, you could make yourself some good tips. And if it's true what they say, that there's to be no more executions now old Robespierre's dead, I know some who'll feel the pinch, in the prison service.

CHARLES. I don't care what they say, those folk had the tipping habit. Those good times are over now, though. Next thing you know they'll be emptying the jails.

JOSEPH (*worriedly*). You may be right . . .

CHARLES. To begin with, the people have had enough of the guillotine. (*He darts an anxious look at the prone figure of* ROBESPIERRE *and goes on darkly.*) There's been protests. It began with the Rue St Honoré. What with the tumbrils going past the whole time – well, I mean! It was upsetting trade! Now it's the districts where the cemeteries are that won't stand for it. They're afraid of epidemics. Well, you can't blame them. The pits were brimming over.

JOSEPH. They put lime in, I heard.

CHARLES. Lime doesn't do anything, it still stinks. I mean

to say, executions are one thing, but you can't go thumbing your noses at the public.

JOSEPH (*looking at* ROBESPIERRE). Hullo, your customer just moved.

CHARLES. With a bit of luck, they'll kill him alive. Are you going along?

JOSEPH (*shrugging*). Puh, executions . . . There's not the same excitement you got at the beginning.

ROBESPIERRE *has suddenly sat up and gone to throw himself into a near-by arm-chair. The two men jump up.*

CHARLES. Hey, citizen! Where do you think you're going?

ROBESPIERRE. I don't want to lie down any more.

CHARLES (*to* JOSEPH. Shall we let him?

JOSEPH. It makes no difference to us. But you just try escaping, citizen, and we'll stick to our orders.

ROBESPIERRE (*says quietly with a faint smile*). Where do you suppose I could run to?

JOSEPH. True. It's guarded here. Not like last night's mess up at the City Hall.

ROBESPIERRE (*looking around him*). How did they get me here?

JOSEPH. On a plank.

ROBESPIERRE (*unexpectedly*). What have I done to you?

CHARLES. To us? Nothing.

ROBESPIERRE (*with a vague gesture*). To them?

CHARLES (*with a like gesture*). That's politics. Danton hadn't done anything to us either. We do what we're told. Seems it's citizen Tallien who's in command now. What do you expect us to do about it?

ROBESPIERRE. I should like some water to stop the bleeding.

The two men look at each other.

CHARLES. I'll see if I can find a basin. Keep an eye on him.

ROBESPIERRE *remains alone with* JOSEPH, *who paces about a bit, then settles himself astride a chair and goes off to sleep.*

ROBESPIERRE (*softly*). I shan't speak. They'll never hear my voice again. Danton shouted right until the last. Play actor! Not me. They'll never know what I was thinking, from the moment that young ruffian fired his pistol full in my face. I looked at him as he pulled the trigger. It's odd, I had plenty of time to look at him. He wasn't yet twenty. He was as handsome as a god. I almost took him for Saint-Just. I didn't move. I let the pain open in me, suddenly, like a great red flower.

A pause. JOSEPH *is snoring now, on his chair.* ROBESPIERRE *goes on softly.*

All the noise, the fury and the agitation, the hatred and the hurts – gone with a pistol shot. As my blood oozed away through the hole in my jaw, I felt, one by one, all my other wounds close up inside me. Just a little more blood, a little more life still left, and then I would be cured, at last.

A pause. He adds mysteriously.

It all falls into place. But it took a long time to learn.

The CLASS MASTER *of the college – a Jesuit priest who has the same features as the King – and the child Robespierre enter upstage. It is the grown-up* ROBESPIERRE *who speaks the little boy's lines, without appearing to notice the Jesuit Father.*

MASTER (*holding the canes in his hand*). Robespierre, you are an excellent pupil, but you are not respectful enough.

ROBESPIERRE. I obey in everything, Father.

MASTER. Your mind is not respectful enough. There is something rigid in your mind which disquiets me. We will teach you pliability.

ROBESPIERRE. Yes, Father.

MASTER. You say 'Yes, Father', but something in your mind is saying no. We will not rest content with your apparent submission, Robespierre. We will chastise you until your mind says yes.

A pause.

ROBBESPIERRE. How will you know, Father?

MASTER (*softly*). For that question, Robespierre, you will receive ten extra strokes of the birch. Now, I shall answer it. We shall know when we no longer feel uncomfortable with you. You are a little scribbler, Robespierre. You are here out of charity. You are by far our best pupil, and yet we are obliged to punish you. You know why the Rev. Father prescribed those ten strokes of the birch, plus ten from me for your insolent question just now? Undo your clothes, if you please.

ROBESPIERRE (*beginning to undress*). Yes, Father, I know why.

MASTER. The very tone of your reply shows that you do not know. Or rather that you do not want to know. You are going to be whipped because you are poor and are making it a cause for pride.

ROBESPIERRE. Yes, Father.

MASTER. Turn around. Settle comfortably under my arm. You are going to be whipped for your obstinate insistence in always coming first. Because we know very well that every first prize you wrench from us is an act of revenge on the part of your pride, to make us pay for our charity.

ROBESPIERRE. Yes, Father.

MASTER. Turn round. Settle comfortably under my arm. We will either break our canes, Robespierre, or your spirit.

He whips him vigorously. Young Robespierre's face remains impassive. ROBESPIERRE *himself has slowly risen from his chair, his face deathly pale.*

The other boys beg for mercy, the proudest of them lets out a cry. We will break your silence, too.

Young Robespierre begins to do his clothes up in silence. The MASTER *studies him for a moment or so. A bell rings in the distance.*

It is nearly time for the visit from our Lord Bishop, who will certainly congratulate you on your remarkable composition in Latin verse. After your little triumph you will come back to my study, bare that ludicrous part of our anatomy where we have placed shame, and receive the ten strokes which I still owe you.

ROBESPIERRE. Yes, Father. Have I leave to go now?

MASTER (*gazing at him*). I should like to make a human being of you, Robespierre. I should like to prise some little failing out of you. You have my permission to beg for forgiveness and the remission of your punishment. I am quite prepared to examine your request favourably in view of that Latin verse composition which will bring honour to our college. (*A short pause.*) I am not asking you for a painful demonstration. A word would do. (*Another pause.*) After all, you are very young . . . You have perhaps not quite understood why I have seen fit to inflict this additional punishment on you?

ROBESPIERRE (*quietly*). Yes, I have, Father.

MASTER. Very well. You may go back to your class. I shall expect you after his Lordship's visit.

He throws down the canes with a hint of pique.

This cane is wearing out. I must put in for a new one.

Young Robespierre goes off towards his classroom. The MASTER *watches him go and calls after him gently.*

Robespierre! If you forget to come, I have a great deal to do now with term ending, I might very well forget, too . . .

Young Robespierre turns at the door.

ROBESPIERRE (*simply*). I shall come, Father.

He goes out. The MASTER *suddenly clasps his hands and says.*

MASTER. O Almighty God, lighten this child's burden of pride.

He crosses himself and goes out on the opposite side.
Left alone, ROBESPIERRE *walks over to the birch, looks at it, touches it with his foot, then picks it up gingerly with a sort of frightened curiosity and sets it down again. He goes to pick up* BITOS'S *bowler hat and little black overcoat which are lying in a corner. He puts them on and goes to sit timidly on the edge of a chair. He seems to be waiting apprehensively for someone. He gets up and says in a drained voice, like someone reciting a speech.*

ROBESPIERRE. I am a young deputy from . . .

His voice dies away with shyness. He sits himself down on the edge of his chair again, and settles down to wait. Suddenly MIRABEAU *walks in swiftly, in a dressing-gown, elegant and spry for all his weight. He is utterly at ease, which makes an even greater contrast with* ROBESPIERRE.

MIRABEAU. (*holding out his hand*). Have I kept you waiting, young man? I was receiving a charming and rather soporific delegation. The ladies of the Paris markets came to bring me fruit and fish to congratulate me on my speech. (*He smiles.*) As you see, the job of a public man has some small advantages: one gets fed. (*He graciously waves him to a seat.* ROBESPIERRE *sits down stiffly.*) You wanted to see me?

ROBESPIERRE (*beginning his prepared speech*). Sir, I am a young deputy from the Constituent Assembly, where I represent the Arras division –

MIRABEAU. Oh yes! You wrote to me. Maximilien de Robetierre.

ROBESPIERRE (*correcting him*). Robespierre.

MIRABEAU (*with a smile and a gracious wave of the hand*). Yes, of course, Robespierre. Forgive me. I have a poor memory for names, but I never forget a face. Have you made a speech yet?

ROBESPIERRE. I had the honour of intervening in the debate of the 30th May.

MIRABEAU (*kindly*). So you did. They didn't take very kindly to you. Voice a little weak, diction rather shaky still . . . I must give you a few tips. We must resign ourselves to cultivating our effects like opera singers. Let's see, what were you speaking about, exactly?

ROBESPIERRE (*with the ghost of a smile*). The marriage of priests. I urged the Assembly to grant them permission to marry.

MIRABEAU *eyes him sardonically.*

MIRABEAU. Most interesting. Of course, there wasn't any particular urgency –

ROBESPIERRE (*quietly*). I beg your pardon. There was urgency.

MIRABEAU (*bursts out laughing*). Do you think they're as frantic as all that? They can go on cuddling their housekeepers for a while yet.

He pats him kindly on the shoulder and takes out his snuffbox.

Believe me, young man, you didn't choose the subject of your first speech very well.

ROBESPIERRE (*insisting*). But I did, sir.

MIRABEAU (*offering him his snuffbox*). Do you take snuff!

ROBESPIERRE. No.

MIRABEAU. You should, it clears the mind. Yes, I can place you completely now. Maximilien de Robenpierre.

ROBESPIERRE (*correcting him*). Robespierre.

MIRABEAU (*not at all put out*). Robespierre. I like you very much. I know they laugh at you a bit, in the Assembly. Assemblies must always find themselves someone to laugh at; it eases tension. Try to arrange it so that this thankless role devolves on someone else. Better diction to begin with. There is also something a little dogmatic in you, a little pedantic, a little starchy, something – let's not mince words – a little boring which tends to put one off. (*He rises.*) Having principles isn't enough, my dear boy. After all, we're in the theatre. You must learn the craft of the tragedian.

He propels him gently towards the door.

Do come again, I shall always be glad to see you. And choose better subjects for your speeches.

ROBESPIERRE (*persistently*). Forgive me for persisting, sir. But I wanted to say that this proposal for the marriage of priests could please a large part of the minor clergy.

MIRABEAU (*a little impatiently*). Yes, yes, I don't doubt it for a moment. And I'll willingly discuss the matter with you some other time, but I am very busy today. (*He smiles and says with a certain amiable condescension.*) To tell you the truth, I haven't had breakfast yet.

ROBESPIERRE (*with a humble smirk*). I know it's uncouth of me to cling on like this. I am uncouth. That's another reason why they laugh at me in the Assembly. I only wanted to say that strength, the strength we need, cannot be the achievement of a single man, even a man of genius, like yourself. The minor clergy in France number some eighty thousand priests who are powerful electors. One may think what one likes of the urgency of their right to marry, but getting them married is the only way to bind them to the Revolution.

MIRABEAU (*who has already opened the door, turns and looks at him*). You are a queer fish. Is that what you wanted to say in the debate? Why on earth didn't you say it then?

ROBESPIERRE (*humbly*). I did. But I couldn't make myself heard. I haven't any genius, you see.

MIRABEAU (*studying him*). Where does strength lie, then, in your opinion?

ROBESPIERRE (*with a soft gleam in his eye*). In the second-rate, since they are the majority.

MIRABEAU (*heavily, after a pause*). I don't like the second-rate.

ROBESPIERRE (*still softly*). We need them. What we have to do will only be done by them.

MIRABEAU (*murmurs, musing*). For them, perhaps. Not by them.

ROBESPIERRE (*more softly still*). Why not?

MIRABEAU. Because they are too near to petty things.

ROBESPIERRE. Is that their fault?

MIRABEAU. No, but it's a fact. To give them power would be to risk having them lose their way in secondary problems. Men who govern must rise a little higher than that. And their lives have not accustomed them to heights.

ROBESPIERRE (*with sudden harshness*). Yet it is those second-rate men who will make the Revolution, whether you and your kind like it or not.

MIRABEAU *looks him up and down, surprised by this change of tone.*

MIRABEAU. Who gave you leave to use that tone to me, my little man?

ROBESPIERRE (*with a venomous hiss which suddenly transforms him*). I'm one of them.

MIRABEAU (*going to him, heavy footed, jovial, and taking his arm*). All right then, you listen to me. I would rather go and live in Constantinople, with the Grand Turk, than see six hundred nonentities make or break France; declare themselves in power for life, perhaps, in the name of the few million nonentities who elected them.

ROBESPIERRE (*hissing*). What if those few millions of nonentities are France?

MIRABEAU (*thundering*). They live in France. But it wasn't they who made it! Do you think France was built the way one runs a grocer's shop? The men who built France had nothing in common with them but the fact of having two arms and two legs, but, I regret to inform you, heads that towered above theirs!

ROBESPIERRE (*dropping the mask suddenly*). In the years that are coming, we shall have to get busy cutting off those towering heads. Might you be unaware of that, Count Mirabeau?

MIRABEAU (*with sudden anger*). Count Mirabeau sends you to hell, you young pipsqueak, where he's been sending all the Mirabeau counts in his family ever since he reached the age of understanding. And he will not allow a little runt to pass judgement on him now! (*He controls his anger abruptly and goes on more calmly.*) Get the devil out of here!

He takes his arm and calmly draws him to the door. ROBESPIERRE *follows, resisting a little.*)

Was it to treat me to drivel of this sort that you asked to see me?

ROBESPIERRE (*distorted with hate*). I came to see you because I admired you!

MIRABEAU (*cheerfully*). Well, that's one load less for you to carry then! Admiration is always heavy!

ROBESPIERRE. I hate you now.

MIRABEAU (*smiling*). Do. That may lend a little tone to your next speech. Cultivate your diction my boy, as well as your hates. And try to be likeable. In France, one can do nothing without charm. Take that poor old Louis 16th, who hasn't any; look at the mess he's in.

ROBESPIERRE (*yelping*). I don't want to be charming! I'll never charm anybody!

MIREABEAU. No, I'm afraid you won't. I'll ring for someone to show you out.

He rings a bell.

ROBESPIERRE (*shouting, contorted with hatred*). I don't need your lackeys to show me to the door!

He spits on the floor.

MIREABEAU (*pained*). My dear boy. One can serve the Revolution and be polite as well.

ROBESPIERRE (*shouting*). No!

MIREABEAU (*shrugging*). To prove it to you, I shall show you to your carriage myself.

ROBESPIERRE. I haven't got a carriage!

MIRABEAU (*lightly, pushing him gently out*). Don't boast about it! It's a great inconvenience.

ROBESPIERRE (*clinging to the door, one doesn't quite know why*). I do boast about it!

MIRABEAU (*resignedly*). Very well.

He looks at him before he goes.

You've taught me a very sad thing, which is that the Revolution could be a bore. I thought it young and gay.

ROBESPIERRE (*shouting after him*). Frivolous! Frivolous, the lot of you! A witty phrase consoles you for everything. France will have to stop being frivolous one day – she'll have to become a bore like me before she's properly clean at last!

He brushes himself down in an abrupt, nervous gesture. SAINT-JUST *has just come in, brilliant, airy, very much at ease. He sees* ROBESPIERRE.

SAINT-JUST. Brushing yourself down again?

ROBESPIERRE *stops guiltily.* SAINT-JUST *sees the birch at* ROBESPIERRE'S *feet and picks it up.*

Have you thought over what we talked about yesterday?

ROBESPIERRE. Yes.

SAINT-JUST. Danton said last night at Vefours – true, he was with women, but Danton always is with women – he said that one day the Republic, once out of danger, could afford clemency and forgive its enemies. It's a mere phrase, of course. But this one, after your speech last week urging the Assembly to greater severity, is downright provocation. Are you going to let it pass?

ROBESPIERRE (*averting his eyes*). Danton was my comrade in arms for a long time . . . Camille is still my friend.

SAINT-JUST (*smiling*). Your friend? Have you read the latest number of the *Cordelier Gazette*? He holds you up to ridicule! Here.

ROBESPIERRE *snatches the paper and starts to read. Then he shouts suddenly.*

ROBESPIERRE. He dared?

SAINT-JUST (*calmly*). Ah. That's roused you. I knew they'd have to wound your vanity as a man of letters to get at you at all.

ROBESPIERRE (*advancing on him, shouting*). Saint-Just, I shan't stand for this!

SAINT-JUST (*still calm and smiling*). God be praised! They're doomed this time.

A pause.

ROBESPIERRE (*dully*). This is a horrible decision to make. True, I've never liked Danton. (*Shouting*.) Danton is a hog, a stinking, rotting, posturing showman!

SAINT-JUST. Save yourself for the rostrum.

ROBESPIERRE. But Camille is a child. Reckless, frivolous, depraved, yes –

SAINT-JUST. One dies for far less than that in France these days. The puppy has a cruel bite. Read the article. It's amusing, as a matter of fact, and well written. He's not without talent.

ROBESPIERRE. No! It may be too soon. We've only just struck at Hébert.

SAINT-JUST. A stroke to the left, a stroke to the right, that's the way to steer a straight course. Did you never go boating on the Marne? Your reluctance does credit to your finer feelings, Robespierre. But we'll give way to sentiment later on, when we've cleaned up the world. Today, our duty lies elsewhere. Danton and Camille stand in the way. You know that as well as I do.

A pause.

ROBESPIERRE (*dully*). You'll have to speak against them, I couldn't do it. Friendship is a sentiment one doesn't flout with impunity.

He brushes himself down nervously, as if driven by a tic.

SAINT-JUST (*gently*). Stop brushing yourself down like that. You're quite clean. (*He pulls out his writing-pad.*) Now. The main points of the Indictment?

ROBESPIERRE *avoids his eyes. Then he pulls a piece of paper abruptly from his pocket and hands it to him.*

ROBESPIERRE. Here. I drew them up a week ago.

SAINT-JUST (*smiling*). You might have spared me the trouble of persuading you. (*He shuts the notebook*). We're supposed to be dining with Danton and Camille at Tallien's. Shall I cancel the engagement?

In the semi-darkness, the dinner guests settle themselves at the table and start to light the candles.

ROBESPIERRE (*after a pause*). No. We will offer up this painful ordeal as a sacrifice to the nation.

SAINT-JUST *bursts out laughing and says, as he moves nonchalantly towards the table.*

SAINT-JUST. You are a splendid character, Robespierre! I

never tire of watching you at work, which may well be the secret of why I stayed faithful to you until my death . . . You amused me.

ROBESPIERRE (*between his teeth*). Take care, Saint-Just!

SAINT-JUST. Of what? One has only one head. I've been gambling with mine in your company for years.

The scene merges into the dinner party.

ROBESPIERRE *has taken off* BITOS'S *overcoat and bowler hat. He walks primly towards the dinner table, where the others greet him mockingly, to the tune of 'La Carmagnole'.*

Shoulder to shoulder
We shall stand
And never fear the enemy.
Shoulder to shoulder
We shall stand
And never fear the enemy.
Fight for the Motherland
Brothers in Liberty.
Ring, ring the cannonade
Death to the foe
Death to the foe
Ring, ring the cannonade
Death to the foe!

DANTON *suddenly stops laughing and singing with the others and looks at* ROBESPIERRE.

DANTON (*shouting*). My friends! There is a traitor in our midst! Robespierre isn't drinking! Robespierre must drink!

ROBESPIERRE. I'm not thirsty.

DANTON. Not thirsty? To the Republic, the One and Indivisible!

EVERYBODY. To the Republic!

DANTON. You're trapped! Tomorrow it will be in all the papers. In letters this high. Leave it to Hébert. 'Patriot's dinner. Robespierre refuses to toast the Republic!'

ROBESPIERRE. I have a stomach ache. I've drunk too much already.

DANTON. Drink all the same, little priest. A pain in the belly is less dangerous in this day and age than a pain in the head. If you don't, I'll tell Hébert and he'll print it in his paper.

ROBESPIERRE. Hébert was arrested this evening.

(*A pause. The singing stops. They are suddenly a little sobered.*)

DANTON. Is this true?

SAINT-JUST (*rocking on his chair*). What Robespierre says is always true.

DANTON. When was this decided? (*Thundering as he bangs on the table.*) Why wasn't I told?

ROBESPIERRE (*coldly*). Where were you last night? We looked for you.

DANTON (*smiling, with an expansive gesture*). At the whore-house, yes, I know. I must tell you about it, little priest. I found an amazing girl at the Palais Royal. A freak . . . She's ugly as sin, but when you undress her –

ROBESPIERRE (*stiffly*). Keep your filth to yourself.

DANTON. Callipygian Venus! She had fleeced some big-wig during the old Régime and do you know where the hangman – who was a humorist – branded his Royal lily?

ROBESPIERRE (*on the verge of hysteria*). I order you – do you hear – I order you to be quiet!

DANTON (*charmingly*). Why? Are you going to accuse me of being a Royalist because of that? Mark you, if the

Revolution had been really vigilant, it should have stamped its cap of liberty on the other cheek. I'm with you there. There's something undercover in the whole affair which you ought to look into, Robespierre. I suspect that bum of being a meeting-place for aristocrats.

ROBESPIERRE (*yelping*). Don't think you can mock everything for ever, Danton.

DANTON (*charmingly, thrusting his face into* ROBESPIERRE'S). What needles you the most, tell me, the Royal lily or the girl's arse?

CAMILLE (*asks suddenly*). Who demanded the indictment of Hébert?

SAINT-JUST (*softly*). I did. In full agreement with Robespierre and with the Committee's unanimous vote. We had to put a stop to rabble rousers. The Committee has approved my list.

DANTON (*into his glass*). And who's on your list?

SAINT-JUST. Hébert, Chabot, Clootz, Sechelles, all proven Royalists.

DANTON (*flinging away his glass with a sudden roar*). Rabbit's piss! (*He chokes and bellows.*) I know we have to kill off a few more and I loathe that bunch as much as you do. But those fellows? Royalists?

SAINT-JUST (*lightly*). Royalists, Danton! Who would have thought it?

DANTON. Dear old Clootz, too – a Royalist? Saint-Just, you elegant viper, until the end of time they'll never know exactly what you were – dandy, imp of mischief, or destroying angel – but one thing is certain, you were very intelligent and –

SAINT-JUST (*interrupting, coldly*). And because I am very intelligent I have contrived to put Clootz on a Royalist list, and likewise Sechelles, your enemy. Oh, yes, and I nearly forgot, Fabre d'Eglantine. In his case it's even simpler; he's a thief.

DANTON. Sechelles is my enemy, but he's no Royalist! I'll shout that from the roof-tops!

SAINT-JUST. You're a child, Danton.

CAMILLE. And Fabre is not a thief! (*Turning to him.*) Robespierre!

ROBESPIERRE. Yes?

CAMILLE. You know that, you know Fabre never stole.

ROBESPIERRE (*inscrutably*). I know the Committee has decided that Fabre has stolen funds.

CAMILLE (*with an anguished cry*). Have we no right to be men any more?

ROBESPIERRE (*coldly*). What do you mean by that?

CAMILLE. That intelligence, that reason of ours, which was going to reshape the world – must we stifle all that now?

ROBESPIERRE (*trenchantly*). When the Committee of Public Safety has so decided, yes.

CAMILLE. When we stood up on our chairs and spoke to the people for the first time in the Palais Royal, we demanded that intelligence and reason should always prevail against tyranny. And that's why the people followed us.

ROBESPIERRE (*quietly*). We killed tyranny, don't forget that.

CAMILLE. We didn't kill it! Where's the difference between the arbitrary rule of Royal ministers and that of a handful of men whom we've made more powerful than ever they were?

ROBESPIERRE (*calmly*). I'm amazed that you can't see the difference, Camille.

CAMILLE (*shouting*). No! I can't see it! I can't see it any more.

ROBESPIERRE (*dryly*). This deficiency of perception could ruin you if you weren't among friends. When the King's Ministers made arbitrary decisions they did so for what they called reasons of state. When the Committee of Public Safety makes decisions which may seem arbitrary to you, it does so for the good of the people. That's the difference.

CAMILLE. Words.

ROBESPIERRE (*tersely*). They will do for me.

CAMILLE. Tyranny is tyranny!

ROBESPIERRE. Must I teach you your catechism? There isn't a ten-year-old dunce in the national schools who can't recite it better than you. The tyranny of kings is a crime! The tyranny of the people is sacred. (*He calms down, and smiles.*) You distress me, Camille.

CAMILLE (*quietly*). Robespierre, we are not on the rostrum now. I've pulled political wires, just as you have –

ROBESPIERRE (*equally quietly*). You watch your words, Camille.

CAMILLE. But we're among ourselves now, friends round a dinner table for an evening's relaxation. Battle companions, too. (*He adds tonelessly.*) And we're even closer, you and I. I was a junior, Maximilien, at school, and you were already in the seniors. But I admired you, I followed you everywhere, I loved you.

ROBESPIERRE (*coldly*). I loved you, too.

CAMILLE. Robespierre, I still admire and love you. Must I beg you on my knees? Don't stay shut in that prison of logic where we can't reach you. It's the little boy you dazzled long ago with your intelligence and your courage who's asking you that now.

ROBESPIERRE (*pulling* CAMILLE *roughly to his feet*). Get up. This is a ridiculous scene. It's late; we must go home. (*He turns smiling to* TALLIEN and THERESA.) My dear Tallien, it's been delightful. Citizeness Tallien really is a marvellous hostess. (*He smiles ambiguously.*) One must say that for ex-aristocrats, they did know how to entertain.

THERESA (*smiling*). Is that a threat? Must I pack my little bundle this evening, Robespierre?

ROBESPIERRE (*kissing her hand*). Dear lady, I was merely paying you a compliment.

DANTON (*with a roar of mirth*). Dear lady! He called her dear lady! And he kissed her hand! Versailles! We're back at Versailles! Oh, now I can die happy! I'll gladly die tomorrow!

SAINT-JUST (*smiling and still nonchalant*). One should never say that, Danton.

DANTON (*going to* ROBESPIERRE *and making his comic little bows*). Kissing the ladies' hands! Maximilien, you old rogue! Red heels to his shoes and we never knew it!

He gives him a hefty slap on the back. ROBESPIERRE *staggers.*

ROBESPIERRE. Imbecile!

DANTON (*putting a friendly arm round his neck*). Well, – it's Tallien's wine, dammit – I'm in an imbecilic mood . . . God, how we've complicated things with these brains of ours . . . and things are simple, Max, my lad, very simple. They obey laws as old as the world, and between ourselves, you and I won't ever change them. We can draw up constitutions until we're blue in the face! Take strength now, physical strength. I take you and I lift you up.

He does so.

Here you are, up in the air; it makes absolutely no sense at all! You're helpless; you'd like to come down. Not a chance! You can't. Now, *that's* a simple thing. *There's* the real inequality between men!

ROBESPIERRE (*wriggling absurdly up in the air and squealing*). Stop it! Stop it, you fool! Put me down!

DANTON (*bawling like a street vendor*). I'm putting you down! But now watch this! I grip him round the throat, so! Still in fun! With one hand, citizens!

ROBESPIERRE (*choking*). Danton, stop it! You're choking me!

DANTON (*softly*). I know I'm choking you. (*He looks at the choking* ROBESPIERRE.) How simple history could be, when you stop to think. But I don't want to deprive us all of Robespierre, friends. We should miss him.

He lets him go.

Simpler still. The arm. Just the arm!

He twists ROBESPIERRE'S *arm behind his back.*

I twist it very gently.

ROBESPIERRE (*sweating in his efforts not to cry out*). Stop it!

DANTON (*softly*). I'll bet you that in three seconds you're going to say you're sorry, Robespierre. Sorry for everything. Sorry for the past, for the future, for whatever I say. Nobody's a stoic when someone has hold of your arm like this.

ROBESPIERRE *grimaces with clenched teeth, and slithers to the floor.*

My friends, the Committee of Public Safety is down on the floor. Now I am master of France! Say sorry, Robespierre. Say sorry, Robespierre. Say sorry. Come on, say sorry.

ROBESPIERRE (*writhing with pain*). Saint-Just . . .!

SAINT-JUST *has risen. Coldly he touches* DANTON *on the shoulder with his cane.*

SAINT-JUST. Danton, I know you're drunk, but either finish him off, or let him go. A semi-game is dangerous.

DANTON (*smiling as he releases* ROBESPIERRE). No. It was only for a little fun, between friends. I couldn't even kill a chicken now. I have a horror of death.

SAINT-JUST *smiles maliciously as* ROBESPIERRE *nervously brushes himself down.*

SAINT-JUST. You're getting old, Danton.

DANTON (*turning suddenly says gravely*). Yes, Saint-Just, I'm getting old. Blood is slowly beginning to turn my stomach. And other things, tiny little everyday things, which I didn't even know existed, are starting to matter to me now.

SAINT-JUST. What things – may one know?

DANTON. Work, children, the sweets of friendship and love. Everything that has always made men what they are until now.

SAINT-JUST (*coldly*). In short, a complete counter-revolutionary programme. (*He turns to* ROBESPIERRE *with a smile.*) My dear Max, we're being very hard on them both. I can quite see now why they are all for leniency. Danton has just married a lovely young wife and Camille is losing himself more and more in Lucille's love. Why cut off their heads just because they don't think our way any more? All we have to do is pull a cotton nightcap over them. Eh, Danton?

He slaps DANTON *on the back. They both laugh.*

DANTON. Pending one or other of these operations, shall I drive you back to Paris, my little Max?

ROBESPIERRE (*still brushing himself nervously*). There's no other carriage!

SAINT-JUST (*softly, from behind him*). You're clean, stop brushing yourself.

TALLIEN (*smiling as if nothing much had happened and picking up a candle to see them out*). Camille, dear boy, you're young and generous hearted. But you'll learn when you grow up that those are no virtues for a public man . . . I knew about the Committee's decision and tonight's arrests, but I didn't say a word during your little argument, did you notice? We all know, and Robespierre best of all, that those men were not quite as black as we have to say they were. But we have to say so. The people need to have things spelled out for them . . . Well, there it is. Those men will have been soldiers sacrificed on a field of battle, lost children of the Revolution. . . . Having obtained the required result, Robespierre himself will make it a point of honour – won't you, Robespierre? – to rehabilitate them one day.

ROBESPIERRE. Every drop of blood I'm forced to shed is wrung from my own veins, I promise you. But there is no friend I would not sacrifice to my duty. I can promise you that, too.

TALLIEN (*smiling and putting a hand on* CAMILLE'S *shoulder*). You understand, Camille?

CAMILLE (*as if lost*). No. I don't. I don't understand anything any more. Let's go home, Lucille, I'm tired.

TALLIEN (*motioning to* THERESA). We'll see you to your carriage . . .

THERESA (*going out on* DANTON'S *arm*). Wonderful night for April, don't you think?

TALLIEN (*softly, as he goes out*). Floreal, beloved, Floreal, not April. You really must remember the new names, my darling, or you'll get us into trouble. (*He sighs.*) Poor Fabre! All there'll be left of him is a calendar and a song. Do you remember, my love, 'Il pleut, il pleut, Bergère' . . . Charming little thing . . .

He goes out humming. ROBESPIERRE *has hung back a little.* LUCILLE *comes back into the room suddenly and stops just outside the circle of light. He has stopped, too.*

LUCILLE (*quietly*). You can't have Camille killed, Robespierre.

ROBESPIERRE (*stiffly, with a faint hint of falseness in his tone*). I would sacrifice myself if necessary. Greatness is very costly.

LUCILLE (*looking at him*). What is greatness?

ROBESPIERRE. The ruthless fulfilment of one's duty.

LUCILLE (*still quietly*). And what is your duty?

ROBESPIERRE. To follow a straight road whatever the cost, towards that clearing in the forest where the Revolution will at last be fully realized.

LUCILLE. What if that clearing receded as it does in fairy tales?

ROBESPIERRE. Then we should have to continue the struggle.

LUCILLE. For ever?

ROBESPIERRE. For ever.

LUCILLE. Without concern for people?

ROBESPIERRE. Without concern for people.

LUCILLE (*still softly*). But it's for people that you want this Revolution.

ROBESPIERRE (*brushing a thought away with his hand*). For other people, without faces.

A pause.

LUCILLE (*gently*). Robespierre. I'm a woman. Women know things that you don't know. Life is made in the depths of their wombs. They have known since always that, in the daytime, there are no men. You've all of you stayed little boys, with your ideas, your assurance which nothing can shake, your fits of violence . . .

ROBESPIERRE (*with an impatient gesture*). Lucille, I have important business . . .

LUCILLE (*smiling*). Of course! Right from the age of fifteen, you've all had so many things to do, always! Becoming generals, discovering the North Pole, building the reign of Justice, taking your revenge . . . Your plans haven't changed since your voices broke. And not one of you set yourself the task of just becoming a man.

ROBESPIERRE (*with another impatient gesture*). Lucille –

LUCILLE. Everything you've just said to me I've heard Camille say, almost to a word. I used to smile and run my fingers through his hair, and I'd go and cook his supper, so that he'd at least eat something. Then the night came and he'd fall asleep at last, defeated, in the hollow of my arm, a man again. I didn't sleep. I looked at my man as he slept, savouring the weight of his head on my shoulder, of his leg across my body. I weighed his real weight as a man, at last, as all silent women do at night. (*A short pause: she asks gently.*) Nobody has ever watched you sleeping, have they, Robespierre?

ROBESPIERRE (*stiffly*). No.

LUCILLE. They'll feel the want of that, when they come to weigh up exactly what you were.

ROBESPIERRE (*with a sudden cry*). Nobody will ever need to know what I was. I was nothing.

He brushes himself down. Another pause. LUCILLE *says very quietly.*

LUCILLE. Give me back Camille's weight on my shoulder, Robespierre. Not because he was your friend at school. Give him back to me because you loved me once.

A pause.

ROBESPIERRE (*stiffly*). If I did that, Lucille, I should be a coward.

LUCILLE (*scarcely audibly*). What is a coward? Past the age of fifteen, nobody knows that either. (*Another pause: she murmurs wearily.*) Very well. I shall go and join Camille alone, since you won't give him back to me.

She moves away gently, already a shadow. On the edge of the circle of light she turns and says.

Poor Robespierre, who kills because he couldn't succeed in growing up . . .

She has gone. ROBESPIERRE *is alone in the middle of the stage, stiff and tense. A spasm distorts his face and he murmurs.*

ROBESPIERRE. No, I haven't grown up. I still hate people. Big fat Mirabeau, with his pot belly and his smile; taking my arm with his stubby ringed fingers and trying to throw me out. (*He rubs his arm.*) And the Jesuit father with his birch: 'Do you know why you are going to be whipped, Robespierre?' And Danton with his big voice and his man's smell. 'Say sorry, Robespierre! Say sorry, Robespierre. Say sorry, Robespierre.'
(*He breaks into sudden, hysterical laughter and yelps.*) Say sorry, Danton! (*He brushes something off his lapel, straightens his clothes and goes on composedly.*) I'll teach them to frighten me. That big Samson who chops their heads off, he stinks too, him and his two assistants with their brawny arms. And they smile fatly down at the girls from the scaffold because they know that the bitches will be waiting for them at night, warm and damp and willing. (*He hisses.*) Whores! I'll widow the lot of you! Wait though, my pretties. Those big lovers of yours, those strong-limbed bulls, those males of yours – you don't know that Robespierre, little Robespierre, has only to look at them, Robespierre who's so thin and ugly – (*He glares with malicious irony and then rocks with mirth.*) So you still want your nightly loving, do you? So you want to look pretty? You want to live a little? Look at me – am I living?

He stares at an imaginary male, then gives a short cackle and spits. He puts on BITO'S *hat and coat. He starts to brush himself down frantically, with a satisfied snigger.* SAINT-JUST *comes in.*

SAINT-JUST. You must stop brushing yourself down like that. It's a ridiculous habit. What were you doing all alone in this empty room? Rehearsing your speech?

ROBESPIERRE *goes to him, panting. This whole scene is played in a tempo of fevered inspiration.*

ROBESPIERRE. Saint-Just, there is in this race of people an incurable bent for fecklessness and easy living. They're more interested in playing bowls or fondling girls than carving out their destiny. I used to loathe the aristocrats, but the lowest workman in France still wears red satin heels. Insolent nation!

SAINT-JUST (*smiling*). Do you want to pass a law against insolence?

ROBESPIERRE. I want to pass a law teaching them to relearn the meaning of respect. (*He sidles over to him.*) We must re-create their God for them. A god of our own making. A God whom we'll keep permanently under control. A decree, that's all we want. Article One: The people of France acknowledge the existence of the Supreme Being. Article Two: They acknowledge that the worship of the Supreme Being is the guiding beacon of man's duties.

SAINT-JUST (*straight-faced*). Are you sure that means anything?

ROBESPIERRE (*unaware of the irony*). Yes. Article Three: The penalty for all blasphemers is death.

SAINT-JUST (*laughing*). Well, that means something anyhow! (*He goes on.*) They'll cheat your God, whatever name you give him. They all cheat. It's in their blood.

ROBESPIERRE (*shouting*). I'll kill them if they cheat! Do I cheat? I'll kill every single one who cheats! I'll guillotine everybody! And I'll rebuild the nation – afterwards. Tomorrow I'll pass a law reforming the Revolutionary Tribunal. It's all too slow! What we lack is the instrument. You write it down. Article One: The Revolutionary Tribunal is set up to punish the enemies of the people. Article Two: The enemies of the people are those who try to annihilate liberty –

SAINT-JUST (*jotting it down in his notebook*). Liberty. I'm not laughing.

He glances up at ROBESPIERRE, *who is looking at him.*

ROBESPIERRE (*goes on, unheedingly*). – Article Three: The penalty for all offenders is death.

SAINT-JUST (*writing it down*). Death.

ROBESPIERRE (*in full creative euphoria*). Article Four: If proof exists, no witnesses will be brought. Article Five: The law gives patriots the defence of patriotic juries! Conspirators will be allowed no jury at all!

He drops into a chair, exhausted by his shouting, and brushes himself down. SAINT-JUST *calmly reads over his notes.*

SAINT-JUST. To take effect retrospectively. Prejudiced juries. No defence. It's a model of its kind. It will be used again. (*He asks.*) Who will arrange for the Tribunal?

ROBESPIERRE. The Committee of Public Safety.

SAINT-JUST. And who will provide the committee with names?

ROBESPIERRE. A Commission, unknown to the Committee, will draw up lists of suspects. The Committee will merely sign them and pass them on to the Tribunal.

SAINT-JUST. And the Tribunal?

ROBESPIERRE. The Tribunal will pass sentence.

SAINT-JUST (*a little taken aback, even so*). But then who will have tried them?

ROBESPIERRE (*mysteriously, as if soothed*). Nobody. The machinery of the law. We must install reliable nobodies, interlock them like cogs in a machine, and dispense as far as possible with the human element, so that everything will seem to decide itself. I myself shall withdraw. The wheels of the law will grind alone.

He brushes himself.

SAINT-JUST (*smiling, as he pockets his notebook*). Where does God come into this? Have you given him up?

ROBESPIERRE *stops brushing and stands up, relaxed and calm.*

ROBESPIERRE. No. We'll start with God. We must give the people back a moral sense. Besides, they need a holiday to help them forget Danton. This evening I shall read the decree on the Supreme Being. I want a celebration, a very fine, very touching celebration. We'll remove the guillotine – just for one day. I want flowers, lots of flowers, girls in white dresses, children – oh, the innocence of children! – choral singers, gymnastic teams, something that will uplift us all! (*He takes* SAINT-JUST *by the arm and leads him off, quite relaxed now.*) I can't do everything!

They have gone.

BLACKOUT *suddenly. When the lights go up again,* CHARLES *is by the table, in ordinary clothes, holding a basin. Everyone crowds round* BITOS, *who is squatting on the floor, nursing his chin. Outside, a heavy rain-storm can be heard.*

BITOS (*holding his jaw, says venomously*). I shall prefer a charge! Attempted murder. Article 117.

MAXIME (*smiling*). No, no, Bitos. You just fainted with fright. The gun wasn't loaded. Robespierre, the real one, was shot in the jaw. But not you. I put a little too much powder in, that's all. Give him the glass, Charles, and let him see for himself.

> CHARLES *hands the mirror to* BITOS, *who slowly and suspiciously lets go of his chin. He looks so funny as he tests the state of his jaw that the others can contain themselves no longer and burst out laughing. He leaps to his feet, shouting.*

BITOS. My hat! My coat!

> CHARLES *hands him his little overcoat and his bowler. Outside one hears the thunder and the rain falling in sheets.* BITOS *gravely puts on his hat after a sort of collective bow and says shortly.*

Thank you.

PHILIPPE (*stepping forward*). You really must let Vulturne and me drive you home. You can't go out in this rain in white stockings and pumps.

BITOS (*vexed, going up the stairs*). I shall find a taxi.

MAXIME (*shouting up at him*). At midnight, in a provincial town, no one has ever found a taxi, Bitos.

> CHARLES *steps forward and says to* BITOS, *who is hovering on the threshold, battling with the door against the wind.*

CHARLES. Perhaps I could lend you my umbrella, sir.

BITOS. Thank you.

He takes the umbrella and tries vainly to open it against the wind.

CHARLES (*crying out anxiously*). It's a little stiff. If you'll allow me, sir?

BITOS (*with a jaundiced smile*). Robespierre may not have known how to boil an egg, but I am still capable of opening an umbrella!

He lunges into the wind.

CHARLES (*increasingly worried, cries*). Careful, sir, please! You have to know the way of it. It's a little nervy, is that umbrella.

BITOS *has forced open the umbrella, determined at all costs to get the better of it. The thing is now inside out.*

There! I knew it! You have to know how to handle it. It's very sensitive.

BITOS *throws the umbrella at him with a baleful look and, clutching his hat with both hands, hurls himself into the storm amid the general laughter, not without the door bashing into his face first.*

A WOMAN'S VOICE. The door! Shut the door!

MAXIME *starts to run up the stairs.* VULTURNE *follows him up.*

VULTURNE (*yelling against the wind and the growling storm*). Maxime! We've got to bring him back! If you let him leave like this, tomorrow he'll prefer a charge and young Delanoue will go back to jail.

MAXIME *looks at him, then snatches off his wig, turns his collar up and starts after* BITOS. BRASSAC, *who has done likewise, joins him.*

BRASSAC. No! Not you, Maxime. I employ twenty thousand factory hands. Pacifying the People is my job. Your gamp, Charles!

CHARLES, *who has mended it, hands him the umbrella.* BRASSAC *seizes it and dashes out, shouting over his shoulder.*

I'll bring him back. You'll have to flatter him. Lila, I'm counting on you. Don't forget, Bitos is a snob at heart and he particularly values the good opinion of the class he's intending to have shot one day.

He vanishes into the night.

MAXIME (*turning to* CHARLES). Charles, bring us some whisky.
CHARLES (*pained*). Between courses, sir?
MAXIME (*firmly*). Between courses, Charles.

CHARLES *goes out with a disillusioned shrug.*

CURTAIN

ACT THREE

Everyone is on stage, waiting anxiously. BRASSAC *pokes his head in through the kitchen door. He has shed his wig. He is wearing a rug over his shoulders and is wiping his hair dry with a towel.*

BRASSAC. He's telephoning for a friend to come and fetch him in his car, but I've persuaded him to come in and get warm. He's soaked to the skin. He's afraid of pneumonia; that's really why he came back. He fusses considerably about his health.

He vanishes again like a jack-in-the-box. DESCHAMPS, *who has been standing a little apart from the others, now steps forward.*

DESCHAMPS. I see you're very wisely trying to smooth things over with Bitos. As my being here certainly wouldn't help, I must ask you to let me leave.

MAXIME (*with a smile*). Yes, one can sometimes make it up with one's class enemies, even after a blood-bath, but never with one's friends.

He rings. CHARLES *appears.*

Charles, M. Deschamps' coat, please.

DESCHAMPS. Before I go, I would like to say that I share André Bitos's political ideas even if I do despise him as a man.

MAXIME. I did realize that.

DESCHAMPS. That's what prevented me from doing honour to your invitation. I haven't been a very entertaining guest. I'm sorry. (*He puts on the raincoat which* CHARLES *brings him.*) I hope this evening will end for the best, for all of you. Good night, sir. I'm very happy to have met you. (*He takes a step, then turns with a shy delightful smile.*) . . . By all means tame 'the people' as M. Brassac calls them – with methods which I would rather not witness . . . What I would like to tell you is that neither André Bitos, nor the ringleaders of M. Brassac's factories, nor incidentally, those figures of the Revolution we tried to bring to life this evening, are the people. Those men are more like yourselves than you can possibly imagine. The people, the real people, have the distinction and the elegance to belong to the race that does nothing else but give. (*He smiles again.*) I apologize if that sounds a bit high-flown, but I didn't quite know how to say this to you and I did want to say it . . . Enjoy your evening, ladies, what remains of it.

VICTOIRE. Maxime, I should like to go, too. I'm sure M. Deschamps would see me home.

MAXIME. My angel, the main thing now is to prevent young Delanoue from footing the bill. You women will have your work cut out, all three of you. (*To* DESCHAMPS, *who stands waiting.*) I'll see you out.

LILA (*to the others as she watches* DESCHAMPS *go.*) He's extremely nice, that young man. Not invitable, but very nice.

AMANDA (*ruefully*). Why did he let him leave? He had the most divine eyes.

BRASSAC *comes in with* BITOS, *who is now without his wig, his hair wet, a towel round his neck and a sort of absurd curtain over his shoulders which gives him a vaguely Roman look.*

BRASSAC. Friends, very sportingly, I must say, Bitos accepts our apologies and has agreed to come and have a drink with us.

BITOS (*still on his guard*). I was anxious to show these ladies that I'm not such a bear as they say. I lost my temper for a second, quite justifiably, as I'm sure you'll agree – and I should like to apologize myself.

LILA. M. Bitos, I knew you had a sense of humour.

MAXIME *comes forward, bottle in hand.*

MAXIME. Here, Bitos, in token of our reconciliation.

BITOS (*with a prudent gesture*). A drop, just a drop.

MAXIME (*pours him a drink and rubs him down*). Are you feeling warmer now? Your friend Deschamps sent his apologies; he had to leave. I thought it best not to try to keep him here. He struck me as curiously hostile towards you.

BITOS. He *is* hostile. (*He drinks and coughs.*) You've made this too strong. Yes, it's a fact, that young man is among the many who cannot forgive me for my success . . .

MAXIME (*giving him a final rub*). What a very ugly sentiment.

BITOS. It's very difficult to rise above certain mediocre individuals and still retain their goodwill.

MAXIME. You know the human heart, I see. (*He exchanges a look with the others and then goes on pouring drinks for all the people grouped around* BITOS.) Personally, I had no idea there had been any trouble between you. Over the young gangster I must plead guilty. I did yield to a certain taste for cheap theatricals in getting him to come here. But I never thought he would indulge in such a dubious piece of foolery. We do all agree, don't we – it was only foolery?

BITOS (*woodenly*). We'll say no more about it. This is entirely my concern.

VULTURNE (*rather too cordially*). Bitos is right! After all, there's no harm done, is there? I behaved none too pleasantly myself. I apologize. Do you know, in the heat of the moment I swear I thought I was Mirabeau –

BITOS (*with an enigmatic smile*). Why not? I certainly thought I was Robespierre.

MAXIME (*filling his glass*). Drink up, friends, and let's forget it.

AMANDA *fills* BITOS'S *glass. He protests laughingly.*

BITOS. Ho, ho there! Steady! You'll make me drunk.

AMANDA (*murmuring in his ear*). I should adore that! You're such a mysterious person, André.

BITOS (*purring, very much the man of the world*). I assure you there's nothing mysterious about me. One can be a 'red', as you call it, and still enjoy a little pleasant relaxation. I've attended quite a few fashionable social gatherings.

He is sitting centre stage in an armchair into which JULIEN *has pushed him, holding court suddenly, with the women fluttering around him, while the men crowd round filling his glass.* LILA *draws up a stool beside him.*

LILA. My dear André, it's just this blend of progressive thought and impeccable behaviour which makes you such a welcome guest.

BITOS (*bowing*). Thank you.

LILA. Are you free on Wednesday week? I'm having a few people to dinner.

BITOS (*pleasantly surprised, while* MAXIME *takes the opportunity of filling his glass*). I should be delighted to be among your guests on that occasion, Countess. (*He drains his glass euphorically and coughs.*) My friend will be arriving soon. I woke him in the middle of the night, poor fellow, and he'll need time to dress. (*A pause. The rain is heard.* BITOS *adds, by way of apology.*) But this weather isn't fit for a dog to go out in. And as I'm a little chesty . . .

BRASSAC *makes a sign to* LILA, *who says quickly.*

LILA. We'll be really sorry to sit down to dinner again without you. Why don't we telephone to tell him not to bother?

BITOS. No, he's sure to be on his way by now.

LILA. Then why don't we ask him to join us?

AMANDA (*taking his arm*). What a good idea! I should so love you to stay.

BITOS (*with a little embarrassed laugh*). Well, he's a very nice young fellow, extremely worthy really . . . but very ordinary. He's the garage man from the market square.

JULIEN. Fessard? But I know him like the back of my hand. Which reminds me, I haven't paid him for my car yet.

BITOS (*with a forced smile*). And as a good tradesman he's bound to have far stricter notions about debt than men of your social set, so . . .

BRASSAC (*very cordially*). My dear Bitos, the thing that delights me most about you is your ability to mix. You tell us that Fessard is a friend of yours, and yet one meets you at Lila's dinner parties, which are the most exclusive in the neighbourhood. You're an amazing man.

MAXIME (*filling everyone's glass*). You're not drinking, friends, you're not drinking.

BITOS, *his glass filled despite his half-hearted protest, goes on very animatedly.*

BITOS. Why amazing? There are good-hearted, interesting people everywhere. I personally make no distinction between a mechanic like Fessard – provided he's not stupid – and a guest at a smart function.

JULIEN. Who isn't necessarily stupid either!

BITOS (*laughing with lordly geniality*). Not necessarily!

BRASSAC (*taking the bottle and refilling his glass as he says with a sigh*). Oh, Bitos . . . We really should get to know each other better. Why this totally false reputation for being a puritan? Do you foster it yourself? Why, you're a very good drinker.

BITOS (*flattered*). Oh, in moderation.

He drinks and then coughs atrociously.

BRASSAC. They say that you're afraid of women, too. But I saw you at Clermont once, in most voluptuous company.

BITOS (*with an inane delighted laugh*). You may have seen me with a lady, I don't say that isn't quite possible, but in most voluptuous company, as you put it – well . . .

BRASSAC. Enough said, Bitos! As one gay dog to another! No need to explain! (*He winks and digs him in the ribs.*) Anyway, she was a very attractive redhead.

MAXIME (*exclaiming*). Lea! My dear Bitos, congratulations. She's the most expensive girl in town.

JULIEN (*patting him on the back*). Lea? Don't tell me the dear creature is playing me false? Are we going to have to fight over her? Bitos, you old scoundrel you!

The three men crowd around him, slapping him on the back. BITOS *drinks, coughs and splutters, in seventh heaven.* JULIEN *tries to refill his glass.* BITOS *refuses. The bottle goes round behind him and comes back to* AMANDA.

BITOS. Gentlemen, gentlemen! I thought one of the rules of your world was discretion over these little . . . escapades – if only out of regard for the ladies.

BRASSAC. Gentlemen, Bitos is reminding us of our manners and he's right.

AMANDA (*refilling* BITOS'S *glass from the other side*). A little more whisky?

BITOS (*blossoming imperceptively*). Thank you. It's most agreeable; this smoky taste.

BRASSAC. Whisky's the most innocuous drink in the world.

MAXIME. Charles, bring another bottle!

BRASSAC. It's made from cereals, did you know? Now, what could be more wholesome than cereals? More socially meaningful? Barley, rye . . .

MAXIME. Wheat.

JULIEN. Collective farms!

BRASSAC. Our daily bread! Brandy, wine, that's suspect. It's the grape. And the grape is Bacchus. And who says Bacchus says Dionysius. And who says Dionysius is already a counter-revolutionary!

BITOS (*amused, says subtly*). I never suspected all this culture, Brassac. But why the devil should Dionysius be a counter-revolutionary?

BRASSAC. Because Dionysius is anarchy. And I hardly need to tell you that when revolutionaries seize power, the first people they shoot are invariably the anarchists. Dammit, you wouldn't want those hysterical maniacs stirring up a whole lot of strikes, would you? Especially when it's the people who govern.

BITOS (*suddenly conspiratorial, raising his glass and drinking with him*). I see there's a lot in the running of this world that hasn't escaped your notice, my dear Brassac.

BRASSAC (*following suit*). Ah, my dear Bitos, one knows instantly, with certain men, that there's everything to be gained by being frank. Intelligence is an Internationale, too; let's not forget that.

BITOS (*beaming and raising his glass*). Allow me to return the compliment, my dear fellow.

BRASSAC (*conspiratorially*). They're always harping on your massacres, but do you think our side ever held our horses, eh?

BITOS (*delightedly*). So you've admitted it at last!

BRASSAC (*winking and putting a finger to his lips*) Shush. Officially one never admits anything.

BITOS (*sniggering*). You said it, I didn't. But then why blame us at the Liberation –

BRASSAC. But we don't! We don't blame you for anything at all! We aren't children! Summary executions are the French national game.

BITOS (*captious suddenly*). Ah, no. No, no. There you're wrong. We always took care – in '93 I'm talking about now – to see that the decisions of the Revolutionary Tribunal were perfectly in order. Always two signatures.

BRASSAC. But so do we, my dear man, so do we! We sign, too. What do you take us for? We aren't savages. Two, three signatures, four if necessary! In France you can always find a general to sign a decree or turn down a reprieve, and if there isn't the right law to hand you pass one, with retrospective effect, naturally! We know the form. We kill, yes, but we do it in the proper manner. Order, always order! The only difference is that when we go home in the evenings we change for dinner and kiss the ladies' hands as we confide, with a smile, a few of those grisly details which they're so scared of and so greedy for . . . And we continue to bring up our darling little children in a good Christian manner. No, we're very concerned – like you – with the future of humanity. You have your hobby horses, we have ours. But one thing's certain whether it's you or us – and we may as well admit the fact – in France we dine off severed heads. It's the national dish.

BITOS (*with an unlovely little gesture*). The Iron fist! That's the whole secret. And no need for the velvet glove either. But wait! (*He lifts a drunken warning finger.*) For the good of the people!

JULIEN (*softly, behind him*). And tell me, who decides that it's for the good of the people?

BITOS (*innocently*). We do!

He says this so seriously that their control breaks and they all laugh. He looks at them a little put out, then joins in. Under cover of this, his glass is filled again.

JULIEN (*slapping him on the back*). Good old Bitos! I like him now.

LILA (*tweaking his ear and laughing*). And he's so clever!

BITOS (*gurgling ludicrously*). You're too kind!

BRASSAC (*raising his glass*). Gentlemen, to Robespierre! A little more whisky, Bitos, to drink Robespierre's health?

BITOS. Delighted, thank you! I've quite grown to like it now!

AMANDA. Neat! And bottoms up!

BITOS (*the gay dog; he cries in his squeaky voice*). Bottoms up! To Robespierre, gentlemen!

ALL (*raising their glasses*). To Robespierre!

BITOS *drains his glass at one gulp and coughs horribly.*

VULTURNE (*moving to* MAXIME). Stop the game now, Maxime, it's going to turn ugly.

MAXIME *has been sitting silently in a corner, pale and malicious.*

MAXIME. You're mad! I've never seen anything so marvellous.

PHILIPPE. Maxime, we must get him to agree not to prosecute young Delanoue now, while he's still drunk.

VULTURNE *exchanges a look with* PHILIPPE *and goes to* BITOS.

VULTURNE. M. Bitos, I should like to ask you a favour –

BITOS (*suspicious suddenly*). Yes? What's that?

VULTURNE. It's about that young man – whom Maxime should never have brought into his lunatic charade in the first place. Any charge brought against him now could get him into serious trouble, as you know –

BITOS (*interrupting, suddenly deadly serious*). Your Grace, I have the greatest regard for you, but I've told you already, this is entirely my concern. The dignity of my robes is at stake.

AMANDA (*winningly*). To please me. I promise you a little reward if you agree not to get that poor boy into trouble.

LILA. It will cause a tremendous stir, you can rely on me for that. Just think!–a public prosecutor dropping a charge! (*She turns to him.*) Besides, pardons are all the rage now, have you noticed?

A pause. Everyone looks at BITOS *as he sits there, embarrassed by the women's caresses. He hiccups with drunken gravity.*

BITOS (*more and more like the great Caesar, draped in his curtain*). Very well. As the ladies all wish it, I incline towards clemency.

ALL. Long live Bitos! Here's to Bitos!

They all drink to him.

MAXIME. Do we have your word, Bitos?

BITOS (*noble and drunk*). You do. I shouldn't be doing this, of course. Clemency towards the enemies of the people is a crime. But tonight's a special occasion. We can stretch a principle or two. (*Holding out his glass.*) Give me some more whisky.

The three men all rush forward with three bottles. Everyone laughs.

AMANDA. Thank you. My turn to pay now. There. (*She kisses him.*) You're very very kind.

BITOS (*bewildered, nervously wiping his lipstick-stained mouth and exclaiming with sudden truculence*). Yes, I am! I'm very kind indeed. Nobody believes I'm a kind man. They hate me!

AMANDA (*cajoling him*). No, they don't. They admire you and like you – everybody does!

BITOS. I was accused of harshness after the Liberation. But we had to sweep up the mess. France wasn't clean. You want France to be clean, don't you?

EVERYBODY (*playing up to him, soothing him and sitting him down again*). Of course we do, M. Bitos of course we do! Now you mustn't worry! France is quite clean.

BITOS (*suddenly voluble, a mass of nervous tics*). It's like that fellow Lucien – the one that rat Deschamps told you about. Do you think it didn't cost me a great deal to demand his death? I made my first communion with him!

EVERYBODY (*soothingly*). Of course it did, Bitos! Of course! It must have cost you a great deal. We understand.

BITOS. Do you think it's funny having to go out at dawn and watch somebody you know being put to death? It's horrible!

AMANDA (*caressing him*). Poor Bitos . . .

BITOS (*shouting*). I bought a doll for his little girl! The most expensive doll I could find! So why do people say I'm not kind?

AMANDA. Yes why do they? It's not fair.

BITOS (*sitting up straight*). No it *isn't* fair! Everybody's unfair to me all the time! And it hurts. (*He shouts suddenly.*) Everything hurts me! (*To* VICTOIRE *who is sitting in a corner pale and silent.*) Mlle de Bremes, your father threw me out like a beggar because I dared to ask for your hand! (*To* LILA.) And you, Countess, at that dinner party you invited me to last winter, you saw what I'd done, you saw that I'd used the wrong fork! Anyway, your butler saw it! Nobody warned me! They let me go right on using the wrong things until when the meat arrived all I had left was my pastry fork! They wanted me to look riduculous! You Maxime, it's true I used to carry your books on our school walks so you could run about. It's true I made myself your valet, it's true I loved you. But you repulsed me. Everybody always repulses me. And yet I'm a kind man! I'm kind! (*He shouts like a madman.*) I wouldn't harm a fly!

He is sombre and crushed. Suddenly he hiccups and drops into a chair which someone has charitably placed under his behind. He says suddenly in a strange voice.

It wasn't my fault I was poor. You never took anything seriously, and yet you succeeded in everything you did. (*He adds dully.*) The world of the poor collapses if people don't take things seriously. It's like a blow in the face.

There is a sort of embarrassment, even in those who were openly enjoying it all a moment before. VULTURNE *looks at* PHILIPPE. *They go to* BITOS.

PHILIPPE. M. Bitos, it's late and you're tired. Wouldn't you like us to drive you home?

He gets up.

MAXIME (*catching him up*). Bitos, you've just upset me very much. I thought we were friends again.

BITOS (*looking at him coldly*). No, I have no friends. I don't love anybody. Not even the people. (*He looks at them strangely and says.*) The iron fist. (*A pause; he adds maliciously.*) That's my only love. (*He brushes himself, dazed. Suddenly he becomes aware of them all, standing silent and a little afraid around him. He breaks into a laugh and says softly.*) Well, well! Little Bitos who was so comical just now, eh? Not laughing now, are we?

The others stand there, dumb-struck. Only BRASSAC *recovers his composure and goes to him, gravely friendly.*

BRASSAC. Bitos, this evening's regrettable adventure has at least accomplished something. It's taught us what you are. Now you said it: the iron fist. If France is to rise again it won't be through systems but through men. Unfortunately men are rare.

BITOS (*contemptuously*). Yes, men are rare.

BRASSAC (*sententiously*). You'll forgive my frankness, but I'm not altogether sure that the political forces which employ you are precisely aware of your true worth. As you probably know, I belong to what is sometimes called 'Progressive Management'. There are a few big employers of labour like myself who put the social question before everything else. Your political beliefs and those of the managerial interests I mentioned just now are almost identical. Our resources are immense, but we need men. A man.

BITOS. I'm not sure I quite understand you, my dear Brassac.

BRASSAC (*the captain of men, very debonair suddenly*). Why don't you telephone me one morning at the factory and we'll have a chat about it over lunch? My syndicate is thinking of creating a job which would ensure contact between the various departmental heads and technical groups on the one hand, and the masses on the other – whole sections of which we are quite unable to reach. A sort of People's Representative, with the most extensive powers – and nothing to prevent it from expanding subsequently to national level . . . (*He has refilled* BITOS'S *glass as he speaks.*)

BITOS. I'm not sure that my functions as an official of the courts would permit me to . . .

BRASSAC (*expansively*) My dear fellow, the courts, like everything else, are made to be got out of. (*He taps him smartly on the shoulder, as if everything were already signed and sealed. Then he becomes bland again.*) But we'll talk about it all later. We're boring these lovely ladies. We're supposed to be enjoying ourselves! (*He claps his hands cheerfully and gathers them closer.*) Friends! Why don't we all go to the Pink Eagle? They say the new band is very good.

MAXIME. Brilliant idea! (*Calling.*) Charles!

BITOS (*suddenly skittish*). The Pink Eagle? I'm told it's a very . . . frisky sort of place. I don't know if I can allow myself, in my capacity as a magistrate –

BRASSAC (*confidently*). My dear fellow, you'll find them there to a man! But there's an unwritten rule, everybody pretends not to recognize anybody else.

BITOS (*clucking*). I must say they've made quite an art of these little niceties in your set . . . (*He drains his glass.*) And very pleasant, too!

A heavy knock is heard. CHARLES *goes up the stairs, opens the door and talks to somebody outside.*

CHARLES. Excuse me, M. Bitos, there's a man here who wishes to see you.

JULIEN (*pretending to panic*). It's Fessard! Hide me! He's going to ask me for money!

AMANDA (*clapping her hands*). Is it the friend? The famous garage man? Do persuade him to come with us. He'll be such fun!

BITOS (*purring*). No, no, ladies. He really is too crude. (*To* CHARLES.) Convey my thanks, my good man, and tell him everything is all right now.

CHARLES. It might be better if you appeared in person, sir. He seems very worried about you, sir.

BITOS (*animatedly*). Dear, dear, dear, how absurd! One second, gentlemen. I'll just send him on his way and then I'm all yours. (*He goes quickly up the stairs, reeling a little, and disappears into the street, calling in his falsetto voice.* Fessard!

MAXIME (*between his teeth*). It's superb! Superb! My dear Brassac, it's better than I ever dreamed! You're a genius!

BRASSAC (*smiling modestly as he lights a cigar*). Of sorts, yes. What will you bet that he telephones the factory within two days to ask me to ask him to lunch?

MAXIME. And will you?

BRASSAC (*softly, into his cigar*). I won't.

JULIEN *steps forward, drunk, powerful, malevolent.*

JULIEN. So we ship this son of the people to the Pink Eagle, right? I must say I'm feeling in great form. I've an itch in the toe of my boot. You should never have let me get a sniff of that Bitos. I absolutely must kill some pauper meat tonight. I'm sick to death of hearing them cry 'Misery me!' as soon as they've eaten their sausage. Sick of it! Death to the weak! Death to the poor and needy! (*He takes them by the arm, his eyes glinting.*) My friends, you leave Bitos to me at the Pink Eagle. I'll pick a quarrel with him – over Lea, for instance, who's bound to be there, she is every night. And this time, I'll smash him. And it won't even be an insult to a magistrate. It will be a settling of accounts between two drunkards, over a whore! Give me another drink.

MAXIME. Julien, you're drunk.

JULIEN (*helping himself*). Not quite!

VICTOIRE (*going to* MAXIME). I'm not going to that club with you.

MAXIME (*kissing her hand affectionately*). You're right, my little pet. It's certain to turn squalid. I'll drop you on the way.

VULTURNE. I'm going home, too, Maxime. I'll drop Victoire.

MAXIME (*with a hard smile*). I thought you would. I've never persuaded you to stay to the end of a bullfight either.

VULTURNE (*quietly*). I don't like to see anything killed. A shot at a bird on the wing, all right. But to watch a cornered animal waiting . . .

MAXIME (*laughing*). Your Grace, there must have been a little hiatus in your lineage. Some amorous young tutor and a great-grandmamma with time on her hands.

VULTURNE (*smiles and says quietly, as he goes up the stairs*). This will surprise you. I rather wish that sometimes . . .

BITOS *reappears, in great form, and shouts down the stairs.*

BITOS. There! The bumpkin has gone. Poor lad, he came with his apprentice, both of them armed to the teeth and ready to do battle. (*He splutters with mirth.*) He wouldn't go, you know! It was priceless! He kept on saying 'Are you sure you're not letting yourself in for anything, M. Bitos?' (*He wheezes with laughter.*)

BRASSAC (*patting him on the back and giving him a cigar*). A severe hangover, at the very most! (*In his ear.*) Or an affair. Our little Amanda has her eye on you, do you know that?

BITOS (*very much the man about town, puffing at his huge cigar*). Easy, is she?

BRASSAC. When she likes you!

MAXIME. Come along, everybody, quickly. We'll take all four cars. (*Calling*.) Charles!

CHARLES. Is everybody leaving, sir?

MAXIME. Yes, everybody.

CHARLES. Joseph, bring the coats. (*Distressed*.) What about dinner? I've kept everything hot!

MAXIME (*putting on his coat*). You two eat it. Eat till you burst!

The coats are handed round, the guests go up the stairs again – one of them opens the door and looks at the weather.

LILA (*from upstairs*). The rain's quite stopped. It's a wonderful night.

BITOS *has put on his Robespierre jacket. He now gallantly helps* AMANDA *on with her things.*

BITOS. Long live the night-time, lovely lady. It's funny, I'm not used to staying up late. After you.

He is about to go up the stairs with the last guests. Then an anxious look crosses his face, he puts his hand inside his coat and calls discreetly to MAXIME *as the others go out.*

My dear Maxime, a stupid accident . . . I seem to have split the seat of my breeches. (*He makes sure they are alone and feels his behind to learn the worst*.) How silly. I shan't be able to go to that club with you.

MAXIME. Nonsense. Charles! Would you do M. Bitos a

small service? A case of mending the seat of his trousers, he's split them. Discreetly, I'm relying on you.

CHARLES. I'll do my best, M. Maxime.

He hurries out.

MAXIME. We'll wait for you in the car, Bitos. A little more whisky to help you through the operation?

BITOS. I'm really going much too far this evening. All that drink, this cigar . . .

MAXIME (*suddenly unaccountably grave*). There are certain evenings when however far one goes, one never goes too far. Make haste, Charles.

He goes out. BITOS *remains alone with* CHARLES.

CHARLES (*calling after* MAXIME). I'll be as quick as I can, sir. (*To* BITOS.) Would you mind removing your overcoat, sir, it would be easier.

BITOS *takes off his coat. He is standing in the middle of the room, smoking his cigar.* CHARLES, *crouching behind him, is sewing up his rear.*

BITOS. I'm very worried about this costume. I borrowed it from the local theatre. They made me pay a very exorbitant deposit. (*A short pause: he adds anxiously.*) I hope they'll give it me back.

CHARLES (*doubtfully*). Well, of course, with this tear . . . You can always point out that the seat was very ripe, sir.

BITOS. An old cast-off, and they hired the thing out at an outrageous price. It did suit me, though, didn't it?

CHARLES (*politely*). You looked very smart indeed in it, sir. Excuse me, sir, but would you mind sticking out your posterior, sir, it would make the stitching easier.

BITOS *sticks out his behind.*

Thank you, sir. That's just right. It gives the stuff a bit of body, as you might say.

VICTOIRE, *who had left with the others, suddenly appears at the top of the stairs and asks, bewildered.*

VICTOIRE. Why, what are you doing?

BITOS (*straightening in panic, his hand on his behind*). Mlle de Bremes! That was unworthy of you! . . . a stupid accident . . . I've split the seat of my trousers. It's very mean of you to spy on me like that.

VICTOIRE (*gently*). I wanted to talk to you.

BITOS (*who goes on clutching his rear throughout the scene*). After what your father did to me this afternoon we have nothing further to say to each other. Anyway, you could have spoken to me over at that club.

VICTOIRE. I'm not going. (*To* CHARLES.) Charles, could you leave us for two minutes? What I have to say to M. Bitos won't take very long.

CHARLES. Very good, mademoiselle. Perhaps you will call me?

He goes out. BITOS *is still standing very stiff and still, his hand on his behind; without looking at her.* VICTOIRE *has come right down the stairs. A horn hoots for them out in the street, then stops.*

VICTOIRE (*suddenly quietly*). You mustn't go with them tonight, M. Bitos.

BITOS (*aggressively*). Is that your business?

VICTOIRE (*gently*). Yes. (*A short pause: she adds.*) They're still planning to make a fool of you.

BITOS (*still truculently, without venturing to meet her eyes*).

Aren't I old enough to see that for myself, if it's true?

VICTOIRE (*with the ghost of a smile*). No. I don't think you are.

BITOS (*with a sudden bark*). Do you think I'm some sort of an idiot?

VICTOIRE (*gravely*). I don't love you, M. Bitos. That's why your proposal this afternoon was unacceptable.

BITOS. Your father threw me out like a common thief!

VICTOIRE (*gently*). I beg your pardon for what my father did . . . If you had spoken to me I would simply have told you that you were mistaken and I couldn't love you . . . For a girl's reasons, which have nothing to do with what you are in the world. (*She smiles kindly.*) You know, there have been a lot of girls who didn't want to marry a man and who told him so. These are small wounds and one forgets them . . . (*She goes on, more gravely.*) Don't go with them tonight, M. Bitos. They'll give you wounds of a different sort and you won't recover from those so easily. They're taking you there so they can make fun of you.

BITOS (*with a terse cackle*). Am I so funny?

The hooters sound again.

VICTOIRE. Quickly, M. Bitos, we haven't much time. They only flattered you so as to destroy you. The proposition Brassac made is probably only a game to get you to make a fool of yourself. But even if he meant it, it would be shameful.

A pause.

BITOS (*heavily*). What do you know about it?

VICTOIRE (*gently*). I don't love you. I could never love a man like you. But I think there's a kind of true courage, a kind of steely worth in you . . . Don't go to that night club with them and have still more to drink . . . (*She smiles kindly.*) In the first place, you can't drink . . .

BITOS (*cackling ironically as he pulls at his cigar*). Indeed?

He unfortunately hiccups at the same time. He throws away his cigar with a shudder of disgust.

VICTOIRE (*goes on, kindly*). Don't go with them to be laughed at, don't go to Lila's to play the social lion, which you're very bad at. Stay yourself. Stay poor. (*A little pause: she adds.*) The only thing I could have loved about you, if I could have loved you, was your poverty. But like all precious things, poverty is very fragile. Keep yours intact, M. Bitos. And never forget that your family crest has your mother's two red arms on it – crossed.

She repeats the little gesture he made earlier in the play when speaking of his mother. She looks at him and smiles. BITOS *is very pale. He stands there, silent, frightening, motionless. Suddenly, he stops clutching his behind and picks up his little black overcoat, swiftly puts it on and sets his bowler on his head, his face set and drawn. The car hooters have started up again outside.*

BITOS (*between his teeth*). Very well, I'll go out the back way.

In the kitchen doorway he turns, lifts up his coat collar and mutters icily.

BITOS. Thank you, mademoiselle, for this little homily. You've saved me from making a blunder. (*He adds heavily.*) But if I can ever get my own back on you all one day, you are the one I shall start with.

He goes out. She has not moved. One can still hear the hooters calling outside. She murmurs.

VICTOIRE. Poor Bitos . . .

And she goes swiftly up the stairs. The CURTAIN *falls as she goes out amid the din of the car hooters, which have all started up together this time.*